Development Administration in Asia

Development Administration in Asia

José Veloso Abueva   Harry J. Friedman
Shou-Sheng Hsueh   Inayatullah
B. S. Khanna   Martin Landau
Hahn-Been Lee   Norman Meller
Fred W. Riggs   Bernard S. Silberman
Edward W. Weidner   Nguyen-Duy Xuan

Edited by Edward W. Weidner

Published in cooperation with the Comparative Administration
Group of the American Society for Public Administration
Duke University Press, Durham, North Carolina   1970

© 1970, Duke University Press
Library of Congress Catalogue Card Number 74–96864
ISBN–0–8223–0221–7

Printed in the United States of America
by Kingsport Press, Inc., Kingsport, Tennessee

Preface

This volume contains the papers, as revised, that were presented and critically discussed at the Seminar on Development Administration, held at the East-West Center, University of Hawaii, during June 13–July 15, 1966. Six Asians and six Americans spent an intensive five weeks together, concentrating on the application of development administration in Asia. They came from seven countries; most had traveled, studied, and worked abroad extensively. Some were administrators, a majority were scholars, and several had observed the development process from both points of view.

It was the first seminar of its kind. It was significant that both Americans and Asians collaborated in this venture. Development administration is a subject that has been of greater concern to scholars in the United States and Asia than elsewhere because of the many universities and the vast resources of the United States and the extensive experiences of Americans in Asia on technical assistance, teaching, and research assignments. Over-all, American scholarship is frequently environmental, experimental, contemporary, and pragmatic in orientation. Development administration —those actions leading to the maximum attainment of development goals—is all of these.

Asian leadership in development administration may in part be explained by the diversity of Asia, where many countries of quite different backgrounds share a chain of interconnected boundaries. Part of the explanation may lie in the stimulus of recent nationhood, as most countries of Asia threw off colonial yokes in the forties or fifties. However, Asia has been a special development case at least as far back as 1950, for its leaders called for development earlier and more insistently than those of Africa or Latin America. Its educational program has matured steadily. Clusters of outstanding research scholars are to be found in most Asian countries. Their development orientation is marked.

The Americans and Asians who participated in the seminar did so under the generous sponsorship of three organizations, the East-West Center, the Comparative Administration Group of the American Society for Public Administration, and the Ford Foundation. These are also the organizations that have been most actively interested and involved in development administration in general, and in its application to Asia in particular. For the Institute of Advanced Projects of the East-West Center, the seminar was the fourth in a series on development. Previous seminars had focused on communication and development, development education, and community development. The institute has had a continuing program in development administration since 1962 in which groups of scholars and administrators from Asia and the United States interested in development administration have spent six to twelve months at the institute each year. A majority of the seminar participants had been thus privileged.

The Comparative Administration Group, formed in the late fifties, turned primarily to development administration beginning in the early sixties. The summer of 1966 was the fourth season of CAG seminars on some aspect of comparative public administration. Several members of the Hawaii seminar had participated in one or more of the previous undertakings, and some fifteen of the CAG Occasional Papers served as common background material for this gathering.

The Ford Foundation's participation was indirect, through its general support of CAG. The foundation has had a long history in development administration. As early as 1956 foundation representatives in South Asia were concerned with the new concept. Later, a substantial portion of the foundation's resources were allocated to enhance development administration both domestically and internationally, with special emphasis placed on Asia.

The seminar represented a milestone in development administration. Preliminary definition and debate, so much a part of the experience of the previous ten years, were put aside. Instead, with the co-operation of the three sponsors, Asian and American scholars considered implications and applications of development administration in Asia. The level of work varied from the highly theoretical to the very applied and from a focus on central governments to a concern for the village. Environmental conditions that sustain particular innovative roles of administrators were identified, and the limitations of an environment on administrative action stressed. In general, the seminar produced a series of essays on administrative cultures in rapidly changing societies in Asia. The overall theme was the distinctive roles and modification of roles of administrators in Asia under the conditions of rapid change and development.

Three essays on the conception and theory of development administration begin the volume. In his essay, "The Elements of Development Administration," Weidner analyzes six sets of conditions leading to development and two sets of conditions resulting in failure of development or a static society. The discussion is basically ecologically oriented, with a pragmatic, experimental approach to development. As such, it goes well beyond a definitional framework. It sets the theme for the collection of essays, a theme which is also fundamentally ecological, pragmatic, and experimental in spirit.

Riggs explores the ecological and dynamic aspects of development administration. Possible foci of interest are examined, leading to the conclusion that the essence of development is an increase in the level of discretion of social systems. A necessary condition for the attainment of an increase in the discretion level is a larger degree of diffraction. Thus the task of development administration concerns both how to implement policies that express discretionary social decisions and how to enhance the continuing development of the social system by further increasing its discretionary powers.

The implications of decision theory for development are considered by Landau. He finds that one major difference between a more developed and a less developed society is the former's greater reliance on a factual basis for decision-making.

The bulk of the essays in this volume present case studies or analyses of development in particular countries. These vary in focus from central, national, state, or provincial governments to field administration and local government. They emphasize the political and cultural as well as the strictly administrative aspects.

The Korean case, presented by Lee, focuses upon the higher civil service. On the basis of a typology of the roles of administrators that is derived from variations of their time orientations, he highlights the innovational potential of higher civil servants who occupy the strategic nexus between the political leadership and the rank and file bureaucracy. This potential, cast in the context of the make-up of the political leadership, he functionally divides into power elite and task elite. Thus, he develops a set of linkage patterns between the higher civil service and different combinations of political elites which he illustrates by drawing on the Korean experience of the last two decades.

Administrative culture and behavior from the viewpoint of middle civil servants are the subject of Abueva's essay on the Philippines. On the assumption that development administration can be successful only in a context of administrative development, he delineates some of the cultural changes—changes in cognitions, values, and attitudes—and behavioral changes that may be required. His description of Filipino administrative culture and behavior is based largely on the perceptions of a panel of fifty-two middle-level civil servants. Varying orientations and behavioral patterns of government personnel are identified. The prospects of administrative development are related to transitional and modern administrators who are potential or actual innovators and acceptors of change and innovation in public administration.

Japanese prefectural governors are examined by Silberman. Analyzing the recruitment and tenure of these officers from 1868 to 1899 and from 1900 to 1945, Silberman concludes that the Japanese civil bureaucracy was achievement-oriented throughout these two periods, although the criteria underwent a marked change after the turn of the century. This orientation occurred even though during the first of these periods the upper civil servants continued to be drawn primarily from the former samurai.

The Indian case, emphasizing personnel administration at the state level, is presented by Khanna. His concern is particularly with selection and recruitment of senior cadres operating at the center as well as at the state level.

A somewhat more comparative paper, with special attention to Pakistan, is Friedman's "Administrative Roles in Local Governments." He posits the view that certain types of programmatic innovations by central governments can increase the level of popular participation in the local decision-making process and that such participation, in turn, has a far-reaching effect on local administrators' roles. For example, Pakistan's administrators are becoming increasingly responsive and goal-oriented on the local level. He concludes that Pakistan has been laying the groundwork for the type of bureaucracy which may eventually possess sufficient technological capacity to support and lead an industrialized society.

Inayatullah, presenting another Pakistan case, discusses one of the most interesting innovations in local administration and local government, the Basic Democracies. Pakistan has experimented with a new method of joining field administration with local government. The arrangement is a compromise between self-government and tutelage. As such, it provides a dynamic element for the future. Field administration can be made progressively more accountable to locally elected bodies as the latter gain strength and experience.

Indigenous leadership in one of the few remaining colonial areas, the Trust Territory of the Pacific Islands, is discussed by Meller. Here on the fringe of Asia, Micronesian participation in governmental policy-making occurs in the territorial legislation. Elected to the recently established Congress of Micronesia has been a new political elite, comprised of relatively young, American-trained communication specialists, as well as named traditional leaders and those possessing ascriptive characteristics. Seemingly basic to the choosing of representatives was a demonstrated competence to deal with American-introduced political institutions, or the possession of attributes connoting that ability.

The last three essays are devoted to how change and innovation can be brought about that will be favorable to development administration in Asia. The first two focus on aspects of technical co-operation and assistance as a force for change. The third, more theoretical in tone, emphasizes innovational roles in general.

A regional view of technical co-operation in development administration is discussed by Hsueh. He reviews various means of technical co-operation, with special attention to the Eastern Regional Organization for Public Administration.

A case study of technical assistance is provided by Xuan in his analysis of the National Institute of Administration in Vietnam. He discusses the assistance given the institute by Michigan State University and other groups with particular concern for its impact on the functioning and role of the institute.

A concluding essay by Weidner on "Development and Innovational Roles" provides an over-all view of innovation. It is argued that there are several identifiable innovational roles, and that there are special opportunities and problems relative to such roles in the public and private sectors. The process of innovation for development can be furthered by strengthening and multiplying the conditions under which innovational roles can be effectively played.

Finally, the seminar was the occasion for the formation of a new organization, the Development Administration Group, Asia, by the six Asian seminar members. DAG promises to be a significant organization for the development and diffusion of new knowledge about development administration in Asia.

EDWARD W. WEIDNER

Green Bay, Wisconsin
April 2, 1968

Contributors

José Veloso Abueva was born in the Philippines in 1928. He was educated at the University of the Philippines and subsequently received the Master of Public Administration and his doctorate in political science from the University of Michigan. He has served in advisory positions for the government of the Philippines and was organizational analyst and staff assistant to the chairman of the Government Survey and Reorganization Commission from 1954 to 1955. He has been a guest lecturer at the Ateneo de Manila University, the Local Autonomy College of Japan, the University of Hawaii, the University of Oregon, the University of Michigan, Duke University, and Cornell University, and in 1965–66 was senior specialist at the East-West Center in Honolulu. He joined the faculty of the University of the Philippines in 1951 and is professor and assistant dean of the College of Public Administration of that university. In 1966–67 he was a visiting professor of political science at Brooklyn College of the City University of New York and in 1969–70 at Yale University. The author of *Focus on the Barrio* (1959), he is co-editor (with Raul P. de Guzman) of *Handbook of Philippine Public Administration* (1967) and *Foundations and Dynamics of Filipino Government and Politics* (1968). He is a contributing author to Edwin O. Stene, ed., *Public Administration in the Philippines* (1955); R. P. de Guzman, ed., *Patterns in Decision-Making* (1963); S. C. Espiritu and C. L. Hunt, eds., *Social Foundations of Community Development* (1964); Lucian W. Pye, ed., *Comparative Politics: Asia* (1969); and Ralph Braibanti and Associates, *Political and Administrative Development* (1969). He has contributed to various learned journals and has served as editor in chief and chairman of the editorial board of the *Philippine Journal of Public Administration*. He has completed a political biography of Ramon Magsaysay resulting from research conducted under a grant from the Rockefeller Foundation.

Harry J. Friedman was born in Trenton, New Jersey, in 1926 and received his doctor's degree in political science from the University of

Pittsburgh in 1956. His army service during World War II included time spent in Europe and in the Philippines. In 1956–57 he was engaged in field research in India. He was a member of the Department of Political Science, Michigan State University, 1957–62, during which period he spent 1959–61 in Peshawar, West Pakistan, as an adviser to the Pakistan Academy for Rural Development. Since 1962 he has been with the Department of Political Science at the University of Hawaii and was chairman of the department from 1965 to 1967. He has served as a consultant to the East-West Center, participating in and conducting several cross-national seminars and training programs, and is a member of the Asia Committee of the Comparative Administration Group. For the 1967–69 period, he is serving as a visiting professor and consultant in the College of Public Administration, University of the Philippines. He has written a number of papers and articles on comparative administration and has published in journals in the United States and in several Asian countries. He has also contributed to three volumes published in Pakistan: S. M. Z. Rizvi, ed., *A Reader in Basic Democracies* (1961) and two edited by Inayatullah, *Bureaucracy and Development in Pakistan* (1963) and *District Administration in West Pakistan* (1964).

Shou-Sheng Hsueh was born in China in 1926. He received his B.A. degree in political science from Yenching University in China and the degrees of Lic. es Sc. Pol., and Doc. es Sc. Pol. from the University of Geneva in Switzerland. He taught for a number of years at the University of Hong Kong and undertook post-doctorate research at Oxford University. He has given occasional lectures and seminars at numerous academic and professional institutions in Asia, Europe, and the United States. From 1963 to 1966 he served as assistant secretary general of the Eastern Regional Organization for Public Administration (EROPA) and visiting professorial lecturer at the Graduate School of Public Administration of the University of the Philippines. At present, he teaches at the Chinese University of Hong Kong. He is author of *L'Organisation des Nations Unies et les Etates Non Membres* (1953) and of *Government and Administration of Hong Kong* (1962). He is editor of *Public Administration in South and Southeast Asia* (1962) and *Political Science in South and Southeast Asia* (1966). He is also a contributing editor of the *Dictionary of Political Science* (1964).

Inayatullah was born at Sialkot, Pakistan, in 1924. He was educated at the University of the Punjab where he received his master's degree in history in 1946. He joined the Civil Service of Pakistan in 1947 on the basis of an All-India competitive examination held in 1945. Thereafter he held a number of administrative assignments in the field and in the Secretariat of the government of West Pakistan.

Inayatullah has edited a number of books on such subjects as statistics and public administration, the administrator and the citizen, pension procedures and methods, Basic Democracies, and the Rural Works Program. While in the National Institute of Public Administration he started a journal on public administration called the *Public Administration Review*, of which he was the chief editor.

In 1959–60, Inayatullah was at Harvard University, where he studied economic development and secured a master's degree in public administration.

In 1962, he was deputed by the government of Pakistan to visit and observe government and private training institutions in public administration in Europe, the United States, and the Far East. Earlier he represented Pakistan on the Economic Committee of CENTO at Ankara in 1959.

In 1965, he was awarded the Senior Specialist Fellowship at the Institute of Advanced Projects at the East-West Center in Hawaii, where he spent about a year. He was recently designated chairman of a committee appointed by the government of West Pakistan to reorganize the structure of municipal administration in West Pakistan.

He is currently a joint secretary in the government of Pakistan. His previous assignment was the chairmanship of a semi-autonomous body concerned with the growth and development of Lahore, capital of West Pakistan—the designation of the post being chairman, Lahore Improvement Trust.

B. S. Khanna was born in India in 1915. He received his master's degree in political science from the Punjab University, Lahore, and the Ph.D. degree from the London University. In 1958 he was awarded a traveling fellowship by the Indian Institute of Public Administration to visit university departments of social sciences and schools of public adminstration in the United States, Canada, Western Europe, and Scandinavia. In 1963 he had a foundation grant to visit universities of Southeast Asia and Japan. He was a senior specialist at the East-West Center, University of Hawaii, from January to August, 1966.

For a number of years he worked as a lecturer in some government colleges as a member of the Punjab Education Service. In 1960 he was appointed professor of political science and also chairman of the Department of Political Science, Punjab University, Chandigarh, and since 1961 has been in the same university. In 1958–60 he was on leave

xiv Contributors

from the university to work as a member of the faculty of the Indian School of Public Administration, New Delhi. He also spent a year and a half in an executive position in a large industrial organization.

He has published a number of papers in the *Indian Journal of Political Science* and *Indian Journal of Public Administration* and has contributed to symposia such as *Aspects of Administration,* ed. A. Avasthi (1964), and *Morale in Public Services,* ed. V. K. N. Menon (1959). Two manuscripts—one on "Rural Institutions in Punjab" and the other on "Municipal Administration in a Punjab City"—are in the press. He has also edited the proceedings of a seminar, *Municipal Government and Politics in India,* which was directed by him in April, 1965.

Martin Landau was born in New York City in 1921 and received his doctorate from New York University in 1952. He served in the United States Army Signal Corps from 1942 to 1946, completing his tour of duty as control chief, United States Ninth Army Multi-Channel Radio Link. He is presently professor of political science at City University of New York—Brooklyn, where he was awarded the Distinguished Teaching Medal in 1963. He has been visiting professor at the University of Michigan, the Graduate Faculty—New School, and the Graduate School of Public Administration, New York University. During the academic year 1969–1970, he taught at the University of California at Berkeley. He has been a Fellow of the United States Air Force Office of Scientific Research (Behavioral Sciences Division) and was a senior specialist at the Institute of Advanced Projects, East-West Center, in 1965–66. He has served as a consultant to various organizations including the New York State Constitutional Convention Commission and the New York City Charter Revision Commission and has lectured often at the United States Civil Service Commission Executive Seminar Center, the New York City Executive Development Program, the United States Naval Applied Science Laboratories and the Institute for Mental Health Research. He is also chairman of the Committee on Organization Theory of the Comparative Administration Group. He is a contributor to *Decisions, Values and Groups,* ed. D. Willner (1962), *Concepts and Issues in Administrative Behavior,* ed. S. Mailick and E. H. Van Ness (1962), *Reapportionment,* ed. Glendon A. Schubert (1964), and is both editor and contributor to *Management Information Technology* (1965). Professor Landau is presently completing *Political Science and Political Theory* and is writing *Decision Theory and the Process of Development.*

Hahn-Been Lee was born in Korea in 1921 and received his doctor's degree in philosophy from Seoul National University in 1967. He joined the Korean Budget Bureau after his graduation from Harvard University Graduate School of Business Administration (coupled with study on public administration at the Littauer School of Public Administration) in 1951 and worked up the bureaucratic ladder from chief of the Budget Section to director of the Budget Bureau and to vice-minister of finance over a period of ten years. During this period he gave visiting lectures in public administration and fiscal policy at both Yonsei University and Seoul National University. In 1962 he was appointed head of the Korean Diplomatic Mission in Geneva; during the subsequent three years he was the first Korean ambassador to Switzerland, assuming concurrent ambassadorial assignments to Austria and the European Economic Community, and was Korea's first minister to the Vatican. During 1965–66 he was a senior specialist, East-West Center, University of Hawaii. He has been dean and professor at the Graduate School of Public Administration, Seoul National University since 1966. Dean Lee is a member of the Executive Council of the Eastern Regional Organization for Public Administration (EROPA) and has been co-ordinator of the Development Administration Group, Asia (DAGA), since 1966. He was also moderator, the Pacific Conference on Urban Growth, Honolulu, in May, 1967. He is the author of *The Way a Small Country Lives: The Case of Switzerland* (1965), *Korea: Time, Change and Administration* (1968), and *A Handbook for Preparing a Curriculum of Development Administration* (1968). He is currently editing (with Abelardo Samonte) a symposium entitled *Administrative Reforms and Innovations in Asia*. Professor Lee is also the author of many articles on development administration and innovational leadership, including essays in Dwight Waldo, ed., *The Temporal Dimension of Administration* (1968); Chongsik Lee and Sung-Chick Hong, eds., *Politics and Society in Korea* (1968); and the *International Review of Administrative Sciences* and *Die Verwaltung*.

Norman Meller, born in California in 1913, has for over two decades considered Hawaii his home. He holds a law degree from Hastings College of the Law, University of California, and is admitted to the California bar; he also has an A.B. from the University of California at Berkeley, and M.A. and Ph.D. degrees from the University of Chicago. He served as deputy legislative counsel to the California State Legislature for seven years, was director of the Hawaii Legislative Reference Bureau for eight years, has been a consultant to legislative committees and director of research for various governmental study groups, has conducted a number of training sessions for legislative staff and orientations programs for island legislators, and since 1947 has been a faculty member of the University of Hawaii. He now holds the post of professor of political science at the university, and served as chairman of his department during 1955–58 and again in 1964–65. He has also taught as a visiting professor at the Claremont Colleges and at the University of California at Berkeley. In 1961 he was acting deputy director of the University of Hawaii's East-West Center while that institution was being established. His first experience with the Pacific Island region occurred during World War II when he was in naval military government in the Mariana Islands. Since then he has traveled extensively and conducted research in Melanesia, Micronesia, and Polynesia. Works he has published both chronologically and topically reflect the changes in emphasis in his professional and vocational interests. While deputy counsel in California he authored a *Survey of California Statutory Provisions Conferring Quasi-Legislative Functions Upon State Administrative Agencies* (1946); as reference bureau director he published numerous studies designed for legislative and executive use; and as consultant he contributed "Political Development in American Samoa" in 87th Congress, 1st Session, Senate, *Study Mission to Eastern (American) Samoa* (1961). His more general works include articles in American and foreign journals: "Three American Legislative Bodies in the Pacific," in Roland W. Force, ed., *Induced Political Change in the Pacific* (1965); *Land and Politics in Hawaii*, with Robert H. Horwitz (3rd ed.; 1966); and *Papers on the New Guinea House of Assembly*, ANU New Guinea Research Unit Bulletin Number 22 (1967). Currently in press are *Fiji Goes to the Polls*, with James Anthony, and *Congress of Micronesia*.

Fred W. Riggs, born in Kuling, China, in 1917, received his doctorate in political science from Columbia University in 1948. He served as a research associate of the Foreign Policy Association from 1948 to 1951, as assistant to the director of the Public Administration Clearing House in New York from 1951 to 1955, and as a member of the Department of Government of Indiana University, where he held the Arthur F. Bentley chair, from 1956 through 1967. Since 1967 he has been professor of political science at the University of Hawaii and a member of its Social Science Research Institute. During 1957–58 he held a fellowship from the Committee on Comparative Politics of the Social Science Research Council for research in Thailand. He often has served as a visiting professor or lecturer: at Yale University during 1955–56, at the National Officials Training Institute in Korea in 1956, at the University of the Philippines in 1958–59, and at the Massachusetts Institute of Technology in 1965–66. He has also been a senior specialist at the East-West Center, University of Hawaii, 1962–63, and a fellow of the Center for Advanced Study in the Behavioral Sciences,

Stanford University, 1966–67. Riggs has been chairman of the Comparative Administration Group of the American Society for Public Administration since 1960 and is a member of the Southeast Asia Development Advisory Group. He is on the editorial boards of *Comparative Political Studies* and *Comparative Politics*. He is the author of *Pressures on Congress* (1950), *Formosa Under Chinese Nationalist Rule* (1952), *The Ecology of Public Administration* (1962), *Administration in Developing Countries* (1964), *Thailand, the Modernization of a Bureaucratic Polity* (1966), and is co-author and editor of *Frontiers in Development Administration* (1969). He is also the author of many articles on international relations and comparative administration, including essays in William J. Siffin, ed., *Toward the Comparative Study of Public Administration* (1957); Klaus Knorr and Sidney Verba, eds., *The International System: Theoretical Essays* (1961); John Montgomery and William J. Siffin, eds., *Approaches to Development: Politics, Administration and Change* (1966); James C. Charlesworth, ed., *Contemporary Political Analysis* (1967); and William J. Crotty, ed., *Approaches to the Study of Party Organization* (1967).

Bernard S. Silberman was born in Detroit, Michigan, in 1930. He received his doctorate in history from the University of Michigan in 1956. At present, he is professor of Japanese History at Duke University. He has been a recipient of Fulbright (Tokyo, 1954–55), Ford Foundation (Tokyo, 1958–59), Carnegie Corporation (London, 1961), and ACLS (Tokyo, 1966) fellowships and was a senior specialist at the Institute of Advanced Projects, East-West Center, in 1965–66. He is assistant editor of the *Journal of Asian Studies* and chairman of the Committee on East Asian Studies, Duke University. He is the author of *Ministers of Modernization: Elite Mobility in the Meiji Restoration, 1868–73* (1964); *Japan and Korea: A Critical Bibliography* (1962); editor and contributor to *Modern Japanese Leadership: Transition and Change* (1966); and contributor to *Political Development in Modern Japan*, ed. Robert Edwards Ward (1968). He is also author of a number of articles on Japanese bureaucratic and political development. He is presently completing *Bureaucratic Development in Modern Japan: 1868–1945*.

Edward W. Weidner was born in Minneapolis, Minnesota, in 1921 and received his doctorate in political science from the University of Minnesota in 1946. He has taught political science at the University of Minnesota, University of Wisconsin—Madison, University of California —Los Angeles, Michigan State University, and the University of Kentucky. He was a member of the Department of Political Science at Michigan State University from 1950 to 1962, serving as chairman from 1952 to 1957 and as director of the Institute of Research on Overseas Projects from 1957 to 1961. He was senior scholar at the East-West Center during 1961–62 and vice-chancellor in 1962–66. After a year as director of the Center for Developmental Change, University of Kentucky, he assumed his present post of chancellor at the University of Wisconsin—Green Bay. He has served abroad in technical assistance and research capacities in 1954–56 and in 1958, and has traveled extensively in Asia. He served as chairman of the Asia Committee of the Comparative Administration Group until 1968 and was chairman of the International Committee of the American Society for Public Administration. He is author of several books and monographs, the latest of which are *Technical Assistance in Public Administration Overseas* (1964) and *The World Role of Universities* (1961).

Nguyen-Duy Xuan was born in Vietnam in 1926. He did his undergraduate studies at the University of Birmingham (England) from 1951 to 1954 and received his doctorate in economics from Vanderbilt University in 1963. He has served the government of Vietnam in many responsible positions: attaché commercial at the Embassy of Vietnam in Tokyo (1955–56), deputy director general of foreign trade (1956–57), commissioner general for cooperatives and agricultural credit (1964), and minister of national economy (1964–65). Since 1960 he has been lecturer in economics at the National Institute of Administration in Saigon. When the University of Cantho was created in 1966 in the Mekong Delta he was offered the deanship of the Faculty of Law and Social Sciences. He is author and co-author of a number of articles on agricultural development and local administration published in Vietnamese periodicals: *Que-Huong, Chan-Hung Kinh-Te,* and *Nghien-Cuu Hanh-Chanh.* He contributed substantially to the translation of foreign textbooks into Vietnamese when he was on the Board of Directors of the Center for Vietnamese Studies (1960–65). Since January, 1968, he has been special assistant to the president of the Republic of Vietnam.

Contents

Tables, Maps, and Figures

Part I

Theory of Development Administration

Chapter 1

The Elements of Development
Administration

Edward W. Weidner

A decade ago, development administration was an unfamiliar and awkward label. Today, it is a term that identifies the professional interest of a substantial portion of the scholars of public administration and related disciplines. Seldom has a new professional focus evolved so quickly. In part, the new focus has flowed from the experiences of scholars and other specialists in technical assistance in public administration. Whether in the role of donor or receiver, scholars were brought into intimate contact with programs of planned change and those who were administering them. In turn, they were asked to contribute to the maximizing of development in one or another country. The limited chance for explicit contributions to development that they could make bothered a considerable number of the colleagues. So little of the lore of administration from one country seemed applicable to another. So little of public administration seemed relevant to development.

The years from the mid-fifties to the mid-sixties were a period of searching and reformulation. New explanations were sought, new theories or skeletons of theories set forth. Even as late as 1960 there was very little literature on development administration proper—some articles but only a few research monographs. Since 1960, hundreds of articles and dozens of books have appeared on one or another aspect of development administration. It is now an accepted problem orientation in the social sciences.

Conditions of Development

As the essays in this volume clearly illustrate, the intensive activity in development administration has not brought unanimity among scholars as to the meaning of the term. In fact, the last ten years have been characterized by more than the usual groping for terms and by substantial semantic debates. What is necessary for a viable definition of development administration is not precise agreement on what each word should mean, but general agreement on the major concepts central to analytical work in this area. Within such agreement, each scholar has a responsibility to make clear how he proposes to use labels and terms. Increasingly, the first of these requirements is being met.

Far more attention has been given to the word "development" than to the word "administration." Much of the literature on development approaches the subject in far too simple terms. One group of scholars has equated development with growth. Another group has thought of it as system change. A third school of thought has argued for goal orientation, especially modernity or nation-building and socio-economic progress. Still another popular approach to development has been to consider it in terms of planned change. Much that is understood to be included in the term "development" by administrators, politicians, businessmen, or scholars can be expressed by a several-faceted definition. Thus, some observers look upon development as planned growth in the direction of modernity or nation-building and socio-economic progress involving substantial differentiation and co-ordination. At the same time, much goal achievement in the direction of modernity would fall outside the definition for the very reason that it prescribes so many different characteristics that must adhere to change if it is to be considered development. It excludes much of what goes on in rapidly developing situations.

Contributions to the discussion of development have come from many sources outside the confines of development administration, e.g., from those interested in the economic, educational, or agricultural aspects of development. Always active and occasionally acrimonious, the discussion has nonetheless served to emphasize three major facets of change pertinent to the student of development administration.

First, a general distinction is now made between change in the output of a system and change in the system itself. Changes in the output of a system that are in the direction of greater quantity are frequently labeled growth, and those that are in the reverse direction, lack of growth or decline. Growth is essentially a quantitative concept. It does not make a qualitative distinction. Thus we may speak of growth of police or military forces, growth of controls on prices or housing, or increases in government reports. Still, growth is not a simple concept. What is growth from one point of view may be decline from another. The growth in income of one business may necessarily result in a decline in another (a zero-sum game). The growth of public services in one society may be twice as slow as similar growth in another. A $50 per capita growth may have entirely different consequences if it is from $500 to $550 rather than from $2,200 to $2,250. The rate or time period of growth, its extent, and whom and what it concerns are all important aspects.

A number of scholars of development administration have looked on change in the social system, and particularly on change in the administrative system of a developing country, as a crucial variable. Riggs, Diamant, and Eisenstadt are among the members of this group, which has set forth two similar formulations. Riggs has emphasized differentiation plus co-ordination as system characteristics that represent the essence of development. Diamant and Eisenstadt have suggested that system capability in handling change is the essential attribute. A choice does not have to be made between these formulations since they are basically different ways of saying the same thing. In the first formulation, differentiation plus co-ordination equals capacity (Riggs). In the other, capability in handling change requires a differentiated and centralized system.[1] However, in neither case is output invariably

1. Alfred Diamant, "Political Development: Approaches to Theory and Strategy," in John D. Montgomery and William J. Siffin, eds., *Approaches to Development: Politics, Administration and Change* (New York: McGraw-Hill, 1966), pp. 15–47.

related to system capacity or differentiation. Capacity can be merely potential and unused. And within limits, growth can occur without alterations in capacity or differentiation. Thus four possibilities emerge: growth with system change, growth without system change, lack of growth (or decline) with system change, and lack of growth (or decline) with no system change.

Second, distinctions have been drawn among the different goals or outputs of an administrative system. Of course no two societies and perhaps no two persons or groups have identical goals or emphases. General directions are discernible. Modernity is a cluster of values that are avidly sought by the less developed societies, and undoubtedly the process of modernization continues even in the most modern country. Daniel Lerner has suggested certain phases of modernity that lead to greater economic and political participation—urbanization, literacy or education, and media production and consumption—which may be considered indexes of geographic, social, and psychic mobility. These indexes might include per capita income and voting participation.[2] An alternative formulation is that of Shils: "Among the elites of the new states, 'modern' means dynamic, concerned with the people, democratic and equalitarian, scientific, economically advanced, sovereign and influential."[3] Other combinations of values have been suggested for modernity. While unanimity on the use of the term is not found, the definitions are substantially compatible with each other. The values they identify may be considered the ultimate goals of development, the ultimate dependent variables in research schemes. There are a number of useful indexes of the values of modernity that can be of important assistance in research.

As a term, modernity is all-inclusive. Other formulations of goals in the developing process have been more selective. Two deserve special attention because of their ultimate, end-product, or consumption aspects. Nation-building is one such cluster of outputs sought in development. Esman defines it as "the deliber-

2. *The Passing of Traditional Society: Modernizing the Middle East* (Glencoe, Ill.: Free Press, 1964).
3. Edward Shils, *Political Development in the New States* (The Hague: Mouton, 1965).

ate fashioning of an integrated political community within fixed geographic boundaries in which the nation state is the dominant political institution."[4] There are several aspects of nation-building among which national identity or solidarity, structuralization, and participation are some of the more important in the less developed countries. The formula for nation-building varies to some extent in each country, and there are extremely wide variations if the entire spectrum of the less developed countries is included, let alone other nations. Still, the important and most relevant fact for the present analysis is that all of the developing nations as well as the more developed countries do have such a formula.

Socio-economic progress is another label for a cluster of values or outputs of a modernizing administrative system. Esman suggests that such progress is "the sustained and widely diffused improvement in material and social welfare."[5] Most of the elements of material and social welfare are rather self-evident and measurable, such as a rise in per capita income, greater number of students completing secondary school and college, and more physicians per capita. Still, there may be substantial disagreement about what constitutes socio-economic progress among two or more groups or individuals within a country or among leaders or dominant factions of different countries. There is great variation in the strategies pursued in regard to the relative balance between consumption and production, and there are many positions on the continuum which has as its poles laissez-faire capitalism and socialism.

Thus in common usage of the term, a rapidly developing country is a goal-oriented country, headed in the direction of modernity, with special emphasis on nation-building and socio-economic progress. This definition accords with the announced objectives of leaders of these nations. While specifics will vary and even be in dispute, the general direction is evident.

Returning to a consideration of the definition of development, we can now attempt a comprehensive statement. A more com-

4. See his extended discussion on this point in Milton Esman, "The Politics of Development Administration," in Montgomery and Siffin, eds., *op. cit.*, esp. pp. 59–87.
5. *Ibid.*

plete description of the development process would be growth, whether under conditions of system change or not, in the direction of modernity and particularly in the direction of nation-building and socio-economic progress. It is a reasonable hypothesis that in order for growth to proceed in this direction very far, system change in the form of increased differentiation and co-ordination, together with appropriate accompanying specialization, would be required. Such changes would be only intermediate dependent variables for the scholar of development administration, however. The ultimate dependent variables would be the goals themselves, the "payoff" in the society. Thus differentiation and co-ordination would be development-related to the extent that they led to the accomplishment of these goals sooner or later.

Third, there is an inherently manipulative aspect to the term "development." It is commonly understood that those engaged in development work are consciously trying to bring about change in a particular direction. An assumption lies behind this common understanding: man can affect the environment of which he is a part as well as be affected by it. A deterministic view of man in relation to environment is thus rejected in favor of a reciprocal view. Riggs and Lee have compared an environmental approach with an ecological one. The former approach is defined as uni-directional, the latter approach as reciprocal. Development administration requires a reciprocal approach. Environmental factors in general and cultural factors in particular are important to those who attempt to bring about major change in a society. Such factors condition the outcome of any governmental program or other innovation. Therefore, changes in man's culture and environment are among the goals of highest priority in the countries most committed to change.

An assumption underlying the selection of goals in planning for national development is that achievement of modernity in general and nation-building and socio-economic progress in particular can be furthered by man through one means or another. The study of development administration proceeds on the same assumption, of course. It is entirely possible that some growth in the direction of modernity or nation-building and socio-economic progress can come about without being specifically planned or even intended. Since extensive progress toward achievement of these goals is likely to require major system change, it is also likely that most development on a major scale will be planned at least to the extent of encouraging environmental factors favorable to unplanned development.

Still, many of the accomplishments of any large organization such as government are clearly not planned or even intended—at least by the authorities that be. And the underlying motivations for actions are normally very diverse and are by no means exclu-

Sets of Conditions Leading to Development

Type	Characteristics		
	Directional growth	System change	Planned or intended
1. Ideal	+	+	+
2. Short-run payoff	+	−	+
3. Long-run payoff	−	+	+
4. Failure	−	−	+
5. Environmental stimulus	+	+	−
6. Pragmatism	+	−	−
7. Crisis	−	+	−
8. Static society	−	−	−

sively developmental or antidevelopmental. It would be unduly restrictive to impute to any government or bureaucracy complete rationality and singleness or duality of purpose. There are almost no occasions when both the power and task elites, much less the bureaucracy, are developmentalist-minded, i.e., single-purpose oriented in the direction of development (Lee). Decision-making involves both facts and values, and there may be ignorance of the one, disagreement concerning the other, and avoidance of the consequences of either (Landau). Some change is planned, other change is largely unplanned. Even within the area of planned change, there are intended and unintended aspects to the results. Some planned change may result in more modernity quite accidentally.

One necessary task for development administration is identification of the circumstances under which modernity or nation-
building and socio-economic progress take place. Several sets of
conditions are possible, using directional growth, system change,
and planned or intended change as varying elements. They are
summarized in tabular form on page 9. Let us turn to an examination of each of these sets of conditions.

The Ideal: Planned Directional Growth with System Change

From an ideal point of view, development is often considered
to be a regular process in which plans for growth in the direction
of modernity or nation-building and socio-economic progress are
made, programs are worked up and implemented, and system
change as well as growth takes place. Changes instrumental to
goal accomplishment such as differentiation and co-ordination
are brought about as necessary. The fact that many planning
commissions have been created in the less developed countries,
often as a matter of high priority, reflects this view of the development process. Among the reasons planning bodies have
been created are to emulate neighboring countries and to help a
country appear modern. They may represent a requirement laid
down by foreign or international aid agencies as a condition of
assistance to the host country. Partly they may represent a desire
on the part of the leaders to maximize the possibility of achieving
development goals. Whatever the explanation for their establishment, the planning bodies represent a judgment on someone's
part (host country, neighboring country, assistance agency) that
planned, intended, and even orderly change is the most likely
way in which development—both system alteration and growth
—can be brought about. A central planning body is thought to be
the capstone of the process.

The planning commissions represent a kind of model or ideal
that is never fully attained in practice. Perhaps land reform on
the island of Taiwan is one of the best approximations of it. It was
planned thoroughly and adopted as policy and when carried out
made basic changes in the system for both the farmers or peas-

ants and the former landlords. The result was directional growth —in this instance, an increase in agricultural production.

The ideal set of conditions of planning, system change, and growth does not often evidence itself. There are two major reasons. First of all, the ability of any political and administrative system to will directional growth and system change is severely restricted. The facts-value decisional framework is simply too complicated and disagreement over values too patent. Because modernity or nation-building and socio-economic progress are not the only major values sought in any society, they compete with many others (Riggs, Abueva, Lee). In any large setting of development administration, a variety of programmatic and expediency values will obtain. Different agencies or other groups will have different combinations of values and so will different individuals. In order to select any development goal authoritatively, a planning commission and associated decisional groups will have to make many compromises. They will have to find the lowest common denominator to obtain maximum support, which is often hard to do. For example, they will probably have to rely on groups and individuals who have strong expediency interests in the projected program, in combination with those with appropriate programmatic interests. From a developmentalist point of view, this is equivalent to saying that in almost all cases many groups or individuals will be supporting programs of growth in a modernity direction for the "wrong" (non-programmatic) reasons. The development of an adequate and stable support base for changes that are far-reaching and long range is difficult under such circumstances.

The ability of any administrative system to carry out a planned program of major change is often severely limited. Successful innovation in an administrative setting is not easily accomplished. Almost all the countries of Southeast Asia have planning commissions that work carefully to put out five-year plans or their equivalent. The great majority of these plans have been complete failures in practice, no matter what their technical quality. Prominent among the reasons for failure is an inadequate administrative system. Planned change is especially difficult to bring about

if it involves heavy administrative burdens as it almost always
does. Even more serious, much planned change requires prior
basic alterations in the political and administrative systems. On
occasion, major changes may be embraced temporarily by politicians or the bureaucracy, for rejecting the past and looking to the
future are popular things to support. When faced with the details
of executing such changes they find the difficulties great. Without
the alterations, the administrative system and the political support base are likely to be inadequate to the task of carrying
through major system change and growth. There are always those
who will gain from a given system change or who may favor it for
other reasons. But the forces that are especially strong, the majority, are those embedded in the status quo; strongly development-
oriented administrators are a small minority.

For this reason much administrative system change is brought
about piecemeal, so that the broad issues of major administrative
change need not be faced. For example, change in the personnel
systems of the less developed countries comes especially hard,
and is normally carried out indirectly piece by piece, rather than
broadside (Khanna).

The Short-run Payoff: Planned Directional Growth with No System Change

The difficulty of introducing major system changes has led
many leaders of the less developed countries to explore the possibilities of maximizing development within the limitations of the
present system. There is also a positive attraction to such a
strategy. It has a maximum payoff in the short run in terms of
consumption or in terms of nation-building and socio-economic
progress. It is the easy way, and is less offensive politically than
system change.

There are at least four circumstances in which planned directional growth with no system change is likely to be the course
selected by leaders. Where the leadership of a country is not
revolutionary and represents a balancing of forces, short-range
results are appealing. Second, if there is little technical assistance

or foreign aid or if such assistance or aid is obtainable without major strings attached, planned directional growth with no system change is attractive. In cases where the country's leadership is experiencing political trouble, there is a desire for stabilization. Finally, in countries where there is a demand to show results or an emphasis on consumption, the short-run payoff is frequently followed. However, in all four cases there may be devotion to the idea of development. Ideally this devotion is reflected in carefully laid plans, suitable goals, and appropriate execution.

An excellent example of planned directional growth with no system change is the promotion of native arts and crafts, such as the cottage industry programs in India and Pakistan. These programs were examined carefully by the respective national planning commissions and adopted as a part of the plans. They did not disturb the existing economic or social structures. Still, economic gains for the countries concerned and for the peasants or others participating have been realized. These gains have been small. That is often true of the short-run payoff strategy; the returns are relatively limited because the basic system remains intact.

Maximizing development within the limitations of the present system does not mean that the amount of differentiation cannot be increased in any way or the level of co-ordination raised. It is a matter of degree. Differentiation and co-ordination present leaders with a tremendous range of possibilities. The creation of an in-service training unit in the personnel agency of the government may not be threatening to anyone, at least initially, even if the function has not been performed previously. Similarly, subdividing an existing bureau of a rather unimportant agency may not be difficult; to add additional units to a branch of an agency may enhance the authority of its chief. These moves are in the direction of differentiation and ultimately require new or supplementary mechanisms for co-ordination. Still, nothing very threatening is likely to come from them in the short run. Changes internal to an agency headed by an innovator that do not involve major system changes can be made rather rapidly and easily. In contrast, the minister or department head who tries to establish fundamentally new rules for the administrative system over which he presides finds many impediments in his path.

In sum, it is evident that substantial growth in output, even impressive growth, can be brought about with no or minor changes in the administrative system, but there are points beyond which such increases in output cannot go.

The Long-run Payoff: Planned System Change with No Directional Growth

Planned system change without an accompanying growth in the direction of modernity or nation-building and socio-economic progress is a common short-run occurrence, and may also obtain over relatively long periods of time. System change does not necessarily result in growth. It may, in fact, have an adverse effect on growth. Some land reform has resulted in lower agricultural production. To accomplish both the socio-political and economic growth objectives behind land reform, two basic system changes are usually required. First, large traditional landholdings must be broken up and the peasants given the land. This may mean a drop in production or a limitation on future growth of production. Second, a means must be found of grouping small holdings into parcels more amenable to efficient production, perhaps through co-operatives or displacement of some farmers.

Of course, political and administrative systems themselves are objects of value. To use Esman's classification, conservative oligarchies, competitive interest-oriented party systems, dominant mass party systems, authoritarian military reform regimes, and Communist totalitarian regimes are political systems that vary widely in regard to differentiation and co-ordination. Each system has distinctive consequences or implications for administration. Each has its vigorous champions, individuals and groups who highly value the system—the system's pattern of differentiation and co-ordination. If the outputs flowing from the system in such areas as socio-economic progress are not as great as desired, the advocates nevertheless are content to continue the system for other values it brings—in some cases expedient, rather than programmatic, values.

Planned system change with little or no immediate growth in a development direction may result from an emphasis on production rather than on consumption. In this context, production is used in the broadest meaning, including the nation's capacity to produce larger outputs in an economic, social, or nation-building direction. A government emphasizing such goals is production-oriented. Consumption may be deferred for a relatively short period of time, or it may be postponed for a generation or more. However, in the case of planned production, growth in the direction of modernity is a future expectation, if not a substantial reality for the present. It is the hard decision. If the leaders seriously seek major growth in the future and have a strong support base, they may decide to pull in on immediate gains so that in the longer view much more can be had.

Behind the plans and accompanying changes in the case of Indonesia was the hope that in the long run basic structural changes would result in achievement of an Indonesian version of modernity or nation-building and socio-economic progress. During most of Sukarno's rule, per capita income showed disappointing trends. This element of socio-economic progress was not achieved. Nor was political participation increased, at least in an orderly manner. Yet the changes that were wrought in the economic and political spheres were extensive. The extent to which these were planned is a matter that is difficult to ascertain, but it is probably not inaccurate to say that during much of the period basic changes in the economic and political system were being planned and carried out in a typically Sukarno manner.

Failure: Planning with No Growth or System Change

A group of Asian and American economists meeting at the East-West Center in Honolulu in 1965 concluded that development planning in Southeast Asia had been a failure. Certainly economic growth had not been accelerated. Economic indicators were unanimous on that point. Apparent growth was barely adequate to cover population increase and inflation. Aside from the system changes forced upon most of these countries by newly won independence and refugees, few system changes were in evidence. Thailand, with no independence or refugee problems, had experienced neither substantial system change nor growth.

Still, it is difficult to render a final judgment of failure. Both system change and growth may be in the making in a country, yet outward signs may not be present. Reverses may be temporary, and what is failure from one perspective may be success from another.

An excellent illustration of the difficulties of determining failure in regard to growth with or without major system change is provided by the experience with budget reform in Vietnam in the late fifties. The budget function was removed from the Ministry of Finance and the foreign aid function from the Ministry of Public Works. A central budget agency was authorized. A highly innovating director was recruited from inside the civil service system. He first embarked upon changing the internal administrative system of the budget agency. Without firing existing employees, or in any way demoting them, he launched a large retraining program and assigned new duties to each. Employees who previously had been guards at the door were trained to run card sorters. More experienced employees were trained as budget analysts. Gradually the entire operation became capable of carrying out complete machine budgeting and accounting, giving the president a comprehensive expenditure balance each month within a few days after the accounting period ended. Program control and budgeting were the focus of internal training. Training sessions were also held for budget officers in each of the several ministries and agencies of the government. Up to this point, a highly innovating budget director with occasional assistance from one or two foreign advisers had made extensive changes in budget procedures largely using the transferred personnel, with very few newcomers. Most of these internal changes were accomplished within a year, with a great increase in output.

The limitations of output increases without major system change external to an agency is illustrated by subsequent events. Ultimately, the budget director was confronted by increasing antagonism on the part of the heads of other agencies, especially when the concepts of program control and program budgeting were introduced. These concepts, carried to their logical end, would have involved a major shift in the decision-making framework of the government. They would have resulted in a substantial change in the role of the budget agency, the presidency, the finance ministry, and others. As he himself had expected, the budget director was eventually removed because the ultimate logic of the reforms involved major government-wide change.

Several propositions relative to innovation suggest themselves:

1. The less an innovation involves a threat to the security of employees or the personnel system, the more probable its success. Perhaps if Vietnam had had a personnel system based on civil service classes together with personnel rotation, as do India and Pakistan, the budget reforms would have been far more difficult to consummate.

2. Changes within an agency headed by an innovator that involve major system changes tend to create resistance because the major changes have implications for those outside the agency.

3. Any proposed major changes in the administrative system of agencies external to that of the innovator will encounter extremely heavy resistance.

4. Innovation short of government-wide change will be inhibited to the extent that central controls are present.

From one point of view, the budget reform was a failure. From another, it was a partial success. Changes had taken place, but some of them were erased. Others remained.

Environmental Stimulus: Unplanned Directional Growth with System Change

That growth in the direction of modernity or nation-building and socio-economic progress involving major differentiation and co-ordination can take place in an unplanned manner or context may seem at first a complete impossibility. Differentiation, co-or-dination, and growth seem to require deliberate acts to bring them into being. In large part this is true. However, such deliber-ate acts are not always the result of planning, and certainly not necessarily the result of long-range planning with the usual con-trols that assure implementation of the plan.

The process of planning on a government-wide basis involves several steps: goals are determined, priorities established, pro-grams of action identified, and implementation devices and con-trols put into effect. Short of government-wide planning or per-haps within it, a similar process can be imaged for each major government agency.

There are several things that make planning in this manner unlikely or at least very difficult. First of all, a strong nation-wide push for developmental change is the most difficult to carry out in practice. It encounters a maximum of resistance. For such a movement to take place, the development politics base of devel-opment administration must be secure, preferably in both the power and task elite, but especially in the latter (Lee). While some planned change can emanate from the center with deter-mined and able leadership, the most extensive innovations are likely to be a product of individual ministries, bureaus, provinces, or districts—and the autonomous pilot project most of all. Central planning may have little to do with many such undertakings. In any event, there is an important distinction between macro and micro planning.

There is also an important difference between planning as normally conceived and planning "unplanned" change. Many of the changes brought about in any society come by reaction of leaders or groups to certain environmental factors. To the extent that such environmental factors can be augmented, non-directed major change may take place. In the obvious case of the private sector an entrepreneur may be encouraged to embark upon a new undertaking because of the "environment" of government policies, even without formal government approval or informal request for establishing a new enterprise. There may be planning for the encouragement of business, but no detailed planning as to who does what where. It is also possible that a government may maintain conditions that encourage business expansion by doing nothing. To the extent that there is reward for effective performance in development activities within or without government, a healthy competition may ensue that will bring about substantial unplanned change.

Within a bureaucracy, even major system changes can be brought about by *ad hoc* pragmatic adaptation to the conditions in which an agency finds itself. These changes may be planned in the sense that actions in regard to them are rational on-the-spot adaptations to particular circumstances, but they may represent no larger commitment to planned development. Such adaptation is especially evident in field administration. Given the same quota of personnel, equal financial resources, and the same generally prescribed terms of reference and set of procedures, twenty field offices will produce widely different results. Some of the differences will undoubtedly be due to variation in the personal characteristics of the public employees stationed in each of the several field offices. Many of the differences will be due to the pragmatic adaptation of the activities of each of the offices to their circumstances or environment. This kind of pragmatic or unplanned adaptation to local circumstances can be accelerated by greater delegation of authority to field offices. However, such delegation is often difficult to achieve because of bureaucratic and political pressures.

Emulation is another force for change that may have an essentially unplanned character, at least from the standpoint of ultimate development objectives. Foreign or domestic models—programs, agencies, procedures, etc.—may be emulated on a wide scale (Hsueh, Xuan). The reasons for doing so may not be explicit. Implicitly or explicitly, prestige may be at stake. When this is so, a milestone of development has been passed, since prestige is often on the side of change. While formalism may be a result of emulation, it is not invariably the result. Emulation is an especially strong force for change in those situations where communication and transportation are good so that opportunities for stimulation from other models are readily available. If in addition a sense of, or a desire for, modernity has become moderately widespread, there may be important stimuli and rewards for those who emulate. An increase in such rewards together with strengthened provisions for travel and communication could bring handsome returns.

Thus, through decentralized initiative, competition, adaptation, and emulation, much change, even of a major kind, can take place although the normal processes of planned change are not utilized. Environmental stimulus is a potent force for change.

Pragmatism: Unplanned Directional Growth with No System Change

Decentralized initiative, competition, adaptation, and emulation are far more likely to be instrumental in bringing about growth in the direction of modernity or nation-building and socio-economic progress if relatively little change in differentiation and co-ordination is involved. A park department increases its outputs because more visitors come. Customs increases its services because the number of visitors to the country sharply increases. If the increase is large enough, major system change may be forced upon both immigration and customs. The output of many government agencies will thus be a function, in part, of the demand for their services.

Even in the case of providing services the demand for which has not increased, unplanned growth in a development direction is a distinct possibility. At a community level, a village worker in one village may have results that far exceed those of his fellow workers in nearby villages. These results may not stem from the planning of any agency. Through decentralized initiative, competition, adaptation, or emulation, the village worker may be encouraged to help secure a significant increase in the level of goal achievement in the village.

Unplanned growth in a development direction accompanied by no system change is probably the most common form of development to be found in mildly liberalizing regimes the world around. It is relatively painless. It produces some short-run pay-off. It does not require complicated planning mechanisms or difficult decisions about priorities. Certainly in countries where integrated attacks on poverty, disease, and social isolation have not been launched, and there is at least a limited desire to adjust to the changing world, unplanned growth in a development direction with no system change is a natural and even an attractive course to follow. Before extensive programs of technical assistance in a less developed country, such a course of action has been a natural pragmatic reaction to events. Without strong controls or "strings" attached to technical assistance, unplanned directional growth is a natural strategy to fall back on. It is also a natural and most important supplement to extensive programs of planned change.

Crisis: Unplanned System Change with No Directional Growth

Unplanned changes largely come about as the result of decentralized initiative, competition, adaptation, and emulation. All of these may be present in unplanned change, but decentralized initiative, adaptation, and emulation are particularly likely to be at work in the case of unplanned system change without directional growth. Emulation can bring changes in a system without developmental growth orientation being present, in which case the system may change in some substantial respects but nation-building and socio-economic progress may not be furthered. A high degree of formalism exists in many societies. Even without development orientation in a society, formalistic system change may eventually lead to greater output and developmental growth.

For the most part, unplanned system change with no directional growth is the result of adjustment to emergencies. The ravages of war, international or civil, have inflicted their misfortunes on many a less developed country, and brought quick unplanned system change in their wake. The shock of newly won or granted independence has had similar effects. Refugee problems, starvation, uncontrolled epidemics, floods, and drought are also types of crises that have required major on-the-spot adjustments. Under such circumstances, decentralized initiative and adaptation, related to the particular nature of a crisis, may produce major system change. Emulation is often found in such cases. It seems to provide a quick solution. Eventually, prolonged crises normally inspire planned as well as unplanned adjustments.

Static Society: No Plans, No Change

Few societies are totally static under the conditions that obtain in the world today. But there are segments of societies that approach a static state. Just as there are pockets of change in developing countries, there may also be pockets of resistance to change. And even under quite favorable circumstances, a certain amount of driftlessness often occurs in larger segments of a nation. Even crises may not arouse a desire for change. They may be viewed fatalistically, not as catastrophes that might be prevented or ameliorated by man.

The introduction of change into a previously static society can take place in a planned or unplanned manner, encompassing the several possibilities outlined previously. Still, all development efforts are likely to be confronted by static conditions that form hurdles to be overcome and by islands or areas of static conditions that exist hand in hand with widespread change.

To be complete, the list of possible sets of conditions under which developmental change takes place could be extended to include conditions under which changes contrary to developmental growth take place, whether planned or unplanned, and with or without major system change. The same kind of analysis could be extended to all kinds of values or goals, not just to those of development. However, enough has been said to serve the heuristic purposes of the present discussion which focuses on the development process.

A review of these eight types will be instructive to both the scholar and the administrator. It is apparent that the conditions under which change takes place are many and varied. The formal planning process has three major strategies: emphasis on production, emphasis on consumption, and emphasis on both. A similar group of three types exists for unplanned change. Each of these six sets of conditions can be further refined to take account of additional strategic and tactical choices. In applying this scheme to an administrative system, a member of the task elite or a policy-concerned administrator would have to make allowance for great variations in the conditions that obtain from one period of time to another and from one part of the administrative system to another. It is possible, even probable, that several sets of conditions will exist to some degree or another in any large agency and certainly in any government as a whole—perhaps all eight, including the two that lead to no change. The decisions to be made are concerned essentially with the balance or mix of the six types with some kind of payoff.

Instead of being a standard prescription for or description of developmental change, planned system change resulting in directional growth is a set of conditions that can be considered one ideal type, never fully attained in practice. Planning and system change are the heart of much hard work in development administration. They are potentially producers of rather sweeping increases in, and alteration of, system outputs. Still, if all change had to rely on the two together, even the most theoretically effective combination, there would be less modernization in the world than there is. Planning and system change are important, but not the exclusive, aspects of the development mix of a government or agency. A government or ministry devoted to modernity or nation-building and socio-economic progress can be expected to consider how to encourage developmental change under each of the six sets of conditions leading to change. Not to do so would be very shortsighted and result in rather heavy-handed planning. Full-scale planning fades into a less vigorous type that eventually melds into a lack of planning or perhaps just maintaining an encouraging environment for modernizing change. Major system change fades into minor system change that eventually melds into a lack of system change. It would be a likely hypothesis that in their efforts to achieve development goals and outputs, public agencies actually prefer to encourage unplanned change and planned change that avoids major alterations in the system.

As for the scholar, development administration, as a part of the policy sciences, could legitimately focus on some of the end results of the policies or goals of the political and administrative systems, such as modernity or nation-building and socio-economic progress. The programs or innovations introduced in developing countries would then be classified among the principal independent variables, the outputs or goal accomplishment the ultimate dependent variables, system changes possible intermediate dependent variables, and environmental or cultural factors intervening or intermediate dependent variables. These would be tendencies, and would not necessarily be true of every research project within development administration.

If he is to have a realistic research model in studying development administration, the scholar would be well advised to take into account the several different sets of conditions under which development outputs can be increased. He is faced with a number of special problems. It is true that using goals, objectives, or outputs as the main dependent variables in a research design does not thereby make the research biased or in any way unscientific. But the variety of goals or outputs encompassed in modernity or nation-building and socio-economic progress is great and may be highly confusing unless operationalized definitions are carefully set forth in each case. The combinations of outputs and goals will also vary from agency to agency and country to country. Goal identification is never simple, and in complex developmental change situations it can be very elusive and difficult. Formal and informal, stated and unstated, intended and unintended, planned and not planned—and goals of whom—these are a few of the dimensions that need to be taken into account.

Finally, the scholar needs to concern himself with a dynamic research model that will assist in answering a basic question: what strategies, policies, or programs make for the most effective growth toward modernity, toward nation-building and socio-economic progress. In answering this question, the social scientist will be aided by the general concurrence that has been achieved from ten years of debate and research on what constitute some of the major elements of the process of developmental change.

Chapter 2

The Idea of Development Administration

Fred W. Riggs

The new field of development administration has raised a host
of theoretical questions which still remain unanswered. The attempt to apply Western concepts of public administration to the
problems of developing countries has revealed major shortcomings in established concepts and doctrines. The efforts of governments in Asia, Africa, and Latin America to promote development through economic planning and large-scale projects have
brought into view many phenomena and relationships hitherto
unknown or at least not well known. It may help us to understand
these phenomena, and to evaluate the limitations as well as the
contributions to be expected of administrative science, if we
focus attention on some of the conceptual and theoretical problems which undergird our thinking in this field.

The implicit premises of administrative thought in the West,
notably in the United States, have been found wanting as a basis
for understanding the problems of development administration in
Asia. In part this is because they are essentially non-ecological in
character, in part because they have been static in their structural
presuppositions. They have been non-ecological insofar as they
failed to relate administrative behavior to its environment. They
have been static insofar as they took the basic institutional patterns of social structure for granted, failing to examine the conditions which brought these patterns into existence, which maintained them, or which caused them to change. Can a developmental frame of reference overcome these limitations? Perhaps
the answer is yes.

It may be that the concept of "development" will provide a key for opening up a new understanding of the nature of administrative processes, not only in Asia and other non-Western areas but also in the United States and other Western countries. For the concept of development is essentially dynamic, not static, in character. Moreover, it can only be understood in an ecological perspective. Unfortunately our ideas about development have been largely formed in terms of some of the consequences of development, not in terms of the essence of the process which generates these consequences.

The point may be illustrated by an analogy with the concept of "life." Such signs of life as breathing, heartbeat, and warmth cannot be equated with life, and yet we say that someone is living if we observe these signs. In the same way rising per capita income, increasing administrative efficiency, and mounting political vitality may be regarded as signs of development, but they do not tell us what development essentially consists of. If we are interested in development—and development administration reflects inherently a concern with the organization and implementation of programs intended to advance developmental goals—then we must not be content with a superficial or "commonsense" idea of what development is.

In earlier writings, the writer has laid a basis for the analysis which follows. He has explored the concept of ecology as applied to the study of administrative behavior[1] and has discussed the meaning of development, with particular reference to political change.[2] Here the discussion will draw on these earlier essays, reformulating some of the ideas, in order to present a theoretical framework for understanding development administration. The hope is that this framework will have a particular relevance to the analysis of problems of development administration in Asia, and that it will also be useful for the study of administrative problems in the United States and other areas.

1. Fred W. Riggs, *The Ecology of Public Administration* (Bombay: East Asia Publishing, 1962).

2. Fred W. Riggs, "The Theory of Political Development," in James C. Charlesworth, ed., *Contemporary Political Analysis* (New York: Free Press, 1967), pp. 317–349.

The first part of the chapter consists of a definition of development in terms of rising levels of autonomy or discretion, in the sense of ability to choose among alternatives, not, of course, in the sense of caution or moderation. The exercise of discretion is one form of autonomy. Later in this chapter two other forms of autonomy are distinguished. This concept, which contains the essential meaning of development, is defined ecologically. In an earlier essay[3] increasing autonomy (discretion) was treated as a consequence of development, but it is more helpful to think of it as the essence of development. This enables us to view increasing levels of "diffraction"—a term defined and discussed at some length elsewhere[4]—as a necessary and perhaps even sufficient condition for development, and the various signs of development (growth, efficiency, etc.) as consequences.

This conception of development overcomes the essentially static quality of systems theory as it has been used in various writings.[5] Yet systems theory provides a necessary foundation for the understanding of diffraction, which is the essential basis for increasing autonomy (discretion). Consequently, the second part of this essay is devoted to a review and restatement of fundamental concepts of systems theory, to the definition of political and administrative systems, and to clarifying the distinction between structure and function on which this whole framework of analysis rests.

The goals of development are multiple. It is concerned not only with raising levels of economic production and consumption, but with freedom, justice, security, and the basic integrity of man as a human being. In this sense the study of development is unavoidably value-oriented. But it does not necessarily assign priorities

3. Fred W. Riggs, "The Ecology of Development," *CAG Occasional Papers* (Bloomington, Ind.: Indiana University, 1964). A further discussion of the ecological framework for studying administrative behavior is contained in Riggs, "Modernization and Development Administration," *CAG Occasional Papers* (Bloomington, Ind.: Indiana University, 1966).

4. Fred W. Riggs, *Administration in Developing Countries: The Theory of Prismatic Society* (Boston: Houghton Mifflin, 1964), pp. 19–27, 416–423.

5. Alfred Diamant, "The Temporal Dimension in Models of Administration and Organization," *CAG Occasional Papers* (Bloomington, Ind.: Indiana University, 1965). Diamant has examined the implicit temporal framework of various writers concerned with politics, administration and change, and finds most of them, including the writer's, to be "static."

among these values. During a period of anti-imperialist struggle, the goals of freedom and equality may be emphasized; at other times increasing production and the alleviation of poverty are given primacy. With development defined in terms of growing autonomy, it involves an increase in the ability of social systems to make choices between competing values, in their capacity to exercise discretion. Therefore, equating development with any of these values must be avoided. But examining the consequences for any social system of the choices that it does make cannot be avoided. In this sense the exercise of increasing autonomy, which is the core of development administration, carries penalties as well as rewards, and it raises some critical dilemmas. These choices, which are crucial for development, create a dialectic which needs to be examined, and this constitutes the subject matter of the third part of this essay.

Development as Increasing Discretion: An Ecological Definition

The concept of development as increasing discretion is essentially non-deterministic and ecological. Yet the misuse of ecological analysis has led to deterministic views of politics and administration which seem to contradict the very idea of development, thereby blocking a better understanding of this difficult subject. Naive interpretations of ecology have suggested that social systems are prisoners of their environment, that they can do nothing to change the conditions which, in effect, predetermine their fate. Just as, perhaps, we might view biological evolution in terms of chance mutations and the capacity to survive in changing natural habitats, so human development can be viewed as the essentially involuntary response of mankind to unplanned and largely unwelcome occurrences outside our control.

Discretion: An Ecological Transaction

Yet such an interpretation is by no means implicit in the concept of ecology. The term, it is true, has been borrowed from biology where there is no room for conscious decision-making on the part of animal and plant species. Even in its sociological applications to urban life, the tendency has been to focus on the unconscious outcome of struggles for survival as determinants of land settlement patterns. But when applied to the relation between politico-administrative systems and their environments, we must add to the traditional conceptions of ecology by recognizing that human groups, unlike plants and animals, can make conscious decisions affecting their own behavior. In this way they can take steps to change the environment in which they live. Thus environments influence without determining the behavior of human groups, and reciprocally, social systems can reshape their environment to such a degree that they can deliberately modify the constraints under which they exist. They exercise discretion to the degree that they can do this.

Unsophisticated applications of the concept of ecology to political science and public administration, applications in which the word "ecology" is treated as a synonym for "environment," have reinforced the view that governments can best be studied as dependent variables. This mind-set provides a misleadingly "scientific" basis for "explaining" the historical emergence of particular patterns of government, but rules out conscious efforts, by deliberate human action, to change either the governments themselves or their environments. A more sophisticated conception of political and administrative ecology arises when government is considered as an independent variable, not as dependent. Then the way in which politico-administrative systems decide (exercise discretion) to change their own environments can be examined.

Perhaps the fact that public administration could be studied non-ecologically in Western societies explains this naive interpretation of ecology. Under the conditions which prevailed in these countries, bureaucracies had gradually been formed and controlled in such a way as to become specialized organs of administration. In a milieu where academic specialization prevailed, it seemed natural enough for one group of scholars to focus its attention on the behavior of national civilian bureaucracies and to consider that in so doing they were encompassing the field of "public administration." They scarcely found it necessary to examine the linkages between the environment of government and bureaucratic behavior which made it possible for these organizations to serve predominantly administrative functions.

It was only when they began to look more closely at the governments of non-Western countries, particularly in Asia, that they started to question the traditional assumptions. They discovered that to a considerable degree public officials—both military and civil—not only served administrative functions but also took a large part in political decision-making. It seemed natural, as a first step in removing the ethnocentric blinders which hampered the ability to see what was happening in these governmental systems, to direct attention to the environmental constraints which appeared to shape public administration in unfamiliar ways.

The writer's efforts to make a contribution at this point led to the formulation of the "prismatic model" as a means of characterizing some of the administrative difficulties which typically arose in societies where new patterns of relatively differentiated governmental conduct were adopted despite the prevalence and persistence of largely undifferentiated structures of power and authority. It was this overlapping of traditional and modern, of ascriptive and achievement-oriented modes of recruitment, of particularistic and universalistic norms, which generated the heterogeneity and formalism that were characteristic prismatic traits.

These efforts were necessary and useful, especially as a corrective at a time when the influence of environmental factors was largely neglected. Not surprisingly, however, the rise of interest in environmental forces affecting administrative behavior led to excesses and misunderstandings, of which the tendency toward environmental determinism was only one. It became difficult to know how to deal with environmental forces, how to discriminate between the relevant and irrelevant, the influential and non-influential. At the one extreme were the historicists or "area specialists" who insisted that everything was relevant, that each case was unique, and that only by including every environmental factor could one hope to understand governmental phenomena in any particular case. Others sought criteria to make the problem more manageable, picking now on this environmental factor, now on another, in the hope that some key variables could be found which would enable us to "explain" behaviors which struck us as mysterious, if not inscrutable. Some, for example, fixed on culture as the key, or on patterns of family organization, on religion, and on "traditional" value orientations. Others sought an explanation in psychological variables, in attitudes toward achievement, power, or self-identification and esteem. Still others found levels of economic growth to be the critical factors, and some thought that differences between democratic and authoritarian modes of political organization might explain variations in administrative performance.

A more satisfactory approach, in the writer's opinion, lies between these extremes. Without taking every environmental condition into account, one must nevertheless consider a wide range of variables, and one needs a basic framework of analysis to bring them into view. Such a framework, for example, would include the temporal-spatial setting, or the historical and geographic continuum of social action; the demographic and psychological contexts, or the human actors in government, considered both quantitatively and qualitatively; and the cultural system, including learned patterns of conduct and the artifacts, which are transmitted from generation to generation, such as language, religion, laws, institutions, currencies, and technologies.[6]

Such an enumeration of environmental categories may prove useful not only as a means of identifying constraints affecting administrative behavior but also as a clue to areas of governmental influence over the environment. For it is primarily this dimension, the capacity of social systems to reshape their environments, which concerns us here. To clarify this point by illustration, one dimension of the environment is the psychological and demographic. If the population in a given society is uniformly illiter-

6. Fred W. Riggs, "Social Change and Political Development" (Bloomington, Ind.: mimeographed, 1964), Parts 3 and 4.

ate, a pattern of administration which relies on written communications cannot be established. Any proposals to reform administrative procedures by introducing written documents would be bound to fail. However, it may be possible to provide education for some members of the population, possibly with external assistance. Once members of the population have learned how to read, the human environment of administration will have been changed. New administrative practices requiring literacy then become possible.

Literacy has been used here as an elementary characteristic, but one could add any other skills and values affecting administrative behavior. For example, the collection of income taxes in the United States depends on the willingness of employers to withhold and submit tax payments, and of ordinary citizens to prepare and submit complicated tax returns. Effective operation of this type of revenue administration depends, among other things, upon the ability and readiness of a large majority of the population to comply with this procedure. In some countries it might be that most of the population would be unable and unwilling to comply. If so, this important type of administrative behavior would not be feasible. It could only be introduced after members of the population had been resocialized to enable them to comply with such a program.

This illustration perhaps clarifies an essential feature of development administration, its two-sidedness. On the one side, it involves transformation of environmental conditions, raising of educational standards, improvement of public health, expansion of economic production, construction of roads, dams, power plants, and irrigation works, conservation of natural resources and their more effective utilization. Such activities are possible to the degree that governments deliberately choose to reshape their human and non-human environments. But on the other side, these developmental activities by government are only possible to the extent that the administrative effectiveness of government can be enhanced.

The reciprocal relatedness of these two sides involves a chicken and egg type of causation. Administration cannot normally be improved very much without changes in the environmental constraints (the "infrastructure") that hamper its effectiveness; and the environment itself cannot be changed unless the administration of developmental programs is strengthened. There is a margin for maneuver, however, such that small increments of administrative growth may make possible environmental transformations which, in turn, will enable administrative practices to be improved some more. The first aspect involves the administration of development; the second involves the development of administration. Neither can proceed alone. Therefore, referring to them both as "development administration" is justified.

Let us speak of relationships between any social system and its environment as *transactions*. It is a transaction, then, for a government to engage in soil conservation, the building of highways, regulation of the calendar, the spread of schools, or the amendment and revision of laws. Each of these transactions brings about some corresponding modification of the environment which generates a feedback to the government as actor. The environment, in other words, is a reactive system. Its character changes, and a changed environment brings about modifications in the character of the social systems contained within it.

A measure of the increasing discretion of a social system is its ability not only to launch programs designed to reshape its environment but also to predict environmental reactions and the influence they will have on the social system itself. Conceivably environmental reactions can cause a reduction in the autonomy of social systems and thereby provoke breakdowns and even stagnation in a developing system.

In this essay not much more is said about the actions and reactions of environmental forces on social and administrative behavior. Not that this aspect of ecological transactions is not important. Quite the contrary, it is basic. But the main focus of this essay is on the other aspect, on the capacity of political and administrative systems to make choices and to exercise autonomy (discretion) to bring about environmental changes by deliberate programs and self-conscious decisions.

Reflection on the transactions between social systems and their environments, then, leads to the definition of development given above. To recapitulate: ecologically speaking, social systems enter into *transactions* with their environments, influencing and being influenced by them. The extent to which a social system can influence its environment and predict how its transactions will affect the environment and its reactions upon the system are a measure of its *autonomy (discretion)*. All social systems capable of making decisions have some discretion, but clearly some social systems have much more discretion than others. The more discretionary a system, the more developed: indeed, *development* is precisely the increase of discretion of social systems.

For further illustration, consider that social systems in industrialized societies, including not only national and local governments but also mines, factories, mechanized farms, and modern fisheries, can transform the raw materials of nature into consumer goods far more effectively than can the social systems of a primitive food-gathering society, or even those of a traditional agricultural civilization. Similarly, a modern society, through schools, public health schemes, family planning, the mass media, and legislative processes, can reshape its human and cultural environment to a much greater degree than is open to the people of a primitive society.

Let us refer to the opposite of discretion as *constraint*, that is, external rather than self-direction. Social systems are never fully discretionary or fully constrained, but they vary on a scale between these extremes. The higher the degree of discretion of any social system on this scale, the more developed it is; the more constrained, the less developed.

Autogeny: A Social Interaction

The word "autonomy" is frequently used in another sense from that of discretion. Since this other meaning is also important for our analysis, we must now take a look at it.

No social system exists in isolation from other social systems, which might therefore be counted as part of the environment. The concept of a social system's environment, however, has been described so as to exclude other social systems. An increase in the ability of one social system to influence or control another therefore may be thought of as an increase in *power,* but not as an increase in discretion. If it were discretion, one social system could increase its discretion relative to another only at the expense of the latter's loss of discretion. In other words, one might think of development as a "zero-sum" game in which the gain of one could be secured only by the loss of another. This would contradict the commonsense idea that development must improve the position of all.

If other social systems are thought of as outside the environment some of these difficulties disappear. One can, indeed, think of all social systems as themselves merely subsystems of one universal or global social system. In this context, the relations between social systems are those between elements of a single system, not those between a system and its environment.

A similar conclusion is arrived at if roles rather than social systems are considered, for social systems are sets of roles. The environment of a role, like the environment of a social system, consists of elements which are not roles, such as the time-space setting, the characteristics of the actors involved, and cultural elements which affect a role. A role is not a person, but a pattern of relationships between one actor, or one kind of actor, and others. Thus roles form a continuous web of relationships. All the other roles impinging on a particular role constitute its nexus, and all the social systems interacting with a given social system also form its nexus.

The relation of a system or role to its nexus should be distinguished from its relation with its environment. Discretion, as defined above, refers only to the latter relationship, not to the former. There is, however, a sense in which any actor or social system may act independently of other actors or social systems. This independence of action is often referred to as autonomy, but clearly it does not mean an ability to reshape environmental conditions. The two forms of autonomy, then, are essentially different, and only confusion can arise from using the same word for two ideas which are so likely to be mixed up. Therefore it seems necessary to use different terms for each of the concepts. The writer proposes, therefore, to use the word "autogeny" to refer to the degree of independence of a role or a social system in relation to its nexus. The degree to which interdependence between roles or social systems prevails may then be referred to as "heterogeny." Clearly no role or social system is ever completely autogenous or heterogenous. We are dealing with a scale in which roles and social systems vary between wide extremes, approaching but never reaching the extreme points on the scale.

Having made this distinction, it is now possible to observe that *although development involves an increase in the degree of autonomy (discretion) of social systems, it also involves a decrease in the degree of autonomy (autogeny)*. The reasons become clear upon reflection. A necessary condition for the increase of discretion of social systems is growing complexity and interdependence. The specialization of labor which is widely recognized to be an essential condition of industrialization implies interdependence. The manager of a factory as much as the worker on an assembly line is tightly meshed in a nexus of linked roles; management no less than trade union leadership must accommodate its conduct to the demands of others. Modern administration similarly requires co-ordination between chief and subordinate. Thus heterogeny increases concurrently with the complexity of human organization which makes discretion possible.

Subjectively, autogeny is valued more highly than discretion, especially by those who have more autogeny than discretion. It is probably true that people in traditional societies normally experience, psychologically, a high degree of autogeny. Although they are subjected to many cultural and material constraints imposed by their environment, they cannot imagine a different state of affairs and do not look upon these conditions as restraints. On the other hand, any imposition of specific demands for a modification in their behavior made by others on the basis of conscious decisions which suspend or modify traditional practices are looked upon as unwelcome interferences with freedom of action. Perhaps one can say that the lack of discretion is compensated for by a strong sense of autogeny.

By contrast, people in a complex modern society have open to them a wide range of choice reflecting substantial discretion, but they must also submit to innumerable limitations on their freedom of action which are imposed by the decisions of others. Subjectively, however, they may well regard their discretion as an inadequate compensation for their lost autogeny since they often find the necessity of making choices itself irksome. No doubt it is not so much the freedom to choose as the freedom from restraints that makes autogeny attractive and discretion seem a poor substitute. In this sense, autogeny is experienced as inherently desirable, but discretion is useful only to the extent that it makes possible environmental transformations which are desired.

Autogeny vs. Discretion: Contrasting Forms of Autonomy

This distinction now permits clarification of the difference between development and growth, and shows how the desire for autogeny can block discretion. Like the word "autonomy," the word "development" is frequently used for quite different concepts. If an increase in discretion, i.e., development, enables a social system to reshape its environment, this means that it can secure from the environment more of the products that it desires, and that it can transform the environment so as to make such increases in production possible. Thus one consequence of development may be rising per capita income. Such increases in production and income are frequently referred to as "economic growth." Let us define growth as any increase in the outputs generated by a social system interacting with its environment.

It is a mistake to confuse the two types of change. A system that is increasingly discretionary may choose not to increase the production of material goods. If so, one could have development without growth. Moreover, a change in the environment, such as a technological innovation, foreign aid, or a climatic change, might bring about an increase in production even though there had been no rise in the level of discretion. One could, therefore, have growth without development.

Since hardship and penury are widespread, it is easy to understand that growth is universally popular. But the conditions requisite to an increase in discretion are not equally popular. They include a decline in the level of autogeny which, as we have seen, is normally felt subjectively as a deprivation. Development can be regarded as universally unpopular in contrast with growth, which is almost everywhere sought after. This helps to explain the "escape from freedom" in some industrial societies which have lapsed into totalitarianism, and the allure of neotraditionalism in some transitional societies which have fallen back from the challenges of modernization. Development, in other words, poses a difficulty familiar in psychological experiments on learning behavior in which a mouse must be willing to experience an electric shock in order to obtain a piece of cheese. Only a very hungry mouse will permit his appetite to overcome his fear, and many will collapse in neurotic frustration. Countries which seek the potential rewards of development in the form of economic growth must also put up with the penalties of development. The confusion of development with growth has made development seem intrinsically desirable to those who do not understand what it costs.

In earlier works the writer has defined development in terms of *diffraction,* as noted above. Here diffraction is treated as the necessary and perhaps the sufficient condition for development, i.e., for increased discretion. But the processes of diffraction typically entail a loss of autogeny which generates resistance at all levels, both from the elite and the mass in any social system. This is the basic reason that, although the fruits of development are universally acclaimed, the costs of development are too great for them to be paid.

In order to explain why diffraction makes increasing discretion possible, and why it also requires a decline in levels of autogeny, some of the key concepts in social science will have to be reviewed and restated. Since diffraction occurs in political and administrative systems, what is meant by these terms must be described more carefully. But since political and administrative systems are a special type of social system, the term "social system" must be explained first. A prerequisite to understanding the meaning of a social system is an ability to distinguish between structural and functional categories. Although this means covering ground that has already been traversed in various ways, the possibilities of confusion and misunderstanding are so great that it seems necessary to take the time and space for examination of these fundamental concepts.

Fundamental Concepts: A Review and Restatement

Traditional theories of public administration dealt primarily with the bureaucratic structures used in performing administrative functions. When these theories were applied to the study of non-Western governments, it became clear that, under the influence of different environmental constraints, governmental structures similar in form to those of the West actually performed in quite different ways. The result was, quite naturally, to discredit the study of administrative behavior in terms of formal structures. A new form of analysis, "structural-functionalism," borrowed from sociology, was adopted enthusiastically as a way of coming to grips more realistically with the administrative problems of developing countries.

This tendency was as necessary for the clarification of thinking about administrative behavior as was the associated stress on ecology. But just as the ecological framework led some to the oversimplified deterministic view that governments were merely "dependent variables," so structural-functionalism led to an exaggerated emphasis on function at the expense of structure. Just as ecology, properly understood, implies the autonomy (discretion) of a system as actor in addition to the dependence of a system on its environment, so structural-functionalism requires an analysis of structures as well as of functions.

The distinction is fundamental, and if it has been blurred it is in part because commonsense practice frequently uses both structural and functional criteria in defining words. Consider the essential ambiguity of a word like "teacher." The term might be defined as including anyone employed on the faculty of a school who teaches students. However, a distinction can be made between the formal role of faculty member in a school and the results of teaching. The former is a structural concept, the latter functional. The former refers to a pattern of institutionalization, a type of bureaucratic office. The latter refers to the consequences of action for another system, namely the students who learn from the teacher.

Structures and Functions

The mixed structural-functional definition gives rise to logical difficulties if there are teachers who do not teach or non-teachers who do teach. This difficulty disappears as soon as two different terms are adopted, one for the structural position of faculty member, another for the functional act of teaching. It is then possible to state the clear proposition that most faculty members engage in teaching. However, some faculty members do not teach —they may engage primarily in administration, research, or other functions. Moreover, it is clear that there are many kinds of people besides faculty members who are occupied in teaching. In other words, not all who teach are faculty members. The logical difficulties inherent in the usual meanings attributed to the word "teacher" now disappear.

Similar difficulties arise when the words "administrator" and "bureaucrat" are used as synonyms, referring in both instances to an occupant of the role of public official (a structure) who administers laws and policies (a function). We have here two different criteria, structural and functional. Clarity is gained if we separate them. A bureaucrat may be defined as any incumbent of a position in a bureaucracy. A bureaucracy in turn may be defined as a hierarchy of positions under the direction of an executive. In these terms the word "bureaucrat" refers to a structure.

By contrast, "administration" may be defined functionally, in terms of the implementation of a policy, law, or norm. It can then be hypothesized that most bureaucrats devote themselves primarily to administrative tasks, i.e., they are predominantly administrators. But this hypothesis also leaves room for exceptions: namely, that bureaucrats also devote themselves to other functions, including political action. Moreover, administrative tasks are sometimes performed by people who are not bureaucrats. Thus, the study of bureaucracy (a structure) includes non-administrative as well as administrative functions; and the study of administration (a function) includes the role of non-bureaucrats as well as of bureaucrats.

The use of the words "structure" and "function" is also confused by ambiguities in their meanings. The word "structure" is often used more narrowly than is intended here, and the word "function" more broadly. Let us examine each term separately.

A function in mathematics is a relationship between variables. Similarly, in social science a function is a relationship between social structures or systems. Thus, whereas one can specify the intrinsic characteristics of a structure, or of A, one cannot attribute a function to it; one can only specify functions as relations between A and B, between two or more structures. A structure can be said to have a function only if the other structure for which it has this function is specified. Thus a function of the United States Civil Service Commission is to recruit personnel for the United States government. To say that the commission's function is recruitment is an incomplete statement, since it does not recruit personnel for state and city governments, for private firms, for trade unions, etc.

This example illustrates another meaning often suggested by the word "function." It may be said that a function of the Forest Service is to prevent forest fires. One can interpret this statement as descriptive of a specialized kind of activity. In this sense, the word "function" is being used as a synonym for "activity." It seems better to use the word "activity" and not to use the word "function" for this meaning. We might then say that fighting forest fires is one of the activities of the Forest Service, but not a function.

The example of the Forest Service illustrates also another common usage of the word "function." The activity of fighting fires has an impact on the physical environment of the service. In this sense, it involves a relationship between a system and its environment, one in which the system is attempting to shape or reshape the environment, to exercise autonomy. Is it justifiable to use the term "function" then to specify this relationship, which is more than the mere activity? By doing so, confusion will be created since system-environment transactions involving discretion ought to be distinguished from system-system relationships involving autogeny. Let us therefore refer to an exercise of discretion designed to affect the environment as a program.

Clearly any activity, by these definitions, may also be a program and a function. Moreover, every program and function is also an activity, but some programs may not be functions and some functions may not be programs. It is possible also to find activities which are neither programs nor functions. Perhaps these possibilities can be clarified by a simple matrix of types of activities as follows:

		Function (system-system relationship)	
		Yes	No
Program (System-Environment transactions)	Yes	A	B
	No	C	D

Note: A = program + function, B = mere program, C = mere function, D = mere activity.

Items in cell A are then activities which are also functions and programs, i.e., they influence both the environment and another system. An illustration might be the collection of taxes by a revenue agency (an activity) which provides resources for a government (a function) and affects the production and distribution of wealth in the taxed population (a program). Since most bureaucratic activities probably also involve functions and programs, it is not difficult to see why these concepts have become confused and why the words "function," "program," and "activity" have tended to be used as synonyms. But if progress is to be made in the analysis of development administration, separation of these concepts must occur by limiting the use of the word "function" to those activities which involve specified system-to-system relationships.

The word "structure," by contrast with the word "function," is frequently used in a narrower sense than the one intended here. Like "function," it refers to a characteristic of an activity, but whereas the word "function" draws attention to the consequences of an activity for other social systems, the word "structure" draws attention to the patterning of an activity, the extent to which it is repeated and recognized as a regularly recurring type of activity. Thus a structure is an institutionalized activity. Any activity recognized as having a distinctive pattern is a structure.

The way in which activities are recognized does raise perplexing problems, which have led to ambiguity. So far as government is concerned, patterns of action carried out by governmental agencies are first likely to be noticed, especially bureaucracies. They may be called *official* structures; other structures are unofficial. Clearly there are many patterns of action carried out by unofficial organizations, such as interest groups, churches, business firms, and families. These activities may be recognized in the sense that there are laws and regulations which govern them. For example, a firm may be incorporated, marriages registered, lobbyists licensed, etc. Insofar as a pattern of activity corresponds to a set of prescribed norms, it may be characterized as *formal,* otherwise as informal.

Some patterns of activity which are not formally prescribed, i.e., informal structures, are nevertheless permitted by formal norms, but others are proscribed. Therefore, it is important to distinguish between structures which are legal and those which are illegal. We can perhaps clarify these distinctions through the following table of types of activities in terms of kinds of recognition.

Column A designates official structures, which are also always formal, legal, and recognized. Column B describes formal structures, which are always legal and recognized, but are unofficial. Column C refers to legal structures which are always recognized, but are informal and unofficial. In column D we find illegal structures which are recognized, and also unofficial and informal. Unrecognized activities, which are therefore not structures, as in column E, are not formal, but they may or may not be official acts, and they may or may not be legal.

	Institutionalized				
	Structures				*Non-structures*
	A	B	C	D	E
Official	+	−	−	−	±
Formal	+	+	−	−	−
Legal	+	+	+	−	±
Recognized	+	+	+	+	−

Note: A plus sign indicates the presence of a characteristic, and a minus sign its absence.

Further statements may be drawn from this table: formal structures can be official or unofficial, and legal structures can be formal or informal. Moreover, structures may be illegal. For example, a criminal activity, such as "moonshining," is a pattern of action and therefore a structure.

The tendency of traditional political science was to focus attention on official structures, notably behaviors of bureaucratic, legislative, and judicial bodies. Subsequently the range of interest expanded to include formal structures, unofficial as well as official (B and A). This brought political parties and interest groups within the purview of analysis. Voting studies and research on organizational behavior, both in public and private bureaucracies, drew attention to informal structures of action as well as formal (C as well as A and B). Illegal structures, however, still remain largely outside the scope of political science and public administration, although they have been examined by sociology. The problems of administration in transitional societies, however, arise in part from the importance of illegal structures, and it is therefore necessary to formulate a theoretical framework that includes them as well as legal, formal, and official structures (D as well as A, B, and C).

Because the concept of structure tended at first to be limited to official structures, and then later to formal structures, confusions arose when the importance of informal and illegal structures was discovered. It was wrongly assumed by some that the concept of structure would not enable one to deal adequately with these important patterns of action, and so the term "function" was seized upon as a rubric under which to study informal and illegal structures. The result was to generate further confusion by mixing the institutional characteristics of a pattern of action with their consequences for other systems. In using the term "structure," therefore, we must broaden it to include illegal and informal as well as formal and official patterns of action, whereas in using the term "function" we must narrow it to exclude mere activities and mere programs.

Systems and Roles

The terms "social system" and "role" have been employed above without definition. It is now possible to comment on these key concepts. First, the distinction between structure and function must be clarified because the confusions which have arisen in dealing with systems and roles result from the mixing of structural and functional attributes in their definition.

The concept of a role arises from theater where an actor is said to perform a role, as when Olivier acts the part of Hamlet. Clearly, in this context, a given actor may play different roles, and the same role may be enacted by different players. It is possible to recognize the role of Hamlet as a distinct pattern of action apart from the person who fills the role. In a more generalized sense, *any recognizable pattern of action which may be performed by different individuals is a role.* As such it is a structure, and may be institutionalized in the various ways that any structure can be institutionalized. An official role, for example, is an *office,* as in a government bureaucracy, legislature, or court. A formal role is a *position,* as in a trade union, church, corporation, or school. Every office is a position, but not all positions are offices: thus a guard in the police force is an office, but a privately employed guard in a store is not. There seems to be a lack of convenient general terms for informal and illegal roles, but examples are common, such as friend, leader, scapegoat, criminal, spy.

As the word "spy" suggests, a role which is illegal in one setting may be quite legal, even official, in another. Thus someone who spies on A for B is filling an illegal role in A, an official role in B. The role as a pattern of action, once recognized, can be described in isolation, but its function can be specified only in relation to a system into which it fits. Thus the function of a spy for A, to steal information, is different from his function for B, to provide information.

Since the functions performed by a role are frequently used in its definition, the concept of a role is often regarded as functional rather than structural. In this sense the role of a spy is to spy, of a teacher to teach, of an administrator to administer, of a politician to engage in politics. Here we find the same difficulty that was discussed above in the first attempt to disengage structure and function. If the word "administration" refers to a function and not an activity, then the word "administrator" cannot be used for a role if a structural definition of roles is desired. Instead, the word "bureaucrat" could be used for the role, and thus the main function of bureaucrats with reference to their agencies would be to administer.

The morphology of words in English is a contributor to our confusion on this score whenever a noun easily changes into a verb, as in the paradigm: teacher, teach; preacher, preach; administrator, administer; legislator, legislate; judge, judge. In other instances, however, this paradigm does not work because the changes in the meaning of the cognate verbs are striking: doctor, doctor; politician, politic. In these instances it is easier to make the analytic distinction required. To say that a doctor doctors is to imply tinkering with or mending rather than healing. Consequently it is likely to be said that a function performed by doctors is to heal, or to help patients get well. But doctors may also try to prevent illness, teach, do research, write papers. Each of these activities may have functions different from those suggested by the word "heal." Moreover, the healing function may be performed by people other than doctors. The analytic distinction between a role and its function, in other words, is real. It needs to be made also between the bureaucratic role and the administrative function, between the role of judge and the judicial function, between the role of legislator and the legislative function.

The concept of role is basic for the concept of a social system. The word "social" is added primarily to designate a system of action by human beings. The word "system" by itself can be applied to computers, automobiles, the human body, a network of rivers, etc. It can also be used for a set of procedures, techniques, equipment, and rules employed by human beings, as in a system of taxation, of budgeting, of inventory control, or of farming. By a "social system," however, reference is made to a set of interacting roles occupied by humans.

Every social system is a collectivity, but not all collectivities are social systems. Any set of roles which share one or more characteristics in common can be called a collectivity. Thus the set of all doctors is a collectivity; so is the set of all bureaucrats; but these collectivities are not social systems unless the roles interact with each other. For example, a set of offices in hierarchical array, working together and constituting a "bureaucracy," is a social system, as is the community of doctors known as the medical "profession." In other words, it is the interaction of roles which distinguishes a social system as a special kind of collectivity.

In this usage, roles have been thought of as structures. But there are some writers who define the constituent roles of a system functionally. They think of social systems as collectivities which include all roles having a specified function. On this basis, for example, they might regard an "educational system" as including all those who teach and learn within a given domain. Similarly, a political social system might include all those who engage in political roles, an administrative social system those who administer and are administered, etc. This functional or analytic way of defining a social system presents, the writer believes, tremendous difficulties. Yet it is the way in which much of the present literature in comparative politics and public administration views this basic unit of analysis.

A structurally based or "concrete" conception of social systems may be illustrated by examining the idea of an educational system. Let us think of a "school system." There should be no doubt in anyone's mind that this term refers to a collectivity of faculty members, pupils, janitors, principals, school superintendents, school boards, truant officers, etc. The interaction patterns among these roles could also be traced fairly exactly. They constitute a recognizable set of formal and informal legal structures—official structures also, if the school system is public. But such a "school system" by no means coincides with an "educational system" as defined in the previous paragraph. Surely some of the activities in any school system have functions for other systems which are not educational, and surely also many of the educational functions for a given community or society are performed outside the school system. When the word "education" is used as a synonym for "schooling," these functional and structural concepts are mixed up and confusion results.

The same confusion may result when a bureaucracy is called an "administrative system" or a legislature a "political system." Even greater confusion occurs if one tries to think of an administrative system as including all the roles in a society which have administrative functions, or a political system as the aggregate of all roles having political functions. Let us now try to specify more exactly, in terms of the social system and role concepts, just what may be meant by political and administrative systems. In doing so the term "component" will be used, meaning any subsystem of a system which has a functional relationship with that system. It will become evident that political and administrative functions can be performed only by components, not by systems.

Political and Administrative Systems

Not all social systems are capable of exercising discretion by deliberately reshaping their environments. Those that do have a special characteristic which we have in mind when talking about "political systems." There are great traps in the use of the word "political," however, which must be avoided, if possible. The term "political system" has been used for the aggregate of the political functions performed by all the roles in a collectivity. This raises the question whether the word "political" refers to a characteristic of a social system or to a characteristic of roles and subsystems, or to relationships between these entities.

Let us first reflect on the concept of decision-making. Individuals are said to make decisions when they weigh alternative courses of action and select one of them. Actions normally occur without the necessity of decisions, as when they are governed by instinct or habit. When a child cries, we can assume that this is an action not based on a prior decision. When a diner picks up his fork to start eating, it should not be imagined that he first made a choice between using chopsticks and a fork, or even between a fork and a spoon. When a driver comes to a stop before a red traffic light, it may be concluded that he did not debate with himself whether to obey the sign. Such actions are based on instinct, cultural norms, and compliance with previous decisions, but they are not properly called decisions unless they involve a conscious weighing of alternatives. When a decision is consciously made, it constitutes an activity. It becomes a program only when it is shown to have consequences for the environment of the actor. It has a function only when it influences another system. The program, then, lies in the consequences of the decision, not in the decision itself. Similarly, the function of a decision is a consequence, not an intrinsic characteristic, of the decision.

Similar statements can be made about the decisions of a social system, bearing in mind that social systems often do not, and cannot, make decisions. If a system is able to choose between alternative courses of action, however, it can be said to have made a decision. But this is an activity, not a function. Nevertheless, it can be referred to as a "political" activity. Accordingly any social system capable of making decisions can be referred to as a political system.

Great care must be exercised to avoid the false conclusion that because a social system can make decisions, and is therefore called a political system, it also exercises a political function. As we have seen, a function is a relationship between structures. Accordingly a structure may be said to exercise a political function only when it influences the making of a decision by a different structure. For example, if A influences the making of a decision by B, then A's activity has exercised a political function by influencing B's political activity. If B's political activity should, in turn, influence the making of a decision by C, then B's political activity generates a political function with reference to C. However, B's political activity is not also a function if it does not affect the political activity of some other system, C. In other words, a political system can engage in political activity, but only its components exercise political functions.

Clearly these two usages of the term "political" are different, and it might be useful to substitute a different word for one of them. In case of ambiguity, therefore, the word "decisional" can be substituted for the word "political." However, no ambiguity need arise in speaking of a "political system" since, in this combination, it can refer only to the activity, not the function. A component, A, which affects decisions by the political system, B, is not itself a political system by virtue of its exercise of the political function. It may, nevertheless, be analyzed as a political system, but then focus is upon how it makes its own decisions, not how it influences the decisions of others.

To illustrate, let us consider the United States government as a political system. A component system which influences the decisions of the United States government is the Congress. When it exercises this political function, the Congress could be thought of as a component of the political system. For convenience it might be even called a "political component," but the relationship referred to is not what would be meant if it should be called a "political system." Of course, Congress could be examined as a political system, but in that case, its own decision-making activities would be studied. Thus, what is meant by Congress as a political system is quite different from what is meant by Congress as a political component.

A political component need not be specialized in political activity, nor need it be "primarily oriented toward" political functions. For example, a bureaucracy might be primarily oriented toward the administrative function, and it may not specialize in political activity, yet it may be a political component in the sense that it influences the decisions of a political system. The federal bureaucracy in the United States, for example, may be regarded as having a significant impact on the decisions of the United States government.

From these definitions we have to conclude that an individual cannot engage in a "political activity," except in the private psychological sense that he may have to wrestle with himself to arrive at a decision. What is called the "political activity" of individuals should, according to our definitions, be referred to as activities having a political function. It can be seen, therefore, that roles, regarded as structures, cannot be intrinsically political, and that a definition of a political system in terms of the activities of individuals or of constituent roles is incompatible with the definitions offered above. It is not contended that the definitions offered here are correct or that they conform with common usage, but it is felt that they can help us to clarify a subject which still remains highly confused.

It should also be recognized that although, by these definitions, no individual engages in political activity, any social system may engage in political activity. It does so to the extent that it makes decisions. This corresponds to common usage in the sense that we think of politics as an interaction process between different people. The decision-making process of one individual does not involve such interaction, and hence is not political, but the decision-making process of any social system is always political, whether it is official or unofficial, formal or informal, legal or illegal.

Individuals, however, may perform political functions to the extent that they influence the decisions made by social systems. We cannot judge from the nature of any act whether it is political or not, but only from the relation of the act to a political system. Consequently individual actions can be judged political only to the extent that they are shown to have a functional bearing on the decision-making processes of a social system. By the same reasoning, a state which engages in political activity cannot be assumed to have any political functions unless it contributes to the decisional processes of another system. When a member state influences the decisions of the United Nations, acting as a component, it is an example of a political function. But the decision by a state on what its policy should be is not a political function, but an activity.

The definition of a political system used here is broad enough to include any kind of social system, including private organizations, trade unions, universities, churches, bureaucratic agencies, even families and private clubs. For the purposes of this chapter, however, it is desirable to limit our discussion to a particular kind of political system, namely the sovereign state, a social system which claims to be the ultimate source of legitimacy in a given domain, to be the final court of appeal, the only system with the right to use violence. For convenient reference let us call any social system of this kind a "polity." Polities, then, are one of many kinds of political systems. Although the illustrations and discussion will be in terms of polities, the propositions offered can be applied readily to subpolities, to private organizations, to bureaucratic agencies, and to many other kinds of social systems.

The word "administration" is subject to as many confusions as the word "politics," but similar propositions apply to its use. Insofar as a social system implements the decisions it takes, it may be said to engage in an "administrative activity." To the extent that other social systems as components implement such decisions, they perform an "administrative function." Strictly speaking, then, a government may engage in administrative activities, relying on components, such as bureaucratic agencies, to carry out the administrative function. Thus, insofar as a unit, A, carries out the decisions of another unit, B, it performs an administrative function. But insofar as A implements its own decisions, it engages in an administrative action.

From this point of view any social system that can make decisions is both a political system and an administrative system. To direct attention to this duality, it may be called a "politico-administrative system." As a political system, it makes decisions; as an administrative system, it carries them out. These are political and administrative activities. But such a system does not necessarily engage in either political or administrative functions. It performs political functions only to the extent that it influences the decisions of another system, and administrative functions to the extent that it implements the decisions of another system. It helps, then, to say of a bureaucracy that it is, intrinsically, a politico-administrative system to the extent that it can make and implement decisions. It performs an administrative function to the extend that it carries out the decisions made by some other system, such as a government.

It should not be said, therefore, that a bureaucracy is "primarily oriented toward administration," but that a bureaucracy may be the most important administrative component of a government. The extent to which a bureaucracy is more of an administrative than a political component is an empirical question to be determined by examination in particular cases, not by definition. It is probably not possible to say of a particular bureaucracy that its political functions are more or less weighty than its administrative. However, one could probably compare the extent to which different components exercise the political and administrative functions in a particular political system. One might then discover that the legislature or the party system, for example, was the most weighty political component, and the bureaucracy the most used administrative component. It can be hypothesized that the degree of discretion of political systems varies directly with the extent to which bureaucracies exercise administrative functions and inversely with the extent to which they exercise political functions.

More will be said about this matter below, but first a few marginal comments on other uses of the word "administration." It is necessary to recognize that it does have other meanings and they will be frequently encountered. The word is sometimes used for any activities engaged in by bureaucrats or officials as a part of their formal roles. It seems preferable to call such actions "bureaucratic activity" or "official activity" but not "administrative activity." However, the reader should be warned that he will find many writers who use the term in this way.

Moreover, it will be found that distinctions are frequently made among different kinds of officials in such a way that some but not all are called "administrative officers" or "administrators." This is particularly true of British usage, where a distinction exists between the administrative class, the executive class, and the clerical class. Consequently the term "administrative activity" may be used for all formal activities by administrative class officers, but not by executive and clerical officers. In the United States, by contrast, the President and Cabinet are sometimes referred to as the Administration. In this context, "administrative action" may refer to an activity of the top political elite. In the Soviet Union administrative action is likely to refer to a particular kind of policy implementation, the enforcement of disciplinary action. Again, in British usage, the term "public administration" is often found meaning the set of policies and programs of government rather than the means by which they are implemented. Indeed, it is probably true that the word "administration" in most contexts is more likely to stand for one of these other meanings than for either administration action or administrative function as defined here. However, in this essay the term is not used for any of these other meanings.

The Administration of Development: Determinants and Dilemmas

If a social system decides to bring about changes in its environment it must then implement these decisions or the anticipated environmental changes will not occur. In other words, discretion can be effective only if it can be administered. But small-scale social systems with limited resources are unable to make much of an impact on their environments. Only social systems capable of mobilizing substantial resources can bring about significant environmental transformations.

Although a polity, or any other kind of politico-administrative system, may have an executive and a small elite of influential members, it can scarcely be expected to succeed if it cannot rely on its components to perform the administrative functions required for policy implementation. Moreover, the elites cannot be expected by themselves to know what should be done, nor can they automatically count on the willing co-operation of large populations. Consequently more components are required for the political functions contributory to decision-making. Since the capacity of any political system for decision-making is limited to some degree, effective discretion in a society also requires that a variety of social systems engage concurrently in specialized political activities (not functions), with some degree of independence of each other, yet with structured interdependence also. These conditions are met to the extent that politico-administrative systems are "diffracted."

By examining the meaning of this term, and studying the conditions under which it can be achieved, something about the requirements of increasing discretion, and hence of development, may be learned. Also it may be discovered why increasing diffraction tends to cause a decline in autogeny (increase in heterogeny) and therefore why it is resisted so strenuously. Finally, this investigation will reveal the nature of the alternatives open to social systems confronted with the hard choices imposed by the desire to reap the rewards of development. Put somewhat differently, it is clear how the need to make painful choices in politico-administrative systems may sometimes lead to development. In this context, development administration will be seen as an aspect of the administration of discretion and the dialectics of development.

Diffraction may be said to exist to the extent that a social system is both differentiated and integrated. Both concepts involve characteristics of a social system, not of the participants in the system. Let us take up each concept in turn.

Differentiation: Specialization and Specificity

The concept of "differentiation" is sometimes confused with "specialization," but the two ideas need to be distinguished from each other. Here again, the difference between structure and function must be kept in mind. Specialization is a structural concept, a type of activity. A doctor, for example, is said to specialize in medicine, or in such fields as cardiology, obstetrics, psychiatry, dermatology. But differentiation involves a characteristic of the functional relationship between components and a system, degrees of specificity. A role or component is said to be specialized if its activity is limited in scope, but a role or component is functionally specific only insofar as it makes a definable contribution to a social system of which it is a part. A politico-administrative system is differentiated to the extent that it contains functionally specific components. Components are functionally diffuse insofar as their relation to other systems are unclear, and they relate to a plurality of systems rather than to one.

In general, a correlation exists between specialization and specificity. The more differentiated a system, the greater the degree of specialization likely to be found among its roles and components. But the relationship is not uniform. For example, among traditional civilizations, such as those of China and India, we can find a striking variation. The centralized bureaucracy of Imperial China was relatively differentiated, but the degree of specialization of roles in this system was not highly marked. By contrast, traditional Indian civilization lacked a centralized and differentiated system of government, but exhibited much greater specialization in the activity of its population, most noticeably at the village level.

The reasons for this striking difference shed some light on the obstacles to differentiation. Specialization in India was reconciled with a relatively high degree of autogeny by being combined with the caste principle. This was the principle of extremely limited social mobility, a high degree of endogamy within caste boundaries, and the inheritance of vocational specializations. The system worked well because of its organic linkages with a particular set of Hindu religious beliefs and values which formed part of the cultural heritage, the environment of the system. Reciprocity in the mutual relationships of specialists, typified in the so-called *jajmani* system, reduced levels of tension and conflict between participants to such a degree that they could be handled without violence in most cases, by those directly concerned, or through appeals to others nearby who were indirectly but closely affected.

A centralized and differentiated social system requires a substantial measure of mobility and communication. The maintenance of a caste system militated against these characteristics, making the appearance of centralized bureaucratic government difficult as well as largely unnecessary in India. By contrast, the creation of such a system of government in China was made possible only because of the imperial examination system which recruited non-specialists, potentially from almost every social stratum, and because of the practice of frequent transfers and advancements, facilitated by the use of a uniform written language and considerable standardization of symbols and etiquette. The emergence of specialized social systems outside this bureaucracy would have threatened its survival, and so the maintenance of the relatively differentiated Imperial Chinese system was necessarily associated with a lower level of specialization throughout the society in general.

These observations are admittedly speculative, but they may illustrate the proposition that, although a general positive correlation between the degrees of differentiation and specialization exists, the two concepts are not identical and should be separated. The tendency to equate differentiation with specialization has prevented a clear perception of the nature of differentiation as a characteristic of social systems having functionally specific components.

Moreover, it has made it difficult to distinguish between the specificity and specialization of components as well as of roles. A component, considered independently as a social system, may be specialized in the activities it undertakes. A fisheries bureau, for example, specializes in fish culture. But it is specific only to the extent that it performs a definite function for a larger social system of which it is a part. Such a function for a fisheries bureau, for example, would be to administer a governmental program. By contrast, the activities of a district officer or a prefecture may be regarded as unspecialized, but the functions of this role or component for the government can be specifically administrative.

It is not only among roles and components in social systems that specialization tends to vary directly with differentiation. The degree of specialization of any social system as such probably also varies directly with the extent to which it is differentiated. This tendency is familiar in Western governments where the process of development was associated with the rise of constitutionalism, by which is meant the imposition of restrictions on the arbitrary exercise of power by a ruler in order that other social systems— parliaments, corporations, political parties, trade unions, churches —might each be given its own proper scope of authority. The phrase "the king can do no wrong" suggests an unspecialized monarchy, but the idea of constitutional monarchy implies specialization of the monarchic role.

The differentiation of politico-administrative systems may enable them to make decisions which are, technically speaking, adequate to solve problems of environmental change, and to administer these decisions through components that are responsive, and populations that are willing and able to co-operate. Specialization of politico-administrative systems also reduces the load sufficiently to make it possible for the system to do well the activities in which it specializes, and consequently to succeed in its programs. Note that differentiation increases the load-carrying capacity of a system, whereas specialization reduces the load. Thus differentiation and specialization complement each other, increasing administrative capabilities and the capacity to exercise discretion.

Integration, Heterogeny, and Universalism

It is by no means easy to make a differentiated system work well, however. It is not certain that a system with a given capability will actually utilize its resources effectively. Will political elites actually limit themselves to those specialized activities which are constitutionally prescribed? Will they give due attention to the proposals of political components? Will populations be willing and able to pay the taxes, obey the laws, and implement the procedures required of them?

Notice that all of these interactions in a differentiated social system depend for their successful performance on the willingness of individuals to perform tasks which are set for them by others, to be responsible in their behavior to standards which they did not personally select. In other words, differentiation requires heterogeny. And, as has been seen, the reluctance to surrender autogeny is universal. No one willingly gives up the right to make his own decisions and accepts the right of others to direct him.

How, then, can any population be induced to accept the degree of heterogeny necessary for the successful operation of a differentiated system? Two conditions which reinforce each other are generally necessary. One involves the acceptance of the legitimacy of the one who prescribes the rule or the directive, i.e., the legitimacy of the superior in administrative hierarchies and the legitimacy of the lawmaker, the judge, the policeman, the doctor, the schoolmaster, the city council and mayor, the expert, the committee chairman. This kind of legitimacy is different from that which is derived ascriptively from birth, the particularistic authority of a hereditary ruler, nobleman, or a "superior man." This is rather a form of legitimacy which is universalistic in character, which is achievement-oriented, which is functionally specific. To accept the decisions of a temporary chairman in a seminar as to who may speak is not to accord him any superior status ascriptively, but to recognize that the seminar can succeed only through communication of ideas, and that this is possible only if speakers can be heard, which in turn dictates the need for a means to limit the autonomy of each seminarian to speak whenever he feels like it. The Weberian idea of a legal-rational basis of legitimacy as necessary for the operation of a differentiated system returns. Heterogeny, in short, becomes acceptable to the extent that it is not arbitrary, not based on discrimination.

Another condition for acceptance of heterogeny is the preservation of as much autogeny as circumstances permit. If the natural interest of everyone in preserving his own autogeny is recognized, it should be possible to increase co-ordination in a differentiated system with a minimum of stress. The "human relations" approach in public administration, although often caricatured, rests at heart upon the understanding that people do what is expected of them more surely and well if their own integrity and autogeny are respected as much as possible.

To the extent that a differentiated system secures an effective linkage of its interdependent components it may be called an "integrated" system. Resistance to heterogeny is probably the most important factor preventing the integration of differentiated systems. It is necessary to add that the most influential actors in any political system, its elite, are the ones whose resistance to heterogeny is the most decisive. Without the imposition of "constitutional" limitations on the power of elites, the political components cannot function properly, and without delegation of authority, administrative components will not function well either. Yet, with rare exceptions, elites do not voluntarily surrender their autogeny. Consequently it has usually been only when extra-elite power has arisen—either endogenously within the social system or exogenously outside—that elites have bowed to necessity and sought to preserve some of their power and prestige by making concessions, accepting constitutionalism. The mere replacement of one elite by another, as in a coup d'état, usually brings no structural change in the degree of differentiation, or even of integration.

Yet it should not be thought that only elite recalcitrance blocks the integration of differentiated systems. Those who are ruled may be as resistant to the rule imposed as rulers are to abridgments of their power. A differentiated system must persuade the ruled that their rights and interests will be safeguarded if they are to be induced to comply. It may be that only if they are given a chance to participate in the making of policies will they consider the policies legitimate and voluntarily comply with them. If force must be widely used, the cost of securing conformity will exceed the rewards.

Members of a developing polity may be encouraged to accept the loss of autogeny (autonomy) inherent in the increasing discretion (autonomy) which signifies development if they simultaneously experience an increase of personal autonomy in yet a third sense, which may be called "detachment." Much current writing, especially from a psychological or social-psychological vantage point, is concerned with this meaning of the word. By detachment (autonomy) one can mean the ability of an ego to stand apart from the roles he plays and view them as alter egos. Thus detachment permits the self to play a variety of different roles just as he might enact several parts in a theatrical performance, or engage in a number of different games. By disassociating himself from his roles, moreover, the personality gains a sense of freedom, almost of autogeny, which makes it possible for him to accept, even humorously, the constraints imposed upon each of his roles.

It is by no means easy for members of a differentiating social system to acquire this sense of detachment (autonomy) any more than it is easy for them to surrender the sense of autogeny (autonomy). Yet the processes of differentiation may continue. When this happens, when differentiation without integration occurs, systems appear which are not so much diffracted as prismatic, a condition which has been discussed elsewhere.[7]

The quest for an increasing level of discretion confronts yet another difficulty. Not only must the resistance to declining autogeny be overcome, but hard decisions must be made about whose autogeny should be sacrificed most. In general, a question always arises in the decision-making processes of a social system as to how much weight shall be given to the preferences of the elite and how much the elite will compromise in order to accommodate other participants in the system. If the elite insists dogmatically on acceptance of its own views, it may find itself confronted by a revolt, ranging from passive resistance to violent upheaval. Such a revolt impairs or prevents the implementation of decisions by a politico-administrative system. But if the elite seeks to accommodate everyone in the system by maximum consultation and participation, differences of interest and opinion may forever prevent a decision. A dilemma therefore faces every social system: how is it to distribute power and authority between leaders and followers, between superiors and subordinates, be-

7. Riggs, *Administration in Developing Countries, passim.*

tween the elected and the electors? This dilemma is not peculiar to any level of development, but its character changes as a social system becomes more diffracted (i.e., differentiated and integrated).

Some components in a diffracted system rely more heavily on hierarchic modes of decision-making in which greater weight is given to the views of superiors than to subordinates, and other components can be essentially polyarchic in character, weighting the opinions of every member equally. In the polities which best illustrate this condition, we find that those components whose functions are primarily political tend to be polyarchic in character and those which are primarily administrative tend to be hierarchic. Political parties and legislatures illustrate the former, bureaucracies the latter. It should be recognized though that parties and legislatures also use the hierarchic principle, and polyarchy can also be found in bureaucracies.

Moreover, there are polities in which the party system and legislature fail to perform the political function effectively, and others—historically speaking—which lack these structures of government. How have they resolved the tension between polyarchic and hierarchic modes of decision-making? This question is fundamental to the present enquiry and leads to a more general investigation of this whole question because it underlies the emergence of autonomy, and hence is basic to development and to development administration.

Hierarchy vs. Polyarchy in Collective Choice

A basic choice which underlies any decision-making procedure, to repeat, is how many people to involve. The question can be seen in its simplest form if a small, undifferentiated group making decisions for itself is postulated. Such groups are found in modern societies, but a food-gathering primitive society composed of small families wandering over the land in search of sustenance can also be imagined. In such a group two extreme patterns of decision-making with a variety of intermediate possibilities can be postulated. At the one extreme, it can be supposed that every member participates equally in making all collective decisions for the group. At the other extreme, it can be supposed that one member is recognized as the leader or chief, and he makes all decisions on behalf of the group, imposing his will upon the others.

In practice, it may be supposed, most groups will find some intermediate mode of decision-making. Even if there is a chief, he may feel obliged to consult with some of his associates before arriving at a decision. Even if a rule of unanimity prevails, the less influential members of the group may be readily swayed in their votes by the others. In practice one might be able to establish a pecking order of relative degrees of influence within the group.

The group might also decide to classify subjects with regard to decision-making procedures. For example, the group as a whole might debate and vote on important matters, leaving secondary questions to the chief for decision. The group might reserve the right to choose its leader by a vote, but then authorize the chief to act during his term of office by authoritarian means. The decisional group might also vary in degree of consistency in its procedures, sometimes resorting to an authoritarian mode of operations, at other times to a more collegial pattern. Indeed, evidence of vacillation between these alternative modes might be regarded as a sign of choice being exercised, whereas groups in which either extreme was regularly used might be thought to have surrendered autonomy in this important matter.

At this level it is probably anachronistic to think of either principle of hierarchy or polyarchy being involved. Instead there is something of an intermediate character which can be called "consensual." A truly consensual politico-administrative system cannot be large simply because of the difficulties involved in communicating fully with every participant.

The problem may be illustrated by a look at the way in which the traditional panchayat system worked in India, or at least in one village described by Ralph Retzlaff.[8] Even at the village level, it was difficult if not impossible to form a single social system capable of making decisions. Accordingly a large number

8. Ralph H. Retzlaff, *Village Government in India* (Bombay: Asia Publishing House, 1962).

of panchayats was found, each of which, in effect, was an undifferentiated social system. Retzlaff recognizes four types of panchayats: caste panchayats, for as many as thirty-six castes in his village; farmer-retainer or *jajmani* panchayats, of which there may have been hundreds; single purpose panchayats, really *ad hoc* groups formed to cope with particular problems; and a general meeting panchayat of the whole village.

These panchayats were not linked together in any hierarchy, nor were they related to each other as components are to a differentiated system. Each panchayat was relatively autogenous, and if it failed to arrive at a decision, the question in dispute would be raised by those directly concerned in some other panchayat. In this sense the general meeting panchayat constituted a kind of court of appeal, and in this setting one might have found a simple elite—the leaders of the main families of the dominant caste of the village—who would have played a major role in formulating and seeking a solution to the problem.

But if the panchayats were not hierarchic, neither were they polyarchic in the sense of having a definite procedure for arriving at clear-cut decisions. Retzlaff says that "in the traditional panchayat system the notion of voting for or against a particular proposition, with a majority carrying the issue and thereby binding the minority to that agreed decision, was and still is completely alien to the system." He goes on to say that

the normal method of decision-making . . . was to initiate consideration of a particular point in the panchayat and continue discussion until a consensus, satisfactory to all the significant groups in the panchayat, could be arrived at. In the event of a stand-off between several equally powerful groups in the village, discussion continued until it was obvious that no agreement would be possible. At that time the panchayat would be disbanded and an attempt would be made to reconvene a similar panchayat at a later stage, when either an alteration in the power status of the two groups involved had taken place or, for some other reason, a compromise seemed possible.[9]

This system of decision-making was not polyarchic in the sense that it did not provide any means for the members to make a

9. *Ibid.*, p. 24.

decision which was opposed by any substantial minority and which they would nevertheless agree to be bound by. Effective polyarchy involves a means by which minorities consent to follow the preferences of a majority, just as effective hierarchy involves the establishment of conditions in which subordinates agree to carry out the decisions of their superiors.

Clearly this mode of consensual decision-making is too slow and cumbersome for the requirements of any large-scale social system. It follows also that the level of autonomy of consensual systems is very low, but the level of autogeny is relatively high in the sense that no one feels obligated to obey the decisions of others—whether of superiors or of majorities—if he does not choose to do so. If the size of a social system is to increase, and if its autonomy level is to rise, more complex and effective means of decision-making must be discovered, and these inevitably mean a drop in the level of autogeny experienced by participants.

It is obvious that if a hierarchy of offices is created, it involves a surrender of autogeny by subordinates, but it is not generally realized that it also requires a surrender of autogeny by superiors. The higher positions in a hierarchy can secure effective co-opera-tion from subordinates only if the subordinates retain some scope for making their own choices, which means delegation of author-ity. Moreover, the "span of control" of any superior has intrinsic limitations so that he can assure effective implementation of gen-eral decisions only by turning over part of the responsibility to others. Insofar as responsibility must be delegated in a hierarchy, there must be some confidence that each subordinate will make his choices so as to implement, not frustrate, the major goals of the hierarchic social system.

A polyarchic decision-making system also involves surrender of autogeny. This is apparent when minorities accept the prefer-ences of a majority, and voters agree to be bound by the decisions of their representatives. It is not so clear that majorities and representatives also must surrender some autogeny if these sys-tems are to work. A majority can expect an overruled minority to accept its preferences only if it manages to reassure the minority that its (the minority's) long-term interests in the system are greater than the short-term interests it sacrifices to the majority's will. In practice this usually means that minorities must be temporary, continually shifting, and therefore that majorities must avoid divisions on any issues which will create a permanent minority. Similarly, representatives must act in the interests of their constituents rather than their personal interests or they will forfeit the confidence of those who chose them and they will not be elected again.

It is easy to think of polyarchy and hierarchy as extremes on a scale in such a fashion that any increase in one involves a decrease in the other, and under certain conditions, it may indeed be true. Particularly at that level where the size of a social system becomes too great for simple consensual techniques of decision-making, it may be forced to choose between monarchic and republican, between authoritarian and equalitarian structures. However, it is possible in diffracted polities to combine a high degree of polyarchy with a high degree of hierarchy simply by linking different components. In other words, instead of seeing hierarchy and polyarchy as opposites or alternatives, they may be viewed as mutually complementary modes of decision-making.

A simple diagram can be used to help clarify the seeming illogic of this statement. Let us treat degrees of hierarchy and polyarchy not as extremes on a single scale, but as two dimensions of variation, as shown in the figure below.

Figure. *Decision-Making Choices at Different Levels*

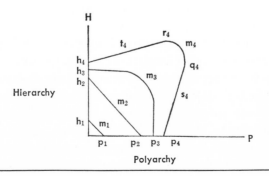

In this figure, any movement to the right on the horizontal axis represents an increase in the level of polyarchy of a decision-making system, and any rise on the vertical axis an increase in hierarchy. The situation of a simple, undifferentiated group is represented by the first curve, m_1, symbolizing a consensual type of decision-making marked by low degrees of both polyarchy and hierarchy. Some movement in either direction on this curve is possible, involving a rise in hierarchy toward h_1 accompanied by a decline in polyarchy, or an increase in polyarchy toward p_1, with corresponding drop in hierarchy. Such changes would be illustrated by small groups either dominated by strong leaders or very equalitarian in nature.

The second curve represents a larger, but still rather undifferentiated system. Here the point m_2 probably represents an uneasy compromise between the principles of hierarchy and polyarchy, and a strong tendency may be imagined for such a system to become more hierarchic or polyarchic, to approach h_2 or p_2. Under these circumstances the idea of a single scale of variation between hierarchy and polyarchy would seem realistic. Counterparts in real life may be found in traditional societies. The Aristotelian picture of a world of city-states fluctuating between monarchic, oligarchic, and republican forms of government provides an illustration.

The fourth curve is designed to show what may well be the situation in a diffracted system, as it may be found in the more industrially developed countries. If one starts from h_4 and moves toward m_4, one can see that the level of hierarchy might increase even as the level of polyarchy also increased. The same would be true if one started from p_4 and worked toward m_4. The point m_4, in this curve, would represent an optimum at the center for both the principles of polyarchy and hierarchy. At this level, however, the degree of hierarchy might be increased somewhat at the expense of polyarchy by moving from m_4 toward r_4, and conversely the degree of polyarchy might be increased at the expense of hierarchy by moving from m_4 toward q_4. A system at r_4 would not move toward h_4, since this would involve a reduction in both hierarchy and polyarchy, and therefore a loss of capacity to make decisions and a reduction in autonomy without compensatory gains. Similarly it would not move from q_4 toward p_4, for similar reasons.

American and Soviet history may be used to illustrate. Let us suppose that the United States, during the Great Depression, found itself in a position, perhaps near s_4, where its extremely polyarchic modes of decision, and limited use of hierarchy, proved inadequate to cope with new economic and social problems. The New Deal may be considered a shift toward q_4, stressing a rise in hierarchy but actually involving some increase also in polyarchic modes of decision-making. A contrasting picture is afforded by the Soviet Union where the difficulties of the Stalinist period could be related to the position t_4, marked by great reliance on hierarchy and a minimal use of polyarchy. The post-Stalinist reforms have probably increased the use of polyarchy in the government, but the level of hierarchy has perhaps also risen, as symbolized by a movement from t_4 toward r_4.

The situation in transitional societies is perhaps more accurately suggested by the third curve. Resembling the second curve, polyarchy and hierarchy may be seen as alternatives in the large picture, but in the short run it may be possible to increase the level of polyarchy without a substantial drop in hierarchy, as by a movement from h_3 toward m_3, and to raise the level of hierarchy without a great drop in polyarchy by a move from p_3 toward m_3. Probably the most commonly encountered situation is one in which a government is run predominantly by a bureaucracy under the rule of a hereditary monarch, a colonial regime, or a military dictator. Such regimes tend to offer little scope for polyarchic components, such as political parties and legislatures. If more representative organs of government are set up, they are likely to promote demands for the overthrow of the elite, the replacement of officials in the bureaucracy by party supporters, or the partitioning of the domain so as to increase the level of autogeny of minorities whose power has been increased by new polyarchic components. Any of these tendencies would, of course, reduce the level of hierarchic decision-making at the same time that the polyarchic level was raised. The alternation between control by political parties and by military officers in some of the new Asian states, as well as in Africa and Latin America, illustrates the possibility of fluctuations between more polyarchic and more hierarchic modes of decision-making in these countries.

Why should these alternations take place? What determines the choices made by a polity as to how its decisions will be made? Why, indeed, should this matter be discussed in the context of development administration? The answer is because the mode of decision-making has profound implications for the values which are served by a social system. Let us turn to an examination of some of these values and goals in terms of their relation to the alternative modes of decision-making.

Right and Left: The Dialectical Dilemma

Two different goals may be regarded as probably universal in all societies: performance and justice. Many other goals are related to these, and they are obviously different in various respects but seem to cluster together. The following table is designed to illustrate some of these goals.

	Goal	
	Performance	Justice
Political	capacity	equality
Administrative	effectiveness	responsibility
Territorial	centralization	localization
Economic	savings	consumption
Time orientation	past	future
Psychological	skill	freedom
Community	security	mobility
Social values	privacy	participation
Attitude toward change (moderate)	conservative	liberal
Attitude toward change (extreme)	reactionary	radical

Normally both sets of goals are attractive to most members of a polity, yet they are sometimes seen to be in conflict with each other. This conflict of norms is related to the antimony between hierarchy and polyarchy. It is related also to a difference in priorities between elite and non-elite. In general, elites give priority to the performance goals, and non-elites favor the goals of justice. Elites are apt to argue that greater hierarchy is needed as a means of assuring the performance values, and non-elites stress the need for polyarchy in order to assure greater justice. The former is identified as a rightist position, the latter as a leftist; the former with conservatism, with a more retrospective orientation toward time, with a greater stress on stability and order; the latter with liberalism, with an orientation toward the future, with a greater stress on the need for change and progress.

Introducing a dialectical frame of reference, it may be argued that the Right represents a thesis and the Left an antithesis. Frequently these tendencies appear to be in conflict with each other, posing dialectical dilemmas. A polity may swing back and forth, pendulum fashion, in cyclical alternations between Right and Left, between thesis and antithesis, stressing first a more hierarchic mode of decision-making, then a more polyarchic mode, first contracting and then enlarging the number of participants in the decision process. This pulsation may easily be associated with stagnation, breakdown, or decline in the development process.

However, synthesis in this dialectical process may arise whenever structural changes occur which permit simultaneously an increase in both the polyarchic and hierarchic principles of decision-making (as in curve 4 of Figure 1), and therefore simultaneous increase in the attainment of both the performance and justice goals. But it should be noted that very often no such synthesis can be found. Even with increased differentiation, a failure to achieve integration can mean that the old antinomy of Right and Left, of thesis and antithesis, persists. It may often happen, moreover, that a polity becomes fixed in an apparently stable form of institutionalization at either the Right or the Left, relying heavily on more hierarchic or more polyarchic means of decision-making.

Conclusion

By introducing the concept of development as an increase in the level of discretion of social systems, and by adding the dialectical scheme of Right and Left (hierarchic and polyarchic) antinomies, it is possible to shed some light on what is meant by development administration. Let us conclude this chapter by commenting first on the idea of development, and then on the meaning of administration.

The most popular idea of development has been increasing outputs, primarily in the economic aspects but also as enhanced capacity to make political decisions and growing administrative capabilities. In light of the theoretical framework presented in this essay, these phenomena can be described as various kinds of growth, made possible in large measure because of the increasing discretion of social systems (development), as indicated by their ability to transform or reshape their environments.

A somewhat different conception of development arises from stress on the rightist (hierarchic) thesis in our dialectical model. This is a viewpoint favored by elites since it involves minimal sacrifice of autogeny on their part. Performance values are stressed, increasing efficiency, reducing costs, improving the machinery of production, of government, of administration. Naturally enough, this is an orientation which makes a strong special appeal to specialists in administration and management.

A contrasting conception of development arises when stress is laid on the leftist (polyarchic) antithesis of the dialectical model. This is the viewpoint favored by non-elites, by those out of power at any given time, since it promises to reduce the degree of heterogeny under which they feel they are suffering. Consequently it stresses the justice values of freedom, independence, equality, change, even revolution. It makes a special appeal to those who think about political processes rather than administrative processes, and to those interested in public opinion, survey research, and rural life.

A fourth conception of development seeks to find a synthesis between the Right and the Left by pointing out that increasing levels of diffraction make it possible for both the goals of performance and justice to be achieved. This involves a study of social structure, of problems of differentiation and integration in social systems. It is dynamic in orientation since it is concerned with the fundamental restructuring of social systems, and therefore with changes in the rules of the game. It is not primarily concerned with either the hierarchic or polyarchic modes of decision-making, but views them as complementary strategies.

A fifth conception, and the one taken in this essay, is that development is seen most fruitfully as a process of increasing autonomy (discretion) of social systems, made possible by rising levels of diffraction. From this point of view, diffraction is not intrinsically significant, but it is a necessary condition for the attainment of discretion. However, increasing discretion is seen as the core of development rather than growth because it directs attention to the capacity of man to make conscious choices among alternatives. The decision to increase outputs is only one of the alternatives which may be selected. Development then involves the ability to choose whether or not to increase outputs, whether or not to raise levels of per capita income, or to direct energies to other goals, to the more equitable distribution of what is available, to aesthetic or spiritual values, or to qualitatively different kinds of outputs.

In this context, administration, as the function of implementing discretionary decisions by components, encounters the difficulty that it characteristically requires a reduction in autogeny, not only for the administrator himself, but also for those administered, and for the superiors who specify goals and norms. Thus the ultimate problem for development administration may be how to implement decisions that express discretionary social decisions, not only through programs that effectively bring about environmental transformations, but also by means which minimize the costs felt by those involved to be a loss of autogeny, and also so as to enhance the continuing development of the social systems by further increasing their discretionary powers.

Chapter 3

Development Administration and Decision Theory

Martin Landau

It is the business of a society to transform sheer behavior into appropriate modes of conduct—-a process we usually refer to as socialization. When a person is socialized, he has learned a set of formulas (which may or may not be consistent with each other) by means of which he makes sense (or nonsense) of the circumstance in which he finds himself. He knows what stimuli to respond to, when and how to respond, and under what conditions he may alter or modify his response. Accordingly, a mode of conduct (or role, whichever terminology is preferable) may be conceived of as a decision system—a conception which is augmented by the fact that all roles, explicitly or implicitly, include both a set of rules by which a decison is reached and the grounds upon which it is legitimated.

There are modes of conduct which are conducive to development and there are those which are not. By way of introductory comment, it suffices to suggest that this difference may be treated in terms of the ground upon which a decision is justified. Whole societies may be so treated; indeed they have been, for the classifications which mark synchronic social analysis are informed by this difference, as is the work of the historian who tells us of the victory of British empiricism or the rise of the Enlightenment. To speak of these events, needless to say, is to speak of a time when the foundations of legitimacy underwent great challenge. "Great challenge" is not to be taken here as hyperbole: we now know that these movements began the revolutionary transformation, the radical alteration, of the decision rules which had previously described European societies. The transformation of what we call "underdeveloped" or "emergent" nations involves a shift of decision rules fully as radical as any which have occurred before.

It may be of interest, therefore, to fix upon the epistemological and methodological presuppositions of both developed and underdeveloped societies, of traditional and modern societies, of backward and advanced societies—however we address them. In turning to this task, I do not imply that this essay is without precedent or that its object of inquiry has not been considered elsewhere. On the contrary, it is prompted by the suggestions of Braibanti, LaPalombara, Spengler, Pye, and others that a prime requirement for development is a change in the "content of men's minds" in the direction of empiricism.[1]

In the context of emerging nations, development administration has come to mean the engineering of social change. The social unit to be acted upon is no less than a "whole society" and the extent of change which is contemplated is "from one state of national being to another."[2] The magnitudes involved here are enormous, roughly equal to the distance between a backward society and a modern one, as we conventionally understand these terms.

The paradigm for the engineering of change is quite familiar: given a state condition A described by the set of properties (PA) at a given time (to) and a desired outcome which shall be a state condition B described by the set of properties (PB) at a time (t), find the set of operations (the instruments, agencies and processes) that will produce B. To Western man, this paradigm is so familiar as to be almost "second nature." It is what he calls "rationality." But the production of a desired outcome, as we well know, is oftentimes not that simple—especially in this area.

In the first instance, clear knowledge or a correct description of the initial state condition is not easy to come by. A failure to

1. Joseph LaPalombara, "Alternative Strategies for Developing Administrative Capabilities in Emerging Nations," *CAG Occasional Papers* (Bloomington, Ind.: Indiana University, 1965).
2. S. Katz, *A Systems Approach to Development Administration*, CAG/ASPA Special Series No. 6 (Washington, D.C.: 1965), p. 2.

produce an outcome or the production of an undesirable outcome is as much the result of inadequate description as of defective praxis. Nor is it often any easier to formulate a clear description of the goal state to be attained. This, of course, is necessary in order to impart direction, to assess feasibility, to provide for indicators and thus to allow for the measurement of achievement. And between the extant state and the goal state there sits the formidable matter of praxis—the means by which the latter is to be attained. In general terms, Simon puts the problem this way: To find the difference between the two states and then to find the means by which this difference can be reduced or eliminated.[3] Reduction or elimination, depending on the goal which is sought, constitutes a solution to the problem. But it is to be emphasized that the entire process is directional: whether we speak in terms of improvement, adjustment, production, or development—a reversal of direction is a sign of failure. So ingrained is this formula in our social habit as to enable us to employ defeat or failure as synonyms for reversal.

In this context, development administration is to be seen as a directive and directional process which is intended to make things happen in a certain way over intervals of time.[4] It is a "causal factor" or "independent variable." And save for the circumstance where its probability value approaches unity, which in the practical world has a probability closer to zero, it must be and usually is treated as a hypothesis. The set of operations designed to bring about a desired outcome has to do with a problematic situation in the future tense. All change agents have as their point of departure a "here and now," a present state of affairs, and their objectives always lie in a tomorrow. Any program is therefore a description of a future state of affairs and the processes that will bring it about. To write such a program is, of necessity, to raise a

3. Herbert A. Simon, "The Architecture of Complexity," in *Proceedings of the American Philosophical Society*, CVI (Dec., 1962), 479.
4. With respect to "emerging nations" the direction is *always* toward "modernization," arguments employing the phrase "culture bound" notwithstanding. Apart from the fact that this tendency, as Marion Levy puts it, is universal, it is also intended. See Levy, "Patterns, Structures, of Modernization and Political Development," *Annals of the American Academy of Political and Social Science*, CCCLVIII (Mar., 1965), 30, for a discussion of "consistency of direction."

hypothesis. To set it into operation is, of equal necessity, to conduct an experiment.

Turning back now to the content of man's mind, it is clear that this mode of conduct is not only conducive to development but may be taken as one of its defining properties. It is what Willbert Moore refers to as the "institutionalization of rationality," some degree of which, he says, "is a condition for even getting started."[5] It is what LaPalombara means in speaking of the need to inculcate empirical and pragmatic approaches to development administration in emergent nations.[6]

Such approaches, however, are disruptive of the most fundamental features of the cultures of traditional societies, and it is questionable whether they can be accommodated at all within the conditions that describe a traditional state. If they are in fact established, if they become modal behavior, then this must mean the destruction of the existing tradition; that is, the reduction or removal of the difference between the epistemology of the initial state and that of the preferred state. It is important, therefore, to turn to the concept of culture.

Culture

However central the concept of culture is to social science, its use does not follow any agreed upon rule. Anthropologists themselves have not been able to settle on a standard definition. Yet it is quite clear that as an anthropological construct it is primarily cognitive in character. To speak of culture as a design for living, as a problem-solving apparatus, as a set of fundamental recipes for everyday living, as a system of "mazeway equivalence," is to speak of a formula which provides relevant questions, appropriate categories, criteria of choice and evaluation, and rules of adequate solution. Common culture thus, in Kluckhohn's phrasing, establishes the "existential and evaluational premises of a society," and the "salient categories" by means of which experi-

5. *Social Change* (Englewood Cliffs, N.J.: Prentice-Hall, 1963), p. 95.
6. LaPalombara, "Alternative Strategies," p. 32.

ence is ordered.[7] Anthony Wallace, in an effort to dispel the notion that *motivational unity is necessary for social integration* (in the further effort to eliminate the confusions which describe the use of "culture and personality"), sees a culturally organized society as one in which organization (or integration) depends upon the *patterned* meanings of stimuli learned by its members. Wallace employs the concept of "mazeway" for the "meaningfully organized totality of learned cognitive representations of people, things, processes and values held at a given time by an individual."

These representations are models of an existential world, cognitive maps, which when "mutually predictable and equivalent" provide for a culturally organized group by establishing the necessary conditions for common social participation. It is not motivational unity (common motives or shared values, as they are more popularly known) that makes for social integration; it is rather the maintenance of mazeway equivalence—a set of standardized models which establishes a system of equivalent behavioral expectancies (modes of conduct). Wallace, thus, defines culture as "those sets of equivalent or identical learned meanings by which the members of society do in fact define stimuli." Culture may accordingly be taken as primal public policy, as rules of behavior which are so fundamental as to constitute the "implicit contract" which governs a community.[8]

A formulation of this order allows us to treat a cultural organization as a decision system. Here, we employ decision in accordance with Simon's use as being based upon sets of factual and

7. Clyde Kluckhohn, "Parts and Wholes in Cultural Analysis," in D. Lerner, ed., *Parts and Wholes* (New York: Free Press, 1963), pp. 120–122.

8. Anthony F. C. Wallace, *Culture and Personality* (New York: Random House, 1961), chap. 1. Also "The Psychic Unity of Human Groups" in B. Kaplan, ed., *Studying Personality Cross-Culturally* (Evanston, Ill.: Row, Peterson, 1961), pp. 129–141. Wallace notes that his views are in sharp opposition to those which make shared interests and motivation a central requirement of common culture. In his conception, shared motivations are neither necessary nor sufficient cultural conditions. The degree to which motivation is shared is a matter of empirical investigation. In some cultural organizations there will be strong insistence upon the necessity for motivational unity (as in societies undergoing revitalization movements) while in others, particularly those which are old, stable and sophisticated (these adjectives do not necessarily imply high technological development) motivational unity will be less important than reliability of performance of those tasks necessary to sustain institutional continuity, however motivated.

valuational premises.[9] Mazeway equivalence establishes the existential and evaluative premises that serve as the legitimate ground for decision.[10] And while ground is always of two orders, explicit and implicit, it is the latter, once again, that are especially important. They remain the unquestioned and unchallenged givens (the implicit contract) of the community—which is to say that there is no conscious awareness of them and they are not, therefore, problematical features of everyday living. For this reason they are of enormous power. In fact, Whorf has urged that the full meanings of explicit or named categories cannot be had without involving the implicit, which he refers to as "cryptotypes." It is interesting that Kluckhohn calls them crypto-categories and treats them as thematic features which possess an "evident primacy" in the sense that they are ultimate or non-discussable.[11] When they become discussable this alone may be a sign of a crucial cultural discontinuity. In any case, the control they exercise is to shape the decisional processes of everyday life—the system of choice or selection by which the problematical features of daily existence are dealt with. Different cultures, different systems of mazeway equivalence, are thus different systems of decision.

For our purposes, we take as the most basic of givens modal responses to time, space, and object. Apart from the fact that the organization of any society is, certainly in part, a function of the way in which these are intuited and represented, this choice is made because they are the most pervasive categories available. Moreover, they offer special utility in the study of development administration or directed social change. Both development and change are constructs reducible to these dimensions; they are temporal processes presupposing a future tense, confined to a

9. Herbert A. Simon, *Administrative Behavior* (New York: Macmillan, 1947), chaps. i, iii.

10. Lest the reader assume a contradiction between "value" premises and "cognitive" maps, values enter the mazeway as phenomena which are represented positively or negatively, etc. That is, they are cognitive data (stimuli) for which there exist learned patterns of response. See *Culture and Personality,* pp. 17–19, for Wallace's content categories.

11. Kluckhohn, *op. cit.;* Benjamin Lee Whorf, *Language, Thought and Reality* (New York: John Wiley, 1956), p. 109.

region of space, and they involve objects acting upon objects. The prior suggestion that we treat the set of operations designed to bring about state condition B as an independent variable is undoubtedly the product of a linguistic model which prescribes that "things do things to things." This patterned response to an object is to be seen in the syntactical rules of the English language (and language is the most powerful carrier of cultural maps) which specify that the form of the English sentence is "actor–action–acted upon." But in the case of development administration what we take as a legitimate *object* of action or manipulation may not in the life-space of host peoples be seen as such; nor are their spatial concepts necessarily equivalent; nor need they entertain the same priority of tenses. Indeed, when we refer to a "traditional society" we may be thinking in terms of future state conditions in a circumstance in which a legitimate future remains the initial state. Similarly, to raise the need for achievement as a crucial variable in the development process presupposes a dissatisfaction with a present-past state of affairs. In our society, generally speaking, the future is always deemed to be of more value than either present or past. The concept "ambition" is indicative of this; to be ambitious really means to place higher value on tomorrow's time than today's or yesterday's. Thus we easily invest today's time so as to reap rewards in the future.

Nor is "investing time" anomalous in a society in which time has been *objectified*. Do we not save and lose time? Do we not make time, allocate time? Is there not real time, time on our hands, no time or lots of time? And, alas, some of us have to "serve time." These idioms transform time into a noun. They make time a thing, and we can therefore understand why we address time by object language or spatial metaphor—long, short, high, low. As Whorf puts it, employing spatial metaphor "is part of our whole scheme of objectifying"; physical bodies (objects) are perceived in a region of space and their outlines in that space "are denoted by size and shape terms and reckoned by cardinnumbers and plurals." By a process of metaphorical transfer that reveals the priorities involved, "these patterns of denotation and

reckoning extend to the symbols of non-spatial meanings."[12] To
see how far this reaches (again a spatial metaphor), all one needs
to do is to look at the face of a clock. The circular shape and
rotary pointer (which are merely matters of design and convenience) should not obscure the fact that time here is represented
as a linear scale. Time is measured by a pointer which traverses
lengths of space, a succession of points along a line in one direction which corresponds to a succession of instants of time. It is by
means of this "mapping" operation (and this is the appropriate
technical term!) that we reckon time. The fact that this process
appears so "natural" is indicative of the power of the cognitive
map which constrains Western man to respond to time as a linear
relation of past-present-future. This, interestingly enough, permits the use of the phrase "backward in time." But there is no
going backward in time. It is the spatial representation of time
that allows us to speak this way, but we can only go backward in
space. "Turning back the clock" is not, therefore, and cannot be a
turning back of time. We merely move the pointer on a linear
scale back toward the zero point.[13] Given a model of time as a
linear scale, however, it does not occasion surprise to see references to past-oriented societies as "backward." We may complete
this statement by noting that in the cognitive map of the Hopi
"the absence of such metaphor . . . is striking. Use of space terms
when there is no space involved is NOT THERE—as if on it had
been laid the taboo teetotal!"[14]

The intent here is to suggest not only that our interpretations
and evaluations are of necessity recorded in terms of a linear
scale *but that we employ this model to establish the primary
features* of the state condition which development administration
is to act upon. Riggs, only one illustration of many, states that the

12. Whorf, *op. cit.*, pp. 145–146. And in the same volume, "An American Indian
Model of the Universe." See also David C. McClelland, *The Achieving Society*
(Princeton: Van Nostrand, 1961), pp. 324–329; R. H. Knapp and J. T. Garbutt,
"Time Imagery and the Achievement Motive," *Journal of Personality*, Vol. XXVI
(1958); E. T. Hall, *The Silent Language* (New York: Doubleday, 1959); and
Dorothy Lee, "Codifications of Reality," in her *Freedom and Culture* (Englewood
Cliffs, N.J.: Prentice-Hall, 1959).
13. W. H. Watson, *On Understanding Physics* (Cambridge: Cambridge University Press, 1938), chap. iii.
14. Whorf, *op. cit.*, p. 146. Emphasis in the original.

elite of traditional societies lack a sense of progress. "Their outlook is retrospective[15] and they seek therefore to preserve, or even
to restore, the norms and way of life of their ancestors." The past
tense defines the concept "tradition" here and we should expect
the action orientation as described. By contrast, the outlook of
the leaders of transitional societies is prospective: they have
effected the transit from past to future. Accordingly, they "have
an image of themselves as molders of a new destiny . . . , as
creators, indeed, of progress . . . it is this sense of self-propelled
change which gives a *distinctive quality* to transitional societies."[16] The future tense, then, defines, if not transitional societies,
the transitional elite. Its members have become Western men.
Western societies, McClelland indicates, exhibit a "forward orientation," a tendency to "think ahead," and their use of "anticipatory
tenses" invokes the concept of an "action forward in time." But
Eastern cultures represent time as a "quiet, motionless ocean."[17]
Knapp's terminology for these responses to time are "vectorial"
and "oceanic."[18] Oceanic time stands still but vectorial time is
"going somewhere" and, like a Western river, it stands still for no
man.

It is the Western crypto-category "vectorial time" that permits
the easy acceptance of the instrumental character of "development administration." Where time is reckoned on the linear scale,
there is little problem attached to the concept of administration
as an independent variable—as a causal factor or directing force.
But in a time zone which is non-linear, the future state condition
projected by development administration may be literally
"unthinkable."[19] That is, oceanic men may no more be able to map

15. I.e., backward.
16. Fred Riggs, *Administration in Developing Countries* (Boston: Houghton
Mifflin, 1964), p. 36. Italics added.
17. *Op. cit.*, p. 328.
18. See Knapp and Garbutt, *op. cit.* Concerning these researches as to the
relation between achievement, development, and the future tense, they appear to
me to be tautologous. In any case, I take temporal orientation as controlling in the
sense that it is a "crypto-category." There is nothing that I can see in the Knapp
researches that bars this proposal. See McClelland for further bibliographical
reference.
19. See the excellent paper of Hahn-Been Lee, "Developmentalist Time, Development Entrepreneurs, and Leadership in Developing Countries," in Dwight
Waldo, ed., *Temporal Dimensions of Development Administration* (Durham, N.C.,
1970), pp. 179–209.

the future than the Hopi can employ an *imaginary space*. In such circumstances, "development administration" easily becomes a literally senseless affair, quite beyond the cultural maps which mark a "here and now." And here lies a paradox, for success means that mazeways have been changed to comprehend or accommodate "anticipatory tenses" and therefore "causal factors," but it is precisely the absence of such changes that marks the maps which demand failure. How to break through is no light task, but we may learn a great deal by failure if we treat it as descriptive of the state condition which actually obtains. Where failure now prompts field reorganization, shifts of personnel, establishment of new offices, in-service training programs, even more money—these in no way tell us about the routine grounds of everyday life,[20] which, in the very first instance, is what is to be changed. If we cannot describe the initial state correctly, praxis is a shot in the dark.

An Illustration

It may be that all of this appears rather abstract, so far removed from the scene of action as to be of doubtful value. But it is well to emphasize that however development and modernization have been thought of (economic, political, social), all commentators establish an empirical outlook as a condition for achievement. Even more, it is technology in all its various forms that is at the base of modernization and it is science which serves as the foundation of technology. When that necessary "redefinition of cognitive categories" (Shils's phrase) occurs, it will have to be in the direction of the scientific orientation because this, as Pye suggests, "is the essence of what we think of as modern life."[21]

Let us then turn to the problem of introducing science educa-

20. If one wishes to see the kind of study that may open new horizons in development administration, see Harold Garfinkle, "Studies of the Routine Grounds of Everyday Activities," *Social Problems*, XI (Winter, 1964), 225–250. Garfinkle discusses the American scene.

21. Lucian W. Pye, ed., *Communications and Political Development* (Princeton: Princeton University Press, 1963), p. 19.

tion to village children in an underdeveloped or traditional society. Here we rely upon the statement of Francis Dart, a professor of physics, and his collaborator Panna Lal Pradhan, a Nepalese colleague.[22]

Now physicists have a curious way of treating problems. They insist upon accurate descriptions of the situations placed before them. If they are asked to solve a problem, they do not act until they know its properties, until they can properly identify it. They do not always succeed in their efforts, but it seems that they cannot proceed otherwise. Indeed, it is they who have established the authority of the problem-solving paradigm cited earlier. We can expect them to be sensitive to initial state conditions.

Working in Nepal, Dart and Lal Pradhan therefore focused upon the notion of "reality" and took as their task the determination of what the villagers of Nepal feel to be reality. To ascertain this they chose three widely separated ethnic communities, each having a different history of external contact, and put a series of questions to school children nine to fourteen years of age. These questions were designed to reveal characteristic concepts of nature, ideas about the control and manipulation of natural phenomena, and the grounds upon which the children validated their statements.

To get at the first problem, the children were asked to account for such commonly experienced events as rain, thunder, lightning, earthquakes, and the like. What is of interest is that in each case, and in each village, such questions elicited both a "folk-oriented" answer (lightning comes from the bangles of Indra's dancers) and a "school-oriented" answer (it comes from the collision of clouds). What is of even greater interest is the fact that despite an evident mutual incompatibility of the two types of answers, both were accepted by the children as correct. This contradiction, Dart points out, "is far more apparent to us than to our respondents who showed no discomfort over it, a fact which should serve as a warning . . . that all is not as it appears on the

22. Frances E. Dart and Panna Lal Pradhan, "Cross-Cultural Teaching of Science," *Science*, CLV (Feb. 10, 1967), 649–656. Professor Dart was my colleague and neighbor at the Institute of Advanced Projects, East-West Center, and I am more in debt to him than he realizes.

surface."[23] Well aware of the widespread use of paradox that Asian philosophies employ and the fact that the majority of textbook writers and teachers are Brahmans (guardians of orthodoxy), Dart and Pradhan allowed for the possibility that the failure to produce a necessary distinction between myth and science is the result of the way in which the children are taught. But they also caution against discounting the possibility of "very deep-rooted patterns of thought" which are not limited to (nor informed by or accommodative of) "the either-or logic underlying western science." An entirely different order of syntactics may be at play here.

So far as the matter of control and manipulation, however, no similar duality was made evident. Control is always at the will of the deities, who may or may not respond to appeals (ritual), and is therefore quite uncertain. By contrast, Honolulu schoolchildren always presented "scientific" answers (even if incorrect), and control and manipulation of natural phenomena were never seen as products of magical and religious practices. And even where control was said to be now impossible, the possibility was expressed that in time it very well might be. Parenthetically, it needs no extended comment to suggest that where causation is taken as a matter of supernatural control, the concept of engineered development and the goals of development administration remain senseless notions—quite incapable of evoking the responses Westerners would naturally expect.[24]

Concerning knowledge itself and the "empirical outlook," Dart and Lal Pradhan indicate that experiment and observation were "never directly suggested to us as an appropriate or trustworthy criterion of the validity of a statement nor as its source." With such an orientation, there can be no such idea as new knowledge. Accordingly, they state: "We were *always* told that such new knowledge is not to be expected. Even when we pushed this question so far as to call attention to such 'new' discoveries as space travel or transistor radios, both of which are known about

23. *Ibid.,* p. 651.
24. Everett E. Hagen, *On the Theory of Social Change* (Homewood, Ill.: Dorsey Press, 1963), pp. 69–70.

all over Nepal, it was *always* held that such things were always known by someone . . . ." The predominant view of knowledge, they report, is "a closed body, rarely if ever capable of extension, which is passed down from teacher to student and from generation to generation. Its source is in authority not in observation."[25] When one examines the epistemology of the American child and the Nepalese child, here indeed are two cultures.

Nor do they respond to space in the same manner. Dart and Lal Pradhan asked the children to draw maps (in a literal sense) showing how to get "from your house to the school."[26] The maps they obtained (which the author has had the opportunity to examine) are all very similar. They "always" include a recognizable picture of "my house" and of "the school" connected by a line which "seems to denote the *process of going* from one to the other, not the spatial *relationship of one to the other*." In all of the cases Dart shows, the two buildings are placed on the same line but they are not in fact on the same street or path and, further, they are separated by several street intersections and other landmarks which do not appear on the map. It is not incidental that maps drawn by American school children (in Hawaii), in response to the same set of instructions, represent house and school by abstract symbols—no pictures—and show a clear effort to present spatial relationships and clues. "The propensity of the Nepalese for making maps (whether verbal or graphic) which are *sequential* rather than spatial constructs is not limited to school children. . . . We too in reply to our inquiries as we travelled were given instructions or 'maps' which, like a string of beads, list in correct sequence the places we should pass through without giving any clue as to distances, trail intersections, changes of direction, etc."[27]

Observations of this kind are of immense practical importance. They point to those basic sets of formulas by which the Nepalese

25. Cross-Cultural Teaching of Science," p. 652; italics added. One group, the Limbus, did assign some power to observation.
26. The reason for this request has to do with the fact that "a map is a fairly simple yet typical example of a scientific model." It therefore constitutes a "representation" of reality and serves, in this case, as a picture of how this reality is perceived.
27. "Cross-Cultural Teaching of Science," p. 653.

villager makes sense of his circumstance. They indicate the existence of crypto-categories which all but make the Western paradigm of problem-solving so alien a concept as to appear a "specifically senseless"[28] procedure to the Nepalese. If we generalize to
those vast numbers of people who are "tradition-bound," this may
well explain the failures of many technical assistance projects. It
would, of course, need further and more refined analysis to secure
full and adequate descriptions of the logics which prevail in
everyday life, yet it is hard to escape the conclusion that they
constitute another world, another reality, which is as hard for us
to grasp as ours is for them. We can note, e.g., that Nepalese
villagers (child and adult) *normally* do not represent space in
terms of co-ordinates. Indeed, by our models, they do not seem to
represent space at all—they use no drawings in the construction
of houses, furniture, and the like. Immediately, we can see the
significance of this for "town planning" or "zoning," and we can
appreciate the conclusion of Dart and Lal Pradhan that Nepalese
school children do not possess concepts (mazeways) conducive
to science education. But it is very difficult for us to comprehend
that "the lack of spatial models may be very natural";[29] as difficult
perhaps as understanding that in many parts of the world the
future tense is not a "natural fact of life."

Where such mazeways do obtain, it must follow as a matter of
course that there will be resistance to change. Receptivity to
change is, after all, a patterned response.

Decision

Mazeway as a system of decision is a feature of all social life
whether traditional, transitional, or modern. What distinguishes
one society from the other is *the ground upon which a decision is
validated,* the rules by which it is assigned legitimacy. Epistemol-

28. This is a term employed by Max Weber. Its import becomes clear on reading
Harold Garfinkle, "A Conception of, and Experiments with, 'Trust' as a Condition
of Stable Concerted Actions," in O. J. Harvey, ed., *Motivation and Social
Interaction* (New York: Ronald Press, 1963).
29. "Cross-Cultural Teaching of Science," p. 653.

ogy, accordingly, may be taken as the salient defining property of a given state condition in the sense that it possesses an "evident operational primacy"; it is the ground upon which decisions are validated.

Suggestions that resistance to change is a function of personality, motivation, drives, and the like may therefore be disregarded. Nor will any credence be paid to such conclusions as "the structure of traditional society has lasted as long as it has because the personalities of the simple folk are authoritarian."[30] Perhaps they are, but the mode of analysis employed here does not require us to psychologize. One may, of course, argue that the principle of mazeway equivalence is a matter of learning and hence of psychology, but concern here is not so much with the psychodynamics of the learning process as with what is learned, i.e., with the "contents of men's minds."

Recall that in Simon's usage a decision is defined as a conclusion drawn from or based upon a set of premises. Premises are of two kinds: factual and valuational. Factual premises are, of course, empirical in character. They contain assertions about an experience. To determine, therefore, the correctness of a factual proposition, one must examine experience. It is for this reason, obvious as it appears, that the rule of observation is indispensable for proposals of this sort. Conversely, the rule of observation makes no sense when applied to value premises since they make no assertions about experience. Technically, value statements are analytic—a fact which is often obscured by the generally elliptical nature of such statements. When fully stated, however, their analytic character can be made abundantly clear and as analytic statements their truth is logical. In short, different criteria of correctness apply in each case.

Generally, a decision is a mix of both types of statements. But often valuational premises are of such importance, they so predominate, that a decision is referred to as a "value judgment." And where we speak of a "factual judgment," the opposite is the case. Facts so predominate, or values are so unimportant or irrelevant, that the decision is a matter of fact. These formulations can

30. Hagen, *op. cit.*, pp. 71–74.

be summarized by noting that while a decision is defined on the basis of both value and fact premises, where values approach zero or are irrelevant the decision may be treated as a matter of fact, and where facts approach zero or are irrelevant the decision may be treated as a value judgment.[31]

In a means-end chain of a complex order, however, whether we can isolate pure factual and pure valuational premises is problematical. But for all practical purposes, this does not seem to present any insurmountable difficulties.[32] We are able to distinguish between factual and value judgments or technical and moral judgments. The fact that a modern society presents so "open" a set of variables as to render synoptic decision-making questionable[33] does not gainsay this distinction. Indeed, were it not possible to establish the distinction, there would be no empirical disciplines.

Thompson and Tuden: Decision Classes

Following Simon, Thompson and Tuden[34] have constructed a classification of decision systems which is based upon (1) the differential consequences of alternative courses of action and (2) the evaluation of potential outcomes on some preference scale. The use of these variables accords with the definition of decision as involving factual and valuational premises. Differential consequences of alternatives constitute an empirical or factual problem and a preference order is a matter of values. Said alternatively, a course of action is instrumental to a preferred outcome or goal; that is, outcomes are dependent upon the instruments selected, they are a consequence of the instrument, which is therefore to

31. $V \to o, D = F; F \to o, D = V.$

32. Where the achievement of a value-goal is instrumental, its relation to a set of ends constitutes a factual proposition. Simon, *op. cit.*, chap. iii, and M. Landau, "The Concept of Decision in the Field of Public Administration," in S. Mailick and E. H. Van Ness, eds., *Concepts and Issues in Administrative Behavior* (Englewood Cliffs, N.J.: Prentice-Hall, 1962). Also Felix Kaufman, *Methodology of the Social Sciences* (New York: Oxford University Press, 1944), chaps. ix, xv.

33. David Braybrooke and Charles E. Lindblom, *A Strategy of Decision* (Glencoe, Ill.: Free Press, 1963).

34. James D. Thompson and Arthur Tuden, "Strategies, Structures, and Processes of Organizational Decision," in *Comparative Studies in Administration* (Pittsburgh: University of Pittsburgh Press, 1959). We rely primarily on the Thompson-Tuden matrix in the succeeding portions of this chapter.

be taken as a "causal agent" or independent variable. A factual proposition is, in this context, an assertion about causation (that A will produce or cause outcome B), while a value judgment states a preference about outcome.

For any social situation, neither causation nor preferences are to be taken as non-problematical. Not only must both be justified, but it is often the case that varying degrees of agreement or certainty (either as to causation or preference) are in evidence. For many problems it is perhaps best to treat agreement or certainty as a continuum. But for purposes of classification, Thompson and Tuden establish the following decision categories:

	Preferences (as to outcome)	
Causation (facts)	Agreement	Disagreement
Agreement	Programmed (computational)	Bargaining (compromise)
Disagreement	Pragmatic	Inspirational

In proceeding with this classification, however, one rather important assumption must be made: the members of any social system will not set it aside for light and transient reasons nor are they able to. We are permitted to make this assumption on the basis of the principle of mazeway equivalence. Psychologists have long noted the defensive character of cognitive maps (stereotypes) which present an ordered, consistent picture of one's world. In that world, we are members, feel at home, know our place, and fathom the rules which govern mutual expectations. As Lippmann once put it, such maps stand as "highly charged fortresses of tradition," and behind their walls we feel safe. We assume, thus, that in any social community continuity is a binding force and consists of the operative sets of standardized models which govern the "habitual workaday" (Max Weber's term).

Programmed decisions: Cell 1. Where agreement exists on both preferred outcomes and appropriate instrumentation, decisions will be computed. Under such conditions, there is no need to do otherwise. Since no doubt obtains as to the outcome which is desired and the necessary knowledge to bring it about is either available or assumed to be available, the correct decision becomes a matter of calculation. The rules which govern calculation constitute a program. Thompson and Tuden refer to this mode of conduct as computational decision-making. But because correct computation is governed by a set of rules (program) we shall refer to this circumstance as "programmed." It illustrates, of course, what is usually meant by "perfect rationality" or "synoptic decision-making."

Pragmatic decisions: Cell 2. Where there exists agreement or certainty about preferred outcome but the knowledge necessary to bring about the outcome is either unknown or unavailable, the decision will be pragmatic. As Thompson and Tuden describe this situation, causation is uncertain, the relative merit of alternative courses of action is in doubt, and there exists no acceptable basis for determining that one alternative will be more efficient than another. Accordingly, a decision cannot be computed and will have to rest on the best judgment of the actors involved. They named this mode of conduct "judgmental," but I prefer to use the term "pragmatic" as Kant originally used it—to stand for contingent beliefs which formed the basis for choice in a means-end network. Here reliance must be placed upon "educated guesses," the "best opinions" of experts, collective judgments in the form of voting, "experienced hands," "wisemen" and the like, depending on the nature of the problem. Trial and error in the face of risk and uncertainty usually describe this circumstance. It is often referred to as heuristic decision-making.

Compromise: Cell 3. Here the opposite holds: there is agreement about the facts, about the consequences of available instruments, and about resultant outcomes, but there is disagreement about the outcome which is desired. Situations of this nature carry the possibilities of schism, of civil conflict and war "for the blunt fact is that if one preference is satisfied, another is denied."[35] To lessen the risk of this order of conflict, some meeting point must be found on the various preference scales involved. But this will occur only under the general assumption indicated earlier. Parties to the dispute will then play something like a minimax game: they will bargain, negotiate, and compromise (so

35. *Ibid.*, p. 200.

that no one wins and no one loses), seeking the highest minimum (the lowest maximum). This mode of conduct, interestingly enough, has been given formal expression in the theory of minimax.

Inspirational: Cell 4. We confront here what appears to be an impossible situation; neither variable finds any agreement. There is no consensus on fact, instrumentation, or expected outcomes and there is disagreement about preferred outcomes. Indeed, it makes sense to refer to this situation as one of social disorganization which is bound to degenerate into strife. If such a circumstance arises with respect to a single issue, following our general assumption, the policy which is applied may be avoidance. But if this condition is widespread, nothing can be avoided and the social organization faces chaos. The problems which confront it cannot be treated programmatically or pragmatically, nor is there any basis for negotiation and compromise. In this condition, often referred to as anomic, charismatic direction and authority easily arise. Problems are then given over to inspirational leaders who are assigned the property of deliverance, who are thought of as possessing a divine touch, an inspired wisdom, or charisma itself —the gift of grace. Here submission to an "inspired leader" becomes a characteristic mode of conduct. It is a mode of conduct which is not so much induced by any "authoritarian personality" as it is a description of a state condition in which the natural reality has been rudely disrupted. When this submission persists over a period of time, when—as the Willners put it[36]—the leader is able to transmit and sustain his "definition of their world" the situation tends to take on the properties of Cell 1 and decisions are programmed. We often call this latter condition "totalitarianism."

Social Types

In employing a decision matrix based upon a double dichotomy, we take due note of the fact that dichotomies are generally frowned upon in development analysis. A sense of unease is

36. Ann R. Willner and Dorothy Willner, "The Rise and Role of Charismatic Leaders," *Annals*, CCCLVIII (Mar., 1965), 77–88.

evident even when Parsonian pattern variables[37] are employed—and there can be little doubt that they are the most influential set of constructs in use at the present time. It is often suggested that pattern variables lead to an "unfortunate theoretical polarization";[38] that as "pure types" they are empty classes—classes for which no empirical cases can be found; that the line they draw is too sharp; that as "limits" they are exaggerated; that the postulate of structural multifunctionality requires that we erect "dualistic," not pure, types. In short, that we need to work with "mixed types."[39]

Such representations may arise, however, from a failure to distinguish between a class and its members, a sign and its referent, an abstract system and a concrete object system. For the fact is that classification is the process of establishing mutually exclusive and collectively exhaustive categories which, not so incidentally, constitute the basis of ordered systems.

Yet it is quite clear that the use of the term "development" directs us toward a *continuous* process. By definition, that is, development is to be taken as a continuous variable. Why then the use of polar types? The answer lies in what is called a "mixed type," which upon analysis turns out to be a position on a scale. Hempel has shown that the logic of extreme (pure) or polar types is "the logic of ordering relations and of measurement." Pure types are not necessarily to be taken as sets which cover real cases but as "poles between which all actual occurrences can be ordered in a serial array."[40] The polar points mark a range of variation within which societies can be ordered in terms of their

37. "A pattern variable is a dichotomy, one side of which must be chosen by an actor before the meaning of a situation is determinate for him, and thus before he can act with respect to that situation" (Talcott Parsons and Edward A. Shils, *Toward a General Theory of Action* [New York: Harper Torchbooks, 1962], Part 2, chap. i).

38. Whatever hesitations appear with respect to "polarization," Parsons's influence is obvious in the work of Almond, Apter, Coleman, Eisenstadt, LaPalombara, Pye, Riggs, and Ward—among others.

39. Gabriel Almond and G. B. Powell, *Comparative Politics* (Boston: Little, Brown, 1966); Gabriel Almond and James S. Coleman, *The Politics of the Developing Areas* (Princeton: Princeton University Press, 1960), esp. pp. 21–25.

40. Carl G. Hempel, "Typological Methods in the Social Sciences," in M. Natanson, ed., *Philosophy of the Social Sciences* (New York: Random House, 1963), pp. 213–216.

"degree of." Intuitively, we have always spoken of societies on a "more or less" basis: more modern, more developed, more industrial, more specialized—more as compared to others which are less. It is, of course, readily apparent that a "backward" society is one which, on some standard scale, lies a good distance away from a "developed" society. If we wish, we can speak of fused and diffracted societies, intermittent and differentiated structures, mobilized and unmobilized societies, and the like. The "mixed" type falls somewhere between the polar points which establish the range of variation. Polarities of this character thus permit the construction (however difficult) of unidimensional scales along which societies may be plotted (described). They are therefore to be construed as attempts to move from nominal to ordinal scales: "from the classificatory, qualitative level of concept formation to the quantitative one." They stand as "ordering concepts of the purely comparative kind representing an intermediate stage."[41]

In this regard, it is interesting that the classical (and closely related) dichotomies of sociological theory (status and contract, gemeinschaft and gesellschaft, sacred and secular, etc.) have also been employed toward this end. Historically, the process has been rather inexact, but the practice of describing societies in terms of their distance from either pole is a commonplace feature of analysis. Indeed, even where formal scaling procedures are not specified, this will be the case: Becker's subdivisions of folk-sacred, prescribed-sacred, principled-secular, and normless-secular are, again, points on a scale.[42] And if each of the classical sociological dichotomies presents a distinct variable as the overarching principle of classification, we can observe, as Lazarsfeld has indicated, that Redfield's folk-urban construction is an attempt to reduce a multidimensional property space to a unidimensional scale—say, the gemeinschaft-gesellschaft continuum.[43] What this

41. *Ibid.*, p. 216.
42. Howard Becker, *Through Values to Social Interpretation* (Durham, N.C.: Duke University Press, 1950).
43. Paul F. Lazarsfeld and Morris Rosenberg, *The Language of Social Research* (Glencoe, Ill.: Free Press, 1955); Robert Redfield, "The Folk Society," *American Journal of Sociology*, LII (Jan., 1947); Horace Miner, "The Folk-Urban Continuum," reprinted in Lazarsfeld and Rosenberg.

suggests is the proposal that each case belongs to the same "family of meanings," that they can be derived from each other, that they are accompanied by the same set of properties, and that the same concept, with minor deviations, is at work. Thus a society which is conceived of as "mechanical" has essentially the same features as one which is sacred, or folk, or gemeinschaft. To illustrate:[44]

1. A mechanically solidary society is one in which beliefs and conduct are alike. People are homogeneous mentally and morally. A totality of beliefs common to all men exists—the collective conscience which is never a product of the members of society at any one point in time, and never open to any challenge. The membership of such a society cannot refute its collective conscience since any questioning constitutes a moral offense and is punishable by repressive law. Communities are thus uniform and non-atomized, unlike the *organic* society where differentiation makes heterogeneous mental and moral sets (Durkheim).

2. The sacred society (isolated vicinally, socially, and mentally) is marked by fixation of habit and neophobia. Social contacts are primary, tradition and ritual govern the life of an individual, and all forms of activity are under the control of sacred sanctions (division of labor, kinship relations, economics, etc.). The value system which operates is impermeable (Becker).

3. The folk society is small, non-literate, homogeneous, exhibiting a strong sense of group solidarity. A minimal division of labor obtains and the concept of everyman prevails—what one person does is what any other can do. Behavior is strictly patterned, patterns are consistent with each other, forming a system of norms which is sanctioned by religion and justified on sacred grounds. Ends, accordingly, are taken as given and tradition determines appropriate conduct. There is no "legislation," no critical habit, no experimental mode: tradition is law and, given its sacred sanction, conduct remains consistent throughout the

44. See J. C. McKinney and C. P. Loomis, "The Application of Gemeinschaft and Gesellschaft as Related to Other Typologies," in Loomis, ed. and trans., Ferdinand Tonnies, *Community and Society* (New York: Harper Torchbooks, 1963), pp. 12–29, upon which I base these capsules.

generations. Should tradition be questioned, negative social sanctions obtain. Briefly, Redfield states, the folk society is a sacred society.[45]

To complete this statement is to note that the opposite pole is explicitly described by Durkheim (organic solidary) and Becker (secular) and is easily constructed in Redfield's case by counterposing the appropriate antonyms. It should be obvious, too, that Parsonian pattern variables are fully consistent with this theoretic continuity. In fact, they were, at least in part, originally formulated in the interest of a comparative analysis of social institutions;[46] and latterly Parsons has referred to them as "modes of classifying the basic structural and processual components of action systems."[47] The pattern variables, as Parsons puts it, "are inherently patterns of cultural value-orientation [which] become integrated both in personalities and social systems."[48] On the one extreme, then, we can establish a societal type (A) which is characterized by affectivity, ascription, diffusion, and particularism; and on the other, a type (B) which is characterized by neutrality, achievement, specificity, and universalism.

Here, my point is to suggest that while each of these dichotomies—down to Parsons—appears to present a different *fundamentum divisionis*, the full statement of any one of them reveals a "conjunction of characteristics" which is similar in almost every instance. There are some differences, of course, but generally they exhibit a central cluster of properties which vary together perhaps to the point of "constant conjunction." Type A, the folk society, stands as one pole, and Type B, the urban society, stands as the other.[49]

What is intriguing, however, is that the pure expression of both types falls into decision Cell 1. That is, the ideal decision—the

45. Redfield, *op. cit.*
46. Robin Williams, Jr., "The Sociological Theory of Talcott Parsons," in Max Black, ed., *The Social Theories of Talcott Parsons* (Englewood Cliffs, N.J.: Prentice-Hall, 1961).
47. Talcott Parsons, "The Point of View of the Author," in Black, *ibid.*, pp. 329–330.
48. Parsons and Shils, *op. cit.*, p. 79.
49. In this context folk, sacred, status, and gemeinschaft can be used interchangeably, as can their opposites. Indeed, it may be said that the pattern variables stipulate the theoretical properties of both polar types.

most legitimate decision of both a folk society and an urban society—is computational or programmatic in character.

Programming: Urban Style

In the case of the urban society, this is rather obvious. Indeed, the continued efforts to provide normative theories of optimal choice are indications of this ideal—an ideal which is represented by the rules of scientific decision-making. These pervade increasingly larger domains of social activity and are retained as ideals, as the most legitimate mode of decision even when not possible. Where this is the case, "satisfactory alternatives" will replace "scientific alternatives," but this in no way departs from the empirical ground and the rules of procedure which validate decisions. On the contrary, the "satisficing" alternative means that we do not possess as yet the necessary knowledge to enable us to treat the situation as a "closed set of variables."[50] Given an objective which is stated in such a manner as to enable the specification of criteria or standards of attainment (itself a scientific rule), it is often the case that we do not know the most effective means of attainment and have to accept, of necessity, a lesser product. Here we stand in the "pragmatic situation," and we know full well that there is much to be learned—that which will allow us to move the problem into Cell 1. It may be that our system of priorities (preference order) does not permit further search at the moment, but we remain cognizant that our knowledge of causation, of appropriate instrumentation, of facts is less than certain.

It is nevertheless clear that the urban order of legitimate decision modes places the scientific-technical procedures in the first rank. Institutions vary in the extent to which they achieve this procedure, yet they continually strive to attain its degree of certainty. Such striving describes the development of the industrial society which at various times "rationalizes" its systems

---

50. In Simon's formulation, rational choice is a function of the ability to treat a problematic situation as a closed set of variables (*op. cit.*, p. 83). Such is the set which describes Cell 1—programmed decision-making.

of production, bureaucratizes (in Max Weber's sense) its systems of administration, and establishes expertise as the premium consideration in the legitimation of role. This last condition suggests that in the social preference order, that vast and complex means-end continuum that marks an urban society, *values are continually instrumentalized, becoming thus questions of fact*. It should not surprise us, therefore, to note the extraordinary power of factual judgments, the pre-eminence of technical schools and the consequent pressure to extend the merit system to all domains of life,[51] and the all-pervasive and powerful effort to reduce uncertainty—indeed, to eliminate it by means of programmed decisions. For some this is liberation; for others, 1984. We forego judgment here and simply note that Parsonian Type B variables describe *the orientation set which enables the technical order to dominate the moral order*. In this context, values tend toward zero and decisions become matters of fact. It is no accident, therefore, that Shils will hold that "professional matter-of-factness" is "modern culture," which, in an undeveloped society, "distinguishes its bearers from all those who do not have it." So too, Pye will state that "modern life . . . is based on a scientific and rational outlook and the application in all phases of life of ever higher levels of technology. It is a reflection of urban and industrial society in which human relations are premised on secular rather than sacred considerations."[52]

In which human relations are premised on secular not on sacred grounds. Observe that this is a difference in epistemology which, in and of itself, *compels the suggestion that certainty describes the state condition of a folk society and that its most legitimate, and perhaps only, form of decision is programmed. It is truly monolithic.*

In the urban society, it is the rule of observation that counts. It is upon experience that a legitimate premise is grounded. And because experience constitutes an "open set," hypothesis and experiment, trial and error, and testing out all become necessary

51. It does not seem that any avenue of life is now exempt. "Marriage and the Family" is a thriving profession these days.
52. Pye, *op. cit.*, pp. 70–71, 19.

modes of behavior. Indeed, in the face of uncertainty, they are taken as both the process and the requirement of correct decision-making. Again, the pragmatic situation presupposes a preference for programmed decisions and is, accordingly, directed toward that end.

Nor is the order of priority any different with respect to negotiation or bargaining—despite continued espousal of democracy. In this situation, it is the difference in preferences that engenders uncertainty. All that separates the actors is a disjunctive situation with respect to demand. They may, of course, pursue the strategy of winner take all, but this is so disruptive to a secularism which generates a plurality of values (pluralism) that theories of the minimax may become more than vehicles for the choice of good strategies—they may become, as they have in the United States, required conduct (as in the case of collective bargaining). If one examines the area of labor-management relations, differences in preferences and fact rarely occur at the same time. When they do, there exists no basis for settlement, and it is possible that the policy of avoidance will be pursued by the larger society—but only if the consequences are negligible. Where not, an outside authority will "seize" control, *dictate* a decision, and impose where necessary punitive sanctions. If the difference is a matter of fact, we observe the use of "fact-finding" commissions which are composed of affectively neutral professionals (a redundant phrase employed only for emphasis). And if the difference is one of interest, we can note a whole battery of devices—now increasingly professionalized—which range from negotiation to mediation and, finally, to arbitration. Here, it is to be stressed, the acceptance by the parties of a common set of preferences means that a solution can be programmed. This "institutionalization" of conflict is required in a society in which decisions are complex precisely because of a secular plurality of values and preferences. What it does is reduce the uncertainty engendered by this plurality to a common consensus—a common denominator. When only values are at issue, achievement of consensus means that solutions can be programmed.

We may, then, picture the condition of the urban society as one in which programmed decision-making stands as the optimal mode and though attainable in only limited domains of institutional behavior nevertheless serves as the ideal form of solving problems. Pragmatics and bargaining are "satisficing" modes of behavior, made eminently legitimate by the uncertainties introduced by an "open environment" and a "secular pluralism."

Programming: Folk Style

But in a folk society, these modes of conduct are illegitimate: *they are sinful and they represent heresy.* Even our capsule descriptions indicate this: any questioning of the collective conscience constitutes a moral offense and is punishable by repressive law. This is Durkheim's phraseology, while Becker tells us that all forms of social activity are governed by sacred sanctions. And Redfield adds that no critical habit, no experimental modes are tolerated. Should tradition be questioned, negative sanctions obtain. In this society, "the moral order predominates over the technical order."[53] But the technical order encompasses so limited a domain as to be virtually non-existent. Behavior "is strongly patterned"; for "pattern" we can substitute the term "program," for there is indeed an axiomatic cast to a folk society. Ends are given; they are not necessarily written, but they serve as first principles, axioms of right in terms of which everyday activities are understood and justified.[54] Folk societies are, despite manifestations of spontaneity, strictly determined, and this determinism is sustained by the force of sacred authority.[55] Constancy of behavior for operational categories and existential and evaluative premises is so great as to suggest that mazeway equivalence approaches identity.

We have here a system in which "facts" tend toward zero and decisions are essentially a matter of values. Hence it is that

53. Robert Redfield, *The Primitive World* (Ithaca, N.Y.: Cornell University Press, 1953), p. 24. Redfield does not hold with my earlier suggestion that the reverse is the case in urban societies.

54. *Ibid.,* p. 11.

55. See Almond and Coleman, *op. cit.,* pp. 103–104, 178, 537, for repeated statements of the force of sacred authority (religion) in their various areas of research.

ordinary commonplace behavior is programmed in strict accordance with tradition.

It may be suggested that this, once again, is a description of an
empty class—that no real societies meet its qualifications for
membership. Yet it is quite apparent that a great many communities exist which must be plotted very close to our type A polar
point.[56] We need not refer only to the Newars of Nepal, or the
"backwardness" of Asian and African villagers, or even those of
ethnographic fame. Here, in the midst of the most urban nation
on earth one can find fundamentalist sects whose behavior is
programmed in strictly doctrinal terms. Among the Mennonites,
the sacred premises of their decision system are guarded with
such care that even remote threats may prompt a relocation to
South America. There, in an "undeveloped" setting, as one
spokesman put it, "we may be able to preserve our way of life." In
the Hasidic community of Williamsburg (Brooklyn), "so strong
are religious sentiments that not only religious affairs but secular
activities as well are controlled and directed mainly by religious
prescription and sacred authority."[57] Few areas of life are exempt
from such control; economics, education, recreation, and the like
are not conceived of as "independent" of the sacred sphere. All
are regulated and controlled by sacred doctrine which "determines the items to be produced, the items to be consumed, and
even the occupations one may hold." Many secular activities are
banned and many secular objects are prohibited (especially those
like television or radio which are deemed to be subversive) and
have, accordingly, been outlawed. Those objects of secular origin
that are admitted are very frequently assigned a sacred character.
A timer will become a Sabbath clock and a pair of heavy gauge
ladies' stockings becomes a "Hasidic stocking"; indeed, almost
every item consumed takes on a sacred aspect.

In this gemeinschaft-like society, religion provides the categories and premises upon which all behavior is founded. The way of
life is programmed, challenge is heresy, and "deviation from

56. McKinney and Loomis, *op. cit.*
57. Solomon Poll, *The Hasidic Community of Williamsburg* (Glencoe, Ill.: Free
Press, 1962), p. 248, and chaps. vii, viii, ix, xii.

prescribed ways," even minor deviation, draws overt and immediate reaction. Where deviation begins to appear with some frequency, it may be concluded that the "tests of secular society" are
of such an order as to make uncertain the raising of a "righteous
generation."[58] And so, it is often said, one group of about 150
families, under the direction of their rabbi, migrated to New
Square (Monsey, New York) where they have literally fenced
themselves off in five square blocks.[59] No one may enter or leave
this area on the Sabbath, television and radio are banned, no
newspapers can be sold, no public library exists, no movies are
permitted, etc. Secular education is kept to the barest minimum
required by law, and it is the rabbi, so exalted[60] for his knowledge
of the law as to be virtually all authority, to whom all problems
are brought—religious and secular alike (taxes, mortgages, etc.).

As regards the decisions which are rendered, these will be
computed. We know this as an exercise in Talmudic scholasticism
in which a conclusion is *drawn* on the basis of logical inference,
and if (axio)-logically incontrovertible, it stands as correct.
When Max Weber dealt with this precise problem,[61] he referred
to the behavior involved as strictly *rationalist* (as distinguished
from rationality) "and at the same time fettered by tradition."
Here we are carried back to an age when the legitimate foundations of decision were "revealed." The knowledge of the learned
rabbi is not fact; it is law, God's law, and this stands as the only
and ultimate ground for a correct decision.

It may therefore be suggested that at the polar points the
distinction to be made is one of epistemology. The ideal solution
to a problem in both instances is programmed, but the difference
is to be seen in the grounds for decision. At the folk end decisions
are virtually value judgments ($F \rightarrow o$, $D = V$), and at the urban

58. One of my research assistants (Israel Singer) working on this group tells me
that there are technical terms, that is, Hebrew words, for the phrases in quota-
tions.
59. "Rate of acculturation," i.e., secularization, is disturbing to many rabbis
(each the prince of a community), and while they wish to follow this example,
they cannot secure suitable rural properties.
60. In another community, the rabbi "sits at a raised platform with the ten most
prominent Hasidim seated at a separate table one level below him."
61. H. H. Gerth and C. Wright Mills, *From Max Weber* (New York: Oxford
University Press, 1958), p. 219.

end the most authoritative decision is a technical judgment
$(V \rightarrow o, D = F)$. The difference is that which obtains between
sin and error. In this context, the requirement for "development"
is a change in the epistemological basis of "mazeway"—i.e., the
construction of mazeways which permit empirical variables to
play a major role in the "trusted" procedures of decision-making.
For development itself, in the modernizing context, is the process
of legitimating technical decisions.

Conclusion

It is possible, if not probable, that this preliminary essay will be
received by some colleagues as another piece of "high-flown"
theory which stands as an impediment to the "kind of clarity"
needed or desired. In the context of "development administration," however, the clarity desired is how to go from state condition A to outcome B in a specified period of time and at a certain
or calculable cost. Consistent failure in this endeavor makes it
clear that we do not as yet, if we ever will, possess sufficient
knowledge to engineer social change as easily as we portray the
process in our paper pictures—and this holds for the antipoverty
scene in the United States as well as for India or Pakistan. But it
is also clear that a good part of our difficulty lies not in process
descriptions alone but in the failure to describe correctly an
existent state condition which is to be the object of the enterprise.
Piling fact upon fact does not make for description, and one need
no longer argue about the utility of simplifying classifications.
One may indeed raise questions about a particular principle of
classification (or measurement), but these can only be answered
empirically. And while this essay is not a statement of findings, its
basic proposal does not appear to run counter to researches which
have been reported—namely, that the primary variable (in
Kluckhohn's usage) in the process of reducing the distance between traditional and developed societies (as these terms are
generally employed) is the trusted ground for decision-making in
everyday life. The Thompson-Tuden matrix accordingly may

turn out to be a valuable device for securing simplified and effective descriptions of existent state conditions. The search for simplicity is a historic stratagem of science, but in this sphere of inquiry it is fortified by the suggestions of anthropologists that some features of a culture are far more diagnostic of the totality than others—so much so that in some cases a single factor is taken as sufficient to establish a "significant" discontinuity.[62]

Finally, we hope that this chapter does not exhibit a "polemical posture" and that it has shown that the proposition that development and modernization require radical breaks from the past need not be derived from the ideology of Marx-Lenin-Stalin.[63] It can be derived from decision theory; in a subsequent essay it shall be extended to meet with what Fred Riggs has called the "critical question"—whether key stages of development can be recognized. In applying the Thompson-Tuden matrix to this question, special attention will be paid to Simon's general theorem that "complex systems will evolve from simple systems much more rapidly if there are stable intermediate forms than if there are not."[64]

62. Kluckhohn, *op. cit.*
63. Joseph LaPalombara, "Theory and Practice in Development Administration," *CAG Occasional Papers* (Bloomington, Ind.: Indiana University, 1967), p. 5.
64. *Op. cit.*, p. 473.

Part II

The Practice of Development Administration

Chapter 4

The Role of the Higher Civil Service
Under Rapid Social and Political Change

Hahn-Been Lee

Constitute government how you please, infinitely the greater part of it must depend upon the exercise of the powers which are left at large to the prudence and uprightness of ministers of state.

Edmund Burke, *Thoughts on the Cause
of the Present Discontents* (1770)

Introduction

This essay is an attempt to analyze the place of the higher civil service in a setting of rapid social and political change and to ascertain those conditions under which it can play a role contributing to administrative development. "Social change" is viewed as the totality of the various and interrelated changes that occur in the political-administrative environment, including changes in the physical and demographic areas and those in the institutional, technological, and ideological realms. "Rapid social change" implies a situation in which many component changes occur in a manner of mutual interaction within a relatively short span of time both in concert and in succession with a significant and lasting general impact upon the political-administrative setting. "Political change" in the present context is the change that occurs in the political sphere in interaction with general social change, including the advance of various new social forces into the political arena, accompanied often by consequent changes of regime.

"Rapid political change" implies a situation in which such political changes take place recurrently in a short span of time.

"Development" is defined as a process of acquiring a sustained growth of a system's capability to cope with new, continuous changes toward the achievement of progressive political, economic, and social objectives.[1] Here development is seen as both process and purpose. In the same vein, "administrative development" is viewed as the growing capability of the administrative system to cope continuously with problems created by social change toward the goal of achieving political, economic, and social progress. The key constituent concepts are change, growth, and continuity. As the capability of the administrators is of crucial importance, the content of that capability must also be delineated. The duality of the function of an administrator who is constantly engaged in both policy formulation or "choice of ends" and policy execution or "employment of means" is widely recognized among students of public administration.[2]

Finally, "higher civil servants" are defined as the relatively permanent top group of civil servants who are placed between the political decision-makers and the rank-and-file bureaucracy and who share, in different degrees, the task of directing the various administrative agencies.[3]

The essay is divided into two main parts. In the first, the writer attempts to build a limited theoretical framework around a typology of bureaucratic roles and a model of political elite structure and bureaucratic roles. The object is to lay out the range of

1. For similar formulations, see S. N. Eisenstadt, "Continuity of Modernization and Development of Administration: Preliminary Statement of the Problem," *CAG Occasional Papers* (Bloomington, Ind.: Indiana University, 1964), pp. 5–7; and Alfred Diamant, "Bureaucracy in Development Movement Regimes: A Bureaucratic Model for Developing Societies," *CAG Occasional Papers* (Bloomington, Ind.: Indiana University, 1964), pp. 4–15. For a formulation stressing the normative aspect of development, see Edward W. Weidner, "Development Administration: A New Focus for Research," in Ferrel Heady and Sybil L. Stokes, eds., *Papers in Comparative Public Administration* (Ann Arbor, Mich.: University of Michigan, 1962), pp. 97–100.

2. See, for example, Fred W. Riggs, "Administrative Development: An Elusive Concept," in John D. Montgomery and William J. Siffin, eds., *Approaches to Development: Politics, Administration and Change* (New York: McGraw-Hill, 1966), p. 229.

3. Fritz Morstein Marx, "The Higher Civil Service as an Action Group in Western Political Development," in Joseph LaPalombara, ed., *Bureaucracy and Political Development* (Princeton: Princeton University Press, 1963), p. 63.

potential roles of higher civil servants and identify the optimum role conducive to administrative development, and subsequently, to examine those conditions in the structural relationship between the political elite and administrative bureaucracy which are conducive to the actualization of such potential as well as those conditions in the same framework which are likely to limit such development with a result of possible regression of bureaucratic role. This part is essentially an extension of an essay on the time dimension in development administration.[4]

The second part of the essay is an application of this theoretical framework to administrative development in Korea in recent years. The main empirical reference is the experience of the writer as a "participant-observer."[5] In addition, liberal use is made of a recent empirical study on the social background of Korean higher civil servants.[6]

Determinants of Bureaucratic Role

A Typology of Bureaucratic Roles

Students of bureaucracy have suggested various typologies on the role of bureaucrats. Categories differ depending on the viewpoints applied. Some emphasize the functional aspect, others single out the structural aspect of the bureaucratic role, and still others inject some normative values into the role. The three patterns of bureaucratic action suggested by Morstein Marx (policy formulation, policy counsel, and public management)[7] are an

---

4. Hahn-Been Lee, "Developmentalist Time and Leadership in Developing Countries," *CAG Occasional Papers* (Bloomington, Ind.: Indiana University, 1965). José Abueva's companion essay that follows in the present volume contains some results of application of my typology of time orientations to the middle civil service of the Philippines.

5. Hahn-Been Lee, *Korea: Time, Change and Administration* (Honolulu: East-West Center Press, 1968).

6. Dong-Suh Bark, "The Problem of Korean Higher Civil Servants: Their Social Background and Morale," in *Some Problems in Public Administration in Developing Countries* (Honolulu: Institute of Advanced Projects, East-West Center, Occasional Papers of Research Translations, Translation Series Number 13, 1966), pp. 1–21. The article was originally published in *Haenchong Kwanli* (*Administrative Management Quarterly*), II, No. 3 (July, 1963), 136–145.

7. Morstein Marx, *op. cit.*, pp. 75–86.

example of the functional approach; Eisenstadt's three categories
of bureaucratic orientation (service, passive tool, and self-aggrandizement)[8] represent a structural-functional viewpoint. More recently, Esman's provocative two poles (creative entrepreneur
and controlled instrument)[9] reflect a pronounced normative bent.
The six major bureaucratic roles suggested by Weidner (innovation, leadership, change agents, administrative process or routine,
specialized or technical expertise, and political or administrative
liaison)[10] present a mixture of various approaches.

The attempt here is to build a typology on the basis of variations in time orientations. I have elsewhere suggested three dominant categories of time orientation: escapist, exploitationist, and
developmentalist.[11] The term "time orientation" used here is a
composite concept incorporating both the time perspective which
is the person's subjective valuation of time and the attitude toward change which influences one's response to external change.
Thus this concept, because of its inherent link to values and
attitudes, possesses considerable potential utility for explaining
and analyzing the behavior of individual actors and groups,[12] as
well as the varying roles of administrators in their interaction
with the environment. Viewed from a time orientation vantage
point, the environmental factors that interact with administration
are not merely a set of facts to be observed but phenomena which
the administrators perceive, develop an image of, and give meaning to, and in relation to which they act meaningfully. Thus *time,*
together with space, is one of the fundamental forms of perception through which meaningful action by individuals and groups
is derived. This has an important bearing on development, because, as Joseph Spengler writes with great clarity, "the state of a
people's politico-economic development, together with its rate
and direction, depends largely upon what is in the minds of its

8. Eisenstadt, *op. cit.,* pp. 24–25.
9. Milton J. Esman, "The CAG and the Study of Public Administration: A
Mid-term Appraisal," *CAG Occasional Papers* (Bloomington, Ind.: Indiana University, 1966), p. 14.
10. Weidner, *op. cit.,* pp. 97–115.
11. Lee, "Developmentalist Time," pp. 4–12.
12. Literature on the relevance of time orientation upon the actor's behavior
includes Georges Gurvitch, *The Spectrum of Social Time* (Dordrecht, The Nether-
lands: D. Reidel, 1964), and Florence R. Kluckhohn and Fred L. Strodtbeck,
Variations in Value Orientations (New York: Harper, 1961), pp. 10–20.

members, and above all upon the content of the minds of its elites, which reflects in part, as do civilizations, the conceptions men form of the universe."[13]

Under conditions of relatively undisturbed continuity, the normal mode of bureaucratic conduct is *routine*. This is mainly due to the temporal and spatial characteristics of the bureaucratic profession. As an occupation, civil service is a stationary business. It is tied to a fixed office, whether a "bureau" or a "sala,"[14] that has more or less regular hours and regular clients. It has familiar or standard procedures and, above all, a regular rhythm of budgetary and program cycles. Regularity, recurrence, and routine are the preferred pattern. Disturbance is shunned. Instinctively, it has an aversion to change, novelty, and crisis. The bureaucratic attitude toward change is normally negative. The time perspective of a typical bureaucracy runs from the past and ends mostly at the present: precedent is greatly valued.[15] As Morstein Marx, a longtime "participant-observer" of a developed bureaucracy, writes, the administrative bureaucracy "responds to the present in the light of the past, confining the future to the immediately foreseeable," and possesses "a professional predilection for the status quo." The higher civil servants, even in well-established bureaucracies, tend to become "emotional defenders of the given order of things."[16] Therefore the time orientation of bureaucracies under stationary conditions tends to be a mixture of "escapist" and "exploitationist" orientations, with an accent on the former. Such orientation tends to produce purposeless ritualism. The bureaucrat in such a situation is conspicuously goal-blind. The "spirit of the clerk"[17] prevails.

Let us introduce now another variable into our typology—the

13. Joseph J. Spengler, "Theory, Ideology, Non-Economic Values, and Politico-Economic Development," in Ralph Braibanti and Joseph J. Spengler, eds., *Tradition, Values, and Socio-Economic Development* (Durham, N.C.: Duke University Press, 1961), pp. 4–5.

14. Fred W. Riggs, "An Ecological Approach: The 'Sala' Model," in Heady and Stokes, eds., *op. cit.*, pp. 19–36.

15. On the hold of precedent and routine in a developing bureaucracy, see Henry Frank Goodnow, *The Civil Service of Pakistan: Bureaucracy in a New Nation* (New Haven: Yale University Press, 1964), p. 137.

16. Morstein Marx, *op. cit.*, p. 87.

17. Lucian W. Pye, *Politics, Personality, and Nation Building: Burma's Search for Identity* (New Haven: Yale University Press, 1962), p. 216.

factor of rapid environmental change—and consider its impact upon the behavior of the bureaucrat.

Under rapidly changing social and political conditions, the "escapist" bureaucrat becomes overwhelmed by the pressure of such change. Often he becomes fearful. Given strong political pressure by the political elite, he is at the mercy of his fear. And when the fear is regressive in character, the bureaucrat becomes a "controlled agent"—a role involving a blind following of the dictates of the political elite without consideration of the consequences of the action taken.

When the "exploitationist" time orientation manifests itself in a static bureaucratic setting the bureaucratic role tends toward opportunism and corruption. The exploitationist bureaucrat is similar to the escapist bureaucrat in being goal-blind, but is different in being self-assertive. He is interested in making short-run gains out of the present circumstances and is therefore given to corrupt practices. William Sheldon designates the role pattern of this category as the "waster," whom he characterizes in these insightful words:

It is the present, his own point in time, that dominates his thought. Of the past and the future he is relatively unaware. He lives intensely *at a point* in the time dimension. . . . He seeks short range adaptation, success at the expense of character. He wants "prosperity," which means to him speed, fast turnover, quick using up of things, and easy money. . . . Above all else he hates "principles."[18]

A useful concept that is related to the "waster" personality type is the idea of "vitiation of social elements." According to Richard T. LaPiere, vitiation of social elements means men's efforts to "maximize personal returns through exploitation of the existing social circumstances" as a means of dispelling tensions of social life. LaPiere suggests that this social behavior occurs "when a society is in a condition of marked incongruence," and when "the tensions produced by severe malfunctioning are in excess of the ability of the system to absorb or dissipate them."[19]

18. William H. Sheldon, *Psychology and the Promethean Will: A Constructive Study of the Acute Common Problem of Education, Medicine and Religion* (New York: Harper, 1936), pp. 61–68.
19. Richard T. LaPiere, *Social Change* (New York: McGraw-Hill, 1965), p. 96.

Thus it is not difficult to see that under conditions of rapid social change and violent political upheavals where external inhibitions are weakened or eliminated, the "waster" could easily "vitiate" the unstable circumstances for self-aggrandizement and could, prompted by his self-assertiveness and aided by his value-blindedness, become a "usurper." This refers to a mode of bureaucratic behavior whereby, in the absence of firm political guidance and direction, bureaucrats use their effective control to advance their expedient bureaucratic interests at the expense of program goals of the government—a process designated by some students of bureaucracy as "negative development."[20]

When a "developmentalist" time orientation manifests itself in a relatively stable condition, bureaucratic behavior conducive to a continuity of essential public service is obtained. This is public management or public housekeeping in the genuine sense. There is a positive, constructive feature in this situation, for the civil servant is goal-conscious and positively adapts to change. Unfortunately, the relative stability of the underlying situation does not prompt him toward extraordinary efforts, and under ordinary conditions, this is the widely expected mode of conduct of the

Table 1. *Typology of Bureaucratic Role*

Environmental conditions	Time orientation		
	escapist	exploitationist	developmentalist
Under relatively stable conditions	routine worker	waster	public servant
Under rapidly changing conditions	controlled agent	usurper	innovator

20. Fred W. Riggs, "Bureaucrats and Political Development: A Paradoxical View," in LaPalombara, ed., *op. cit.*, pp. 120–167, esp. pp. 125–129. Also S. N. Eisenstadt, "Problems of Emerging Bureaucracies in Developing Areas and New States," in B. F. Hoselitz and W. E. Moore, eds., *Industrialization and Society* (Paris: UNESCO, 1963), pp. 159–174, esp. pp. 172–173.

civil service. It provides the continuity of government operation, the foundation for any sustained development. Under normal conditions, therefore, this is the very *raison d'être* of bureaucracy.

Under conditions of rapid environmental change, a higher civil servant with this orientation can become an "innovator." This stems from a latent attitude to adapt to and overcome change coupled with a general trust in time and in the future.

Table 1 is a recapitulation of the typology of bureaucratic roles developed on the basis of differences of time orientation and environmental conditions.

Conditions for Emergence of Administrative Innovation

What are the "innovational" characteristics that can be applied to an administrative process and can potential innovators be identified in a bureaucratic setting? Elsewhere the writer has discussed three different subtypes of innovators in the generic sense: "original innovators," "advocates," and "initial adopters."[21] The innovational role expected of a higher civil servant is rarely that of an "original innovator"; it is either that of an "advocate" or an "initial adopter" of some new or revised measures—program, organizational design, method, or procedure—that will bring improvement and progress in administration. Obviously, an "advocate" role would involve more policy formulation, while an "adopter" role would imply more policy execution.

Broadly speaking, there are two major conditions for innovation within a bureaucracy. One is administrative, the other is political. The administrative condition in turn consists of two elements, (1) personnel and (2) organizational structure.

First, there must exist in the higher civil service some "advocates" of new programs, procedures, methods, and organizations, *plus* a sufficient number of "initial adopters" who would support the "advocates" as the introducers of change. What is operationally important is that some minimum proportion of advocates—often a small but significant minority—must exist before innovation can be effectively introduced and carried on. Such a mini-

21. Lee, "Developmentalist Time," pp. 24–30.

mum might vary from one bureaucracy to another, but it must be proportionately large enough to sustain the innovational fermentation up to the point of adoption. Creative elements in bureaucracy expectedly are always in the minority,[22] but there must exist some enclaves of creativity before such elements can come to the fore.

The question how can higher civil servants with an innovational potential be identified arises at this point. Our hypothesis is that those higher civil servants are likely to be innovational who possess developmentalist time orientations which include both a future time perspective and a positive attitude toward change. How can these potential innovators be found? At the present level of sophistication in the study and practice of administration, various social background studies could be useful. Attention may be given to such positive features as middle-class and lower-middle-class backgrounds, indicative of a drive for achievement; high merit in terms of competitive examinations; youth; sufficient educational background; postentry in-service training; and exposure, including foreign travel.

Second, the structure of administrative bureaucracy must be flexible for the innovational germ to be engendered. Victor Thompson, in writing about innovation in bureaucracy, emphasizes these structural requirements for bureaucratic innovation: (1) structural looseness (even some redundancy) and (2) integrative group processes, including such features as multiple group membership (e.g., task forces) and group problem-solving methods on the basis of interprofessional and interdisciplinary grouping. Thompson further advises against using hierarchical positions as prizes or rewards and assigning innovation to any isolated jurisdiction such as a research and development department. He stresses that "the innovative organization is innovative throughout."[23] It is clear that excessive rigidity in organizational structure, which is the rule in many bureaucracies in developing countries, stifles innovation within. As a provocative thinker on the problems of policy-making and leadership remarked:

22. A. J. Toynbee, *A Study of History,* Somervell Abridgment (New York: Oxford University Press, 1947–57), Part III, chap. xx, p. 533.
23. Victor A. Thompson, "Bureaucracy and Innovation," *Administrative Science Quarterly,* X, No. 1 (June, 1965), 19.

the greatness of a society derives from its willingness to chart new ground beyond the confines of routine. Without organization every problem becomes a special case. Without inspiration a society will stagnate. . . . Too much stress on organization leads to bureaucratization and the withering of imagination. Excessive emphasis on inspiration produces a tour de force without continuity or organizational stability. . . .[24]

In short, structural flexibility, toleration for some autonomy, and protection and cultivation of "innovational enclaves"[25] are structural prerequisites for emergence of innovation within administrative bureaucracy.

The existence of innovational enclaves within the bureaucracy does not automatically lead to diffusion of administrative innovation. A small minority, they must be actively discovered and identified. Otherwise, they are apt to be submerged under majority elements with different orientations which are given to routine and often corruption.

The crucial condition for enabling innovational enclaves to come to the center is the existence of strong political elites that are ready to take up the task of identifying and fostering potential innovators among the civil servants. Once there is a significant minority of potential innovators within the higher layers of the bureaucracy, the extent to which their potential becomes actualized depends to a substantial degree upon the composition and quality of the political elite and the structural relationship between that elite and the higher civil service.

Influence of the Political Elite upon Bureaucratic Roles: A Model

A political elite is seldom monolithic in composition or in function. In terms of role distribution, a division of the political elite into two subcategories is useful: (1) the power elite—the effective power holder or holders at the center; (2) the task elite —task-oriented leaders. Rarely are these two identical. A normal pattern sees older, charismatic, amateur leaders becoming the

24. Henry A. Kissinger, *Nuclear Weapons and Foreign Policy* (New York: Harper, 1957), pp. 246–248.
25. S. N. Eisenstadt, "Social Change, Differentiation and Evolution," *American Sociological Review*, XXX (June, 1964), 384–385.

power elite, with younger, technocratic and professional leaders forming the task elite. The former are the "solidarity-makers" and the latter the "instrumental leaders."[26] In cases where these two types are either identical, which is very rare, or are in harmonious mutual association, the political elite is strong and can elicit spontaneous support from the bureaucracy. When the normal structural pattern is reversed, the effective strength of the political elite becomes compromised.

In institutional terms, a power elite usually includes the chief executive, members of the directorate of the ruling party, and the caucus of the ruling party in the legislature. A task elite usually includes members of the cabinet and their politically appointed deputies.

Normally, the higher civil service is more easily influenced by the task elite than by the power elite. This is mainly due to propinquity and relative homogeneity of outlook and experience. This relationship sometimes puts the higher civil service in trouble in its relations with the power elite. When the task elite is in proper association with the power elite, there is no problem for the higher civil service. But when this is not the case, the higher civil service is liable to invite suspicion from the power elite. But if the task elite is strong enough, the problem will not arise. It is only when the task elite is dissociated from the power elite and therefore weak that the higher civil service suffers.

Table 2 shows a model built on the basis of the composition of the political elite and its impact upon the role of the higher civil servants under conditions of rapid change. This deals only with that fraction of the higher civil servants who are potentially innovational. One of the focuses of this model is upon the possible tendency of regression of the bureaucratic role under adverse conditions in terms of political elite structure.

Several propositions may be advanced from the various relationships in the model. The following propositions are posed in terms of the relationship of political elites to the civil servants. Reverse propositions may also be constructed, and additional

26. S. N. Eisenstadt, "Breakdowns of Modernization," *Economic Development and Cultural Change*, XII, No. 4 (July, 1964), 352–356.

Table 2. *A Model of Political Elite Structure and Bureaucratic Roles under Rapidly Changing Conditions*

| | Political elite structure and time orientations | | Higher civil servants' roles | |
	Power elite	Task elite	Potential role	Actual role
1.	D	D	(i)	i
2.	D	E	(i)	i—
3.	D	X	(i)	i—
4.	X	D	(i)	i—
5.	X	E	(i)	c
6.	X	X	(i)	c
7.	E	D	(i)	i—
8.	E	E	(i)	u
9.	E	X	(i)	c

Note: D = developmentalist time orientation, X = exploitationist time orientation, E = escapist time orientation, i = innovator, u = usurper, c = controlled agent.

To elaborate on the model:

1. (DD/i) This is only logical and is the most desirable type: close identity or harmony between the power and task elites would enable the innovational higher civil servants to actualize their full potential.

2. (DE/i—) Developmentalist power elite aided by weak political lieutenants would still allow potentially innovational higher civil servants to realize

hypotheses generated. The following, however, will serve as a beginning.

1. The full innovational potential of the higher civil service can be realized only when the power elite and the task elite both have developmentalist orientations. (Full role actualization)

2. As long as at least one of the two elites possesses developmentalist orientation, some room for actualization of innovational potentials of the higher civil service exists. (Partial role actualization)

3. The higher civil service is more influenced in its behavior pattern by the task elite than by the power elite. The more developmentalist the task elite is, therefore, the more innovational the higher civil service tends to become. (Role harmony) By the same token, when a developmentalist orientation of the

some of their potential.

3. (DX/i—) A really developmentalist power elite would seldom surround itself with an exploitationist task elite. But even if such were the case, the former would in time either assimilate or eliminate the latter. At any rate, innovational civil servants under such a combination of political elites would have a reasonably good chance to do justice to their potential.

4. (XD/i—) Exploitationist power elite supported by developmentalist task elite would still leave some room for potentially innovational bureaucrats to realize their innovational potential. (In this case, the higher civil service may invite suspicion of the power elite.)

5. (XE/c) When an exploitationist power elite controls a weak, captive task elite, then the top bureaucrats would tend to assume the role of controlled agents of the ruling power elite.

6. (XX/c) This combination amounts to a monolithic political elite with an exploitationist orientation. Under such a political leadership, the top civil servants would have little chance to escape from the role of controlled agents of the monolithic ruling elite.

7. (ED/i—) When an escapist power elite is supported by a developmentalist task elite, then the innovational potential of top bureaucracy would be given some free play. (This is especially the case when the power elite is headed by a past-oriented charismatic leader.)

8. (EE/u) When both the power elite and the task elite are escapist, then the potentially innovational elements in the top bureaucracy would get frustrated, and under conditions of acute tension, might become usurpers.

9. (EX/c) This case is one step before XX/c above; the exploitationist task elite would sooner or later swallow or replace the escapist power elite and become itself the power elite. Even potentially innovational civil servants would become easily the controlled agents of the exploitationist elite, perhaps not as rapidly as in the case of XX/c but sooner than in the case of XE/c.

The differential rate of regression is due to the greater propinquity to the task elite.

---

task elite is sanctioned and shared by the power elite, the innovational tendency of the higher civil service is maximized. (Complete role harmony.) This approximates the case in Proposition 1 above.

4. When such harmonious association between the elites is not obtained and when the task elite is impotent or weakened, the innovational tendency of the higher civil service is compromised. (Role regression)

5. When the power elite is highly exploitationist and the task elite itself becomes the controlled agent of the power elite, even innovational higher civil servants would be coerced to become the controlled agents of the power elite. (Role regression)

6. When the power elite has an escapist orientation and when a task elite does not exist, the top bureaucrats, even those with

innovational potential, would tend to become exploitationist and may become potential usurpers. (Role regression)

The Case of Korean Bureaucracy

A Bureaucracy under Transformation

Let us now turn to Korea, using it as an example of a bureaucracy undergoing rapid external change and intensive internal transformation in recent years. We shall first examine the social background and motivational aspects of the higher civil servants in this bureaucracy in order to get indications, even indirect, of the time orientation and the internal weight of potentially innovational elements in it. We shall then draw some examples of different patterns of the structural relationship in the politico-administrative nexus from recent political and administrative history.

A study of the social background of higher civil servants conducted by Dong-Suh Bark in 1962[27] has some interesting revelations concerning developments in the Korean bureaucracy during the rapid social and political change since the 1960–61 period. Most indicative of a general internal transformation is a marked trend toward rejuvenation at the top level in comparison with the subordinate levels.

Table 3 shows the age characteristic of the Korean bureaucracy as of 1962. The average age of officials of Grade 2A (which corresponds to the level of bureau directors in the central ministries) was only forty, and this was lower than that of their immediate subordinates in Grade 2B (corresponding to the level of directors of field offices) which was forty-six, and also lower than that of Grade 3A (corresponding to the level of central division chiefs) which was forty-two.

One can easily see from the table that something very unusual has happened in the Korean bureaucracy in recent years. The deeply rooted traditional pattern of seniority was radically upset by the political upheavals of 1960–61. Major thrust points were created at the top (Grade 2A) and at the bottom (Grade 4B).

27. Bark, *op. cit.*, Chart 7.

Table 3. *Age Characteristics of Korean Bureaucracy*

Grade	Average age	Description of grades
1	44	Assistant vice-minister, planning co-ordinators, provincial governors, directors of independent institutes
2A	40	Central bureau directors
2B	46	Directors of field offices
3A	42	Central section chiefs, heads of large field offices
3B	39	Central subsection chiefs, heads of small field offices
4A	39	Senior clerks
4B	34	Senior clerks (new)
5A	34	Junior clerks
5B	32	Junior clerks, patrolmen, postmen

Source: Dong-Suh Bark, "The Problem of Korean Higher Civil Servants: Their Social Background and Morale," in *Some Problems in Public Administration in Developing Countries* (Honolulu: Institute of Advanced Projects, East-West Center, Occasional Papers of Research Translations, Translation Series Number 13, 1966), Chart 7.

The thrust at the top was made both by bringing in new blood[28] (including selected military officers) and by promoting relatively merit-oriented civil servants from the middle ranks. On the whole the latter were more numerous. There was a definite indication that higher civil servants recruited on the basis of merit were increasing in number, especially at the Grade 3A level. Table 4 shows the relative proportion of higher civil servants at several grades by the channel of promotion.

It is noteworthy that the percentage of those who occupied higher posts through open competitive examination is greater at Grade 3A level than at Grade 2 levels. This is indicative of the upward thrust of younger, more merit-oriented civil servants. The thrust at the bottom at Grade 4B level, noted in Table 4 above, reflected to a large extent the influx of new university graduates —a process which started in 1960.

Side by side with these points of thrust were some "clogging points" of relatively older bureaucrats: Grades 2B, 4A, 5A, and

28. Bark's survey showed that 20.5 per cent of Grade 2A officials had less than two years of government service to get to that grade (*ibid.*, Chart 8).

Table 4. *Recruitment Pattern*

Grade	Open competitive examination	Limited examination upon nomination	No examination	No answer
2 administrator	16.7%	54.2%	20.8%	8.3%
2 technician	12.2	34.1	48.8	4.9
3A administrator	23.2	46.3	22.9	7.5
3A technician	8.6	54.3	26.9	10.1

Source: Bark,   "The Problem of Korean Higher Civil Servants," Chart 1.

5B. Thus, by 1962 there were signs that the bureaucracy was torn between two conflicting forces—relatively change-attuned forces on the one hand, and relatively status quo-oriented forces on the other.

This transformation from a seniority-based bureaucracy to a merit-based bureaucracy was also manifest in the divergence in career outlook of different civil servants. Bark's study showed that the majority of Korean higher civil servants of all grades felt insecurity over pay and position.[29] Most of them also assigned a lower current value to government positions in comparison to jobs in industry, commerce, and banking[30]—a value in direct contrast to the traditional status scale where commercial occupations ranked at the very bottom.

But side by side with such an insecure and dissatisfied majority, there was emerging a significant minority who showed an unwavering motivation for government careers in spite of a general change in the occupational value scale.[31] There was also a similarly significant minority who apparently had a relatively long-range career outlook coupled with a relatively high achievement motivation, so that they felt that the pension they would get was dependable.[32] Although these various indexes of the social

29. *Ibid.*, Chart 15.   30. *Ibid.*, Chart 14.
31. *Ibid.*
32. *Ibid.*, Chart 13. Currently the pension is very modest. But as the amount is predicated on the salary level at the time of retirement, and as the present salary scale is somewhat progressively steep, there is a valid reason for relatively highly motivated civil servants who look forward to attaining high positions before retirement to take the pension scheme more seriously than those who have no expectation of higher positions.

background characteristics and bureaucratic motivations and morale are not correlated in Bark's survey, there is good reason to hypothesize that a close correlation does exist between the various findings, such as merit thrust, postentry training and exposure, service morale, and career outlook. One can also hypothesize that in the higher civil service in Korea around 1962 there was a small but significant minority, roughly around 20 to 25 per cent, who represented a pool of potential innovational elements.

José V. Abueva's study on the service orientation of some middle civil servants of the Philippines sheds an interesting parallel light. According to this study, 33 per cent of the respondents are "indifferent to relatives and friends who measure personal ties by willingness to accommodate requests." Abueva suggests that in the Philippine bureaucracy, which is deeply "entangled" with relatives and friends, it is among these "disentangled administrators" that innovational potential can be expected.[33]

Although the two studies mentioned above do not lend themselves to direct comparison, they are useful because of their common indication of the existence and emergence of a potentially innovational minority in each of the two bureaucracies studied.

A composite portrait of the higher civil service of Korea which can be drawn from the foregoing analysis is one of a bureaucracy undergoing a rapid transformation. This reflects the underlying social change as well as the recent political upheavals. Although a corps of bureaucrats oriented toward seniority and the status quo remains as the backbone, two significant thrusts are making the bureaucracy more responsive to external change. One is an influx of new blood at the top, the other is an upward thrust of younger and merit-oriented civil servants from within the bureaucracy. To what extent these two thrusts are in harmony and in mutually complementary relations is problematical. There are elements both of conflict and of mutual stimulation. The crucial question from the point of view of administrative development is the extent to which the more genuinely innovational elements in both

33. See chap. v, below.

groups can be identified and nourished in order to exert an ever greater influence upon the entire bureaucracy. They are, to be sure, in the minority, but they are a significant minority—significant in innovational potential.

Changing Political Elites and Bureaucratic Roles

In an earlier section, we saw the important theoretical implications that the structure of a political elite has for the bureaucratic role. Now let us apply the model of political elite structure and bureaucratic roles to the recent political and administrative history in Korea. In the Korean experience since 1945, one can identify at least four of the six types suggested in the model: ED/i—, XD/i—, XE/c, and EE/u.

ED/i— model. A case in point is the Rhee administration during the period of recovery after the war of 1950–53.[34] The period runs from 1954 through the first half of 1958.

The effective power elite at this period was President Rhee himself. During the early years of the Republic, beginning with the establishment of its government in 1948 and through the war years, this charismatic leader contributed greatly in building basic solidarity and collective loyalty among the population. But his obsessive claim to be the sole repository of leadership in the independence movement together with his senile irritation at the many pressing problems of a war-torn nation made him more "escapist" than "developmentalist" in his orientation. An index of such orientation was his recurring failure to use his charisma to build up potential leadership, and specifically to identify and foster potential understudies. On the contrary, he did not waste time in eliminating any political lieutenants who showed ability and stature.

Such orientation was related to his highly authoritarian style of leadership and resulted in a series of constitutional crises which gradually eroded his charisma. Although his charisma began to

34. See my *Korea: Time, Change and Administration,* chap. v.

decline in the postwar period under consideration, the war dislocation and urgent demands for quick action for economic recovery forced President Rhee to pay some attention to pressing economic problems. While trying slowly to consolidate his political power by building a political party of his own to counter his strong political opponents, he surrounded himself in his cabinet with a succession of task-oriented ministers who were to tackle the major task of economic recovery. The time orientation of these task leaders was generally "developmentalist"; their program orientation was generally toward production and economic stabilization. They were largely responsible for bringing about industrial recovery—especially expansion of coal production, beginning around 1956, and control of inflation and general price stability beginning around 1957—and for making an important start in marshaling talents for long-term development planning around 1958.

Until then, the bureaucracy was virtually a closed institution staffed at the top by Japanese-trained former colonial civil servants whose dominant orientation was clerical, ritualistic, routine-loving, and seniority bound. There had been very little influx of blood with a modern orientation until the latter part of the fifties. And it was only through the sponsorship of the new task elite in the cabinet that the first real dent was made. These task-oriented ministers were generally exposed to current Western influence through travel or residence abroad just before this time or through frequent contacts with foreign officials in economic assistance. Bent on discharging their tasks and interested in getting results, they decided to recruit into their staff some young men with specialized knowledge and a professional outlook, but naturally met staunch built-in resistance from the existing bureaucracy. In the face of this resistance, the task elite often broke existing bureaucratic red tape and rules in order to secure new talents at the relatively higher positions of the bureaucracy where their specialized knowledge and relatively modern outlook could be effective. By this time, some of the younger men, who had received advanced education both in Korea and in Western coun-

tries between 1945 and 1955, were available in various specialized fields such as public health, agriculture, forestry, geology,
engineering, public finance, and economic planning.

To be sure, these new recruits formed merely a single corps
against a wall of seniority-based bureaucracy. Yet the new blood
that was brought into the higher civil service at this time not only
played an active role in helping the task elite in planning and
implementing economic recovery around 1956–58 but also constituted the scattered innovational enclaves of the bureaucracy.
When the political and bureaucratic structures became more
flexible after the violent upheavals in 1960 and 1961, many members of these enclaves and their internees played vital roles by
underpinning the administrative transition and by providing specialized knowledge and the many skills that were required to
formulate and implement various development-oriented action
programs of the changing administrations. At a time when there
were few innovational elements in the task elite and in the higher
civil service, this illustrates at least partial role actualization by
the bureaucracy under an ED (escapist-developmentalist) type
of political elite structure.

XD/i– model. The turbulent conditions in recent years created
two versions of this situation: the second half of the Democratic
administration—from November, 1960, to April, 1961; and the
first year of the military administration—from May, 1961, to May,
1962. Let us examine each of these cases on the basis of time
orientations of the respective elites.

The Democratic administration came to power in August, 1960,
in the aftermath of the April Revolution (student uprising)
which toppled the twelve-year Rhee administration. Although
the Democratic party was the sole organized political force in the
power vacuum after the Rhee regime ended, the new ruling party
suffered from a serious limitation in effective power because it
was not directly instrumental in causing the change of administration—the students and the intellectual community, not the
Democratic party, were directly responsible for the decisive political change in April.

The weakness of the new political elite was magnified by a

nagging factional scramble for power within the Democratic party that was largely traceable to the regretful "exploitationist" time orientation which the power elite of the party possessed. It was further aggravated by the newly adopted parliamentary-cabinet type of government in which the effective power was thinly diffused among a large number of politicians in the cabinet and in the National Assembly. Thus, the power elite of the Democratic administration was diffused and very weak.

However, this administration had a task elite which was as enlightened and task-oriented as any before that time. Under the initiative of some members of this task elite in the cabinet an imaginative action program was shaped and implemented. This program became the National Construction Service—a large-scale multipurpose public works program including a Peace Corps-type youth recruiting program designed to absorb the newly emerging social energy into constructive channels and eventually into the bureaucracy.

Under such a "developmentalist" task elite, the higher civil service, which was going through a process of major adaptation to rapid social and political change, was generally encouraged to play an active role in the formulation and implementation of the regime's major action program. But the scope and effect of such contribution were inevitably limited by the fragmentation of the effective power at the center.[35] Thus, this illustrates a case of partial role actualization under an XD (exploitationist-developmentalist) type of political elite structure.

The military administration which assumed power by a coup in May, 1961, after a state of general unrest had a singular type of elite structure. The power elite consisted of relatively junior military officers who had attained a tactical-operational skill level below the field grade, whereas the task elite was mostly composed of generals who had attained a skill level that reflected a strategic-managerial outlook. In terms of time orientation, the power elite was relatively "hasty" and the task elite relatively "developmentalist"; in terms of program orientation, the former

35. *Ibid.*, chap. vii.

was preoccupied with basic control framework, while the latter was oriented toward economic development. When the regime consolidated its power after the first hundred days, there was a strong program initiative at the task-elite level. Such an initiative was largely responsible for emergency economic measures designed to bring recovery from the stagnation caused by repeated political upheavals, as well as to plan for long-range economic development.

The higher civil service was actively utilized by the task elite in formulation and implementation of such substantive programs. But the tension inherent in the situation of role conflict due to the different orientations of the power elite and the task elite, together with the tension caused by an attitude of suspicion on the part of the power elite toward the higher bureaucracy, compromised the full realization of the innovational potential of the bureaucracy.[36]

XE/c model. The last period of the Rhee administration, the period of the "liberal oligarch"—from the latter half of 1958 until the downfall of the regime in April, 1960—was the time when the charisma of the old President had considerably eroded.

Although the President retained nominal power until the last day of his regime, a substantial part of the effective power moved to the Liberal party oligarchs whose main background was legalistic-bureaucratic and whose dominant time orientation was "exploitationist." This oligarchical power elite had acquired a tight control over the cabinet through long years of constitutional and legal manipulations. The cabinet which had had some innovational ministers in earlier years became itself a controlled agent of the highly "exploitationist" power elite in the ruling party. Under these circumstances, members of the higher civil service, at the mercy of the power elite and following their immediate superiors, the impotent task elite, became controlled agents as well.[37]

EE/u model. The initial period of the Rhee administration, from 1948 to 1953, included the period from the establishment of the government until the end of the war of 1950–53. The effective political power was in the hands of President Rhee whose time

36. *Ibid.*, chap. viii.   37. *Ibid.*, chap. v.

orientation was a mixture of "retrospective-escapist" time and "inheriting-developmentalist" time, the former outweighing the latter as years went by. This was reflected in his failure to cultivate his lieutenants and task elite. He was jealous of any lieutenants of stature and ability, so that potentially capable members of the task elite were successively eliminated from positions of responsibility. A vacuum of leadership within the task elite was created. Meanwhile, the retrospective leader decided to create a political party of his own following, whose directorate was filled mainly by former bureaucrats with a highly "exploitationist" orientation. As the charisma and power of the senile leader declined this bureaucratic core group by the end of the regime became virtual usurpers of state power.[38] It may be added that the u in this model eventually became the X group in the XE/c model above.

Summary and Conclusion

What is the role of a higher civil servant? Is he a controlled agent or an innovator? Is he a usurper? Under normal conditions of relative stability he is none of these; he is usually a defender of the status quo. With this basic tendency, his orientations can fall roughly within three types: routine, waste, and conscientious housekeeping. But under rapidly changing conditions his behavior will show a degree of intensity, and he would exhibit one of the three potential roles: (1) controlled agent, (2) usurper, and (3) innovator.

The innovational potential is related to a "developmentalist" orientation of the bureaucrat. This means that the bureaucrat must combine a forward-looking perspective and a positive attitude toward change. Factors such as his personality, social background, education and exposure, and job motivation are intimately related to his time orientation. Existence of a sizable portion, even though a minority, of such elements within the bureaucracy is the necessary condition for administrative innova-

38. *Ibid.*

tion. To be operationally important this minority must be identified, fostered, and properly utilized. This is basically the function
of political leadership.

A further condition for the innovational potential of the bureaucrats to be realized relates to the quality and structure of the
political elite. Two distinct groups of political elite can be analytically distinguished: the power elite group which holds the effective control and the task elite group which takes charge of the
action program of the regime. When the two are in a positive
harmony, the portion of the higher civil service that works closely
with them tends to display its full innovational potential without
undermining due control by the political elite. At least one of the
two political elite groups must be "developmentalist" in order to
obtain even a partial measure of administrative innovation. It is
particularly important that the task elite be "developmentalist,"
for the higher bureaucracy is more influenced by this group than
by the power elite. Some of the illustrious Korean cases of relatively good administration in the recent past were those in which
the task elite was enlightened and reasonably strong vis-à-vis the
power elite, or when the former obtained even grudging support
from the latter.

Bureaucratic role regression occurs when the pattern of the
political elite structure exhibits a regressive combination. This
could be either a redundance of "escapist" orientations (EE) or a
match of an aggressively "exploitationist" power elite with a
captive task elite (which is tantamount to non-existence of such
an elite) (XE). In the former case, the bureaucracy is degraded
to a controlled agent, while in the latter case there is the danger
of its becoming a usurper.

What can we do for the emergence of innovation in administration? Innovation is related to "developmentalist" time, and this is
the function of a longer time perspective and a positive attitude.
Thus, talents related to the development of a longer view and
those related to adaptability to change must be tapped. In terms
of personnel policy, this includes "catching young" and sufficient
exposure to change. Exposure can be gained through systematic
in-service training, but over a period of time it can also be gained
through systematic promotion of well-trained civil servants to

positions of higher responsibility with wider citizen exposure. A judicious and balanced injection of new blood from constantly new emerging groups and from various strata of society is also essential for a continuous growth of adaptive capability of the bureaucracy. At the same time, in order to allow innovation to emerge within the bureaucracy, the organizational structure must be reasonably flexible. Some measure of autonomous development of innovational enclaves must be tolerated. Contacts and cross-fertilization among such enclaves within the bureaucracy and between these and any external centers of innovation must be encouraged. Such flexibility would allow innovators to emerge and help them until they become a significant minority with enough momentum to sustain themselves for eventual exertion of innovational influence.

In the political sphere, the basic requirement is again flexibility in the political system, so that free-floating resources can be engendered in the polity that will eventually provide both adaptability and stability. One crucial condition is a kind of differentiated harmony in the structure of the political elite, namely between the power elite and the task elite. Ideally, both of these elite groups should be "developmentalist." But in real political life, this does not happen often and does not have to be the case. A working association of a charismatic power elite with an enlightened and capable task elite would be a sufficient minimum condition for a substantial realization of the innovation role of the higher civil service.

The essence of administration in developing countries is smooth and creative management of rapid social and political change. This requires among other things a major innovational role on the part of the higher civil service which is the crucial link between the political elites and the rank-and-file bureaucrats. To secure such a contribution from the higher civil service, however, takes more than the mere presence of some innovational elements within it. It requires a parallel presence of enlightened political leadership with an adequate measure of "developmentalist" orientation. Only under such political elites can higher civil servants with requisite qualities realize their full innovational potential in the task of managing rapid social and political change.

Chapter 5

Administrative Culture and Behavior and Middle Civil Servants in the Philippines

José Veloso Abueva

Introduction

For two decades, concern for accelerating the development of many old and new nation-states has been worldwide. This concern has yielded a prodigious array of theories, strategies, and practical devices regarding various aspects of the development process: economic, social, cultural, political, administrative. It is mainly with the last of these interrelated aspects, administrative development, that this essay deals. The assumption is that if "development administration"—the administration of specifically *developmental* programs—is to be successful, it must take place within the context of administrative development.

Administrative Development

"Administrative development" is the increasing ability of the political system or polity of any country to implement its collective decisions. The bureaucracy is the major structure for performing this implementing function, and it may also play a role in making those decisions. But many actors other than those who populate the bureaucracy, headed by the chief executive, are often implicated in administration: the legislators and other elected officials, the party members, perhaps the military, the members of organizations and associations, the citizens—all of whom participate in one way or another in making and carrying out decisions for the nation and who are also subject to their application. This concept of development, in its political and administrative aspects, has been elaborated by Fred W. Riggs.[1]

The more developed a polity, according to Riggs, the higher the level of its *diffraction*: the differentiation (specificity) of its political structures and functions *and* their integration (co-ordination). The level of diffraction makes possible a given combination of *capacity* for and *participation* in the decision-making or problem-solving processes of the polity. Both attributes are values which are constantly sought, in varying degrees, by the elites and the citizenry of every country. Yet they seem to be basically antithetical since, structurally speaking, capacity takes the form of *hierarchy* while participation assumes the form of *polyarchy*. Particularly at lower levels of diffraction, attempts to increase participation are bound to be at the expense of capacity, and vice versa. This dilemma is implicit in what Prime Minister Nehru and President Magsaysay said about the development of their respective countries being complicated by democratic institutions.[2] The only way to increase both capacity and participation is to raise the level of diffraction of the polity.

In turn, the greater the capacity and participation characterizing the polity, the greater its *autonomy* in relation to its environment. By autonomy, Riggs means the ability of the polity to shape and influence its environment of human actors, their culture, and the physical setting, while at the same time being affected by them. Ultimately, the polity does aim to provide services to its citizens, influence their values and attitudes, modify their individual behavior, regulate their group activities, and exact their support, as well as help them transform the material and physical aspects of the environment to make it more amenable to human life.

1. See chap. ii above.
2. For Nehru's statement, see José V. Abueva, "An Interview with Nehru," *Sunday Times Magazine* (Manila), June 14, 1964, pp. 28–29. For some of Magsaysay's statements on his difficulties in introducing reforms, see Abueva, *Focus on the Barrio: The Story Behind the Birth of the Philippine Community Development Program* (Quezon City: Institute of Public Administration, University of the Philippines, 1959), pp. 54–55, 397–402.

This generalized discussion may be applied to one of the important structures of the polity whose principal function is administration: the bureaucracy. The more developed a polity as a whole, the higher the level of administrative development. Within this context, and as the major instrument for administration, the bureaucracy is integrated into or co-ordinated with the functioning of the other political structures—the legislature, the parties, the interest groups (or their structural equivalents), the citizenry. Internally, the bureaucracy in a developed polity is also both differentiated and able to integrate its various specialized agencies and functions, whether programmatic (e.g., agricultural extension) or managerial (e.g., budgeting) in nature. This makes possible the internal efficiency and external effectiveness of the bureaucracy. In other words, it has a high capacity for making its decisions and solving its problems. Likewise, it is able to relate to its programs more and more interested outside individuals and groups. Consequently, the bureaucracy also partakes of the autonomy of the entire polity by being able to influence the values, attitudes, behavior, and relationships of appropriate human actors—including its own members and all other persons with whom they interact in performing their official roles.

Within this theoretical framework, an analysis of the administrative development of any country, such as the Philippines, must look into the operationalizing of diffraction, capacity, participation, hierarchy, polyarchy, and autonomy, among others. Pending these formulations, and as one short step toward making them, answers to another related and large question may illuminate the analytical problems. The question is: What are the historically derived ways of behaving characteristic of most actors or role-players in the Filipino administrative system? The desired answers, in the form of generalizations, constitute the Filipino "administrative culture."

It is helpful to distinguish between the polity and the administrative system of any country. The polity is the nationwide social system concerned with both the making and enforcing of collective decisions for its members. Ultimately, the polity is backed by force which is usually legitimate. The administrative system is that aspect of the polity which is primarily concerned with its implementing or administrative function.

Administrative Culture and Administrative Behavior

The administrative culture is but an aspect of the political culture, which in turn is a part of the total culture of a given society. The components of administrative culture are cognitions, evaluations, and affect which together form the subjective orientations to the administrative system and its ecology (interactions between the administrative system and its environment).[3] All actors or role-players in the administrative system have orientations—not only the administrators who occupy the bureaucracy and perform its roles, but also the politicians, the members of interest groups, the operators of the mass media, the rank-and-file citizens, and even those foreigners who (through technical assistance or international loans) somehow perform roles in the administrative system under consideration.

What is the relation between the administrative culture and administrative behavior?[4] The former is abstracted from and manifested in the latter. The prevalent existential beliefs, values, norms, and feelings that make up the administrative culture are the subjective links between the events of politics and administration and the behavior of the actors in the administrative system. In other words, it is in terms of the meanings and interpretations given to those events by the actors that they act or react in concrete situations. The administrative culture defines the desirable, proper, required, permissible, tolerable, and prohibited kinds of behavior among the actors in the administrative system; it therefore performs a regulative function in relation to administrative behavior. The administrative culture, along with other values

3. This concept of "administrative culture" is adapted from "political culture" as defined by Gabriel A. Almond and Sidney Verba in their *The Civic Culture* (Boston: Little, Brown, 1965), pp. 12–26. The definition of "ecology" is from Riggs, chap. ii above.

4. The analysis here draws heavily on that of Sidney Verba in Lucian W. Pye and Sidney Verba, eds., *Political Culture and Political Development* (Princeton: Princeton University Press, 1965), pp. 516–519. The distinction between culture and behavior is discussed in Ralph L. Beals and Harry Hoijer, *An Introduction to Anthropology* (3rd ed.; New York: Macmillan, 1965), pp. 269–271.

and norms of the society, shapes the policy, and organizational, procedural, and technological preferences for the administrative system. In general, the administrative culture also determines the ways in which administrative agencies and programs change: how they are stabilized, modified, developed, or dissolved. It is apparent that administrative development, in its functional and structural aspects, would likewise be influenced by, even as it is reflected in, the administrative culture of the time.

The administrative culture may be said to consist of two types of patterns: (1) the *ideal patterns* which define what the actors in the administrative system would do or say in particular situations if they conformed faithfully to the standards evolved by the on-going administrative culture; and (2) the *behavioral patterns* which are abstracted from observations of how the actors in the administrative system actually behave in specific situations.[5] In transitional or partially modernizing societies, like the Philippines and other Asian countries, we expect to find marked incongruencies and conflicts within the ideal patterns which are in turn reflected in contrasting behavioral patterns. In the more integrated cultures of either the traditional or the modern societies, relatively fewer incongruencies and conflicts may be found within the ideal patterns and therefore in the behavioral patterns as well.

The usage of "administrative culture" herein is adapted from the anthropological concept of "culture" and from the latter's prior adaptation as "political culture" by Gabriel Almond and his associates.[6] It is consistent with that of Dwight Waldo in his

5. The concept of "ideal patterns" is from Clyde Kluckhohn, "Patterning in Navaho Culture," in Leslie Spier, ed., *Language, Culture and Personality* (Menasha, Wis.: Sapir Memorial Publication Fund, 1941), pp. 109–130, as cited by Beals and Hoijer, *op. cit.*, pp. 271–272. The companion concept of "behavioral patterns" is defined by Beals and Hoijer (p. 272). Their definitions have been adapted to the particular usage herein.

6. This definition of "administrative culture" is based on Clyde Kluckhohn's definition of "culture" as the "historically derived system of explicit and implicit designs for living, which tend to be shared by all or specifically designated members of" society. See Clyde Kluckhohn and William Kelly, "The Concept of Culture," in Ralph Linton, ed., *The Science of Man in the World Crisis* (New York: Columbia University Press, 1945), p. 97. The definition here has also been influenced by the essays of Edward B. Tylor, Alfred Louis Kroeber, and Clyde Kluckhohn which are reprinted in Lewis A. Coser and Bernard Rosenberg, eds., *Sociological Theory: A Book of Readings* (New York: Macmillan, 1964), pp. 18–21, 21–32, and 40–54, respectively.

essay, "Public Administration and Culture."[7] Although Waldo suggests several dimensions of an administrative culture, a more specific approach has been devised here in the hope of operationalizing the concept.

This study is concerned with various actors in the Filipino administrative system. However, it explores the existential beliefs, values, norms, and feelings of just one set of public administrators with regard to their administrative roles, to the roles of other participants in the Filipino administrative system, and to other aspects of that system. These orientations are then related to the perceivable behavior of the administrators in their particular administrative and political situations, as well as to the larger Filipino culture, social structure, national character, and political organization. Beyond all these, an attempt is also made to delineate what facets of the Filipino administrative culture and other factors tend to obstruct, modify, or enhance administrative development, particularly the variables of administrative capacity, administrative autonomy, and administrative participation.

Functional Integration and Social Change

For an appreciation of the evolution of contemporary Filipino administrative culture—which is an uneven blending of traditional and modern elements—Richard T. LaPiere's models of functional integration can be adapted.[8] In his terms, any social system, such as Filipino society or, within it, the Filipino administrative system, is composed of three sets of interacting social elements: ideology (roughly corresponding to "culture"), organization, and technology. These elements interact in such manner that any social system may be regarded as more or less integrated.

In a condition of "stable congruence" of the functionally interrelated elements mentioned above, the motivations, interests, attitudes, sentiments, and beliefs of all actors involved are in bal-

7. Roscoe C. Martin, ed., *Public Administration and Democracy: Essays in Honor of Paul H. Appleby* (Syracuse, N.Y.: Syracuse University Press, 1965), pp. 39–61.
8. *Social Change* (New York: McGraw-Hill, 1965), pp. 88–102.

ance. Since it is thus unlikely that this stability will be altered by internal forces, the system will persist unaltered from one generation to another. The pre-Spanish congeries of unamalgamated settlements known as *barangays*, with their population of less than half a million, their traditional culture and social organization, and their primitive technology, were probably nearest to this first model of functional integration.

In a condition of "static incongruence," incompatibilities within and among the three social components of the social system (the consequences of dysfunctional changes) emerge and persist for a relatively long time. Although here social arrangements are functionally ineffective, the members of society live with them, because not enough among them have been motivated to correct the situation and usually also because the ideological and organizational components of that society stifle individual initiative and thereby discourage significant changes. Filipino society under Spain, from the mid-sixteenth to the early nineteenth century, with a peak population of probably some six million, might be a case in point. For example, the Spaniards largely brought the Filipino communities under unified political control. They introduced a bureaucracy and legal system, a common religion, a common language, restricted education, and, gradually and unintendedly, a common nationalist cause.[9] But it took a few more generations for the appropriate combination of libertarian ideology, a Westernized Filipino intelligentsia, an organized revolutionary group, some modern weaponry, and the intervention of another foreign power, among other things, to begin the significant transformation of Filipino social and political life—perhaps a mild condition of the third of LaPiere's models: "dynamic incongruence."

Some of the elements contributing to the significant social changes under American colonial rule were: (1) a tutelage democracy—affording substantial Filipino participation in the judiciary, the bureaucracy, the legislature, the political parties, and

9. The best single work covering the entire Spanish period and after, consisting of an integrated series of primary sources, is H. de la Costa, S.J., *Readings in Philippine History* (Manila: Bookmark, 1965).

the local governments; (2) English as a second common language, public education, and transportation and communications which created widening opportunities for national integration, learning and travel, and consequently, increasing social, spatial, and psychic mobility; (3) an agricultural export industry, encouraged by its protected American market, that made possible some accumulation of capital (although this in itself discouraged diversification of the economy); and (4) expanding Filipino contact with the outside world, largely the United States, with all its implications for continuing cultural diffusion. This period of fairly rapid change had seen an upsurge in population from 7.6 million in 1903 to 16 million in 1939. There are over 30 million at present, of which 70 per cent reside in rural areas.[10]

It is only in the condition of "dynamic incongruence" that the characteristics of the social system allow the psychological tensions produced by the incongruences to be directed to eufunctional or corrective changes. Out of the malfunctioning of the social elements—the weakening of organizational, ideological, or cultural constraints—emerge the asocial, marginal, and deviant individuals; these are the potential innovators or advocates and adopters of new ideas, new modes of organization, or new techniques developed indigenously or borrowed from abroad. In contrast, in the state of "static incongruence" the prevalent tendency is to exploit the dysfunctional situation rather than to rectify it, thus perpetuating the social imbalance.

In contemporary Filipino society varying conditions corresponding to LaPiere's three ideal-type models are found to coexist. Among the "transitional" and "modern" residents in metropolitan Manila and in the bigger provincial centers a degree of "dynamic incongruence" obtains in their culture, in their interrelations, and in their technologies. With them changes are most rapid compared to the rest of their countrymen. In most of the smaller towns, despite some influences felt from the urban centers, conditions vary so slowly and imperceptibly as to reflect

10. See "The Population and Other Demographic Facts of the Philippines," prepared by the National Economic Council, Republic of the Philippines, for the Asian Population Conference in New Delhi, December, 1963, p. 3.

"static incongruence." Both the inhabitants in old communities that have lost a good number of their more venturesome members and the cultural minorities and tribes in the remotest areas lead their lives in much the same way as did their ancestors, in virtual "stable congruence." In the same general way, the scope and intensity of political and administrative action and the differentiation of corresponding political and bureaucratic structures vary widely from the center to the periphery of the country. Some of these generalizations will come into focus as we examine the selected orientations of our subject Filipino administrators and elaborate upon their implications.

A Profile of the Administrators

Social Backgrounds and Status

The respondents or informants of this study are fifty-two administrators who were then either studying for the master's degree, or participating in a training course of the Philippine Executive Academy, all within the Graduate School of Public Administration, University of the Philippines. Questionnaires were filled out by them during April and May of 1966.[11]

The respondents may be called the "middle civil servants," as

11. The questionnaire consisted of a few open-ended questions; one scale which was adapted from the Self-Anchoring Striving Scale devised by Hadley Cantril and Lloyd A. Free; many items consisting of statements of cognitions, evaluations, and expressions of feeling concerning the self-roles of the respondent-administrators, the roles of other actors in the administrative system, and various aspects of the administrative environment; multiple-choice questions evoking attitudes and opinions; and the usual questions to elicit socio-economic backgrounds.
The bulk of the data used in this chapter consists of responses to the cognitive, evaluative, and affective items. The responses have been collapsed into two categories and are reported as agreements or disagreements to individual items; actually the questionnaire allowed four responses: strongly agree, slightly agree, slightly disagree, and strongly disagree. It is important to bear in mind that a report of, say, 60 per cent of the respondents agreeing to a particular statement does not mean that all the remaining 40 per cent disagreed, although as a rule "no answers" rarely went beyond 4 per cent and never beyond 13 per cent. Neither all agreements nor all disagreements are homogeneous in nature, even allowing for variations in the intensity of the response. For example, a "strongly disagree" could mean that the item is unimportant or irrelevant in the respondent's opinion. However, the aggregate responses, collapsed into and reported as simply "agrees" or "disagrees," do indicate the tendencies in orientations and behavior which are all we need in the data for this article.

distinguished from those known as the "higher civil servants," who would comprise appointive officials from administrative officer to secretary of a major department. The differentiation and specialization of the bureaucracy is partially reflected in the diversity of the programs the respondents represent, which can only be sampled here: agricultural productivity, reforestation, telecommunications, highways, bacteriology, science promotion, civil aeronautics, revenue, central banking, civil service, social security, community development. In rank or position the respondents ranged from unit head to assistant director of a bureau. For every ten of them: eight were at the level of division head or section chief; eight were males; seven were between thirty and forty-five years old; seven had government jobs as their first full-time occupation; between four and five had begun in a professional or technical type of work; five had been in the government service from sixteen to thirty years, with three others from six to fifteen years; five were born or at least lived their first twelve years in metropolitan Manila or in the adjacent provinces of the Central Plain or the southern Tagalog region; and a total of nine were reared on the main island of Luzon, which accounts for only half of the entire population.

Despite their study or training in the University of the Philippines Graduate School of Public Administration, random observations regarding the nature of many other government administrators at comparable levels, many of whom have had previous exposure to the graduate school, suggest that collectively the informants are probably not very atypical of their category. As long as no hard generalizations are made from them to the universe of Filipino middle civil servants, the danger of bias is minimized. The greatest value in the use of their collective perceptions is to multiply and validate the author's own limited perceptions concerning Filipino administrative culture and behavior, considering that the respondents "represent" some forty agencies within the bureaucracy. In any event, insofar as the research objectives are to discover the kinds of incongruencies and conflicts in the administrative culture, behavior, and environment which might stunt or promote administrative development, and to explore the presence of potential bearers of administrative change, the selected group satisfies the needs of an exploratory study.

Comparisons among the respondent middle civil servants, the higher civil servants, and the legislators are marked.[12] The respondents are a much younger group: two-thirds are below forty-five years, as against about 20 per cent of the higher civil servants and the representatives and 13 per cent of the senators. Insofar as susceptibility to innovation is a function of younger age, this is a significant fact to bear in mind about the respondents. The preponderance of respondents originating from Manila and environs, and the overwhelming numerical advantage of those from Luzon, are consistent with the origins of two-thirds of the higher civil servants and an equal proportion of the senators. The latter are supposed to represent the nation at large by whom they are elected biennially for staggered terms of six years; but somehow the senatorial candidates from the most urban and developed areas of the country have a distinct advantage over their fellow candidates and rivals who are deliberately nominated to "represent" other regions. Finally, from existing data we find the Visayas and Mindanao better represented among the middle civil servants than among the two other leader categories.[13]

Considering that Filipinos coming from the center are apt to have a more modern socialization, and thus are more amenable to change, the environmental origin of most senators and administrators is working to the advantage of the whole country. This proposition is further supported by the great educational, occupational, financial, and travel advantages enjoyed by the respondent middle civil servants and other leader groups compared to

12. Comparative material on the higher civil servants and the legislators are from José V. Abueva, "Social Backgrounds and Recruitment of Legislators and Administrators in the Philippines," *Philippine Journal of Public Administration,* IX (Jan., 1965), 10–29. For a more comprehensive study of Filipino legislators that analyzes their changing backgrounds and the range of interests they represent, see Robert B. Stauffer, "Philippine Legislators and Their Changing Universe," *World Politics,* XXVIII, No. 3 (Aug., 1966), 556–597.

13. Behind this distribution pattern are the unprecedented spread of educational opportunities after the war and the sheer increase in numbers of positions from the higher civil servant category downward. Survey data on the geographic distribution of middle civil servants are supported by data available in the files of the Philippine Civil Service Commission.

the vast majority of the citizenry. It appears that the expanded postwar opportunities for college education have given the respondents and other middle civil servants an edge over some of their older administrative superiors and some of the representatives. As many of the younger informants as the older higher civil servants hold graduate degrees, about one-fifth. This is a higher proportion than that of the representatives, although one-third less than that of the senators who are also the most well-to-do and prestigious of all the categories being compared. It should be remembered that while the Filipinos have a higher literacy rate than most of their fellow Asians and while the Philippines ranked second only to the United States in rates of enrolment in higher education among 121 countries in 1957, still only about 6.3 per cent of Filipinos fifteen years and older had had at least a year of college education in 1960.[14]

The pattern of education and training of Filipino officialdom is interesting. An education in law is a salient characteristic of the political and administrative leaders: from 80 to 90 per cent of the legislators, 57 per cent of the higher civil servants, and 42 per cent of the respondent middle civil servants. The last category consists of the widest variety of professional and technical skills, which seems appropriate to their more direct responsibility for administering the diverse programs and operations of the bureaucracy. A reflection of the popularity of in-service training and executive development programs in the Philippine government is that close to one-third of the respondents had undergone formal training twice before the survey was conducted and about half had participated in three or more such on-the-job learning activities.[15]

14. Rates of enrolment in higher education and literacy are reported in "Basic Data for Cross-National Comparisons: Provisional Profiles," Research Monograph No. 1, Yale University Political Data Program, 1963, and cited in Carl H. Lande, "The Philippines," in James S. Coleman, ed., *Education and Political Development* (Princeton: Princeton University Press, 1965), p. 335. The figure of 6.3 per cent for persons who have had at least one year of college education was computed from data in the 1960 census, as follows: total number of persons reporting at least one year of attendance in college (927, 266) divided by total number of persons aged fifteen years and over (14,710,445).

15. See the record on training abroad as summarized below in the section on the administrators' view of government and politics. No up-to-date figures were available on government training participants since the early fifties. However,

The informants exemplify social mobility in Filipino society. More than half obtained their college degrees as working students, most of them after having joined the government service. They belong to a burgeoning group of "self-made men" who take justifiable pride in their rise from humble beginnings. A similar pattern applies to the higher civil servants.[16] To a somewhat lesser extent, legislators have also experienced upward mobility.[17] Two-thirds of the informants believed that they were now better off financially in relation to their fathers, at least one-fourth of whom had been or are of lower-class status.[18] Supportive of their claimed financial position is their family income, which places most of them within the upper less than 2 per cent of Filipino families earning P10,000 and more. Of every ten informants, seven own their homes, six own a car, and four to five have traveled to an industrialized country (three to the United States). These facts are consistent with the urban, middle-class status of the informants. As for the higher civil servants, one-third of their fathers were laborers, small farmers, or fishermen.[19] A number of representatives, in contrast with the senators, have also risen from lowly origins.

On the whole, however, it is clear that the administrators have relatively humbler social origins and lower social status at present compared with the representatives, and especially the senators, a factor which contributes to the observed vulnerability of the

some impressions may be gained from the following figures on direct and indirect training conducted by the University of the Philippines Institute of Public Administration until 1962. From April, 1953, to September, 1954, the institute trained 2,599 administrators, and 400 others attended training courses in government agencies with the assistance of institute staff. By 1961, the institute had trained 322 training officers from the national and local governments. Since the mid-fifties, when the institute began the training of trainers, most national agencies have been running their own training programs. For the institute's training record, see Ramon M. Garcia, "Training Government Personnel: IPA's Changing Role," *Philippine Journal of Public Administration,* VI (Oct., 1962), 306–310.

16. Gregorio A. Francisco, "Higher Civil Servants in the Philippines" (unpublished doctoral dissertation, University of Minnesota, 1960), pp. 205–211.

17. Abueva, "Social Backgrounds," pp. 21–22.

18. The information on the respondents' fathers suggested that 25 per cent belonged to the category described as "unskilled and semi-skilled laborers, peddlers, *sari-sari* store owners, tenant farmers, and owner-cultivators without tenants." The basis of the comparison is the father's financial status up to the time the respondent was eighteen years old.

19. Francisco, *op. cit.,* p. 168.

administrators to the legislators and other important politicians.[20] But the common attributes of a Westernized college education, Catholicism, urban upbringing, metropolitan residence, ability to communicate in both English and Tagalog, access to the mass media, among other things, should be considered, along with the differences in background and status, in comparing the political and administrative elites in the Philippines and in analyzing their interrelationships. To be sure, they have far more in common, socially and culturally, than when as a group they are compared to most other Filipinos.

We now turn to associational membership as one index of the degree of differentiation and specialization in the society and its bureaucracy. As a group, the middle civil servants studied are joiners of associations: more than half belonged to at least five associations; 60 per cent were members of employee or labor organizations; 85 per cent were members of professional organizations; and, as an indication of the persistence of ethno-linguistic ties, about a fifth belonged to provincial or regional organizations of residents in metropolitan Manila. These associational affiliations also make them different from most of their provincial cousins who rely mainly on face-to-face contacts.[21]

Not surprisingly, level of political interest and amount of political information are variables in which the respondents score much higher than would most other citizens. Behind this, certainly, are differentials in access to political events, personally or through the mass media, and in mobility, income, and education. All respondents follow political events in the newspapers. A great many watch television programs featuring public figures, take part in informal discussions about political affairs, and initiate

20. Abueva, "Social Backgrounds," p. 29.
21. For the major findings in studies of social stratification and social mobility in the Philippines, see Frank Lynch, S.J., "Trends Report of Studies in Social Stratification and Social Mobility," *East Asian Cultural Studies*, IV (Mar., 1965), 163–191. For an analysis of social inequalities and the efforts of President Magsaysay to redress them, see José V. Abueva, "Bridging the Gap Between the Elite and the People in the Philippines," *Philippine Journal of Public Administration*, VIII (Oct., 1964); a slightly revised version of this article appeared earlier in Theodore Geiger and Leo Solomon, eds., *Motivations and Methods in Development and Foreign Aid* (Washington, D.C.: Society for International Development, 1964), pp. 48–60.

conversations on politics with friends. About half attend political rallies in public places. More active forms of political involvement and the reasons for the high political interest and knowledgeability are analyzed below in connection with the administrators' perception of the politicians.

Individual Aspirations, Work Orientation, and Change

In general the levels of individual aspirations fall as the distance increases from the urban centers to the remote hinterland, and as one moves from the upper to the lower classes. Likewise, we could hypothesize that family-centered notions of success are strongest in the rural areas and among lower-class members.

Significantly, the following were ranked by the informants as the four highest measures of personal success: (1) "achieving something really significant in my chosen field of work," (2) "contributing to the welfare of my country and people," (3) "affording myself and family a comfortable home and standard of living," and (4) "giving my children a good education and leaving them some money to get started in life." Also revealing are the lowest-ranked and least-mentioned measures of personal success: (9) "helping needy relatives get an education and a start in life," and (10) "becoming rich or wealthy."

It seems that the informants are fairly individualistic in their concept of success. They tend to identify with the nation as a whole, while desiring to afford their children a level of living above the average and a more than ordinary readiness for striking off on their own upon reaching adulthood. There is a hint that most of the informants now wish to be responsible mainly for members of the nuclear family and less and less for other relatives in the extended bilateral kinship system. This evolving normative and structural pattern is a deviation from that characteristic of most Filipinos outside the big centers of population and below the educated middle class.[22]

All the respondents agreed that their individual success "de-

22. Extended familism is explained by George M. Guthrie in "Philippine National Character," unpublished mimeographed manuscript, pp. 8–18.

pends more on ability and industry than on luck" and that one "could create opportunities for himself by alertness and fore-sight." Four in five believed that people are challenged by the success of others and that those who trust mostly to luck "are lazy and lack ambition." Yet a certain ambiguity and ambivalence are evident, certainly a function of their environment and experience, when 42 per cent also agreed that their success depended "entirely on God"[23] and when 31 per cent believed that their advancement depended "most of all on having the backing of important persons," presumably politicians and other well-placed patrons. However, admission of one's total dependence on God could well be in the sense of the oft-quoted saying among Filipinos: "God helps those who help themselves."

Orientations toward change, time, and planning are important for the accomplishment of development programs and projects. Accordingly, some measures of these orientations were incorporated in the study. Two-thirds identified with the statement: "Although there may be something we can learn from the past and we must be concerned with the present, all of our efforts should be directed towards the future." About half the remaining one-third would also look to the future in the belief that "things are changing and improving." The rest were of the opinion that "the most important thing is what we do here and now." In Hahn-Been Lee's terminology, subject to further check, the first two groups could probably be labeled "developmentalist" and the last, "exploitationist."[24] None could be classified as "escapist" or yearning for "our good old days" and "the traditional ways." Likewise, 85 per cent were of the opinion that the Filipinos had "too much" of rituals and ceremonies, including inaugurations, anniversary celebrations, and perhaps expensive feasts. Most of

23. The Filipino expression of this is "Bahala na." It means literally "It's up to God," but it has become secularized to mean simply "Let's see what happens." Catholicism impresses on its believers that they should be humble; humility is often expressed by ascribing to God all good things, without denying free will and the duty to make the most of one's endowments and opportunities. Other forms of social control are discussed in Mary R. Hollnsteiner, "Social Control and Filipino Personality," *Philippine Sociological Review*, XI (July–Oct., 1963), 184–188.

24. "Developmentalist Time and Leadership in Developing Countries," *CAG Occasional Papers* (Bloomington, Ind.: Indiana University, 1965).

the respondents were aware of the high birth rate (3.2 per cent per year). And being mostly Catholics, it is remarkable that 48 per cent believed that family planning and birth control were "urgently needed," with another 35 per cent saying that such devices for curbing population growth were "moderately needed."[25]

Nuances in time orientations emerge in relation to more specific indexes. There was unanimity among the respondents that "time is probably the most precious resource because once it has passed, you cannot recover it." With few exceptions, they realized that time pressures mounted as one rose in the bureaucratic hierarchy. Four out of five disagreed that, given the "present stage of development," it was unnecessary "to use time through tight plans, schedules, and appointments." The actual behavioral pattern in the bureaucracy in regard to time may be visualized from various perceptions of the environment. In effect, 75 per cent agreed that "most government employees" do not "appreciate the value of time." Two items suggest the respondents' departure from their own ideal temporal norms: 77 per cent indicated that "time is valuable but I often cannot move fast because most people are accustomed to a slower pace"; and half agreed that "our climate does not permit us to work hard and fast."

In other words, the respondents assign a high value to time as a scarce resource, but they have a lower affect in regard to it, perhaps partly because they find their ideal difficult to realize in practice. What they had to say regarding the prevalent attitude toward time seems valid: some two-thirds agreed that "to most Filipinos one day is not very different from the next one, so they don't want to move fast" or "most Filipinos don't worry about taking their time in doing things." The foregoing analysis is in line with the common observation that in metropolitan Manila the tempo of life is fast and still accelerating, that the sense of time

25. The high positive effect on family planning and birth control indicated here should be qualified because it is in response to a direct question. The fact that only 13 per cent regarded population growth as a major national problem in reply to an open-ended question suggests that it is not as salient as the position stated above may suggest.

of government officials and employees varies considerably, and that a much slower pace marks most Filipinos, who live and work in the rural areas.

There are varied indicators of the informants' high evaluation of efficiency as a proper norm of administrative behavior. To begin with, half of them mentioned "efficiency" and a third ranked this quality, along with "economy and dependability," among the top three principles that ought to guide the government. Practically all, 90 per cent, conceded that business administration is more efficient than public administration. This means their generalized concept of efficiency is applied in the environment by a number of business corporations—as it is undoubtedly by some government offices as well. For example, close to two-thirds claimed that in their respective agencies there are objective standards for measuring efficiency. Contrasting levels of efficiency in the government, viewed against an environment of relative business efficiency, heighten the informants' awareness of the efficiency factor in administration. Thus three-fourths among them accepted these appraisals: (1) "most agencies accomplish not more than 60 per cent of what they plan to do in any fiscal year"; (2) "most government workers do not take their work seriously"; or (3) "in general, government workers just take it easy." Moreover, half agreed that "probably, at least one-third of all employees are dishonest in filling out their time-record or in punching their bundy clock."

Through our informants' eyes we also see some circumstances relating to the incongruencies between efficiency and time utilization as ideals and how they are actually internalized and translated into behavior. Again, ambivalence is manifest and qualifications concerning claims of efficient performance are called for. On the one hand 81 per cent agreed that "even without political backing, you will get recognition if you are efficient," and on the other 69 per cent agreed that "it is not enough to be efficient, you must also have political backing to get what you deserve." Related to this is the view of one-third of the respondents: "in my agency, you rarely get credit for what you do because many want to take credit for it."

More evidence of the formalistic adoption of efficiency standards is at hand. Upward of 80 per cent believed that "most of the efficiency ratings are not being used as the real basis for promotion" and that "practically no one ever gets a rating of 'unsatisfactory' because of our tendency to pity the employee and not to embarrass him." Also more than eight in ten agreed that "the legal and political difficulties of firing inefficient employees" and the "giving and taking of bribes" contribute to the inefficiency which they recognize. The sense of pity or *awa* mentioned is consistent with the respondents' nearly unanimous perception that as a people Filipinos "tend to be personal and emotional," and with the social science findings that Filipinos have a heightened sense of self-esteem (*amor propio*), go to lengths to avoid causing anybody shame (*hiya*), and in general seek to maintain smooth interpersonal relations partly through euphemism (such as avoidance of giving a rating of "unsatisfactory").[26] Considerable unemployment and consequent economic insecurity are also behind the charitable attitude toward inefficient government workers.[27]

The informants also generally agreed that agency or program success is most certainly not a matter of luck or chance, that a good plan makes it easier to obtain support, and that the more the agency has to depend on co-operation and co-ordination for the realization of its program, "the more planning you have to do." Yet an underlying sense of disappointment and even frustration with planning experience is discernible. Almost half felt "it is useless to plan when you don't have full control over the resources you need," and two in five felt that "planning just makes you unhappy because the best plans are never carried out." But still almost two-thirds believed that "most agencies know where they want to go." Undoubtedly, partly because of the strong competition for very limited funds, agencies are compelled to

26. Frank Lynch, S.J., "Social Acceptance," *Four Readings on Philippine Values*, Frank Lynch, comp. (2nd rev. ed.; Quezon City: Ateneo de Manila University Press, 1964), pp. 1–21. Also see Guthrie, *op. cit., passim*.

27. The common Tagalog expression is "Kawawa na man." (This means, in effect, "Pity him because he and his family will really be miserable in these hard times.")

plan for at least the ensuing fiscal year, and performance budgeting has had some salutary effects.

The Administrators' View of the Nation

Three interrelated dimensions of the respondents' orientations are juxtaposed in Table 1: the things or aspects about the Philippines they were most proud of, those they could not be proud of, and what they regarded as the nation's major problems. The elements of what Filipinos cannot be proud of, nationally speaking, are also considered objects of national shame.

Implicit in the citing and ranking of specific objects of national pride is a degree of comparison with certain other peoples and cultures. The accent on "scenic beauty and natural resources" recalls the lingering claim of literate Filipinos, still being inculcated by schoolteachers, that the Philippines is the "Pearl of the Orient." Alluding to the abundance of natural resources is perhaps an optimistic way out of worrisome economic problems that have the highest salience for middle civil servants whose task it is to help solve them. Coincidentally, psychologists regard "optimistic fatalism" as part of the Filipino national character.[28]

The equally top position of "democratic ideals and institutions" is evidently in relation to the political instability and the unacceptable political ideologies and regimes in the Asian vicinity. More important is the indication that a great deal of consensus on democratic ideals and basic procedures (popular sovereignty, civil liberties, elections, majority rule, etc.) exists among Filipinos, largely as a result of over six decades of practical experience in choosing leaders, bargaining with them, and resolving a few political crises.[29]

The "democratic syndrome" is further depicted in the finding that from 85 to 90 per cent of the informants affirmed the following cognitions and evaluations: "by and large, our elections have been free and honest, in spite of the reported cases of violence

28. Guthrie, *op. cit.*, p. 23.
29. For an analysis of the role of education and practical experience in the Filipino commitment to democracy, see Lande, *op. cit.*

Table 1. *Objects of National Pride, Objects of National Shame, and Major National Problems as Mentioned and Ranked by the Respondents*

Objects of national pride[a]	Objects of national shame[c]	Major national problems[d]
1. Scenic beauty & natural resources (81/62%)[b]	1. Graft and corruption in government (90/58%)	1. Economic problems (228/165%)[e]
2. Democratic ideals and institutions (81/50%)	2. Political partisanship and interference (82/52%)	2. Graft and corruption in government (66/56%)
3. Friendliness and hospitality (75/54%)	3. Lack of civic consciousness, national discipline, and nationalism (65/48%)	3. Lawlessness and criminality (59/50%)
4. Christianity and morality (61/42%)	4. Laziness and aversion to manual labor (55/40%)	4. Political partisanship and interference (34/29%)
5. Cultural and historical heritage (59/40%)	5. Lawlessness and criminality (49/35%)	5. Inadequate public services and community facilities (23/27%)
6. Close family ties (38/33%)	6. Poverty and underdeveloped economy (44/36%)	6. Lack of civic consciousness, national discipline, and nationalism (22/23%)
7. Literacy and desire for education (37/36%)	7. Poor leadership (contemporary leaders in general) (36/29%)	7. Government inefficiency and red tape (15/15%)
8. National heroes and outstanding leaders (19/15%)	8. National inferiority complex (22/19%)	8. National security (14/13%)
9. Intelligence, creativity, and receptivity to change (18/12%)	9. Inadequate public services and community facilities (15/15%)	9. Low tax payments and collection (9/8%)
		10. Rapid population growth (8/13%)
		11. Laziness, apathy, and indifference (7/12%)

a. Based on responses to the open-ended question: "I-1. Speaking generally, what are the things (or aspects) about the PHILIPPINES that you are most proud of?"

b. Inside the parentheses the first figure is the weighted score; the second is the percentage of respondents citing the response. The respondent was asked to rank the three objects of which he was most proud. His first choices were given weights of 4, 3, and 2, respectively, while the rest of his choices were each given a weight of 1.

c. Based on responses to the open-ended question: "I-2. Speaking generally, again, what are the things or aspects about the PHILIPPINES that you cannot be proud of?" The same weighting method described in note b was used.

d. Based on responses to the open-ended question: "I-8. What do you consider the most important problems facing the country today?" The same weighting method described in note b was used.

e. The percentage exceeds 100 because several responses on economic problems were combined.

and fraud," "you can depend upon the Supreme Court to uphold the rule of law or the supremacy of the Constitution," and "on the whole newspapers do more good than harm." Seven in ten agreed that "the Armed Forces have abiding faith in the supremacy of civilian rule over the military," a statement backed by the fact that the Philippines is one of the few Asian countries which have not experienced military domination or takeover since independence. Also, some two-thirds disagreed that most citizens "are too poor and ignorant to vote intelligently."

Yet the obverse of the claimed successful borrowing of Western constitutional democracy, basically American, is projected in bold relief. "Graft and corruption in government," "political partisanship and interference," and "lack of civic consciousness, national discipline, and nationalism" are cited as the top three objects of national shame. *Nakakahiya* (shameful or disgraceful) is the label that many informed Filipinos would use in regard to these among themselves. Moreover, 82 per cent of the informants joined in lamenting that "the trouble with a democracy is that we spend too much time and money arguing and too little time for the work that must be done."

Here is a large and complex incongruence of ideas, values, behavior, and social organization which we shall further analyze below. Suffice it now to point out that the high degree of personalism in social relations and the emphasis on family solidarity in Filipino society, as reflected by prideful citation of "friendliness and hospitality" and "close family ties," is suggestive of the difficulty (arising from dysfunctions and incongruences) of transplanting foreign ideas and institutions into a different cultural milieu. On the other hand, pride in a common belief in God ("Christianity and morality") among 85 per cent of the people, pride in a fairly high "literacy" (72 per cent), and pride in a flaming "desire for education" help to explain the broad political consensus already mentioned and the absence of deep cleavages in the body politic.

The nice fit between the perceived major national problems and the perceived objects of national shame broadly defines the

continuing tasks of nation-building and socio-economic development in the Philippines.[30] The problems that directly impinge on
the respondents' role performance as public administrators, in
varying degrees, seem to be the perceived irregular official behavior, political interference, deficiency of public services, inefficiency and red tape, lack of appropriate citizen conduct and
response, and fiscal inadequacy. Parenthetically, it would take a
comparison with a similar group of administrators in two or more
under-developed countries to appreciate fully the perceptiveness
and candor of the respondents in describing the problems that
make up the context and target of their daily tasks as public
administrators.

The tacit cross-cultural comparison discussed above surfaced
when the respondents were made to rank the Philippines among
nine other selected countries.[31] In "economic development" they
ranked the Philippines in fourth place: the countries ranked
above as first, second, and third, respectively, were the United
States, the Soviet Union, and Japan. Ranked below, also in de-
scending order, were Taiwan, Mainland China, Malaysia, India,
Thailand, and Indonesia. In "political development," initially defined as "the way in which these countries are governed," the
respondents elevated their country to third position. This is a
clear reflection of their pride in the nation's "democratic ideals
and institutions." Only the United States and Japan surpassed the
Philippines, with the Soviet Union, a world power the respondents surely recognize, ranked close behind the homeland. From
fifth to tenth places were Taiwan, India, Mainland China, Thai-

30. Milton J. Esman's discussion of the individual developmental goals and tasks
he subsumes in the grand categories of "nation-building" and "socio-economic
development" has great relevance to the Philippines. See his essay, "The Politics of
Development Administration," in John D. Montgomery and William J. Siffin, eds.,
Approaches to Development: Politics, Administration and Change (New York:
McGraw-Hill, 1966), pp. 59–65.

31. The technique used in this ranking of selected countries was a seventeen-
rung "ladder," with "Philippines" written on the middle rung. The respondent
was asked to rank the nine other countries above or below the Philippines according to his judgment of their relative "economic development" and their relative "political development." The composite ranking by the respondents was based
on a weighting system which multiplied the top position by ten, the second position by nine, and so on with the next lower position multiplied by the next smaller
multiplier, the bottom or tenth position being assigned one point.

land, Indonesia, and Malaysia.[32] Although obviously subjective—based on varying mixes of knowledge, ignorance, and ethnocentrism—the comparison is significant. Along with the pronounced predilection for democratic ways, the rankings help determine the foreign models the respondents would emulate in the process of modernization and development. With respect to political and administrative reforms this will become evident below in the section on orientations toward politics and government.

The Administrators' View of the Citizens

The informants' images of the citizens are consistent with the ambiguities and ambivalence noted earlier in the respondents' view of the nation and the country as whole entities. Nine in ten respondents recognized a tendency toward egalitarian expectations of citizens regardless of their gross inequalities in social status. One perceived manifestation of this is the citizens' sense of electoral potency: three of four respondents agreed that "if the citizens don't like an elective official, they can easily vote him out of office." Circumstantial support of this civic power is the high turnover of national and local elective leaders and a voting turnout of 75 to 85 per cent since independence in 1946.[33] Yet half of the respondents doubted whether the citizens are sufficiently informed to judge the government's "effectiveness and honesty," and about a third believed that most citizens "are too poor and ignorant to vote intelligently." And three in four struck the not unfamiliar note: "The trouble with the country is that most of our

32. "Economic development" was left undefined. In a subsequent question the respondent was asked to indicate what he meant by the term. The four most frequently cited meanings were: (1) national or per capita income, (2) industrialization, (3) productivity and GNP, and (4) self-sufficiency in essential needs.

In the questionnaire, "political development" was defined simply as "the way in which these countries are governed." In reply to a subsequent question, by far the most frequently cited interpretations of the definition were: (1) government stability, effectiveness, or efficiency regardless of political ideology, (2) people's participation in political, governmental decisions, and (3) democratic government.

33. The changing role of the expanding electorate is discussed in José V. Abueva, "Filipino Politics: Problems and Trends," paper presented at the Golden Anniversary Conference of the Political Science Department, University of the Philippines, June 14, 1965; the paper, in slightly modified form, was published in the Manila *Times*, Sept. 13–16, 1965.

people don't care what happens to the government and how we stand beside other nations." These perceptions give us glimpses of the gaps between the urbanized "political-administrative culture"[34] of the administrators as a group and the rural "political-administrative culture" of most citizens.

In sharp contrast to the citizens' sense of potency in regard to the politician, they seem to be relatively impotent vis-à-vis the unresponsive administrator. Thus, two in three respondents perceived most citizens to have difficulty in making "an indifferent official (who has permanent tenure) provide them with the service they need" and to "feel helpless and do nothing about it" when "officials and employees are indifferent or discourteous." One clue in explaining this paradox lies in the personalization of the interacting roles by both actors in the administrative scene: the official and the citizen. Thus two-thirds of the respondents agreed that "instead of providing service or benefits as a matter of duty, most government officials feel that they are doing these things as personal favors to citizens." Conversely, three-fourths agreed that "instead of expecting services or benefits as a matter of right, most citizens feel that they are asking a personal favor when they approach government officials for service or benefits." Another clue to the explanation is that while citizens, as individual voters, with their relatives and dependents, can directly influence the outcome of a highly competitive election, they cannot so influence the status or advancement of a government administrator unless they work through associations—in other words, unless they are organized as an interest group.[35] Note, however, the significant numbers of those respondents who took exception to the generalization about the personalization of the interrelated roles of official and citizen—one-third and one-fourth, respectively.

Put in the role of prescribing the duties and responsibilities of citizens in a democratic political system, the respondents empathized in a revealing manner. As shown in column one, Table 2,

34. "Political culture" is used in the sense of Almond and Verba, *op. cit.*, pp. 12–26. "Political-administrative culture" incorporates into the former concept the derivation of "administrative culture" from this study."
35. Abueva, "Filipino Politics: Problems and Trends."

the respondents collectively stressed the passive "subject role" (obedience to law and authority) over the active "participant role" (political participation) of the citizens.[36] Thus the three most frequently mentioned ideal attributes are "obey laws and help enforce them," "pay taxes," and "be loyal, patriotic." The first is related to the cited problem of "lawlessness and criminality"; the second brings to mind the cited problem of "low tax payments and collection" caused by rampant tax evasion, most evident among educated non-salaried professionals; the third is linked with the first in such forms as government corruption, smuggling, and buying of smuggled goods. Unconsciously, the administrators are saying that before the citizen can be really made to perform his vital "participant role" in a democracy, more has to be done to divert him from his engrossing "parochial role" (private activity in the context of primary groups) to his "subject role."[37]

When the impersonality of bureaucratic roles remains more of an ideal than a behavioral pattern internalized in the personalities of the administrators, the consequences are predictable. In a society that normally stresses kinship values, friendship based on the unending reciprocity of personal favors (*utang na loob*), and other variants of social segmentation, politics and administration inevitably assume particularistic and ascriptive ways as well. Forty per cent of the informants admitted their "difficulty in refusing relatives and friends who do not deserve to get what they want from the government." As far as administrators in general are concerned, kinship and friendship pressures are felt in various forms. Almost half of the informants felt that if they do not go out of their way to help their relatives and friends, misunderstanding is bound to result. Many more anticipated that relatives and friends "will feel . . . you are cold, proud, or ungrateful," an image that the "entangled official" would anxiously avoid.[38] Moreover, given the customary reciprocity and the extent

36. Almond and Verba defined these concepts fully in their book, *The Civic Culture*, pp. 16–26, 117–121, 176–185, 339.
37. *Ibid.*
38. The usage of "entangled" and "disentangled" administrators, in relation to their primary groups, was suggested by Frank Lynch in his essay, "The Less Entangled Civil Servant," *Philippine Journal of Public Administration*, V (July, 1961), 201–209.

of political interference, accommodation to primary group members could be conceived by administrators as an investment for the future. For example, eight to nine respondents out of ten believed that recipients of favors may be expected "to be more willing to help you to return" and that most people remember "the good things you've done for them." Furthermore, there is the felt pressure of daily example. Some 80 per cent of the respondent administrators admitted these descriptions of administrative behavior to be valid: (1) "In case of conflict between the merit system and the demands of their relatives, most officials would rather please their relatives"; (2) "The truth is that most officials

Table 2. *Duties and Obligations of Citizens, Principles and Standards for the Conduct and Administration of the Government, and Common Qualities of Good Administrators as Mentioned by the Respondents*

Duties and obligations of citizens[a]	Principles and standards for the conduct and administration of government[c]	Common qualities of good administration[e]
1. Obey laws and enforce them (42/81%)[b]	1. Honesty and integrity (113/69%)[d]	1. Honesty and integrity (31/60%)[f]
2. Pay taxes (42/81%)	2. Merit and political non-interference (83/63%)	2. Professional or technical competence (28/54%)
3. Be loyal and patriotic (33/63%)	3. Responsiveness to the people's welfare (59/42%)	3. Concerned with employees' well-being (27/52%)
4. Participate in public affairs (30/58%)	4. Sense of duty and service (58/42%)	4. Leadership (25/48%)
5. Participate in civic and community activities (21/40%)	5. Efficiency, economy, dependability (57/50%)	5. Enthusiastic, determined, energetic (25/48%)
6. Educate themselves and children (10/19%)	6. Progressive, farsighted, firm leadership (31/27%)	6. Strong moral character (22/42%)
7. Co-operate in government programs (10/19%)	7. Rule of law (27/35%)	7. Skilful in public relations (17/33%)
8. Work (11/21%)	8. Loyalty and dedication to country (25/19%)	8. Intelligence (17/33%)
9. Conserve natural resources, economize wealth (9/17%)	9. Determined and sustained action for economic development (18/15%)	9. Concerned with agency goals, decisions, results (15/29%)

would rather go around the merit system than antagonize a close friend or relative."

This analysis of personalism leads to more insights into the unequal or discriminatory treatment of citizens by government officials and the modes of citizen access to decision-making under the circumstances. The general assumption is that "who the person is makes a big difference in most government offices." Consequently, the normal impulse is "to ask the help of someone you know in a government office." This requires a personal follow-up which interferes with intended routines. By some kind of mutual understanding, most citizens do not observe "first come, first served" in dealing with the government, and most government

---

10. Protect public property (5/10%)

11. Patronize Filipino products (3/6%)

10. Employee welfare and morale (9/10%)

10. Imaginative, resourceful, far-sighted (13/25%)

11. Assumes responsibilities or takes risks (11/21%)

12. Flexible, receptive to ideas, progressive (11/21%)

13. Good physical attributes (10/19%)

14. Loyal to the service or organization (7/13%)

15. Consults or shares authority with others (6/12%)

---

a. The actual question was: "I-7. What do you think are the duties and obligations that every citizen owes to the country?"

b. The first figure in the parentheses is the number of respondents citing the duty and obligation mentioned; the percentage refers to the proportion of that number to the total number of respondents, which is 52.

c. Based on responses to the open-ended question: "I-3. In your opinion what five or six principles or standards should guide the conduct and administration of our government?"

d. The first figure in the parentheses is the weighted score of the principle or standard mentioned; the percentage refers to the proportion of the respondents who mentioned that principle or standard to the total number of respondents. To compute the weighted scores, the respondent was asked to rank the three principles or standards he considered the most important. His first three choices were given weights of 4, 3, and 2, while the rest of his choices were each given a weight of 1.

e. Based on unranked multiple responses to the open-ended question: "I-4. In your judgment, what particular qualities or characteristics do good executives or administrators have in common?"

f. The first figure in the parentheses is the number of respondents who mentioned the particular qualities or characteristics; the percentage refers to those respondents in relation to the total number of respondents.

workers disregard this impersonal rule. In any event, the respondents are virtually unanimous regarding the personal follow-up of pending papers as effective in obtaining favorable and faster action.

But of course not all citizens can know somebody in every office—the larger Filipino society becomes, the fewer relatives and friends most citizens will have in the proliferating agencies of the bureaucracy—so personal intervention has its limitations. In offices where government workers feel they can ignore ordinary citizens and strangers with impunity, it becomes necessary at times to have big "influence peddlers" and petty "fixers." The intercession of such third parties in administrative decision-making also happens to be natural in a social setting where intermediaries or go-betweens are daily being used to maintain smooth interpersonal relations.[39]

The Administrators' Views of Government and Politics

It is no surprise that the informants share the rather widespread expectation of a large, positive scope and role for the government. In a pampered free-enterprise economy where socialism is almost synonymous with communism, and therefore a pejorative word, traditional paternalism and American New Deal influences on Filipino leadership and the Constitution have nevertheless favored the welfare state—in the abstract. The actual willingness to pay the cost of "big government" is rather low, as measured by taxation and the ratio of public expenditures to the national income.[40] It is for these reasons that most respondents felt that the present size and scope of the government are either

39. *Ibid.*, pp. 202–206; also see Lynch, "Social Acceptance," pp. 12–15.

40. To the extent that total appropriations represent aggregate pressures for desired magnitudes of government operations, the government was willing to pay for only 35 to 46 per cent of what it desired during the five years ending on June 30, 1965. See Table 1 in José D. Soberano, "Philippine Fiscal Planning—Quo Vadis?" *Philippine Journal of Public Administration*, X (Jan., 1966), 8. Public expenditures as a percentage of the GNP (average of 12.61 per cent in the decade of the fifties) was lower than in several countries in a similar state of underdevelopment; see Amelia B. Abello, *Patterns of Philippine Public Expenditures and Revenue, 1951–1960* (Quezon City: University of the Philippines, Institute of Economic Development and Research, 1964).

"about right" (40 per cent) or "too large" (38 per cent), and yet they would also like to see a greater governmental role than at present in planning, promoting, and regulating the national economy.

Cogency marks the orientations of the informants in regard to venality in office and political intrusion into the administrative domain. The middle and right columns of Tables 1 and 2 show this. "Honesty and integrity" are deemed the proper governmental norms for counteracting "graft and corruption." "Merit and political non-interference" are likewise prescribed as antidotes to "political partisanship and interference." Accordingly, the two highest qualities idealized for good administrators are "honesty and integrity" and "professional or technical competence." To some extent these perceptions must be their idealized self-image as role-players in their administrative world.

Beyond merit and expertise, the respondents singled out the democratic ideals of bureaucratic "responsiveness to the people's welfare," "sense of duty and service," and the "rule of law" as guiding principles that seemed most in need of elevating, given the administrative context. Administrative "efficiency, economy, or dependability" were mentioned by half of the respondents as a performance standard. An equal number pointed out that administrators ought to be concerned with the employees' "well-being," in the same measure perhaps that the government should be responsive to the people. The usual vagueness surrounding notions about what makes "a good administrator" is apparent in the citing of "leadership" and "intelligence" as characteristic qualities.

All told it is true that secondary emphasis was given to what might be called entrepreneurial or development-oriented qualities of administrative leadership. Thus while upward of 52 per cent mentioned "rectitude, competence, and employee-centeredness," 48 per cent mentioned "enthusiastic, determined, energetic," 33 per cent mentioned "skilful in public relations," 29 per cent mentioned "concerned with agency goals, decisions, results," 25 per cent mentioned "imaginative, resourceful, far-sighted," and 21 per cent mentioned "assumes responsibilities or takes

risks" (see Table 2). It would seem that these middle civil servants are constrained by the low standards of public morality and
a weak merit system while being engaged in development administration. Yet we cannot minimize their significant awareness of
action-mindedness and goal-accomplishment which Edward W.
Weidner considers to be crucial characteristics of development
administration, defined by him as "the process of guiding an
organization toward the achievement of development objectives."[41]

Insofar as explicit models guide efforts at political and administrative reform, it is interesting to note the ready availability of
both foreign and local examples. In thinking about improving the
government in general, the following countries were cited as
models by varying percentages of the respondents: the United
States (50 per cent), the United Kingdom (40 per cent), Ger-
many and/or France (19 per cent), Taiwan (8 per cent), and the
Scandinavian countries (6 per cent). When they think of improving their own agencies, their preferences were distributed as
follows: Philippine government agencies (29 per cent), non-governmental organizations in the Philippines (23 per cent), international or world agencies (6 per cent), and United States government agencies (4 per cent). Resort to foreign models is clear
evidence of the impact of bilateral or multilateral foreign aid and
technical assistance,[42] as well as the fact that nearly half the
respondents had traveled abroad. By 1965 more than three thousand Filipino administrators had participated in training activities in the United States, many other administrators were among
the more than a thousand who had enjoyed Colombo Plan fellowships, and over a hundred officials had trained abroad under
United Nations auspices. The record up to 1965 was tersely
summarized by David Wurfel: "Since 1951 the Philippines has

41. *Technical Assistance in Public Administration Overseas: The Case for
Development Administration* (Chicago: Public Administration Service, 1964), p.
200.
42. The fluctuating impact of United States foreign aid is assessed by David
Wurfel in his paper, "Problems of Decolonization," prepared for the American
Assembly on Philippine-American Relations, February, 1966. Also see his "Foreign
Aid and Social Reform in Political Development: A Philippine Case-Study,"
American Political Science Review, LIII (June, 1959), 456–482.

received more than 2,000 man-years of technical advice from all donor agencies and 5,000 man-years of training for Filipino technicians abroad."[43]

Equally significant for the prospect of administrative development is the perceived availability of indigenous models, undoubtedly a sign of Filipino administrative change for the better. The perception of business organizations as being in general more efficient than government administration, coupled by increasing mobility of outstanding public administrators and military men into private business and industry, is in itself a big organizational and managerial incongruence in the respondents' administrative culture which could motivate further administrative development and development administration.

The Administrators' Views of the Politicians

In order to focus on the more specific orientations regarding the relations between the respondent middle civil servants and the politicians with whom they interact, it would be useful to employ an analytic scheme portraying types of bureaucratic roles under varying equilibria of political and bureaucratic power. For heuristic purposes, Riggs's distinction between a "bureaucrat" and an "administrator" is relevant. The former is a structural definition stressing one's membership in a bureaucracy; the latter is a functional definition stressing one's primary function of carrying out policies determined by politicians.[44]

Where the politician is superordinate (political superordination), the bureaucrat is held accountable or subordinated to the politician. If theory and tradition have made the two roles specific and complementary in practice, the bureaucrat is a *partner* of the politician: his role is to implement policy and *assist* the politician in shaping that policy. If belief and circumstance make the politician regard the bureaucrat as an expendable adjunct

43. "Problems of Decolonization," p. 21. The most comprehensive study on the subject is *A Survey of Foreign Economic and Technical Assistance Programs in the Philippines*, by the United States Agency for International Development Mission to the Philippines (Manila: October, 1964).
44. Riggs, *op. cit.*

whose position and advancement are entirely subject to the politician's control, the bureaucrat is a *dependent*: his role is to serve and please his politician patron.

Where the relationship between the politician and bureaucrat is in favor of the latter (political subordination), the politician has become the dependent and the bureaucrat assumes the role of *patron*. This happens because politicians and bureaucrats vary in their status and power in the governmental hierarchy and in their other political resources.[45] Thus, for example, a neophyte politician may actually be more dependent on the authority and discretion of a bureaucrat than the latter is on the former's power and influence. Because ideologically the politician is supposed to

Table 3. *Bureaucratic Roles in Relation to Politicians*

| | | Bureaucratic roles | |
		Differentiated	Undifferentiated
Political-bureaucratic relationship	Political superordination (bureaucratic responsibility)	Partner	Dependent
	Political subordination (bureaucratic irresponsibility)	Patron	Antagonist

be superior, but in fact he may be subordinate, he may assert his ideological supremacy. At the same time, however, the bureaucrat resents what he regards as encroachments on his perceived domain by the politician. The conflicting relationship impels the bureaucrat to become an *antagonist* to the politician: overtly or covertly, the bureaucrat deliberately seeks to enhance his authority and discretion and undermine the politician's power. These ideal-type bureaucratic roles are presented graphically in Table 3.[46]

45. The concept of "political resources" is defined by Robert A. Dahl in *Modern Political Analysis* (Englewood Cliffs, N.J.: Prentice-Hall, 1965), pp. 15–16. The sources and uses of power in the Philippines are analyzed in Jean Grossholtz, *Politics in the Philippines* (Boston: Little, Brown, 1964), pp. 162–164.

46. The roles of interacting bureaucrats and politicians are clearly reciprocal. Thus, in our scheme when the bureaucrat is a "partner," the politician is also a "partner," a senior partner if you will. When the bureaucrat is a "dependent," the politician is the "patron." When the bureaucrat is the "patron," the politician is a "dependent." And when the bureaucrat is an "antagonist," so is the politician.

In "real life" situations the bureaucratic roles and attitudes vis-à-vis the politician are often mixed types involving variations in emphasis in the course of time—such as "partner-dependent," "dependent-partner," "patron-dependent," "dependent-patron," "dependent-antagonist," etc. The incidence of the various combinations depends on a number of factors. One major factor is the degree of differentiation of functions between the politician and the bureaucrat which the culture, the political structure, and the personalities will permit. (Here we resume our common usage of the term "administrator" as meaning a bureaucrat who performs more or less administrative and political functions.)

The ideal bureaucratic roles are of course exemplified in the Constitution and the Civil Service Law and their implementing rules. The respondents probably had this in mind when three-fourths among them gave their assent to the statement, "It always pays to be politically neutral or non-partisan in doing your work as an administrator," and when even more identified themselves as non-members of parties and as voting "for candidates regardless of party considerations." All politicians have publicly held to the ideal norms and even to the idea of "partyless voting" because of the nature of the party system.[47]

What role combinations do the Filipino administrative culture and the structure of political-bureaucratic relationships permit? The informants provide us some answers, but we have to infer still others. Seven in ten agreed that "most politicians get what they want even if it is against existing policies and rules." Two more believed that "if you don't play ball with politicians, they will give you a rough time." "In my experience," three-fourths of the informants agreed, "legislators influence the actual implementation of the law, and not just its enactment." As if to compensate for all these, however, the informants had also experienced that "administrators not only influence how the law is executed but also actually help make the law." They voiced greater agreement on the important generalization that "administrators have . . .

47. The most valuable analysis of the Filipino party system is Carl H. Lande, *Leaders, Factions, and Parties: The Structure of Philippine Politics* (New Haven: Yale University Southeast Asia Studies Monograph Series, 1965), pp. 69–75.

discretion in implementing the laws and rules governing their agencies." Certainly, some case studies document the varying discretion and resources which administrators could employ in dealing with politicians.[48]

Nevertheless, the loud refrain about political partisanship and interference in administration mentioned earlier sums up, as it were, the undifferentiated, diffuse, and dominant character of the politician's role in general. Indeed, anyone familiar with the Filipino president or the average Filipino legislator or governor knows how he is constantly driven beyond his idealized role, in a legal-rational sense, to embrace a compromised role as defined by his constituents and more or less accepted by him. This latter role is normally a composite of expectations that he behave variously as official, patron, sponsor, employment agent, moneylender, charity dispenser, financier, educational foundation, father-surrogate, transporter, and food provider. The fusion or "agglomeration"[49] of multiple roles in one complex official role—of president, legislator, or governor—is a function of the combined power, wealth, popularity, and prestige in the person of the politician which most citizens perceive. Consequently, few politicians would disagree, as did two-thirds of the respondents, that "it is a politician's duty to get what he can for those who support him."

Again, all these points add up to the supremacy of the politicians, especially the president and the legislators. It would therefore be the exceptional middle civil servant, of great personal prestige and political potential, who could act as a "patron-dependent" in relation to the legislator. This exceptional role is reserved for powerful politicians turned administrators—as exemplified by a few members of the president's cabinet. Most administrators would be at best a "partner-dependent." More likely, they would be a "dependent-partner," a "dependent-patron," or a

48. Among the available case studies perhaps the most striking is the one entitled "The Fifty-Fifty Agreement," which tells the story of legislative-executive bargaining over patronage; the case, written by Gregorio A. Francisco and Raul P. de Guzman, is in Raul P. de Guzman, ed., *Patterns in Decision-making: Cases in Philippine Public Administration in the Philippines* (Manila: Institute of Public Administration, University of the Philippines, 1963), pp. 91–120.

49. See the pertinent discussion in Fred W. Riggs, *Administration in Developing Countries: The Theory of Prismatic Society* (Boston: Houghton Mifflin, 1964), pp. 124–132. On these pages Riggs analyzes the interaction of power, wealth and education in the prismatic society.

"dependent-antagonist." Only if courageous and secure enough in their own right would they be an outright "antagonist." Now and then news stories feature a heroic administrator standing up to and exposing an erring politician, to the applause of urban public opinion, editors, and columnists.

The extent to which the respondents assume the role of "partner-dependent" or "dependent-partner" is suggested by two ways of looking at a set of five role indicators or tasks. One is to note that from 35 per cent to 50 per cent of the respondents (1) helped prepare bills to be introduced in Congress, (2) contacted legislators for support of pending agency legislation, and (3) asked the help of two or more legislators with whom they are personally close; that (4) 25 per cent had been asked by their chief to seek political support for him or for their agency; and that (5) only 8 per cent had been specifically asked by legislators for help in preparing bills. Another way is to consider that one-fifth of the respondents had performed three or more of the five tasks and may be therefore called "bureaucratic politicians," as distinguished from those who performed less than three of the tasks, who may be called "functionaries." (If those who performed two of the tasks are to be regarded as "bureaucratic politicians," those in this category would be doubled in number.)

What makes the dependency relationship to the legislator desirable, or at least tolerable, is not only the common ideal of bureaucratic responsibility but also the transparent symbiosis and reciprocity involved. "By giving in to a politician," two-thirds of the informants agreed, "you make him more helpful in obtaining funds, passing your bill, or getting you a promotion." About the same proportion also agreed that "if we cannot get enough funds from the Budget Commission, some friends of my agency in Congress usually help us out." In fact, almost a third asserted that "with the strong backing of members in Congress, we can get funds for my agency even if the Budget Commission or the President is not enthusiastic about our program." Recall the assent of as many informants that their personal success depended "most of all on having the backing of important persons" and of 69 per cent that political backing was needed on top of efficiency to get what one deserved. Along with the personalistic and fragmented party system, this beneficial alliance between individual administrators and legislators contributes to the paradoxical inability of the president, despite his ample constitutional authority as chief executive, to direct, co-ordinate, and control the numerous agencies of the bureaucracy effectively.

The frustration and exasperation of some or most respondent middle civil servants is again manifested in specific terms. As against the 53 per cent who felt the politicians they knew were "usually reasonable in their demands," 44 per cent felt otherwise. "The more I deal with our legislators," confessed two-thirds of the respondents, "the less respect I have for them." Even among those who acknowledged the support and assistance of the legislators, apparently the resentment ran deep, to the point of their becoming extremely ambivalent in their attitudes toward democratic values. Thus did eight in ten agree to the bureaucratic utopia and irresponsibility implied in this remark: "In the long run, public administration will be more effective if politicians will leave administrators alone to decide what programs to carry out and how to carry them out."

The latent paternalistic-authoritarian disposition that leads to submission and dependency on the one hand expresses itself in tendencies toward dominance and aggressiveness on the other. While three in four informants believed "a few strong leaders could make this country better than all the laws and talk," half would go so far as to assert, "what we probably need is a dictator, at least for some years." Relevant here is a personality study reporting that male Filipino college students scored higher than their American counterparts on need for dominance and need for aggression, as well as on need for abasement and need for deference. The latter could be a source of profound personality conflict. However, the same Filipinos were lower on need for autonomy and need for exhibitionist expression.[50] To the degree that

50. Jaime Bulatao, S.J., "Personal Preferences of Filipino Students," *Philippine Sociological Review*, XI (July–Oct., 1963), 168–184. That suppression of one's identity may be a source of personality conflict is discussed by Lee Sechrest in his mimeographed paper, "Philippine Culture, Stress, and Psychopathology," presented at the Asia-Pacific Conference on Mental Health, March 28–April 1, 1966, East-West Center, Honolulu, Hawaii.

the model personality of a nation is conditioned by culture and social structure, we may hypothesize that the typical Filipino administrator—and the typical Filipino politician—would exhibit need patterns similar to those of the students studied. There appears to be empirical basis for this hypothesis.

A brief digression into the social structure would be helpful. Most Filipinos still find their identity, status, and social security within the extended bilateral family. Their social relations are usually patterned by segmentation. In-groups and out-groups are organized along such boundaries as kinship, social position, generation, language, locality, and power—although we must again hasten to add that social stratification is far from being rigid, since considerable social mobility occurs.[51] The basic relationship —even in such nationwide organizations as the Nacionalista party and the Liberal party—is dyadic, oftentimes between one person of superior status and another one of lower status. It is commonplace to observe the prevalence of nepotism, regionalism, factionalism, and clique-formation in Filipino politics and government.

Caught up in such a social web, the mobile and ambitious administrator would wish to extricate himself from a subordinate position and move on to a superordinate one, hopefully with the help of a congenial patron or protector, who not infrequently would be a politician. Since the national politician is a prominent and dominant figure—an opulent and dominating father-surrogate in the administrator's world and beyond—for the administrator to become himself a politician is a ubiquitous allurement which is lessened only by its costs and risks. Short of running for public office, something akin to the American pragmatism, "if you can't lick 'em, join 'em," seems to operate. The "bureaucratic politician" or "dependent-patron" or "dependent-partner" are perhaps cases in point.

More apropos is the involvement of one-third of the respondent middle civil servants in questionable political partisanship which they themselves, in their idealistic moments, so roundly criticize.

51. Segmentation and ranking are discussed by Frank Lynch in his cited essay, "Social Acceptance."

Their irregular bureaucratic conduct consists of the following: attending a political caucus or strategy meeting; helping a political candidate in his public relations; giving time to a candidate's campaign; having frequent contacts with politicians; distributing campaign handbills to friends, neighbors, and fellow workers. Indeed, some of these activities are plainly illegal. Also germane, albeit hardly questionable, is supplying ideas for the speeches of political leaders, as one in four of the middle civil servants reported doing.

The impact on the administrators of the high degree of politicization of the administrative culture is best illustrated by their developing political proclivities. Twenty-seven per cent of the middle civil servants affirmed, "I will be a candidate for public office if circumstances are favorable!" Rather consistently, more than one-third intimated that their "associates and friends consider them persons with strong political connections" and that they are regarded by their "relatives and folks back home . . . as potential politicians." In fact one in five had been encouraged by political leaders "to become a candidate for public office." How gratifying it must be to these political dependents to become political patrons, as have some senators and even more representatives within view.[52] So much so, barely a majority of the respondents would foreclose their potential political future by agreeing to the projection: "As far as I can see, I really think I won't be a candidate for public office."

The Administrators' Views of Superiors, Equals, and Subordinates

The previous generalizations on segmentation and dyadic ties in the society at large find concrete application within individual agencies. The administrative culture takes note of this. Cliques and factions are recognized by the respondents as normal features of organizational life. Some 40 per cent felt they had to belong to the right clique or faction in order "to get ahead." Half believed that by being outside the ruling group they would not know "what's going on in the organization" because "some per-

52. Abueva, "Social Backgrounds," pp. 23–24.

sons withhold information from their associates . . . to gain power and control." Half also conceded: "Whether you like it or not, in order to advance, it is more important to get along with your group (*pakiksama*) than to have ability or a sense of duty." The tendency toward conformity with their "in-group" among about half of the informants is paralleled by their inclination to be deferential and personally loyal to their superiors. In the first place, the familial model is highly salient even for our group of urbanized, middle-class civil servants, 84 per cent of whom agreed that "supervisors should act like a good father because an organization is just like a big family."[53] Consistent with this paternal image, most superiors were seen by three-fourths of the respondents as persons who "expect a lot of personal respect and loyalty from their subordinates."

This style of interpersonal relations may be illustrated by certain observations on status symbols and appropriate behavioral responses within the bureaucracy, which are a reflection of the degree of status consciousness and the desire for group solidarity among Filipinos. Normally, Tagalog-speaking subordinates punctuate their oral communication with superiors with the expression *ho,* a variant of the deferential *po* reserved for parents and elder relatives. As with their elder kin, most subordinates greet their superiors with a slight head bow. Subordinates usually contribute to a gift and/or join the *asalto* (a group courtesy call complete with brought-over food and perhaps some entertainment) during the birthday or special anniversary of the big boss. Many field men entertain their traveling superiors rather generously and give token presents of local specialties when visiting their bosses in the central office. It is not uncommon for an official or employee, except the lowliest, to invite several of his fellow workers to a party at home or in a restaurant during his birthday or to celebrate a promotion. An occasion for a similar solidarity get-together is the annual fiesta in the hometown of an associate or fellow worker in the agency.

53. The idea of the "family" is undergoing change, and along with it the role of the "father." The family as a model for other social relationships is treated at length by George Guthrie in "Philippine National Character," pp. 10–18.

The emphasis on solidarity of the segment (or "informal organization") and on personal loyalty and deference are by no means shared by all respondents in the same degree, or in a simply passive and subservient manner. In an important sense, the orientations are conscious adjustments to the perceived administrative situation, and these orientations vary from supine resignation to calculated manipulation. A good deal of resignation and subservience is probably expressed by 42 per cent of the respondents who concluded that "if you just follow the leader, you'll be a happier man in the government." Anxiety and insecurity are patently evident among the 37 per cent who felt "life in the government is so rough, you can never be sure who your friends are."

But the manipulative aspects of the respondents' accommodation to their superiors emerge when other perceptions are considered. For instance, when half disagreed that "most of my superiors and associates will put merit above personal relationship in filling up positions," it made sense for them at least to simulate agreement with and obeisance toward their bosses. The desire for effective communication upward in the hierarchy seemed to have impelled the respondents to show respect, acquiescence, and loyalty because in their estimate their superiors would then "be more receptive to . . . ideas and criticism" than otherwise. Furthermore, two-thirds sensed that, in general, if they did anything without the knowledge and participation of their chief, he was likely to be resentful. After all, in a society where open suggestions and criticism, however honest and well-meaning, are liable to be misunderstood because most persons would prefer euphemistic indirection in communication, the respondents did admit, "Most superiors I know welcome suggestions and criticisms if these are offered constructively and diplomatically."

Analytically, only one in four respondents confused loyalty to the organization with loyalty to its head; half did not believe in belonging to the right clique as a prerequisite to advancement in the organization; 44 per cent believed most of their superiors and associates would prefer merit to personal equation in making appointments; 56 per cent disagreed that simply following the leader is the path to happiness in governmental life; about one-third believed competition for higher positions in their agencies "is so keen that most rivals will break any law or rule to advance"; half disagreed that in order to get promoted conformity to the group is more important than ability and a sense of duty; and an equal proportion thought their active participation in staff meetings would be regarded positively by their fellow workers. Moreover, as any perceptive observer of Filipino behavior would know, verbal agreements and commitments are frequently modified if not disregarded in practice, and most persons involved would understand why.

Insofar as the example of their superiors conditioned the respondents' willingness in turn to delegate their authority to subordinates, it is illuminating to know that although three-fourths regarded most administrators they knew as being "very jealous of their prerogatives," half agreed that most of these administrators were in fact "willing to delegate authority to their subordinates." Likewise, insofar as their perceptions of subordinates in general, including themselves, influenced the respondents' willingness to delegate authority, those perceptions are significant. Ninety per cent agreed that "the more friendly and trusting you are toward your subordinates, the more likely they are to act responsibly." Conversely, however, slightly fewer (65 per cent) disagreed that "the more friendly and trusting you are, the more likely subordinates would abuse or take advantage of their superior's positive bent." As an alternative measure, a mere 14 per cent agreed that "when you delegate authority to your subordinates, most of the time things go wrong."

Despite all these orientations favorable to the delegation of authority, however, it is important to know that about two-thirds would in practice want to delegate authority "only to subordinates who measure up to [their] standards." Given the respondents' low evaluation of the seriousness and efficiency of government workers as a whole, actual delegation of authority might be less than the verbalized orientations would suggest. Their own criticism of government inefficiency and red tape, as mentioned above, is pertinent. In addition, the respondents divided fifty-fifty over this generalization: "Most administrators tend to be excessively concerned with legal procedures as if every problem were a case in court." Even the lawyers among the respondents (who comprised 42 per cent) subjectively agreed that "lawyer-administrators" are especially guilty of such a legalistic approach to administration, because 81 per cent of the respondents so declared.

Administrative Culture and Administrative Development

Conclusions are presented in two parts. First, a summary about the respondents as a category is given and some observations are made on their potential for contributing to administrative development. This is followed by several generalizations, largely based on their orientations, which form a part of the Filipino administrative culture. At the same time these generalizations are offered as hypotheses regarding the conditions of administrative development in transitional societies similar to the Philippines.

The Administrators and Administrative Development

Taken together the respondents are middle-level administrators who are mostly male and under forty-five years old, college educated and administratively trained, interested in the acquisition of advanced administrative know-how and joiners of associations. They have been continually exposed to modernity through education and training, urban upbringing, metropolitan residence, ability to read, speak, and write English, domestic and foreign travel, and intercourse with their professional peers. From lower origins most of them have ascended to their present middle-class status in the metropolis by working their way through college and via government employment. Apparently, most of them are ambitious, pragmatic in their approach to their job and relationships, far-sighted in their outlook, and rather critical of existing conditions and customary practices.

As a category, their concept of personal success is progressively individualistic, occupationally oriented, and manipulative. Like many other middle-class members, it seems that their kinship commitments are being more and more limited to their immediate family. They probably have more than the usual appreciation of the need for work efficiency, for rational utilization of time, for goal orientation and action-mindedness, for delegation of authority, and for reforms in general. Being the beneficiaries of social change and being younger than their political and administrative superiors, a number of them are likely to be actual borrowers, advocates, and adopters of innovations, although only a few might be innovators themselves.[54] Their susceptibility to new ideas and roles is a function of their exposure to modernity and of their ambition to improve their marginal status (between the dominant upper class and the lowly lower class).

As a whole the respondents exhibit considerable deviant orientations from most other administrators and citizens with whom they subjectively compared themselves. Thus, if we accept that most officials are still deeply "entangled" with their relatives and friends, we may find exceptions among some of the respondents. Who among them are "disentangled" administrators? They are to be found among the 56 per cent who do not find it difficult to turn down undeserving relatives and friends; among the 38 per cent who feel that their relatives and friends, who must have changed their own orientations, would be just as close to them personally without receiving favors or despite being refused; among the 33 per cent who seem indifferent to relatives and friends who measure personal ties by mutual willingness to accommodate requests; among those who, like more and more city residents, do not care about being called by their elders and provincial cousins bad relatives, *hindi na nakakakilala* (he no longer cares for us), *walang utang na loob* (ungrateful), *nagiba na* (he has changed), *walang delicadeza* (no subtlety), or even that most opprobrious label, *walang hiya* (shameless).

54. The respective roles of the innovator, the advocate, and the adopter are the subjects of chaps. iv, v, and vi, respectively, of Richard T. LaPiere, *op. cit.*, pp. 103–211. With respect to innovation in the administrative setting, see Edward W. Weidner, "Development and Innovational Roles," chap. xiii below.

Almost in the same breath as the respondents agreed to many of the dysfunctions and deficiencies afflicting Filipino public administration in general, they wished to draw the line. Presumably with their own agencies and themselves in mind, 46 per cent asserted that administrative decisions are nonetheless made objectively and without regard to the persons involved, one-third denied that most government officials feel they are dispensing personal favors to citizens, one-fourth disagreed that most citizens are unmindful of their rights to the services and benefits they seek from the government, and one-third disagreed that government employees can get away with their indifference or discourtesy toward ordinary citizens. Their rationalizations aside, it does seem that, like many other educated Filipinos, the respondents are highly critical of the government. In fact their acute awareness of the many departures from the ideal bureaucratic rules and styles, which is shared by the articulate press, might very well bolster their will and skill to help rectify the situation.

Perhaps the most significant single quality of the respondent middle civil servants that their total responses reveal is their empathy and ability to identify with the nation and the government, in their past, present, and future aspirations and behavior and in relation to other nations and governments. Daniel Lerner has defined empathy as "the inner mechanism which enables newly mobile persons to operate efficiently in a changing world . . . the capacity to see oneself in the other fellow's situation . . . an expansive and adaptive self-system, ready to incorporate new roles and to identify personal values with public issues."[55] Indeed, most of the respondents personify a high mobility—social, psychic, and spatial. To the extent that "transitionals" and "moderns," like many of the respondents, exist elsewhere in and outside the bureaucracy, administrative development will be enhanced. Not surprisingly, the variables we have associated with administrative development are more evident in the large concentration of government agencies in metropolitan Manila than

55. *The Passing of Traditional Society: Modernizing the Middle East* (New York: Free Press, 1958), p. 51.

elsewhere in the country, for in the metropolis social change is most rapid.

Conditions of Administrative Development and the Filipino Administrative Culture

The Filipino administrative culture that emerged from an analysis of the respondents' orientations is a fascinating and somewhat paradoxical admixture of elements thrown together in complex and shifting interrelationships. There are pronounced incongruencies and wide variability in the orientations toward the respondents' self-roles, the roles of their fellow actors in the administrative system, and other aspects of the administrative system and its ecology.

In the nature of propositions or hypotheses, some generalizations relative to part of the Filipino administrative culture are possible. These same propositions, *mutatis mutandis,* have a descriptive, analytical, and explanatory utility for the comparative study of many transitional societies and their efforts to bring about administrative development.

1. The identifications of government workers and citizens vary from an almost exclusive parochialism to a widening set that includes identifications with the government and the nation in an international context—with a preponderance of parochialism (primary group orientation).

2. Concepts of personal success of government workers vary from professionalism and individualism to the idea that success is undeserved, being a stroke of good fortune, and must be shared by the extended family. The latter idea is still prevalent.

3. Concepts of individual success of government workers vary from an accent on achievement and the manipulativeness of success to fatalistic dependence on external forces, notably politicians or the supernatural. The prevalent accent is on fatalistic dependence, which tends, however, to be optimistic rather than pessimistic fatalism.

4. Change-time orientations of government workers vary from preoccupation with the present to increasing concern with the

future of the individual, the agency, or the country; from full utilization of fixed time to temporal prodigality. Traditional change-time orientations prevail in most agencies.

5. Merit and efficiency consciousness tend to be relegated to secondary importance in the priority of concerns of middle and higher officials, because of distractions caused by "graft and corruption" and "political partisanship and interference."

6. Merit and efficiency norms and measures tend to be formalistic because of such incongruent values and conditions as familism, personalized reciprocity, *hiya* (shame) and *awa* (pity), scarcity of job opportunities in a situation of high unemployment, and widespread economic hardships. Program goals and results tend to be displaced by legal and procedural technicalities as apparent ends in themselves. Yet the latter may be arbitrarily disregarded if and when the administrator so wills it.

7. Workloads fluctuate sharply as between the overburdened, capable, and/or serious government workers and the many who are reluctant to make decisions or who consider their work as sinecures or otherwise take it lightly and unprofessionally, and as between the higher-level administrators and staff specialists on the one hand and the lower-echelon workers on the other.

8. Among middle and higher officials there is an underlying sense of futility toward the otherwise positively valued concept of planning. A chasm exists between glaring failure in comprehensive planning and reasonable success in agency planning and programs.[56] Agency and government-wide planning in the budgetary sense is considered essential for obtaining political support.

9. There is popular consensus about the desirability of democratic ideals, institutions, and procedures in the familiar sense of government as an instrument for the people's welfare, civil rights, election of leaders, and access to government services. However,

56. While there is consensus among economic planners and scholars that comprehensive socio-economic planning schemes in the Philippines have failed, there appears to be much less feeling that, consequently, the individual agencies have failed. As the volumes of physical production, the growth of the manufacturing sector, the Filipinization of the economy, and the emergence of several Filipino entrepreneurs would indirectly show, public policy and public administration have in fact been crucial factors fostering national economic development. See Frank H. Golay, "Obstacles to Philippine Economic Planning," *Philippine Economic Journal*, IV (2nd semester, 1965), 284–309.

these are reinterpreted largely in personal and particularistic terms when most citizens deal with officials. The more informed officials and citizens take pride in the democratic consensus in relation to what they regard as less politically fortunate nations around them.

10. Political leaders are legitimized through elections, but considerable skepticism and cynicism about their motives and conduct are in evidence. Many informed officials and citizens react to the malfunctioning of Filipino democracy with considerable ambivalence; they hold patently antidemocratic attitudes along with their democratic attitudes.

11. The popular acceptance of a democratic political system has yet to be complemented by the necessary differentiation and integration of the political and the administrative structures and functions, by the appropriate citizen response and support, and by the requisite level of public morality. Nevertheless, the political system is capable of self-correction which in turn feeds the observed pride in the nation's democratic ideals and performance.[57]

12. Government services are generally deficient in amount if not always in quality. Fiscal conservatism and irresponsibility in the face of ostensibly progressive intentions regarding programs and services have been hallmarks of elite behavior.[58] These are incongruent with the objective financial requirements of the government and its formal plans. The citizens' low tax-consciousness is matched by inefficient tax collection. The resulting lack of resources aggravates the limited capacity of the polity to solve national problems. Here we might recall the "inadequate public services and community facilities" which the respondents recognized as a major national problem.

57. This self-corrective capacity was demonstrated in a dramatic way by the introduction of reforms as part of the government's successful suppression of the Communist-Hukbalahap rebellion in the early and mid-fifties, and by the nationwide movement, led by civic organizations, for insuring free elections in 1951 and 1953, following the notorious presidential and senatorial elections of 1949.
58. In the words of Frank H. Golay, "Philippine fiscal policy has been unrealistic in terms of the avowed objectives of public policy and the failure of policy-makers to exploit potential productive tax bases" (*The Philippines: Public Policy and National Economic Development* [Ithaca, N.Y.: Cornell University Press, 1961], p. 187).

13. In an important sense the citizenry is highly politicized. Conscious of their bargaining influence through their votes, and encouraged by the competitiveness of elections, citizens have little hesitancy in approaching politicians with particularistic demands. These become pressures on the administrators for jobs, concessions, and exemptions from the rules.

However, most citizens comprise an amorphous, undifferentiated mass of people who are poorly integrated with the functioning of the legislature and the bureaucracy. Largely unorganized as members of associations with common interests, and unable to perceive their individual interests in policy terms, they are ineffectual in influencing legislation or demanding proper conduct from administrators. In other words, the citizens have developed only the electoral aspect of their "participant role," are too entangled in their "parochial role," and yet have to learn their "subject role" as well. In their predominantly undifferentiated and poorly integrated state, most citizens can neither exert the necessary policy demands nor contribute the required public scrutiny and support. Unorganized and undisciplined participation of citizens in administrative decision-making lowers the capacity of the bureaucracy for achieving results.

14. Subject to the qualifications mentioned in paragraphs 19 and 20 below, society-wide emphasis on primary group values, interests, and techniques tends to bias administrative decision-making away from the idealized norms of merit and equal treatment of citizens—and, again, this lowers the over-all capacity of the bureaucracy. Relatives and friends tend to be favored. The more numerous uninfluential persons and strangers tend to be ignored. Oftentimes founded on personalized reciprocity, the relationships among citizens, politicians, and administrators tend to be corrupted. Weakly internalized distinctions between "public" and "private," if at all existent—coupled with overriding egocentric or family-centered loyalties and tenuous identifications with the nation—result in rather rampant privatization of public property and resources.

One resulting mood in and out of the government is to exploit the dysfunctions arising from the incongruencies in values, in norms, and in behavior. The more the people observe official discrimination and corruption, the more they want to take advantage of existing weaknesses and arrangements in the government. In sum, here is a conspicuous instance of environmental factors acting as severe constraints on the capacity of the political system. The upshot is also a low degree of system autonomy:[59] politics and administration are being shaped compellingly by the citizens' values, attitudes, and demands, and this fact restricts the reverse process. The respondents' mention of lawlessness and criminality, lack of civic consciousness, and low tax payments are further evidence of the low degree of system autonomy.

15. By and large, interpersonal relations in and outside the bureaucracy are paternalistic and authoritarian. They are usually structured along segments which define for their members the in-group and the out-group. Patron-dependent types of dyadic relationships are also common among members of an agency and between some of them and their politician allies. To a greater or lesser extent, segmentation and patron-dependent dyads affect the flow of communication, individual access to superiors, and individual opportunities for advancement within an agency.

16. Most government workers regard their agency as the family writ large in which the head, like the father of a family, deserves personal loyalty and deference. But actually the idea of "family" itself is undergoing change, and with it the rights and duties of the "father." Although hierarchical relationships are often marked by acquiescence and subservience by subordinates, government workers can act rather independently of their superiors and even manipulate them. Lateral alliances with politicians and vertical relationships with an influential superior somewhere in the bureaucracy can enhance the position of fairly junior officials vis-à-vis their bosses.

17. Centralization of legal authority in the bureaucracy results in the common administrative delays without always insuring direction and control by top administrators. Behind this paradox

59. In Riggs's theory, the more autonomous the polity, the more it can shape the environment; when the environment—here the citizens' values, attitudes, and demands—exerts a strong influence on the polity, the polity's autonomy is being correspondingly reduced.

is the dispersion of power among politicians and their personal allies up and down the bureaucracy who manage to decentralize effective authority and discretion from time to time. Here is a conflict between hierarchy and polyarchy resulting alternately in the enhancement or the diminution of bureaucratic capacity.

18. Under heavy pressures of a personal or political nature, government decision-making tends to be *ad hoc,* face-to-face exchanges in the form of mutual *cathexis* and *individual bargaining*—in either of which, values loom large and facts recede to the background.[60] In Martin Landau's analysis, administrative decisions vary in their content from an emphasis on value premises in the folk society to an emphasis on factual premises in the urban society.[61] In a modern bureaucracy the pervading modes of exchange are based on official *duty or obligation* and *collective bargaining* between the decision-maker and the subject of his decisions. (In this context "collective bargaining" means bargaining by *representatives* of the interested parties.)

19. Generalizations about decision-making in the Filipino bureaucracy need ample qualification, however. There are decisional areas of known unmitigated cathexis and individual bargaining, such as patronage in semiskilled and unskilled labor in public works projects. There are decisional areas where rules are explicitly set and known, but frequent exceptions or preferential treatment occur, such as in the issuance of business licenses, permits, financial loans from government banks, and in tax collections. There are decisional areas where favoritism is resorted to occasionally but the minimal legal requirements and rules are

60. How the terms of exchange between members of a group are determined is analyzed in Harry C. Bredemeier and Richard M. Stephenson, *The Analysis of Social Systems* (New York: Holt, Rinehart and Winston, 1964), pp. 48–49. They examine three major kinds of exchange which may be institutionalized: *cathexis, duty or obligation,* and *bargaining.* Cathexis is based on mutual love or regard between members of a primary group. Duty or obligation depends on membership in a bureaucracy, without regard to mutual cathexis between the parties involved. In bargaining each party to the exchange is supposed to get what he needs by making it worth the other's while to meet that need; the parties act on the basis of mutual inducement.

For an extended analysis of Filipino politics as bargaining, see Jean Grossholtz, *op. cit.* In her view, "Philippine political culture is a bargaining culture, which is made evident by the Filipino way of perceiving and responding to power, conflict, and human interaction" (p. 159).

61. See chap. iii above.

observed; an example of this is the making of appointments to the classified civil service. Then there are decisional areas where rules are observed with hardly any deviation because officials discharge their defined duties and obligations—all legally qualified persons do get the service or benefit due them but certain persons are chronologically favored, for example, in extending loans and benefits accruing from government insurance or social security. Finally, there are decisional areas where, generally, rules are applied and services are rendered in an objective and universalistic manner, where official duties and obligations clearly transcend cathexis and bargaining as the form of exchange among the parties concerned in the official transaction. Examples are public education, public health services, postal services, emergency hospitalization, and the obvious public use of certain facilities such as roads and parks.

From the first to the last decisional areas, we find a shift in the definition of the decision-making situation: (1) from cathexis to individual bargaining to collective bargaining to official duties and obligations; (2) from personalism to impersonalism; (3) from inequality to egalitarianism; (4) from particularism to universalism; (5) from ascription to achievement; (6) from diffuseness to specificity; (7) from mere self-involvement to the involvement of collectivities such as the government, the nation, or the country, as these are subsumed in such entities as "the law" or "the rules."

20. An objective appraisal will likely disclose the widening observance of modern bureaucratic criteria in certain agencies and offices, in contrast to most other agencies and offices where, with few exceptions here and there, the modal conditions and tendencies analyzed earlier apply with greater force. And depending in part on the reputation of the different agencies and offices and on the primary decision-making orientations of the administrators, the citizens who approach them for service or action will also tend to perceive them, in Harry Friedman's terms, as either "policy-oriented" or "administrative-oriented."[62] Just as

62. See his essay, "Administrative Roles in Local Governments," chap. viii below.

many government workers and citizens realize the superior rationality and efficiency of business administration compared with public administration, they also learn to discriminate among various government agencies in these terms.

21. Besieged by "interfering" politicians and importuning citizens and compelled by them to accommodate political and personal pressures, high-minded administrators are torn between their ideal values and norms and their individual and programmatic survival, causing them varying anxiety, shame, or guilt. Increasing assumption of political roles by some of them is one form of adaptation to the relatively undifferentiated and unintegrated roles of bureaucrats vis-à-vis politicians. Equally high-minded politicians suffer some of the same feelings although their widely perceived roles, which are greatly diffuse, allow for the compromises they make.

22. Many citizens do not see, or prefer not to see, the administrative implications of their particularistic demands and their inattention to policy questions; they may therefore join in the recurrent outcry against "graft and corruption," "political partisanship and interference," "the spoils system," or "government inefficiency and red tape." The resulting public mood is often negative: "Change the leadership!" The high turnover in political office and the regular alternation of the parties in national power indicate this; so do the usual campaign attacks against the political incumbents and the ruling party.

23. In an earlier paper, some of the incongruencies we have analyzed led Mary R. Hollnsteiner to hypothesize that two whole and unintegrated and often conflicting value systems or patterns, both of them regarded as legitimate, co-exist in the bureaucracy: (1) the traditional norms typified by segmentation, personalism, and reciprocity, and (2) the Weberian bureaucratic norms articulated in the laws, rules, and administrative lore of the Westernized officials and citizens.[63] Her proposition is this: "The norms of Western bureaucracy in the Philippines constitute an essential

63. [Philippine] "Bureaucracy: The Interplay of Two Legitimate Value Systems," paper read at the third session of the Philippine Executive Academy, Baguio City, February 9, 1966.

part of Filipino life because their chief function as reinterpreted by Filipinos is *to strengthen the traditional norms of the society* through evolution of a unique synthesis of the rational and the traditional."[64] Thus, she illustrates: "those in power tend to favor traditional goals [e.g., welfare of one's in-group] through the use of traditional means [e.g., appointing one's loyal allies to important positions]; those out of power also favor traditional goals but find that these can be achieved by means of bureaucratic norms. By providing a legitimate lever for combating the actions of the traditional policies of those in power, bureaucratic norms allow more equal distribution of power between the in-group and the out-group. This equalization sets the stage for the reversal of the power locus at some future date, placing the former out-group in an in-group position now able to pursue its traditional goals."[65]

24. Hollnsteiner's proposition has great validity especially when applied to local governments and certain national agencies where traditional values and norms persist as decisional premises, and where traditional reciprocity remains the predominant mode of exchange. However, it does not adequately account for the various other agencies in which decision-making patterns take on more and more of the modern bureaucratic characteristics. Just as citizens vary in their circumstances and in their perceptions of and demands upon the government and its bureaucracy, we also find that administrators vary in their internalization of the modern values and norms to which they are increasingly being exposed by observation and experience. The more modern bureaucratic values and norms are not without staunch defenders who have incorporated them in their personalities. They are unlike other administrators who invoke the law and rules mostly for expediency reasons. And where ideological and organizational constraints are not as strong as in other agencies, these deviant bearers and defenders of modernity have been fairly successful.

25. To the extent of the physical and social distance from familial, provincial roots and of the internalization of the modern bureaucratic values and norms, for whatever reasons, administrators will be sufficiently freed from primary group attachments

64. *Ibid.*, p. 12. Italics mine.   65. *Ibid.*, p. 8.

José Veloso Abueva

and enabled to act as their modernized outlook dictates. In a sense the observed independence of administrators from the citizens, in contrast to the politicians, might be an index of a desirable social disentanglement, from the viewpoint of administrative development. Administrators do not have to be popular because they have tenure. They may also find reinforcement in their adherence to the rules among their peers in their profession and agency. The perceived helplessness of the citizens in relation to the "indifferent" or asocial administrator becomes less of a drawback wherever the citizens are actually demanding illegitimate favors that lessen bureaucratic capacity.

Chapter 6

The Role of Prefectural Governors in Japanese Bureaucratic Development

Bernard S. Silberman

The development, since the end of World War II, of the concept of development administration has resulted in the growth of interest and research in the role of civil and military bureaucracies in the so-called developing societies. Whatever Weber himself may have intended, it has been the general assumption, with some recent exceptions, that rapid and successful political, economic, and social development could not occur unless bureaucracies possessed the characteristics of the "legal-rational" type—hierarchy, responsibility, discipline, achievement orientation, specialization-differentiation, contractual participation, secular fixed compensation, and careerism.[1] More specifically, in terms of role, this assumption embraces the view that the policy-making and especially the administrative functions of a polity bent on "modernization" must be carried out, if it is to be successful, predominantly by a structure in which roles are: (1) allocated on the basis of performance, (2) defined on the basis of differentiated and specialized activity, (3) structured on the basis of hierarchical authority and responsibility, and (4) integrated through a universal commitment to a relatively well-defined career as set forth in a "career contract." It is this kind of structure which is usually termed rational bureaucracy.

1. Max Weber, *The Theory of Social and Economic Organization*, trans. A. M. Henderson and Talcott Parsons, ed. Talcott Parsons (New York and London: Oxford University Press, 1947), pp. 329–340.

Recent investigation and observation, however, have indicated that at certain stages of economic, political, and social development, a civil bureaucracy need not exhibit all of the characteristics of Weber's legal-rational bureaucratic type to be successful in development policy-making and administration. Indeed some research suggests that possession of these attributes by a civil bureaucracy at beginning stages of development may in fact be a hindrance rather than a help.[2]

The Japan Case

A primary obstacle in testing the validity of these assumptions lies in the fact that very few societies outside of the West have progressed beyond the beginning stages of political and economic development. In this sense Japan represents an excellent case study. After the Meiji Restoration of 1868 a newly formed civil bureaucracy recruited ostensibly from a traditionally oriented society was successful in introducing and implementing far-reaching changes with great success and rapidity. Analysis of Japanese bureaucratic development after 1868 thus represents a means of testing the validity of: (1) whether the key elements of the Weberian legal-rational type must be present if a civil bureaucracy is to be successful in carrying out programs of change and (2) whether the persistence of non-legal-rational bureaucratic characteristics and orientations renders a bureaucracy less effective in making "developmental" policy decisions and implementing them. If it is true that the persistence of non-legal-rational characteristics is an obstacle to rapid and successful development, then in view of Japan's success we should expect to find

2. See, for example, Ralph Braibanti, "Bureaucracy and Judiciary in Pakistan," and J. Donald Kingsley, "Bureaucracy and Political Development with Particular Reference to Nigeria," in Joseph LaPalombara, ed., *Bureaucracy and Political Development* (Princeton: Princeton University Press, 1963), pp. 360–440, 301–317. Also, Bernard S. Silberman, "Criteria for Recruitment and Success in the Japanese Bureaucracy, 1868–1900: 'Traditional' and 'Modern' Criteria in Bureaucratic Development," *Economic Development and Cultural Change*, XIV (Jan., 1966), 158–173.

that the new national civil bureaucracy which emerged after 1868 was characterized by a lack of such tendencies. We should also expect to find that bureaucratic development in Japan between 1868 and 1945 was characterized not by changes from a non-legal-rational type to a legal-rational one but by the existence and refinement of the legal-rational type from the very beginning of the period of development. Essentially it is the testing of this hypothesis with which this study is concerned.

An attempt to examine Japanese civil bureaucratic development in the light of all the Weberian characteristics for the entire period from 1868–1945 would entail a study of considerable length. For the present a partial answer with considerable validity may be obtained by analysis in terms of one of the most critical standards of bureaucratic development—the criteria for allocating bureaucratic roles. That is, whether bureaucratic roles are allocated on the basis of performance or ascriptive-oriented criteria. Since the two major aspects of role allocation in terms of bureaucratic structure are recruitment (the allocation of bureaucratic rank) and advancement (the allocation of bureaucratic office) we are here concerned with the criteria for eligibility recruitment and advancement in the Japanese civil bureaucracy.

The importance of role-allocation criteria in the analysis of bureaucratic development lies in the fact that they are both a reflection and determinant of bureaucratic role definition, structure, and integration. When roles are allocated primarily on the basis of ascriptive criteria, for example, the definition of role activity and the requirements for performing that activity will tend to be diffuse and non-specific since ascriptive criteria such as family social status have little to do directly with preparation for differentiated and specialized activity or their requirements. Again if ascriptive criteria are predominant then bureaucratic hierarchical structure will tend to be determined by such extra-bureaucratic attributes as family and/or stratum social status and prestige. The highest bureaucratic offices are not, then, filled with regard to performance of functions associated with the bureaucracy but rather on the basis of family and/or stratum status and prestige.

Under these conditions appeals by inferiors to decisions from a higher level may be made on the basis of extrabureaucratic criteria. Much the same may be said for integrating values. The predominance of ascriptive criteria may result in the commitment of the official to those extrabureaucratic norms and values associated with determining his status and prestige, and these will tend to be dysfunctional for bureaucratic role integration. Under these conditions there is no bureaucratic career, only bureaucratic avocation, since the commitment to bureaucratic office and values is secondary or tertiary to perhaps family, tribe, caste, or social stratum. Analysis of the criteria for role allocation, thus, can provide insight into the presence or absence of the other major characteristics of the legal-rational type.

For the purposes of this study analysis is focused on an examination of the backgrounds of a sample of upper civil servants.[3] The choice of this method was dictated by two considerations: (1) prior to 1887 there were no formal criteria for recruitment or advancement and it was not until 1899 that the formal structures of recruitment and advancement were stabilized; (2) the presence after 1899 of a stable recruitment structure and path of advancement was no assurance that the reality approximated the ideal as embodied in the formal requirements. In view of these considerations, analysis of the backgrounds of a group of upper civil servants spanning the entire period from 1868–1945 was considered to be the best technique for laying bare the nature of and changes in the criteria for recruitment and advancement.

The choice of a population from which the sample was drawn was determined by a number of factors: (1) because of the relatively long time span included in the study a more limited population than all upper civil servants between 1868–1945 was considered desirable; (2) the nature of the population was delim-

3. The use of the upper civil servant as the category of analysis is based on the view of the bureaucracy as an acting force in deciding policy and strategy of implementation. To the extent that this is true "it makes sense to think primarily of the groupings of advanced rank . . ." (Fritz Morstein Marx, "The Higher Civil Service as an Action Group in Western Political Development," in LaPalombara, ed., *op. cit.,* p. 63). "Upper civil servant" is defined here as one holding either *sonin* or *chokunin* rank in the pre-1945 civil bureaucracy. These designations were legally termed the upper civil service.

ited also by the desire to examine a group of upper civil servants who were not located entirely in the national central ministries. The main purpose of this delimitation was to center the analysis on a group of upper civil servants who were actively engaged in both policy-making and implementation of policy at "line" levels. This was a primary consideration since a major aspect of this analysis is the determination of whether the presence or absence of certain characteristics was important in the success of both planning and implementation.

The only group which seemed to meet these qualifications was the prefectural governors. The prefectural governor was a civil servant of high rank (governors belonged to the two highest ranks in the permanent civil service) but was not located in the central ministerial bureaucracy of the Home Ministry which was responsible for local government. From the beginning of the new regime in 1868 the governors performed a dual role. On the one hand they were highly placed officials of the national bureaucracy, while on the other they were the chief local officials.[4] It was through the governor that implementation of policy occurred. His reactions to specific policies and policy suggestions helped in the formulation of policy both explicitly and implicitly. The population of prefectural governors was also small enough to be manipulable. The entire population of prefectural governors between 1868 and 1945 numbered 862, from which a simple random sample of 25 per cent or 215 was selected.[5]

Categories of data for analysis of backgrounds were derived from a set of propositions concerning ascriptive and achievement-oriented criteria which emerged from the following analysis

4. Kurt Steiner, *Local Government in Japan* (Stanford, Calif.: Stanford University Press, 1965), pp. 43–44. Also Steiner's "The Japanese Prefecture, A Pivot of Centralization," paper delivered at the 1956 meeting of the American Political Science Association. Summary in *Toshi Mondai*, XLVIII (Apr., 1957), 107–116.

5. The population was determined on the basis of: (1) all those who were appointed by the central government as governors of officially designated prefectures in the period from May, 1868, to September, 1945; (2) the exclusion of the 273 daimyo who retained their positions until their domains were created and amalgamated into new prefectures by the end of 1871. The incumbents were determined by use of the following sources: Ijiri Tsunekichi, *Rekidai kenkanroku* (Tokyo: Naikaku Insatsukyoku, 1925); Naikaku Insatsukyoku, *Shokuinroku* (Tokyo: Naikaku Insatsukyoku, 1886–1945).

of the historical changes in the structure of the Japanese civil bureaucracy from 1868 to 1945.[6]

Propositions

Prior to 1868 the basic criterion of eligibility for recruitment to domain (*han*) or central *Bakufu* office was birth within the traditional political elite strata. Ostensibly unless one was a member of a family of at least samurai rank bureaucratic service was out of the question. Within the broad stratum of the governing elite there was a further stratification based on family rank. The position of the family in this system of stratification determined the range of offices one might attain. Family rank was associated with and reflected in a specific family income or stipend assigned by the daimyo or shogun in the case of the national bureaucracy. This income was used as the formal measure of eligibility for specific offices—offices required men of families with a certain range of income. Birth within a family of specific samurai rank, however, was not synonymous with office-holding. For every office at the domain or *Bakufu* level there were at least several families whose heads were eligible for that office.[7]

The criteria for choosing among the various eligibles for appointment to office was in large part performance-oriented. This was reflected, for example, in the widespread custom of adopting

6. The biographical data were derived from a large number of sources, of which the major ones are: Heibonsha, eds., *Dai jimmei jiten*, 10 vols. (Tokyo: Heibonsha, 1957–58); Igarashi Eikichi, *Taisho jimmei jiten* (Tokyo: Toyo Shimposha, 1914); Ishin Shiryo Hensankai, *Gendai kazoku fuyo* (Tokyo: Nihon Shiseki Kyokai, 1929); Osaka Mainichi Shimbunsha, eds., *Gendai jimmeiroku*, 10 vols. (Osaka: Osaka Mainichi Shimbunsha, 1926–35); Jinji Koshinjo, *Jinji koshinroku* (Tokyo: Jinji Koshinjo, 1903, 1908, 1911, 1915, 1918, 1921, 1925, 1928, 1931, 1934, 1937, 1939, 1941, 1943, 1948, 1951, 1953, 1955, 1957); Asahi Shimbunsha, *Asahi nenkan*, 26 vols. (Osaka: Asahi Shimbunsha, 1920–45); Kaneko Nobuhisa, *Hokkaido jimmei jisho* (Sapporo: N.P. 1923); Noyori Hideichi, ed., *Meiji Taisho shi: jimbutsu hen*, Vols. XIII–XV (Tokyo: Asahi Shimbunsha, 1930); Okamoto Takeo, ed., *Shiga ken jimbutsu shi* (Otsu, Shiga ken kyoiku kai, 1930); Matsuda Gensuke, ed., *Bocho jinshi hatten kan* (Yamaguchi, Yamaguchi ken kyoiku kai, 1932). In addition to these a large number of regional biographical dictionaries, prefectural histories and biographies were also used.

7. This was even true for the position of daimyo and shogun. In cases of lack of heirs or incompetence of existing heirs, a new daimyo or shogun might be chosen from the collateral families, the chief function of which was to provide possible alternates.

children and adults from lower-ranking families if there were no heirs or nature had not endowed one's heirs with competence. Performance orientation was reflected more noticeably in the increasing tendency on the part of *han* and *Bakufu* governments after the first quarter of the eighteenth century to give additional stipends to men of presumed competence in administration so that they might become eligible for higher-ranking offices than their family rank allowed.[8]

Broadly speaking, in 1868 at the time of the Meiji Restoration, the basic criterion of eligibility for office in the traditional bureaucracy was ascriptive-oriented, but within the confines of status and rank, achievement-oriented criteria were important. What constituted adequate performance, however, was never clearly defined in the Tokugawa period. By the beginning of the nineteenth century the intensification of economic crises and pressure from the West to open Japan resulted in considerable discussion and controversy over what constituted adequate performance or competence. A general consensus emerged that *jitsugaku*—experience and performance in actual affairs—constituted the best criteria for appointment to office.[9] With the advent of the Restoration, experience and performance in actual affairs presumably came to mean two specific criteria. Participation in the Restoration itself, since it was successful in overthrowing the *Bakufu,* would cast an aura, whether deserved or not, of competence over the participants. In this sense the Restoration was a test of competence—those who had participated on the winning side had shown themselves to be competent in "actual affairs." The second criterion was related to the pressure of the Western nations on Japan to accept the basic values of contract and defined authority then governing the relations between Western states. This pressure had finally resulted in the "opening" of Japan and had contributed heavily to the collapse of the *ancien régime.* The

8. Sakata Yoshio, "Meiji ishin to Tempo kaikaku," *Jimbun Gakuho,* II (Mar., 1952), 1–26. Also, Naito Masanaka, "Hansei kaikaku no shakaiteki kiban," in Horie Eiichi, ed., *Hansei kaikaku no kenkyu* (Tokyo, Ochanomizu Shobu, 1955).

9. Harry D. Harootunian, "Aspects of Elite Ideology in the Late Tokugawa Period," in Bernard S. Silberman and Harry D. Harootunian, eds., *Leadership in Modern Japan* (Tucson: University of Arizona Press, 1966).

desire of the Japanese to free themselves from the humiliation of extraterritoriality which had accompanied the opening appears to have resulted in the emergence of Western learning and knowledge as the other major aspect of "actual affairs."[10]

In the period after 1868 the desire, almost amounting to an obsession, on the part of the Japanese leaders to gain juridical autonomy and to create a strong united and centralized state led to the adoption and implementation of widespread political, economic, and social changes. Foremost among these was the complete reformation along primarily Western and specifically Prussian lines of the political structure. Between 1885 and 1900 there emerged a highly centralized political system, the mainstay of which was a "modern" bureaucratic structure. A series of ordinances and laws promulgated between 1885 and 1900 established a civil service structure which remained largely unchanged for the next forty-five years.

The major formal consequences of these reforms in terms of recruitment and advancement in the civil bureaucracy may be summed up briefly: (1) the establishment in 1887 and strengthening, in 1893, of a civil service examination system which distinguished between a lower and an upper civil service; (2) the establishment of an upper civil service examination based on an extensive knowledge of jurisprudence and various types of law such as administrative, commercial, civil, and constitutional law requiring in effect a university degree in law; (3) the practical elimination, with some exceptions, of entry into the upper civil service other than through examination; (4) the establishment of civil service autonomy reflected in the practical exclusion of non-civil servants from all but a few posts of the highest ranks of the civil service; (5) the establishment of prior upper civil service experience as the major criterion for appointment to the highest ranks of the civil service.[11] Out of the various ordinances

10. Bernard S. Silberman, *Ministers of Modernization: Elite Mobility in the Meiji Restoration, 1868–73* (Tucson: University of Arizona Press, 1964).
11. The civil service examination system is defined in the following statutes (all references are to the *Collected Statutes* (*Horei zensho*): Imperial Ordinances 37,

and laws defining the structure of the upper civil service there emerges a picture of a higher bureaucracy trained primarily in law, oriented toward performance as the criterion for recruitment and promoted or advanced by the criterion of experience in a defined career.

From this brief description of the historical background of the changes in the recruitment and advancement structure in the higher civil bureaucracy between 1868 and 1945 the following propositions may be presented as the basis for collecting and analyzing the data on the backgrounds of the selected sample: *There will be significant differences in the sample with regard to the criteria for recruitment and advancement of those appointed as prefectural governors between 1868 and 1899 and those appointed between 1900 and 1945, and these differences may be explained in terms of the following subpropositions.*

1. For those in the sample appointed as governors prior to 1900 we will expect that: (*a*) the criterion of eligibility for recruitment will be the possession of status in the traditional governing elite (samurai status at least); (*b*) to the extent family rank determined eligibility for specific offices then prefectural governors will be drawn from the ranks of former daimyo, the pre-1868 equivalent of prefectural governor; (*c*) within the limits of the group defined in (1) and (2) the criteria for recruitment and advancement will be participation in the Restoration and/or possession of Western languages, military and civil technology, science, history, and political economy; (*d*) the absence of a direct relationship of the criteria for recruitment and advancement to any formal bureaucratic requirements or formal experience in a

38, Cabinet Ordinances 8, 19, and 20, July 23, 1887; Imperial Ordinance 57, Nov. 5, 1887; Imperial Ordinance 58, Nov. 7, 1887; Cabinet Ordinance 25, Dec. 1, 1887; Imperial Ordinances 63, 64, Dec. 24, 1887; Cabinet Ordinance 28, Dec. 28, 1887. The revisions of 1893 are contained in the following: Imperial Ordinances 126, 183, 187, 197, Oct. 31, 1893; Imperial Ordinance 54, May 24, 1894; Cabinet Ordinance 2, May 7, 1894; Foreign Ministry Ordinance 7, June 22, 1894; Imperial Ordinance 7, Jan. 18, 1918; Imperial Ordinance 15, Mar. 28, 1929; Imperial Ordinance 1, Jan. 6, 1941. The major ordinances defining appointment, advancement, discipline, and dismissal are as follows: Imperial Ordinance 183, Nov. 30, 1893; Imperial Ordinances 61, 62, 63, Mar. 28, 1899; Imperial Ordinance 261, July 31, 1913.

bureaucratic structure will be reflected in the absence of a consistent career pattern among the appointees.

2. For those in the sample appointed as governors after 1899 we will expect that: (*a*) the basic criterion of eligibility for recruitment will be a university education in law; (*b*) since entrance to universities was on a universalistic basis, birth in a family belonging to the traditional political elite will be of relatively little significance; (*c*) to the extent that university training required relatively high economic status the majority of governors appointed will have come from middle and high income families; (*d*) passage of the upper civil service examinations will be the criterion for recruitment into the upper civil service, and this will be reflected in the fact that all or nearly all of the governors in this group will possess this attribute; (*e*) to the extent that the criteria for eligibility, recruitment, and advancement were directly related to a formal bureaucratic structure and formal requirements of the structure, there will be a significantly consistent career pattern for those in this group.

Analysis

Turning to analysis of the data we may begin by testing the basic proposition of whether there existed significant differences in the criteria for recruitment and advancement to the post of governor in the two periods 1868–99 and 1900–45. This may be done by testing one or more of the subpropositions explaining the significant differences. Subpropositions 2*a* and 2*d* are especially suitable for this purpose. Analysis of the data on university education and passage of the upper civil service examinations in the sample shows that of the total number, those with university education number 132 while 83 were without university education. Those who passed the upper civil service examinations totaled 127 while 88 did not (see Tables 1 and 2). Tables 1 and 2 indicate that there were significant differences in the criteria for recruitment and advancement in the two periods.

What then were the criteria for eligibility, recruitment and

appointment as governor in the period 1868–99? The first proposition we may examine is that regarding traditional elite and
daimyo status as criteria of eligibility. Table 3 presents the data
in terms of pre-1868 socio-political strata origin. Only 2.5 per cent
were of commoner origin, indicating that traditional political

Table 1. *University Education by Appointment Period*

Appointment period	University education Number	%	No university education Number	%	Total Number
Pre-1900	2	1.5	78	94.0	80
Post-1899	130	98.5	5	6.0	135
Total	132	100.0	83	100.0	215

$R = +1.00$ $X^2 = 185.708$ $P < .001$

Table 2. *Civil Service Examination by Appointment Period*

Appointment period	Passed examination Number	%	Non-examination Number	%	Total Number	%
Pre-1900	0	0.0	80	91.0	80	37.0
Post-1899	127	100.0	8	9.0	135	63.0
Total	127	100.0	88	100.0	215	100.0

$R = +1.00$ $X^2 = 183.427$ $P < .001$

elite status was the basic criterion of eligibility for recruitment.
However, since 86.25 per cent of governors appointed prior to
1900 were of samurai origin and only 1.25 per cent were recruited
from former daimyo, it is clear that family rank was no longer a
significant factor in determining eligibility for recruitment to
specific offices. The predominance of those of samurai origin also
indicates a high level of mobility within the traditional elite.[12] It
may be concluded that within the boundaries of the traditional
political elite, the criteria of eligibility had become much more
universal in character. The pool of possible candidates for any
given office was enlarged considerably.

With the enlargement of the pool of possible candidates for

12. This supports the data on mobility of upper civil servants in the central
ministries as reported in Silberman, *Ministers of Modernization.*

positions, especially high-ranking ones, in the new civil bureaucracy, the problem of employing more explicit and clearly defined criteria for recruitment emerged. Since family rank no longer served to delimit the numbers eligible for recruitment to specific offices, more emphasis had to be placed on defining, at least informally, the content of recruitment criteria. It has been proposed (subproposition 1c) that two clearly identifiable but informal criteria emerged at the time of the Restoration and persisted until approximately 1900: (1) participation in the activities leading to the Restoration and (2) possession of Western knowl-

Table 3. *Pre-1868 Social Stratum Origin of Pre-1900 Appointees*

Social stratum	Number	%
Imperial household	0	0.00
Court aristocracy (Kuge)	8	10.00
Daimyo	1	1.25
Samurai	69	86.25
Commoner	2	2.50
Others	0	0.00
N.A.	0	0.00
Total	80	100.00

edge and/or education. The data, when analyzed on this basis, indicate that participation in the Restoration was an important criterion since 73.75 per cent had this attribute (see Table 4). Western education appears to be clearly secondary (22.5 per cent). Only 11.25 per cent had neither characteristic, indicating that the two criteria taken together were the basis for recruitment and appointment as governor.[13]

As has been suggested (subproposition 1d), given the fact that the criteria for recruitment and appointment as governor were extrabureaucratic in character—not directly the consequence of a formally defined bureaucratic structure or formal requirements

13. The presence of 11.25 per cent with neither of these attributes suggests the possibility of a third criterion for recruitment and advancement. The only significant correlation which emerges with other variables is that of seniority. We may conclude that these 11.25 per cent represent a transitional group.

Table 4. *Participation in the Meiji Restoration by Western Education Pre-1900 Appointees*

Education	Participation in Restoration		Non-participation in Restoration		Total	
	Number	%	Number	%	Number	%
Some Western education	10	12.50	8	10.00	18	22.5
Traditional education only	49	61.25	9	11.25	58	72.5
N.A.	0	0.00	4	5.00	4	5.0
Total	59	73.75	21	26.25	80	100.0
	R = +.675		X^2 = 17.735	P < .001		

of a bureaucratic structure—we may expect to find that career patterns among those achieving the rank of governor prior to 1900 will vary widely.[14] The variables used in this analysis to determine consistency of career pattern are: (1) age of entry, (2) mode of entry, (3) ministry of first office held, (4) level of first office held, (5) number of ministries of service, and (6) number of offices held before governor's appointment. Tables 5–10 present data on these variables. Examination of the data reveals that career patterns varied widely in terms of a number of variables. Age of entry varied all the way from eighteen to fifty-seven, with at least 50 per cent entering after the age of twenty-nine. Furthermore, ages are relatively well distributed over the whole range with the exception of 23.75 per cent in the twenty-three to twenty-seven range. Mode of entry was consistent, as one might expect, since the examination system was not established until 1887. But as we have seen, mode of entry was appointment on the basis of two performance-oriented criteria. The absence of a consistent career pattern is clearly noticeable when civil service

14. The term "career pattern" is defined here as the movement of the individual into various roles throughout his lifetime. A bureaucratic career is then defined as the progression of the individual through a series of various offices and roles within a hierarchically arranged system of offices and roles either horizontally or vertically. When career patterns of a majority of those holding office in a particular area of the bureaucratic structure are similar—begin at the same age and move through a similar series of hierarchically arranged offices—we may conclude that the criteria for progression are internal rather than external. When the career patterns of a majority of those holding office in a particular area of the structure are dissimilar, we may conclude that the criteria for progression are external to the structure.

Table 5. *Age at Entry of Pre-1900 Appointees*

Age in five-year periods	Number	%
18–22	6	7.50
23–27	19	23.75
28–32	6	7.50
33–37	8	10.00
38–42	6	7.50
43–47	3	3.75
48–52	2	2.50
53–57	4	5.00
N.A.	26	32.50
Total	80	100.00

Table 6. *Mode of Entry of Pre-1900 Appointees*

Mode of entry	Number	%
Examination	0	0.0
Non-examination	80	100.0
Total	80	100.0

Table 7. *Ministry of First Office Held of Pre-1900 Appointees*

Ministry of first office	Number	%
Cabinet Secretariat	2	2.50
Imperial Household	1	1.25
Foreign Affairs	3	3.75
Home	54	67.50
Finance	1	1.25
Education	1	1.25
Agriculture	2	2.50
Commerce-Industry	0	0.00
Communications	0	0.00
Army-Navy	9	11.25
Justice	7	8.75
Total	80	100.00

Table 8. *Level of First Office of Pre-1900 Appointees*

Level of office by civil service rank	Number	%
Lower civil service (*Hanin* rank)	11	13.75
Upper civil service (*Sonin* ranks 8–6)	16	20.00
Upper civil service (*Sonin* ranks 5–3)	17	21.25
Upper civil service (*Chokunin* ranks 2–1)	20	25.00
Military service	7	8.75
N.A.	9	11.25
Total	80	100.00

Table 9. *Number of Ministries of Service by Number of Offices Held*

Number of ministries of service	\ Number of offices held 1	2	3	4	5	6	7	8	9	10	11	Total
1	24	4	4	3	8	5	0	1	0	0	0	49
2	0	5	3	5	2	3	1	0	0	0	1	20
3	0	0	3	1	3	1	2	0	0	0	0	10
4	0	0	0	0	1	0	0	0	0	0	0	1
Total	24	9	10	9	14	9	3	1	0	0	1	80

Table 10. *Age at Retirement of Pre-1900 Appointees*

Age	Number	%
20–24	0	0.00
25–29	3	3.75
30–34	5	6.25
35–39	5	6.25
40–44	8	10.00
45–49	3	3.75
50–54	8	10.00
55–59	16	20.00
60–64	9	11.25
65–69	2	2.50
70–74	1	1.25
N.A.	20	25.00
Total	80	100.00

Bernard S. Silberman

rank of first office held is examined. First office varied from lower civil service rank to the highest ranks, with 25 per cent being appointed as governor in their first office. The view that career patterns were not consistent tends to be supported by the data in Table 9, which indicates the relationship between the number of ministries in which the appointees served and the number of offices held. Of those who served in only one ministry, one measure of consistent career patterns, nearly 50 per cent held only one office. In other words, the extent of their careers was one office. Of the entire group, only 35 per cent held more than four offices, while 55 per cent held three offices or less during their careers. In

Table 11. *Number of Ministries Served, by Length of Service*

Number of ministries of service	Length of service by five-year periods							Over 35	Total
	1–5	6–10	11–15	16–20	21–25	26–30	31–35		
1	17	12	6	1	4	1	0	2	43
2	2	2	2	3	4	4	2	1	20
3	1	2	0	1	0	4	2	0	10
4	0	1	0	0	0	0	0	0	1
N.A.	—	—	—	—	—	—	—	—	6
Total	20	17	8	5	8	9	4	3	80

terms of ministries of service, more than 38 per cent served in more than one ministry indicating considerable variation in career service. Indeed it appears from this tabulation that number of offices held tended to increase with the number of ministries served, indicating that longer careers were associated with movement from one ministry to another. This proposition can be further examined by relating the data on length of service with number of ministries served (see Table 11). These data indicate that this conclusion is generally true. Service in one ministry tends to be correlated with short career spans; of those in one ministry only, more than 67 per cent have less than eleven years service. The opposite is true for those serving in two and three ministries; less than 26 per cent of this group have less than eleven years of service.

Regarding the men who were recruited and appointed as governor and, by extension, upper civil servants generally in the period 1868–99 the following specific conclusions may be drawn: (1) the criteria of eligibility for recruitment continued to be largely ascriptive-oriented, and at least samurai rank was necessary for eligibility; (2) family rank was no longer a criterion for either eligibility or recruitment; (3) the criteria for recruitment appear to have been participation in the Restoration and/or possession of Western knowledge; (4) the extrabureaucratic character of the criteria appears to have resulted in the absence of a consistent career pattern. Careers tended to vary in regard to age at entry, number of ministries served, level of first office, number of offices held, and length of service; (5) the one consistent career element appears to have been the criteria of eligibility and recruitment. To the extent this is true these men were united on the basis of their social origins and their commitment to innovative behavior.

If we now turn to the analysis of data with regard to those recruited and appointed as governors in the period 1900–45 a number of significant differences emerge. As we have seen (Table 1), of those recruited and rising to the position of governor in this period 98.5 per cent had a university education. The great majority (91.1 per cent) were graduates of law or jurisprudential curricula (see Table 12).[15] The criterion of eligibility for recruitment, it may be concluded, was acquisition of a university education emphasizing legal training. Restricted generalist training rather than specialist training predominated among governors and quite likely among upper civil servants generally. Although the criterion of eligibility seems to have been a university education in law, it has often been noted and suggested that with regard to the upper civil service, university education and education at Tokyo Imperial University in the pre-1945 period were synonymous. Tabulation of data on university attended confirms these observations (see Table 13). The number recruited from Tokyo Imperial University far exceeds that possible on a purely random basis. This is especially significant when it is noted that

15. In the prewar university system political science and law were taught by the same faculty and shared a large number of courses as well as outlook.

Table 12. *University Specialization of Post-1899 Appointees*

Specialization	Number	%
Law	89	65.9*
Political science	34	25.2*
Economics	2	1.5
Agriculture	1	0.7
Engineering	0	0.0
No degree	5	3.7
N.A.	4	3.0
Total	135	100.0

* Law curricula.

Table 13. *University Attended by Post-1899 Appointees*

University	Number	%
Tokyo Imperial	115	85.2
Kyoto Imperial	10	7.4
Hitotsubashi	2	1.5
Hosei	1	0.7
American-European	2	1.5
No degree	5	3.7
Total	135	100.0

there were a larger number of recognized universities than are represented in the sample. Consequently, we may conclude that education at Tokyo Imperial University was almost a criterion of eligibility for recruitment and advancement to the position of governor and in the upper civil service.

Access to university education was ostensibly universalistic. There were no formal ascriptive restrictions on entrance to universities. Consequently we should expect to find birth in a family of traditional elite origins to be of negligible significance. Social stratum origin in pre-1868 terms is represented in Table 14. The expectations with regard to significance of traditional elite family origins are not fulfilled. Almost half (48.1 per cent) came from families of traditional elite status. The representation of this group in the sample is far larger than their distribution in the general population. In 1868 the traditional elite population was approximately 5 per cent of the total population. Assuming that despite large increases in the population after 1868 the traditional elite population remained relatively the same proportion of the total, then this group is overrepresented in the sample. Yet, because of the large number of those of commoner origin, traditional elite origin does not appear to be a criterion of eligibility, recruitment, or advancement to the position of governor. The overrepresentation of those of traditional elite origins can perhaps be explained in terms of economic status and motivation.

Table 14. *Pre-1868 Social Stratum Origins of Post-1899 Appointees, by Pre-1868 Social Strata*

Social stratum in pre-1868 social strata	Number	%
Traditional political elite	65	48.1
Commoners	62	45.9
N.A.	8	6.0
Total	135	100.0

Those from former elite families, it is suggested, would be more likely to have the economic means to finance an education through the university than the vast majority of the population. Finally, members of this group were perhaps more highly motivated to seek education in order to maintain the prestige style of their fathers—a style which laid great emphasis on education as an aspect of high prestige.

To the extent that this is true, the significant differences in social origin in terms of pre-1868 social status should be explained by common economic stratum origins. The assumption is that commoners with sufficient economic status would seek to raise their prestige by acquiring the style of the traditional elite, while those of traditional elite origin with sufficient income would seek to maintain their traditional family status and prestige. Economic

Table 15. *Economic Status of Families of Origin of Post-1899 Appointees*

Economic status	Traditional political elite		Commoner		Total	
	Number	%	Number	%	Number	%
High income	19	15.0	34	26.8	53	41.8
Middle income	35	27.6	22	17.3	57	44.9
Low income	0	0.0	0	0.0	0	0.0
N.A.	11	8.6	6	4.7	17	13.3
Total	65	51.2	62	48.8	127	100.0
		Social strata unknown = 8		P < .001		

status of families of origin is tabulated in Table 15. While data on income are not of the highest accuracy, economic status based on father's occupation indicates that all members of the sample belonged to higher- and middle-income groups. The slightly higher percentage from former elite families in the middle-income group perhaps indicates higher motivation among former elite families. However, the significance is not strong enough to support these generalizations. Economic status does appear to explain the differences between the groups generally—all belonged to income groups capable of financing a prolonged education. Economic status was apparently a qualification necessary in order to attain eligibility.

The recruitment and advancement structure which had come into existence by 1900 implied the presence of a consistent career pattern for governors and upper civil servants in general. The same measures were used as were employed for determining consistency of career patterns for those appointed prior to 1900 (see Tables 16–21).

When Tables 5–10 are compared with Tables 16–21 the differences in career patterns are dramatic. For those who advanced to the position of governor after 1899 there is a clearly consistent career pattern. Entry into the upper civil service occurred largely between the ages of twenty-three and thirty-two (83 per cent) with a large majority entering between the ages of twenty-three and twenty-seven (see Table 16). This tends to support the

Table 16. *Age of Entry of Post-1899 Appointees*

Age in five-year periods	Number	%
18–22	3	2.2
23–27	95	70.4
28–32	17	12.6
33–37	1	0.7
38–42	0	0.0
43–47	0	0.0
48–52	0	0.0
53–57	0	0.0
N.A.	19	14.1
Total	135	100.0

Table 17. *Mode of Entry of Post-1899 Appointees*

Mode of entry	Number	%
Examination	127	94.1
Appointment	8	5.9
Total	135	100.0

Table 18. *Ministry of First Office Held by Post-1899 Appointees*

Ministry	Number	%
Cabinet Secretariat	1	0.7
Imperial Household	0	0.0
Foreign Affairs	1	0.7
Home	120	88.9
Finance	2	1.5
Education	0	0.0
Agriculture	4	3.0
Commerce-Industry	0	0.0
Communications	3	2.2
Army-Navy	0	0.0
Justice	4	3.0
Total	135	100.0

conclusion that university education was essentially part of the career pattern of upper civil servants since university graduation occurred largely in this age group. Mode of entry was also consistent for this group, with 94.1 per cent entering via the upper civil service examinations (see Table 17). This consistency is

Table 19. *Level of First Office Held by Post-1899 Appointees*

Level of office	Number	%
Lower civil service (*Hanin* ranks)	0	0.0
Upper civil service (*Sonin* ranks 8–6)	111	82.2
Upper civil service (*Sonin* ranks 5–3)	13	9.6
Upper civil service (*Chokunin* ranks 2–1)	0	0.0
Military service	0	0.0
N.A.	11	8.2
Total	135	100.0

upheld by the other data. For 88.9 per cent of the members of this group the Home Ministry was the ministry of first office, while 86 per cent served in the same ministry throughout their entire careers (see Tables 18 and 20). The variation in number of offices held prior to appointment as governor is also quite limited, with 54.1 per cent holding from six to eight offices and

Table 20. *Number of Ministries Served by Number of Offices Held Prior to Appointment as Governor, by Post-1899 Appointees*

Number of ministries														Total	

Number of ministries	1	2	3	4	5	6	7	8	9	10	11	12	N.A.	Number	%
1	0	0	2	1	6	16	28	20	13	9	6	3	12	116	86.0
2	0	0	0	0	1	5	3	1	1	3	3	2	0	19	14.0
3	—	—	—	—	—	—	—	—	—	—	—	—	—	—	0.0
4	—	—	—	—	—	—	—	—	—	—	—	—	—	—	0.0
Total	0	0	2	1	7	21	31	21	14	12	9	5	12	135	100.0

$P < .001$

none holding fewer than three. Only three individuals achieved the rank of governor without serving in at least five offices. Nor do there seem to be any significant differences in the number of offices held by those who served in more than one ministry, with the exception of a slight tendency to hold more offices prior to appointment. Careers apparently came to be structured so as to limit the possibilities of transfer to more than one other ministry. Or, to put it another way, advancement to high rank would probably have been seriously retarded or impossible for those who transferred to more than one other ministry before arriving at the Home Ministry.

Table 21. *Age of Retirement of Post-1899 Appointees*

Age in five-year periods	Number	%
20–24	0	0.0
25–29	0	0.0
30–34	3	2.2
35–39	0	0.0
40–44	16	11.9
45–49	48	35.6
50–54	42	31.1
55–59	15	11.1
60–64	5	3.7
65–69	0	0.0
70–74	0	0.0
N.A.	6	4.4
Total	135	100.0

When level of first office of the appointees in this group is tabulated, consistency of career pattern is substantiated. None of the members of this group in the sample entered the upper civil service via the lower civil service route (see Table 19). The great majority (82.2 per cent) entered at *sonin* ranks 8–6, with a small minority entering in the next three highest *sonin* ranks. Especially significant is the fact that no one was appointed directly as governor or to *chokunin* rank generally, as compared with 25 per cent in the pre-1900 group.

Finally, age at retirement fills out the picture of a consistent career pattern (see Table 21). While the median age for those appointed before 1900 and those appointed after 1899 was almost the same (fifty-one and fifty, respectively) the distribution of retirement ages for the latter group is centered on a ten-year span, forty-five to fifty-four, in which two-thirds of the entire group retired. Only three individuals (2.2 per cent) retired before the age of forty and 3.7 per cent retired after the age of fifty-nine as compared with 16.25 per cent and 15 per cent, respectively, for those appointed prior to 1900.

A major question which arises for those appointed as governors after 1899 is on what basis they were advanced. Since, presumably, all those entering the upper civil service in this period shared with this group similarities in age at entry, first ministry of service, mode of entry, and level of first office, advancement must have been dependent on some other factor. The data indicating the number of offices served prior to appointment as governor offer a major clue. There appears some variation in the number of offices held prior to appointment (see Table 20). Although the majority were appointed after holding six to eight offices, there were a considerable number appointed after holding nine to twelve offices. The differences may be explained by length of service. That is, length of service prior to appointment may have been similar for all members of this group although some held more offices than others. The fact that 79.3 per cent of this group reached the position of governor between eleven and twenty years of service (Table 22) while a similar percentage (85.2) covers the range of five to eleven offices held (Table 20) indicates that seniority rather than number of offices held tended to determine advancement. It may be concluded then that experience was the major criterion of advancement, but that the content of this criterion was length of service or seniority rather than a wide range of offices served.

With regard to those who were appointed as governors (and by extension upper civil servants as a whole) after 1899, several specific conclusions may be drawn. (1) The criteria of eligibility had shifted from pre-1868 traditional political elite status to university education emphasizing law and more specifically to at-

Table 22. Years of Service by Number of Offices Held Prior to Appointment of Post-1899 Gubernatorial Appointees

Years of service prior to appointment	Number of offices held prior to appointment												N.A.	Total Number	%
	1	2	3	4	5	6	7	8	9	10	11	12			
0– 5	—	—	—	—	—	—	—	—	—	—	—	—		0	0.0
6–10	—	—	1	—	—	—	—	—	—	—	—	—		1	0.7
11–15	—	—	1	—	5	10	14	9	2	2	—	—		43	32.0
16–20	—	—	—	1	2	10	13	10	10	9	6	3		64	47.3
21–25	—	—	—	—	—	1	4	2	1	1	3	1		13	9.6
26–30	—	—	—	—	—	—	—	—	1	—	—	—		1	0.7
31–35	—	—	—	—	—	—	—	—	—	—	—	1		1	0.7
Over 35	—	—	—	—	—	—	—	—	—	—	—	—		0	0.0
N.A.													12	12	9.0
Total	0	0	2	1	7	21	31	21	14	12	9	5	12	135	100.0
			(1.5)	(.75)	(5.1)	(15.4)	(23.0)	(15.4)	(10.0)	(9.0)	(6.5)	(3.7)	(9.0)	(100.0)	

tendance at Tokyo Imperial University. The criterion of eligibility was no longer ascriptive-oriented but had largely become achievement-oriented. (2) The shift from an ascriptive to an achievement-oriented criterion of eligibility resulted in considerable mobility within the political elite. (3) The criterion for recruitment was passage of the upper civil service examinations, indicating that formal requirements and actuality were not widely separated and that performance was the criterion for recruitment. (4) The bureaucratic character of the criteria of eligibility and recruitment was reflected in the emergence of a clearly consistent career pattern. (5) Advancement was apparently accorded on the basis of seniority, and to this extent experience defined as length of service was a basic criterion for advancement.

Conclusion

A number of general as well as specific conclusions may be drawn from the data and the specific conclusions drawn from the analysis of the data presented here on the role of prefectural governors. First, it may be concluded that the Japanese civil bureaucracy was achievement-oriented from 1868 on in terms of recruitment and advancement. However, the content of the criteria underwent a marked shift after approximately 1899. The achievement-oriented criteria which prevailed before 1900 were characterized by their extrabureaucratic origins. Participation in the Restoration and possession of some Western knowledge were not only extrabureaucratic in origin, but they may also be termed innovative since neither activity was sanctioned by the traditional institutional structure or the norms associated with these structures. The men who became the high-ranking civil servants were thus not innovative bureaucrats but rather innovators who by nature of their activity and their ascriptively determined eligibility for office-holding became bureaucrats. Perhaps because of this quality they were able to improvise and devise "developmental" policies—they were not constrained by commitment to routine or to bureaucratic hierarchy.

The very similarity of the social origins of the upper civil service in the period 1868–99 perhaps also sheds some light on the reasons for the effectiveness and rapidity with which new programs were formulated and implemented in this period. The upper civil servants, drawn primarily from the former samurai stratum, shared a common set of values, norms, and patterns of behavior. At the same time they belonged to a stratum whose other members continued to exert wide influence and hold a majority of the positions at the local level of government and administration.[16] There was, then, a community of shared values and patterns of behavior between the members of the new national upper civil bureaucracy and local leadership which made for continuity of communication. Furthermore, the commitment of both groups was not to a bureaucratic structure or bureaucratic values but to their social stratum and its values, which happened to include political power and participation as a major value.

The ascriptive nature of the criterion of eligibility also indicates that a "successful" bureaucracy in developmental terms need not adhere to the principle of democratic or society-wide universalistic recruitment in order to be effective. Perhaps it may also be concluded that it was the very nature of the exclusive criterion of birth in the traditional political elite which made possible the rapid acceptance and, consequently, implementation of reforms passed down by the bureaucracy. Had the governors, for example, been recruited entirely on the basis of universalistic criteria of eligibility, the new government would not have had the prestige or status necessary, in a still predominantly traditional society, to gain acceptance of the reforms by local leadership and the great masses of the society.

The innovative and extrabureaucratic nature of the criteria for recruitment and appointment to the upper civil service prior to 1900 also suggests one explanation for the emergence of the unique system of decision-making, called the *Genro,* which dominated policy-making for the entire civil and military bureaucracy and the government as well. An oligarchy composed of approximately twelve men, all of whom, with one exception, were former

16. Local governmental and administrative offices continued to be dominated by local ex-samurai. See Harry D. Harootunian, "The Progress of Japan and the Samurai Class, 1868–1882," *Pacific Historical Review,* XXVIII (Aug., 1959), 255–266.

samurai, emerged in the 1880's to make all of the major political
and military decisions. Although the *Genro* had no legal or constitutional status, by virtue of the high positions they held in the
civil and military bureaucracy and their relationships with others
in the two bureaucracies, they maintained tight control over all
major decisions until approximately 1900. The origins of this
mechanism do not appear to lie in Japanese institutional history
—no such group existed in the preceding Tokugawa period. Its
emergence, however, may be explained in terms of the bureaucratic expertise available to help make policy and devise means of
implementation. If, as seems likely, the upper civil service in this
period was recruited and advanced on the basis of participation
in the Meiji Restoration and possession of Western knowledge,
then the very existential and random character of this type of
training must have produced a considerable lack of consensus on
how to achieve the "rich country and strong nation." In the
absence of uniform training and common outlook the only means
by which decisions could be arrived at without continual conflict
was to create a system for making judgments as to which facts,
means, and technologies would produce the desired results. Since
there was no individual charismatic leader who, by his mystique,
could make such choices, responsibility devolved on those in the
bureaucracy with the highest prestige and access to the most
important offices—men such as Ito Hirobumi, Yamagata Aritomo,
Matsukata Shogi, Katsura Taro, and Saionji Kimmochi. The size
of the group was probably determined by trial and error until a
number was reached which could make choices of techniques
and means, which were binding on the rest of the upper civil
service. Not much is known concerning the actual pattern of
decision-making within this group, but it is clear that certain
rules were created and abided by. For example, once a choice
had been made the opponents of the decision united with the
proponents to form a common front.[17] Majority rule also seems to
have governed the group, decisions generally being binding

17. For a description of this period in English, see W. W. McLaren, *A Political
History of the Meiji Era, 1867–1912* (London: Scribner's, 1916). Also, Robert A.
Scalapino, *Democracy and the Party Movement in Prewar Japan: The Failure of
the First Attempt* (Berkeley: University of California Press, 1953).

when a majority had agreed to a specific decision. At any rate there emerged a collegial system of decision-making which maintained control over all major day-to-day decisions until, significantly enough, around 1900 when the *Genro* retired to participate only in major over-all decisions.[18]

The turn of the century was a critical point in the development of the civil bureaucracy. As we have seen, there emerged after 1900 new criteria of eligibility and recruitment. The criteria were directly related to the attempts to create a stable bureaucratic structure in which conflict over means and techniques of achieving major goals would be reduced to a minimum.[19] The means chosen by the leaders of the bureaucracy prior to 1900 to achieve this uniformity of outlook was uniformity of training and career. Underlying the choice of legal training was, apparently, the assumption and belief that generalist training in the method of applying the principles and specifics of law to situations of decision-making would create a corps of officials capable of functioning in a wide variety of positions, especially after passing through a period of years and offices. The consequences of this belief were reflected in the emergence of a university education in law as the basic criterion of eligibility for recruitment and the development of an upper civil service examination system emphasizing a wide knowledge of law as the chief test of performance for acquiring upper civil service rank and seniority as the major criterion for advancement. The emergence of this achievement-, generalist-, and career-oriented upper civil service undoubtedly reduced, for a time, the range of conflict over questions of techniques and technologies for achieving goals. One might well explain the continuity of Japanese political and economic development be-

18. The *Genro* is startlingly reminiscent of Thompson and Tuden's model of decision by majority judgment (James D. Thompson and Arthur Tuden, "Strategies, Structures, and Processes of Organizational Decision," in James D. Thompson, *et al.*, *Comparative Studies in Administration* [Pittsburgh: University of Pittsburgh Press, 1959], pp. 199–200).

19. It is significant that Yamagata Aritomo, one of the *Genro*, stated in 1900, "We have reached the point where laws are already highly developed, where there is little room left for arbitrary decisions by officials and where at last, administration is becoming a specialized technique" (quoted in Naikaku Kanchokyoku, *Gikai seido nanajunenshi: Kenseishi gaikan* [Tokyo: Okurasho Insatsukyoku, 1963], p. 134).

tween 1900–20 in terms of the replacement of the innovators by the university bureaucrats. As the complexity of developmental problems increased, so there emerged a group of upper civil servants and, quite probably, lower civil servants capable of handling these complexities by virtue of their uniform and extended education and their commitment to career. However, one might also suggest that it was the persistence of these criteria which, in the period after 1920, led increasingly to the failure of the civil bureaucracy externally to maintain social, political, and economic integration and to the failure internally to maintain bureaucratic integration. The increasing complexity and range of services performed by the bureaucracy after 1900 and especially after 1920 led to increasing recruitment of specialist-trained bureaucrats.[20] The increasing ineffectiveness of the civil bureaucracy, it is suggested here, may be seen in part as the consequence of a growing conflict between generalist and specialist.[21] The conflict was quite probably exacerbated by the legal focus of generalist training with its emphasis on the use of jurisprudential principles as the method for decision-making. With rapid increases, after 1920, in the number of specialists who made decisions in terms of technological or specialist expertise, the uniformity of agreement on the nature of decision-making and the facts pertinent to decision-making was shattered. The extent to which this interpretation is true, however, requires considerable research on other aspects of bureaucratic development in the period 1920–45. Nevertheless, the fact of civil bureaucratic ineffectiveness in decision-making is not essentially debatable—it is reflected in the military usurpation of decision-making in the 1930's.

Finally, several broad generalizations might also be drawn from this analysis regarding the pertinence of "legal-rational" orientations to developing and development bureaucracies. First,

20. For example, after 1920 a large number of specialist positions were created at the prefectural level. See Imperial Ordinance 248, Aug. 10, 1920; Imperial Ordinances 435, 436, Jan. 11, 1921; Imperial Ordinance 113, May 5, 1926.

21. The existence of this type of conflict in the military service has been noted by James B. Crowley, "Japanese Army Factionalism in the 1930's," *Journal of Asian Studies*, XXI (May, 1962), 309–326.

the restriction of eligibility to relatively small groups of the population in both the pre- and post-1900 periods, although on the
basis of differing criteria, suggests that in developing and even in
well-developed societies restrictions on eligibility do not necessarily hinder effective program planning and implementation.
The experience of Japan and the Communist party regimes in
China, Russia, and Eastern Europe all seems to support this
conclusion. Furthermore, in societies in which traditional orientations are still strong, it may be desirable to use traditional ascriptive-oriented criteria as the basis of eligibility so long as the
criteria are not so restrictive as to make it impossible to have a
pool large enough to provide sufficient competent personnel. Traditional social status and prestige may provide the element necessary to get traditionally oriented local leadership to accept new
programs of change.

A second generalization regarding the necessity of achievement orientation in developing and developmental bureaucracies
also appears possible. From the Japanese experience it would
seem safe to conclude that at least some of the major elements
suggested by Weber in the legal-rational type must be present,
implicitly or explicitly, if a bureaucracy is to be successful in
introducing and implementing broad programs of change. The
Japanese case also suggests that in societies undergoing the process of development, bureaucracies may possess some of the legal-
rational characteristics which, however, are masked by the continued persistence of traditional criteria of eligibility for political
and bureaucratic role performance.

Finally, the Japanese experience prior to 1900 also suggests the
possibility that ascriptive and achievement-oriented criteria for
bureaucratic role allocation are not mutually exclusive. The rise
in one need not lead, at least in some stages of development, to
reduction in the other. This would seem to be true for societies in
the early stages of political and economic development where
ascriptive criteria may continue to exist while achievement-oriented criteria emerge and become increasingly explicit. In this
case, ascriptive criteria of eligibility, for example, may delimit the
field of competition in a situation where more sophisticated and

universalistic criteria are not available or well developed. At the same time the persistence of ascriptive criteria may well reduce role conflict by using a restrictive mechanism which the majority of a traditionally oriented society understands and accepts.[22] One basic problem, thus, for students of development administration is to develop means of carefully distinguishing between criteria of eligibility and criteria for recruitment and to determine their respective political and bureaucratic functions. Else we may end up by throwing out the baby with the bath water in a situation where both may be absolutely necessary.

22. I am indebted to Fred Riggs for his suggestion with regard to the possibility that ascriptive and achievement-oriented criteria might not be mutually exclusive at certain stages of political development.

Chapter 7

Bureaucracy and Development in India

B. S. Khanna

Introduction

Problems of developing countries of Asia, Africa, and Latin America have been receiving increasing attention of the social scientists in the postwar period. The three major problems are nation-building (democratic or non-democratic), social progress, and economic growth. There is a realization among the social scientists that these problems are continuously interacting among themselves and, therefore, none of them can be studied in complete isolation, though for a deep analysis the main focus may be on any one of them. Moreover, there is also an appreciation that there is continuous interaction between the environment (both physical and social) and the various social systems (including political systems). While a social system may appear to make decisions or implement them in the light of its own knowledge, reasoning, and inclinations, these decisions and consequent actions bear varying interactions with other systems and the environment.

There are three chief constituents of a political system: (1) the citizens, the political elite, and the legislators; (2) the political executive and the bureaucracy; and (3) the judiciary. These three interact continuously with one another, while they interact, though somewhat less intensely, with other systems and the environment. Our interest here is with some aspects of the second constituent, i.e., bureaucracy. Bureaucracy itself has a number of aspects—its capability, its ethics, and its relationship with the political executive, the citizens, the political elite, the political institutions, and the judiciary. Its performance depends upon its internal capacity, its ethical standards, and the nature of this relationship and the varying degree of interaction with other social systems and environment, both internal and international.

Capability of a bureaucracy has to be studied in relation to the responsibilities and tasks which confront it. Are these primarily concerned with law and order, revenue collection, and security against external aggression, or are these also concerned with a limited degree of promotion of welfare of the citizens? Perhaps these are concerned with burgeoning and complex problems of nation-building, social progress, and economic growth among people who are underdeveloped politically, socially, and economically according to their own understanding and from the international standards which are being evolved by the international organizations and European–North American nations.

Since Independence (August, 1947) India has been engaged in the threefold development of its vast number of underdeveloped inhabitants. Nation-building processes along democratic lines are being accompanied increasingly by bold and gigantic measures for social progress and economic growth in a semitraditional society of a huge size. These present great and complex challenges to the government, political elite, and the people of the country. Bureaucracy is one of the chief instruments in the hands of the government to deal with these challenges of new political process and socio-economic development. Hence, it will be instructive to study the capability of this instrument to play its role, both old and new. Emphasis will be upon changes in the structure and recruitment of the bureaucracy as these affect its talent and skills as well as its morale and development orientation.[1]

1. The literature on modern India's administrative system, while not yet voluminous, is quite extensive. A general analysis integrating historical forces with contemporary problems is Ralph Braibanti, "Reflections on Bureaucratic Reform in India," in Braibanti and Joseph J. Spengler, eds., *Administration and Economic Development in India* (Durham, N.C.: Duke University Press, 1953), pp. 3–69. See also Hugh Tinker, "Structure of the British Imperial Heritage"; Bernard S. Cohn, "Recruitment and Training of British Civil Servants in India, 1600–1860"; David C. Potter, "Bureaucratic Change in India"; chaps. 2 (pp. 23–87), 3 (pp. 87–141), and 4 (pp. 141–209), respectively, in Ralph Braibanti and Associates, *Asian Bureaucratic Systems Emergent from the British Imperial Tradition* (Durham, N.C.: Duke University Press, 1966).

Public bureaucracy in India is comprised of a number of constituents—Union government bureaucracy, state government bureaucracy (sixteen states at present), local authorities bureaucracy, quasi-government bodies bureaucracy. In 1963 the numerical strength was as follows:

Union government employees	2,406,200
State government employees	3,317,600
Quasi-government bodies employees	1,062,800
Local bodies employees	1,682,100
Total	8,268,700

Source: Statistical Abstract of India.

This essay will confine itself to changes in a segment of the Union
bureaucracy and state bureaucracy. This segment includes the
personnel engaged in administrative executive and housekeeping
activities relating to the policies and programs of the Union and
state governments. In 1963, within the Union bureaucracy, for
instance, 330,953 out of 2,406,200 were thus engaged. The exact
number of such employees under the state government is not
known at present.

Features of the Civil Services before Independence

From the mid-eighties of the eighteenth century the British in
India began to build a new system of civil services, and this
process was practically completed by the second decade of the
present century. While the British approach was mostly pragmatic, there was some impact on this process from two sources at
least—the basic characteristics of the Mogul system of bureaucracy and the thinking of the Utilitarians in England about the
role of the government and the position of the individual.

1. Initially the only civil service organized was a multifunctional, higher-echelon, generalist civil service which was needed
for the chief purposes of maintenance of law and order and
collection of taxes. This civil service, called the Covenanted Civil
Service in the beginning but later named the Indian Civil Service
(ICS), was at the apex of the other civil services which were
formed later and set the general tone and style for the Indian

administration as a whole. In the course of time it began to be recruited on the basis of a stiff competitive examination held exclusively in Britain for which Indians were made eligible from 1853. Remaining mostly British in its social makeup, it was highly trained both at the universities and in the practice of administration. A member of this civil service had a good deal of spatial mobility along with vertical mobility. In charge of a local administration, he could later move between provincial government departments and central government administration or local administration. He enjoyed great prestige, very attractive terms of employment, and a good deal of administrative power and discretion. A substantial degree of intellectualism and integrity characterized many members of this elite corps.

2. The other higher civil services, formed from the second half of the nineteenth century, were, like the ICS, mostly recruited in Britain on the basis of merit. They were well trained to carry on their specialized tasks, which were not of great complexity or magnitude in those days of laissez faire and limited government through foreign rule in India. Liberal terms of employment attracted many able young men from the British universities and to a smaller extent from the Indian universities. Their prestige and power were high, though they took a secondary place in an administration where the dominant place went to the ICS. Control over them was shared between the secretary of state for India in London and the central government in India.

3. Middle-level civil servants also began to appear in the nineteenth century, both for general administrative tasks and specialized tasks. Organized into well-knit services in the closing decades of the nineteenth century, they were recruited in India itself. While they included a few British, their social makeup was mostly Indian. Their training and terms of employment were well regulated. Their prestige and power, though less than that of the first two categories, were substantial.

4. The lower civil servants, concerned with clerical, minor, and semiskilled work, were considered to be of inferior rank by the first three categories but enjoyed prestige among the people. They were a part of a powerful bureaucratic system and the

common man came more in contact with them than with the higher categories of civil servants. Their standards of integrity were less inflexible.

5. The higher civil services served as an integrative factor of considerable importance in a very extensive and highly populated country. Administrative unity of the country, maintenance of law and order, reasonable standards of integrity, systemization of the tax system, and also formalization of the relationship between the administration and the people in place of arbitrary dealings as in the past were the main achievements of the civil services. Besides, the civil services came to be interested in the construction of public works (roads, railways, canals, etc.), as well as in the development of public social services (education, hospitals, etc.).

6. Power was highly centralized within the bureaucracy. It lay largely in the hands of the ICS and partly in the hands of the other higher civil services. Despite the recommendations of a royal commission in the first decade of the twentieth century, no significant deconcentration of powers within the bureaucracy took place. Moreover, there being no elected political executive and rarely an elected legislative body (even after the reforms of 1909 there was only a very weak legislature), the higher bureaucracy's power regarding formulation of public policies and the administration of these policies was great (though not altogether unrestrained). The British Parliament was too busy with other matters to spend much time and energy in scrutiny of the work of the Indian bureaucracy. The secretary of state for India (a British minister), assisted by a number of advisors, was too distantly situated from India to exercise any effective control. Members of the governor-general's councils, many of the governors, and the members of the governors' councils were drawn from the ICS and were therefore not averse to the concentration of power in the hands of the higher bureaucracy. There were, however, some restraints on the bureaucratic power in the form of judicial review of administrative action, both in the context of the existing laws and in the provisions of the Constitutional Acts passed by the British Parliament.

7. The higher bureaucracy (especially the ICS) operated under a number of restraints. Since it was a part of an alien imperial administration, it could not undertake any steps which were inconsistent with the British imperial interests or which did not seem to be acceptable to the majority of the inhabitants of India—not a difficult requirement, since political and social consciousness was low as a result of inadequate politicization and the near absence of strong political organizations. Moreover, since the bureaucracy was not motivated by any nationally oriented political elite in power, its only source of inspiration was from within itself, despite the high standards of intellectualism with the ICS. No wonder, then, that social change and economic growth in the country took place at a slow tempo in the largely traditional and static Indian society.

The higher bureaucracy, especially, was not sympathetic—even antipathetic at times—to the participation of the representatives of the Indian people in the government and administration of the country. They saw in this a threat to their own power; their protest against it was based on their argument that the Indians were not fit to man the key positions in the administration and to share substantially in the power of law-making, the public purse, and overseeing administration. This highly conservative attitude toward the political advancement of the country was a further deficiency of the bureaucracy.

Growth of Self-Government and Transformation in the Civil Services

From 1919 to 1947 the pace of political and constitutional developments in the country began to quicken. The Constitution Act of 1919 first brought a portion of provincial administration under the substantial control of the Indian ministers and the general direction of the reorganized provincial legislatures. This process was carried forward by the Act of 1935 when the whole provincial administration came under a greater extent of political control. Provision also was made for a similar change in the central administration. This necessitated the replacement of many of the existing higher imperial services that had been recruited and controlled mostly by the secretary of state by higher central and provincial services, now controlled by the central and provincial governments within India. Most recruitment to these services began to take place in India, though recruitment to a few of these continued partially in Britain. Indians began to enter these services in increasing numbers, so that a change in the racial makeup of the services that affected even the social composition of the ICS began to take place. This process of the transfer of administration to Indian control brought the Indian bureaucracy face to face with the Indian politicians who formed the political executive and indirectly into contact with politicians in the legislatures and outside. Protection of civil servants against the excesses of politicians was provided not only in the Constitution but in the strong tradition of the services themselves. The civil services were exhorted to adjust themselves to the new constitutional setup, but complete adjustments were not always easily effected in a satisfactory manner.

Second, the standards and orientations of the bureaucracy began to be affected by the increasing tempo of the national agitation for independence. The political sea was no longer calm, and political struggles created ripples and later storms. The civil services were under strong political challenge. Although some within them were confused, and a few sympathized with the nationalist struggles outside, while others acted as pliant tools of repression in the hands of an imperial power struggling to retain its hold, some became the architects of the repressive policy and action. This weakened the internal unity of the civil service, sapped its vitality, and brought down its prestige among the people.

In the third place, interreligious rivalries and disorders accompanied the last stages of the Indian struggle against the British imperial rule and began to bring the neutrality of the civil service under some shadow of distrust. By fixing quotas of recruitment on a communal basis and by making it a consideration in promotion to higher posts within the administration, the standards of the civil services were diluted.

World War II also exerted an impact on the composition and standards of the civil services. Stoppage of recruitment in Britain brought the British quota practically to an end. Overwork told on standards. The great increase in the bureaucracy recruited on an *ad hoc* basis brought about a weakening of ethical standards. The independence of the country accompanied by its partition weakened the numerical strength of those available to the higher bureaucracy. The exodus of Europeans and many Moslems from the civil services of India, especially the higher ones, marked this period. This decline in numerical strength of the higher bureaucracy was bound to affect administrative efficiency.

In short, independent India inherited a bureaucracy efficient in its limited tasks, conservative in orientation, weakened by communalism, distrusted by the politicians for having served as the tool of the dying imperialism, somewhat authoritative in its attitude within as well as to the people, and weakened in the ranks at its higher levels.

Civil Services after Independence

The new governments of independent India not only had to deal with immediate complicated political problems but also had to devote attention to the pressing problems of consolidation and some reorganization of public administration. Special recruitment of experienced persons from outside the administration and quick promotion of subordinates to superior administrative positions were undertaken to fill the gaps in the higher civil services created by the exodus of the European and Moslem civil servants. Some controversy about the suitability of this new personnel for coping with complex administrative responsibilities developed.

A second problem related to unrest among the civil servants (including many of the middle level and almost all of the lower level) was because of deteriorating purchasing power of their salaries caused by the inflationary trends set into motion by the Second World War and continuing into the postwar period. The Union government and several of the state governments appointed inquiry bodies and then adopted measures to implement many of their recommendations for the improvement of the terms of employment of the civil servants. Things did not work out very satisfactorily because of the further rises in prices. Morale of the employees of the government suffered by the worries caused by the rise in prices, which subjected the low-paid especially to hardships.

A third personnel problem concerned the integration of the personnel systems of over five hundred princely states into the personnel system of the rest of India consequent to the redrawing of the political map of the country and the mergers of these states into what used to be called British India. The personnel systems in most of the princely states were underdeveloped and their reorganization to fit into the national personnel system was neither easy nor free from tensions among the personnel concerned.

A fourth main problem related to the lack of an adequate adjustment of position and of understanding between the civil servants on the one side and the political elite, especially the ministers, legislators, and office-bearers of the ruling political party (the Indian National Congress), on the other. The civil servants had served as the strong arm of the British imperial power and had adopted an attitude of superiority (which varied according to their status) in their dealings with politicians, intelligentsia, and the common man. Thanks to the leadership of some imaginative and progressive politicians and administrators, adjustments between the civil servants and the ministers as well as the political elite began to be attempted.

In 1950–52 two very significant developments began in the country. The Constitution of India was inaugurated in January, 1950, while the first general elections in the infant but very populous country took place in 1951–52. Processes of politicization on democratic lines began to produce political articulation, political recruitment, political pressures, and political tensions in increasing degree, which had an important bearing on the civil services. They were no longer to function in a political milieu of complacency as before 1921 or of agitation as between 1921 and the date of the country's independence (August 15, 1947). They were now to function in the context of political control by ministers, of their accountability to the legislature through the cabinet, of increasing public discussions and criticisms about administration, and of political rivalries among various groups and of general political pressures.

The second development related to the formulation and introduction of the first five-year plan in 1951 with a total investment of 33.6 billion rupees—the share of the public sector being 15.6 billion rupees. This was followed by a second plan in 1956 with an investment of double the size of the first plan; this was succeeded by a third plan with an investment nearly equal to the first two plans. The basic objectives of these plans were to bring about social and economic change by planned development in order to reduce poverty and social backwardness. This has posed a continuous and increasing challenge to the political elite and the bureaucracy. No longer can the administration be concerned largely with law and order and tax collection, but it has to undertake complex, burgeoning, and new responsibilities.

The question of bringing about changes and modifications within the bureaucracy and administrative organizations has aroused the attention not only of the Planning Commission for the five-year plans but also of the legislatures, which have had, however, only vague and at times contradictory views on it. Foreign experts brought in to observe Indian efforts at socioeconomic change have also made suggestions for administrative changes. Both Indian administrators and scholars have been thinking, though not very dynamically in many cases, about the problems of administrative reforms.

The government of India, partly on its own initiative and partly under the pressure of legislative and public comments and criticisms, has appointed committees and commissions to inquire into either the specific problems of administrative inadequacies or the general problems of administrative reorganizations. The recommendations made by them, as well as by some administrators in governmental agencies themselves, have led to a number of changes in the administrative organizations and the bureaucracies. These administrative changes have not been altogether satisfactory. The lack of extensive research and evaluations in the field of public administration that might throw up new and bold ideas of reforms, the inability of most of the members of the inquiry bodies to think outside the set concepts and contours of an administration with a long past, and the traditional conservatism of an Indian bureaucracy which is unwilling to implement the recommendations of the inquiry bodies both in letter and spirit—these are responsible for this state of affairs.

It is now possible to examine critically the changes in the structures and the recruitment of a part of the bureaucracy.

Structure

The civil services serving under the Union government and the state governments are officially classified as: (1) All-India Services, (2) Central (Union) Services, and (3) State Civil Services. The civil service which occupies key positions in the administration both under the Union and state governments is the Indian Administrative Service (IAS). This generalist and multifunctional service is the sum total of cadres allotted to various state governments. The Union government draws the number of officers it needs from the state cadres in which a definite provision has been made to send IAS officers on deputation to the Union government. The IAS civil servants perform not only higher administrative functions but also higher executive functions. While in Britain the generalist civil servants (called the administrative class) perform only administrative functions, both in India and Pakistan (the Civil Service of Pakistan) the administrative and executive functions are combined in the same generalist civil service. This combination of the two functions adds to the richness of the administrative experience of the generalist civil servant. The remnants of the ICS have been merged into the IAS.

Within the structure of the civil services two main changes have been taking place in recent years. First, there has been a continuous increase in the numerical strength of each class and in that of most of the civil services within each class. This increase may be illustrated by a reference to the figures regarding the IAS and the total number of employees of the Union government services excluding the railways and the Indian mission abroad. The total expenditure for the salaries and allowances of the civil servants has also been enlarged with the increase in their numbers and the raising of allowances to compensate for the rise in prices. This can be illustrated by reference to the expenditure increase for Union government employees for which figures are readily available.

Table 1. *Number of Union (Central) Government Employees (Excluding Railways and Indian Mission Abroad)*

	Administrative and executive	Clerical (commonly called ministerial)
1950	51,860	132,003
1960	79,292	251,661

Source: Statistical Abstract of India.

Table 2. *Indian Administrative Service*

	Sanctioned	Actual
1948	803	—
1964 (December)	2,470	2,145

Source: Estimates Committee, 93rd Report.

Table 3. *Pay for All Union Government Employees (Excluding Railways) in Rupees (millions)*

	Amount of pay and allowances	Total civil expenditures
1956–57	873.5	4,699.7
1960–61	1,352.3	9,541.5
1965–66 (revised)	2,317.2	15,058.7

Note: 1 Rs is equal to 1/15 dollar.
Source: Estimates Committee, 93rd Report.

The increase in the numerical strength of the civil services is mostly due to the continual increase in the scale of administrative activity. The bigger and bigger developmental plans and programs as provided in the successive five-year plans have been the underlying cause. Only to a small extent does it reflect the increase in population of the country and the political reorganization of the map of India in 1948 when the civil services of the princely states were merged (as a result of the political reintegration of the country) into the civil services of the rest of India.

The second important change which has taken place in the structure of the civil services is the growing and rapid specialization of high and medium skills. Not only more specialists of existing types are needed but specialists of new types are also increasingly needed. For instance, the number of statisticians needed by Union government departments increased substantially during the last several years, and in 1966 a new civil service—called the Indian Statistical Service with a cadre strength of 185—was constituted. Again, the demand for specialists in engineering, forestry, and medical sciences on the part of both the Union and the state governments has been increasing so rapidly that joint civil services (commonly called the All-India Services) —the Indian Medical and Health Service, Indian Forest Service, and Indian Service of Engineers—were set up in 1966 in place of small and separate Union and state services in these fields of specialization. These are some indications of the growth of specialization taking place within the civil services so that they can handle the increasingly complex developmental tasks.

We may now discuss a number of questions relating to the structure of civil services in terms of the needs of development administration.

1. Is the supply of qualified manpower adequate for the needs of the rapidly expanding structures of the civil services? While there is no difficulty in finding an adequate supply of manpower for the generalist, semispecialist, and specialist positions at the middle and lower levels of civil services, it is becoming less easy to find able persons in adequate number for the higher generalist posts and still more so for higher specialist posts, especially in

certain categories. The educational system has been expanding substantially in the country in recent years, but the expansion of the facilities for high scientific, technical, and specialized education remains inadequate, in terms of the rapidly expanding demand, for such types of university-educated persons from public enterprises and private industrial undertakings, along with the increasing demand for them from the civil services. The higher civil services do not have the prestige or the attractive terms of employment they had in the past; hence it is not surprising that they no longer attract so large a share of available talent as before.

Accordingly, three steps have been taken in recent years. One is the setting up of an Institute of Applied Manpower Research on the initiative of the government of India. On the basis of research into the country's total need of specialized personnel over a period of time for both the private sector and the public sector, it tenders advice to the Planning Commission, and the authorities concerned with the manipulation of the educational facilities, for providing the supply of required personnel in the country.

The second step taken relates to the establishment of the Directorate of Manpower within the Union Ministry of Home Affairs which is concerned with personnel management problems of the Union government directly and of the state governments indirectly. This directorate is concerned with guiding the various departments of the Union and state governments in drawing up comprehensive manpower plans for meeting their needs over a period of time. At the state level, too, units of manpower planning have been set up within the administration. But the units in many of the states have not been active in formulating integrated manpower plans or collaborating with the Union Directorate of Manpower and the Institute of Applied Manpower Research in a meaningful way. Moreover, there has been little liaison between the administrative manpower planning units and the educational authorities and universities.

A third measure is the creation of the Pool of Indian Scientists

and Technologists in 1958, chiefly for providing temporary place-
ment of well-qualified Indian scientists and technologists returning from abroad. The total strength of the pool is five hundred at
present. This pool provides scientific and technical manpower not
only to the governments and public enterprises but also to private
undertakings in need of highly qualified personnel.

2. Does the existence of too many civil services stand in the
way of the growth of an adequate professional sense of unification among civil servants that hinders effective teamwork among
them? Some critics are of the view that the existence of many
organized civil services within each class (I, II, III) tends to
generate some feeling of parochialism among the civil servants
belonging to each of these services.[2] There seems to be substance
in this view, for even the civil servants themselves complain of
the existence of service and class consciousness among themselves. This is apt to generate jealousies and a feeling of separate-
ness which is injurious to teamwork among civil servants engaged
in developmental work. Paul Appleby and a number of other
observers have suggested the formation of one common higher
civil service with different wings and a common system of recruitment, uniform terms of employment, and equal professional perquisites and rights. Mobility of personnel could take place among
wings providing that the person had suitable qualifications, aptitude, and willingness.[3]

The higher non-specialist civil service of France has four wings
—general administration, social administration, economic and financial administration, and foreign service. Recruitment and
training are carried on jointly, differentiation of candidates takes
place during the second half of the period of training, and terms
of employment are uniform.

All five All-India Services could be constituted in a higher civil
service with different wings, while all Class I civil services could
constitute a higher Union civil service or state civil service. Even

2. A. K. Chanda, *Indian Administration* (London: Allen and Unwin, 1958);
see also Paul H. Appleby, *Public Administration in India: Report of a Survey*
(New Delhi, 1953).
3. *Ibid.*

now entry is the same—by competition through examinations and tests conducted by the Public Service Commissions. Uniform syllabuses could be evolved easily.

While much of the training of Class I civil servants is now under one roof, the National Academy of Administration, terms of employment and professional perquisites could be standardized. If the experiment proved successful in promoting better teamwork and lessening of interservice jealousies, it could then be applied to Class II and even Class III civil services, hopefully generating a feeling of unification among all the civil servants.

3. What are the implications of the increasing number of All-India Services? Only two All-India Services (under different names) out of the four were retained after independence. However, a provision in the Constitution made it possible for the government to create more All-India Services on the basis of the mutual agreement between the Union and state governments. Thus three new All-India Services (Indian Medical and Health Service, Indian Service of Engineers, and Indian Forest Service) have recently been brought into existence, and two more (Indian Agriculture Service and Indian Education Service) are likely to be formed in the near future if the present negotiations between the Union government and the state governments succeed.[4] These steps have been taken to supply highly qualified personnel to both the state and Union governments. Earlier some of the state governments failed to obtain high-quality personnel largely on account of stereotyped and timid personnel policies and practices. If a uniformly attractive salary is offered, if the gate of entry is the same (the Union Public Service Commission as the selecting agency), if the basic disciplinary control is in the hands of the Union government, which enjoys a higher reputation for impartiality than several state governments, more adequate numbers of highly qualified personnel are likely to be attracted to the public administration of the country as a whole. Moreover, the utilization of these personnel will tend to be more effective for developmental tasks for they can be moved back and forth from

4. Ministry of House Affairs, *Annual Report, 1964–65* (New Delhi: Government of India, 1965).

the Union level to the state level or from one state to the other as the needs of various developmental projects and programs demand. Furthermore, the existence of an All-India Service in preference to both a number of state services and a Union service concerned with the same field of specialization will provide better promotional avenues to civil servants and will act as an incentive to good work. Moreover, the formation of All-India cadres provides opportunities for the rotation of personnel between the Union government and the state governments, thereby adding to the richness of their professional experience, which, in its turn, tends to improve the efficiency of the administration.

Some, including legislators, have also welcomed the formation of these All-India Services on another ground.[5] As politicization has proceeded in India since independence, and more particularly after the inauguration of the new constitution, political articulation of new regional and local groups has tended to increase regional and local pulls, retarding the growth of a national consensus. The role of solidarity-making in the country, which is mainly the responsibility of the governing political elite, is reinforced by having a few civil services which, being recruited and controlled by the Union government and being mobile across the state boundaries within the country, have an All-India loyalty and outlook.

On the other hand, most of those who believe in strong federalism in an extensive and densely populated country like India believe also that the formation of additional All-India Services weakens the requisite autonomy of the constituent states within the Indian polity. Members of these services look up to the Union government first and cannot be expected to be scrupulously loyal to the state governments which exercise only day-to-day control over them. In keeping with the idea of semiautonomous states in a federal system, the higher rungs of state administration should be manned by personnel recruited and controlled by the state government.

In balance, the administrative advantages of having a certain

5. Estimates Committee (1965–66), *93rd Report on Ministry of Home Affairs Public Services* (New Delhi: Lok Sabha Secretariat, 1966).

number of All-India Services outweigh any political detraction from the system of federalism. The availability of high quality, developmental skills, and the integrative value associated with these All-India Services are very crucial in a developing country. If the existence of All-India Services affects the political division of power within the federal system, the developmental gains are still very high, even in terms of any political detraction from the powers of the states.

4. Is there enough spatial, vertical, and horizontal mobility within the civil services to provide enrichment of experience and also incentives for good work? Within the civil services there is a substantial degree of spatial mobility. The members of many Class I and Class II services especially are transferred periodically from the district (local) administration to the regional and headquarters agencies and vice versa. There is also movement from state administration to Union administration in regard to the All-India Services and some state services. This spatial mobility has two advantages. It is enriching and refreshing for civil servants to move from one area to the other; it is also conducive to the maintenance of the impartiality of administration—the higher- and middle-level personnel do not develop strong links with an area or with any of the groups of people living within it.

In terms of developmental requirements, however, too much spatial mobility is not desirable. Development projects and programs require a longer time for execution than in the past when they were of smaller dimensions and represented limited financial investment. If the higher personnel in charge are transferred frequently, responsibility for proper execution of the projects cannot be fixed in a definite manner. Evasion of responsibility and inadequacy of commitment have been complained of in recent years, which has led to some reviews of the practice of transfers and resulted in the important personnel staying at one place, so far as possible, for the duration of a five-year plan.

Automatic transfer of the generalist civil servants from one agency to the other is no longer desirable because developmental tasks require some elementary specialization even among non-specialized personnel. It is preferable to have "linking" of experience by restricting the movement of the generalist civil servants within agencies that have some common elements. For instance, the agencies of health, education, and welfare can be grouped together for the purposes of interagency transfers that provide a "linking experience"; transfers of the generalist civil servant from the education department to the agriculture department would not do this. If, however, the generalists can be put into a unified service with different wings, as suggested earlier, this type of "linking experience" will take place automatically.

Vertical mobility between one class of civil services and another has been improving in recent years. Twenty-five per cent of the vacancies in the IAS are now filled by promotion from the state generalist civil service (called the state administrative service), while 20 per cent of the vacancies in the ICS were allotted to the provincial administrative service in the past. Again, quotas set aside for promotion from several of the Class II services to the requisite Class I services both at the center and in the states are bigger than before, though these differ from one state to another and also from one civil service to another. This change has provided more incentive within the civil services, and has tended to provide some social bridge between the higher and subordinate services where the social distance tends to be larger than in a developed country because of the big disparity in pay scales and powers.

The vertical promotional avenues do not, however, seem to satisfy the civil servants at the subordinate positions. They ask for a larger quota for promotion and a smaller one for direct recruitment to the higher levels of civil services. On the other hand, there are some who warn against such bigger quotas for promotion on the ground that this would dilute the quality of the personnel as well as increase inbreeding within the civil services. Nevertheless, there seems to be justification for more liberalization of promotional quotas, particularly through a well-planned training program. Promotion at the higher levels could be mostly by merit, while at the middle levels seniority indicative of administrative experience could continue as an important consideration along with merit.

5. Does the increase in the number and importance of the specialists within the Indian administration create any problem of adjustment between them and the higher generalist civil servants? There are frequent indications of a growing restlessness among the specialists over the traditional hegemony of the generalists in the Indian administration; but there is less than in the past when the ICS dominated all the civil services working within this administration. The IAS civil servants are less rigid, less snobbish, and less assertive of their position than were those of the ICS because there has been more than one gate of entry into the IAS; the new officers have been educated in the postindependence social atmosphere, fewer of them come from privileged families, and more of them possess science degrees than the members of the ICS had. But the specialists today are also more conscious than before of the significance of their respective skills that show various levels of sophistication which are needed for the execution of development projects and programs.

This enhanced feeling of position is not only true for the higher specialist civil servants in the IAS, but is also true, in varying degrees, for middle-level specialist civil servants both in state-level administrative agencies and field administration (commonly called the district administration). A similar situation exists in the new developmental bureaucracy in the rural areas (the Block Development Officer competing with the block level specialists). Two steps seem to be indicated in regard to hierarchical rearrangements. Direct dialogue should be possible between the specialist civil servant and the generalist civil servant without the intervention of the large secretarial staff. The latter, through its lengthy noting of comments, creates a certain administrative stuffiness and even some distortion of the original proposals, which hinder good understanding between the two. Also, it should be possible for the specialist civil servant to have direct access to the minister in charge of the agency both for general discussions and for explanations of his point of view when he and the generalist civil servant disagree on an important matter. The generalist civil servant has an access to the minister since he generally advises him on departmental policies and programs.

There has been an improvement in the emoluments and perquisites of the specialist civil servants at the center as a result of the recommendations of the lay commissions, especially of the second one (the DAS Commission reporting in 1959), that brings these almost to the level of those of the generalist civil servant. However, in many states this development has not taken place and the specialist civil servants suffer from sullenness and jealousy because of the better financial position of the generalist civil servants. Actually, it takes longer and involves higher investment of funds for a specialist to complete his education and training than is the case for the generalist. The importance of the skills of the specialists to several types of administrative projects has also increased. There is thus no known reason for his being paid less than the generalist civil servant of the same level within the hierarchy.

Finally, the civil service rules relating to the Union administration and several state administrations make a provision for the appointment of some outsiders to any level of civil service on a contractual basis for a period of time. Up to now, no substantial use of this provision has been made. The provision allows men of high entrepreneurial skills, or men with a special knowledge of and commitment to a certain developmental program, to be brought into the services. Such men have been very useful to the American administration, but in India their utility has not been fully realized. Yet the need is greater in a developing country in which the governmental administration plays a more crucial role in development than it does in a developed country. The conservatism of the civil services and their fear about their own position and prospects have brought forth their resistance, both direct and subtle, against the appointment of outsiders who have distinguished themselves as experts in non-governmental fields of activity. Moreover, the practice of referring all important appointments to public service commissions, either for recruitment or for approval, discourages many such experts from offering their periodic services to the administration in the interest of promotion of the developmental tempo in certain fields of activity.

It is also to be noted that political stresses and strains as well as rival political demands have continued to increase in India in recent years. The processes of political socialization and political articulation are taking place among wider sections of people—most of whom are inadequately educated and many of whom suffer from certain political allergies and prejudices because of traditional ideas or poverty. The civil servant finds himself subjected to more political demands and pressures in recent years than he did in the preindependence days. Thus, his political neutrality may suffer or much of his time may be spent resolving political tensions and disputes regarding administrative matters and projects. The few ministers do not have sufficient time and energy to deal with the situation. The American practice that has Schedule C appointments, made partly on political grounds to provide a shield for the career civil servants engaged in administrative activities, needs to be seriously considered by some Indian states on an experimental basis. It may make some feel that India is adopting a restricted version of the spoils system. Yet it seems desirable to try this experiment in the interest of making administration more effective in the midst of growing political pressures and for shielding the career civil servants against any political aggrandisement.

Recruitment

The structure of a civil service is given meaning and substance by its personnel. Recruitment thus complements structure. The bases for direct recruitment to the higher-level and middle-level civil services (both generalist and specialist) in India are: (1) equality of opportunity for public employment, (2) semiautonomous commission for conducting recruitment, and (3) recruitment of persons who have just finished their education and are still in their early youth.

Equality of Opportunity for Public Employment

Article 16 of the Indian Constitution states that there is to be equality of opportunity for public employment, irrespective of religion, caste, sex, or place of residence within the country. This *eg.* constitutes an important step toward the implementation of the principle of merit as the basis of recruitment to civil services which form an important and comprehensive segment of public employment in India. Earlier there was reservation of certain percentages of posts in civil services (as in the case of membership of the legislatures) for Moslems and other important religious minorities. For recruitment to the state civil services there was also the condition that to be eligible for it a person must have lived for a prescribed number of years within the boundaries of the state concerned. These two considerations tended to detract from the principle of merit as the basis of recruitment. Their disappearance as the result of constitutional and legal provisions contributes to the efficiency of civil services since recruitment to them can be on the basis of a more rigorous and open competition than before.

For a temporary period, however, there is a small reservation in certain civil services for the Anglo-Indians in order to afford them time to have occupational adjustments instead of depending mostly on certain sectors of public employment. More important than this, however, is the reservation of appointments in almost all services under the Union government and the state governments for the members of the two socially depressed classes of Indians—the scheduled castes and the scheduled tribes. The Union government, for instance, has fixed 12.5 per cent and 5 per cent of posts in civil services for the members of these two *affirmative action* social classes so long as their appointment does not cause any injury to the efficiency of administration. In actual practice, there is so much political pressure in regard to the filling of the prescribed minimum quota of posts by members of these classes that not enough attention is paid to the question of the maintenance of administrative efficiency. In the interest of administrative efficiency, it is hoped that using recruitment to civil services as a lever for the social uplift of the scheduled castes and tribes will not last for long.

Public Service Commission

The Constitution of India has tried to provide for strengthening the position of the Public Service Commission, which came into existence from the mid-twenties of this century onward. At present there is a Union Public Service Commission and a number of state public service commissions. Their functions can be divided into two main categories: (1) to advise the government regarding rules and regulations concerning recruitment and structure and discipline of civil services as well as in regard to specific cases of promotion and discipline, and (2) to conduct recruitment tests and examinations for various posts and to recommend candidates for appointment under the government. These functions are not so extensive as in the case of the American Civil Service Commission, as some aspects of public personnel management are outside the direct purview of the commissions of India.

Members of the commissions are appointed by the president for the Union Public Service Commission and by the governor for state public service commissions. Half of them are to be, according to the Constitution, from among those who have had at least ten years' experience in public employment, since this would insure possession of administrative experience among a substantial number of the members. Members have been drawn not only from the field of public employment but from the fields of politics, business, professions, and education. There has been a complaint that sometimes the appointments to vacancies in the state public service commissions have been made not on merit but on the basis of political considerations. The result has been that such appointees have not displayed strict standards of integrity but have submitted occasionally to the influence of a state government or a powerful political lobby. Since the opportunities for employment are restricted in India and the number of candidates in need of jobs tends to be increasingly large, pulls and pressures are exerted by the influential ones to get jobs for their protégés or relatives. A public service commission in India, therefore, must operate in the midst of such pressures, and it is important that its members should have inflexible standards of integrity. A suggestion has been made in certain quarters that the president of India, who alone at present has the power of removing a member of any public service commission in India, should also be empowered to make appointments to the state public service commissions as he does in the case of the Union Public Service Commission. If this is thought to be out of tune with federalism in the country, the alternative can be that the governor should make appointments to a public service commission without consulting the chief minister of the state. In short, in the interest of better recruitment, the members of the state public service commissions need to be selected with more care than has occasionally been the case.

The work of every public service commission has grown rapidly as more posts have to be filled because of the rapid expansion in the size of the administrative system. But the commission has not been able to cope with it effectively, with the result that long delays have occurred at times in filling civil service appointments. An increase in the membership of the commission and in its secretarial staff seems to deserve more attention on the part of the government concerned than has been the case so far. Nor have the commissions made adequate use of research in the field of behavioral sciences to reorient their testing and examining techniques as much as seems to be indicated in view of the need for probing into the personal traits of candidates, besides their skills and formal qualifications.

Development administration requires speedy and sophisticated testing in the recruitment of specialists. For this purpose the public service commissions and the governments need to review the existing recruitment arrangements. It appears that a public service commission should be strengthened numerically and reorganized functionally so that it can play an effective role in recruitment for an expanding and changing administrative system.

It was Macaulay, toward the middle of the nineteenth century, who put forward the idea that the higher administrative service (then called the Covenanted Civil Service and later the ICS) should draw its candidates from among those who had given an evidence of intellectual brightness in one academic field or another. This idea was adopted and the recruiting competitive examination was modeled in such a way as to provide for testing the candidates in their respective fields of education. Over the years these arrangements have continued with certain minor modifications made from time to time.

The educational background of the candidates who have been successful in the IAS and allied services examinations reflects these recruiting policies. The allied services include the Indian Foreign Service and a number of other higher Union generalist and semigeneralist services. It has been found that in 1961–62, of 116 persons selected for IAS and IFS and 256 selected for the Indian Police and Union Services the educational background was as follows:

	IAS and IFS	IPS and Other Services	Total
M.A./B.A. (Honors)/B.A.	92	202	294
M.Sc./B.Sc. (Honors)/B.Sc.	20	34	54
M.Com./B.Com. (Honors)/B.Com.	4	13	17
Law degree	—	7	7
Total	116	256	372

Source: Union Public Services Commission (1961–62), Twelfth Report (New Delhi, 1962).

Out of the total number of candidates (372), 211 appeared with British history as one of the optional subjects, 130 with Indian history, 169 with political science, 113 with general economics, 112 with international law, 30 with English literature, 16 with pure mathematics, and 14 with statistics. The number of candidates who offered each of the remaining subjects was less than 10. Furthermore, out of the 116 candidates recommended for IAS and IFS who had taken two additional options, 40 appeared with political theory as an optional subject, 38 with

European history, 28 with constitutional history of Britain, 24 with advanced Indian economics, 22 with Indian history, 18 with political organization and public administration, 17 with advanced economics, and 11 with ancient Indian civilization and philosophy. The number of candidates who offered each of the remaining subjects included in the syllabus was less than 10.

This analysis shows that the overwhelming majority of candidates had university degrees and had taken up subjects in the fields of social sciences, history, and English literature. The science graduates and the candidates taking up science subjects in the competitive examination were fewer. This has made some observers remark that the examination syllabuses seemed to be oriented more to the arts subjects than to the science subjects. This, coupled with the lesser number of candidates with qualifications in science appearing in the examination, has restricted the entry of such persons into the IAS and the semigeneralist civil services. These observers feel that since even the general administrators and other generalist civil servants have to make decisions which may concern knowledge of the utility of science for developmental projects, the syllabuses should be remodeled to "afford a fair chance to students with scientific background" and the supplementary interview should be reoriented to test scientific knowledge of the candidates. There is a good deal of substance to this viewpoint. It can also be supported on the basis of the additional argument that if general administrators and specialists are to get on well in the interest of administrative teamwork, among the several measures which can make it easier is the induction of science graduates into general administration on the basis of either initial recruitment or later transfer.

It has also been pointed out that the educational qualifications and the general intellectual caliber of the successful candidates in the examination have shown a tendency to decline over the years. The intake of candidates for the IAS and the semigeneralist higher Union services has increased because of the expanding numerical strength of civil service. The following figures have been cited in support of this view:

	1960	1961	1962	1963
Number of B.A./B.Sc. and M.A./M.Sc. passing out of Indian universities	99,967	113,646	121,822	N.A.
Number of applicants for combined competitive examination for IAS and other generalist civil service	10,376	9,182	8,432	7,113
Number actually appearing in the competitive examination	5,873	5,659	5,391	4,282
Number of candidates possessing Class I out of the number appearing in the competitive examination	634	593	527	N.A.
Number of candidates recommended for appointment by the commissions	338	440	480	457

Source: Estimates Committee, 93rd Report (New Delhi, Lok Sabha, 1965–66).

While the intake of candidates has increased, the number of those competing with Class I degrees has been going down. This seems to support the viewpoint of the Union Public Service Commission that there is a qualitative decline among the candidates in spite of the increase in graduates from the universities. While the long-term remedy lies in improving university education in the country, other remedies include the elimination of delays in recruitment and actual appointment, and improvement of the terms of employment, both in view of the inflationary trends and the attractiveness of the terms offered by the private sector.

There are two important problems in regard to the recruitment of higher specialists into the Union civil services. First, the recruitment examinations and tests are not adequate and the rigidity of procedures in making actual appointments leads to the loss of some of the selected candidates. There is urgent need for dealing with both aspects of this problem. Second, there is a lack of availability of highly qualified specialized persons, particularly in certain fields. In 1961–62, personnel for 112 vacancies in certain types of highly specialized posts under the Union government were not available. This shortage affects the capability of the administration for developmental work. Remedial measures need to be effected to deal with this problem in the development administration of India.

What has been said in regard to the higher Union services and the two of the five All-India Services applies in varying degrees to the state civil services.

The social base of the higher civil services in India, both at the Union and state levels, is broader than before but is still much narrower than that in an educationally developed country such as the United States. University education and general literacy have increased in the country more rapidly after 1950 than before. The following figures are illustrative:

	Number of universities	State university students	Percentage of literacy		
			Male	Female	Average
1950–51	27	403,519	—	—	—
1962–63	54	1,150,769	34.5	13.0	24.0

Source: *India—1965: A Reference Annual.*

With the spread of education in the country and the increasing financial assistance available to talented children from low-income families, it is more possible for children from a larger number of social classes to compete for the higher social services. This is also borne out by information available about the economic status of the parents of the 615 IAS candidates who were successful in the competitive examinations held between 1948 and 1960.[6] All told, 32.9 per cent came from the upper-income families each with an income of 900 rupees and above per month, 58.2 per cent came from middle-income families each with an income of between 300 and 899 rupees per month, and 8.9 per cent came from low-income families with a monthly income of less than 300 rupees.

Most of the successful candidates (nearly 90 per cent) came from families engaged in non-agricultural pursuits in a country where the bulk of the population is engaged in agricultural pursuits and do not have the educational opportunities of the urban families and areas.

Some believe that as the higher civil services build up a

6. D. N. Rao, "Disparities of Representation in I.A.S.," an unpublished paper contributed to a conference on Problems of the Public Services held in March, 1962, at the Indian Institute of Public Administration, New Delhi.

broader social base, the services will have a deeper appreciation of the developmental problems of the different social classes in the community. While some substance cannot be denied to this viewpoint, merit must not be given a secondary place in recruitment. It should remain the primary criterion, while socialization should be the result of the evolution of educational development.

The age limits prescribed for candidates to compete for the civil services are based on the idea that civil service is to be treated as a lifelong career and it is thus desirable to recruit persons at a young age when they are easily molded into the traditions and ethos of administration in general and the agencies in particular. The age limits for entry into the IAS and the higher Union services tend to be twenty-one to twenty-three and twenty-one to twenty-four years. Generally, twenty-five is the maximum age limit for entry into the non-specialist posts and twenty-five to thirty-five for specialist posts, though in some cases it may be raised to forty-five.

If persons with entrepreneurial skills or political skills or with a high degree of some unusual type of specialization are to be inducted into the civil service, age limits will have to be made still more flexible. While it is perhaps not possible to expect that the age limits should be abolished altogether in India—this would radically change the character of the civil service as a long-term career for its members—there is a need for relaxing the existing rigidities to find men with special qualifications for development administration on a short-term (as compared with the present life-term basis).

Conclusions

The organization and ethos of the Indian civil services were fashioned in the earlier days of semicolonialism and restricted governmental action in the fields of social welfare and economic growth. Since independence, and especially since 1950–51 when the developmental processes began to grow and proceed in definite directions, a number of changes have been introduced into the civil services. In the preceding pages, the nature and effects of these changes have been discussed in only two fields of public personnel administration in the country—structure and recruitment. Also examined have been the deficiencies in these fields which need to be remedied if the civil services are to become more capable of coping with innovative and complex tasks of development. To summarize briefly:

1. The structure of civil services has been changed to accommodate more skills within it. There is still more need for entrepreneurial skills, innovative types of leadership, and political skills. Persons with these attributes must find an adequate place within the services.

2. There is more vertical mobility than before because of less restrictive promotional opportunities. This has improved morale to an extent. But promotional policies are still unduly restrictive in certain categories of the civil services.

3. There is a good deal of spatial and interagency mobility of the generalist civil servants. But this needs to be made more meaningful by the suitable interlinking of the administrative experiences of each of these civil servants.

4. The need for new adjustments between the expanding number of the specialists and the generalist civil servants has led to some changes in attitudes and organizational arrangements. But for removing the dissatisfactions among the specialists about their position vis-à-vis the dominant one of the generalists, as well as for fuller utilization of the skills and knowledge of these specialists for developmental tasks, more changes in attitudes and organizational arrangements seem to be indicated.

5. The increase in the number of All-India Services promotes efficiency of administration for developmental purposes and for strengthening national integrative processes. Though it is not in keeping with the spirit of constitutional federalism, it is in accord with the spirit of co-operative federalism.

6. The social base and the manpower reservoir for the recruitment of civil services have tended to broaden with the rapid educational development in the country. The process is still far short of the one in a developed country like the United States,

and it will take time for it to reach the requisite stage of development as education spreads more widely among the people.

In short, both the organization and ethos of civil services need
fresh thinking. Civil servants generally prefer the status quo and
slow change. They must become the effective agents and leaders
of an innovational and dynamic administration which can cope
with developmental tasks of rapidly growing magnitude and complexity. And this must be carried out in a country that has considerable poverty and illiteracy but is wedded to the ideals of
democracy and planned change on the basis of egalitarianism.

Chapter 8

Administrative Roles
in Local Governments

Harry J. Friedman

The study of development in the contemporary world is likely
to focus more often on analysis of national political systems or
activities of central governments than on analysis of subnational
systems or activities of local governments. There are forceful
reasons, becoming increasingly apparent, however, for making
local jurisdictions the objects of research in the development
field. Indeed, a reawakened interest in comparative local government has occurred in the past few years, with studies in local
development not far behind.

In the first place, patterns of local politics and administration
have been more stable than national ones over longer periods of
time in many countries. Only in recent times has the impact of
national development begun to make essential changes at the
local level. Particularly in village politics, but sometimes also in
larger units, the patterns of conflict resolution, the means of
establishing public policy, and the distribution of power and
authority have remained essentially the same for exceedingly
long periods, even centuries. This factor alone should provide
clues to the fundamental nature of political and administrative
dynamics in a particular society, clues which can be applicable at
the national level as well.

Second, units of local government can, in many cases, provide
more compact subjects for analysis than total national systems,
frequently offering more manageable locales for the purposes of
collection, testing, and evaluation. The process of theory-building

in the social sciences still has a long road ahead and a larger number of empirical testing grounds can accelerate that process.

For the purpose of generating development theory, there may be an even more compelling reason for focusing part of our attention on local government. Most development programs, policies, and plans are initiated by national government officials. Most governments today contain a fairly substantial number of individuals who are skilful at formulating and communicating the background, goals, measurements, and techniques of development plans. Most complain, however, of the difficulty in implementing plans, of meeting targets at the local and even individual level where the greatest needs may be found.

Bertram M. Gross has described the process of overcoming the problems of plan implementation in terms of the concept, "activating."[1] But it is not the purpose here to repeat the problems and analyses of plan implementation; rather, it is to describe and analyze the nature of administration at the local level on the supposition that a clearer understanding of local government is a prerequisite for understanding and implementing national development programs, policies, and plans.

For the purposes of this chapter, local government and local administration refer to jurisdictions smaller than states or provinces, and since Pakistan will be drawn upon for examples the term "local," for all practical purposes, will mean the district level and below as found in that country.[2]

1. "Activating National Plans," *CAG Occasional Papers* (Bloomington, Ind.: Indiana University, 1964).
2. Elsewhere, my colleague and I have defined local government in a way which includes state and provincial governments but that was for the purpose of outlining a broad strategy for theory-building. That definition is:

Local government is a *pattern of binding rules, rule making, rule obedience and rule enforcement activities*, which is characteristic of a *territorially defined collectivity* of human beings, and which meets three additional criteria: (1) there is some set of binding (enforced and obeyed) rules applicable to membership of the collectivity under consideration; (2) there is at least one other set of binding rules applicable both to the collectivity under consideration and to at least one territorially more inclusive collectivity of which it is a part; (3) when rules appertaining solely to the collectivity under consideration conflict with rules appertaining to the more inclusive collectivity (or collectivities), then rules heretofore binding only on the collectivity under consideration cease to be binding.

(Robert S. Cahill and Harry J. Friedman, "A Strategy for the Comparative Study of Local Government," *Thai Journal of Public Administration*, VI, No. 1 [July, 1965], 114–115.)

The concern here is with the changing roles of local administrators as development takes place in their environment. The administrators themselves may play an important part in bringing about the development which, in turn, contributes to their own role changes.[3]

Herein, development means both the achievement of modernity and those changes in a society's economic, social, political, and administrative spheres which tend to move the society closer to modernity. Development is both a goal and a process. The goal, modernity, is defined broadly to include both socio-economic progress and nation-building. The process, those changes which tend to move the society closer to modernity, takes place in all four systems—economic, social, political, and administrative. In every case, the achievement of modernity is the ultimate dependent variable.

Although development as a process may take place in all four systems, this chapter is concerned with aspects of development administration or the relation of the administrative system to development. There may be privately administered programs contributing to development, but we are here dealing with public administration, the effects of programs administered by government agencies.

Some programs may be designed to help move the society closer to modernity within the context of the existing system. In this category may be found many capital-improvement projects and those which attempt to increase the level of resources, such as supplying additional seeds to farmers. Some programs are designed to create basic changes in the administrative system and other systems. These systemic changes, in turn, may tend to move the society closer to modernity on a planned or unplanned basis. In this category may be found such examples as creation of those new structures which alter the communications patterns in administration. Local councils and voluntary associations fall into this category.

3. The emphasis here is on the interaction between the administrator and his environment, or the ecology of administration, as Fred W. Riggs has stressed in his chapter for this volume as well as in other writings.

In both instances, whether there are systemic changes or not, government programs are an independent variable, with the achievement of modernity a dependent variable. In one case, however, a change in a system may also be a dependent variable and the system change, in turn, may become an independent variable for the achievement of modernity, as illustrated in the diagram below.[4]

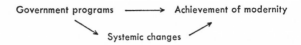

For summarizing purposes, then, development administration is here defined as including two elements: (1) the implementation of programs designed to bring about modernity and (2) the changes within an administrative system which increase its capacity to implement such programs.

In this chapter, the changes to be discussed are in the nature of the decision-making process at the local level and in the roles of local administrators.

The Context of Administrative Behavior

In order to have relevance to explanations of development, local administration cannot be thought of as simply a combination of offices, agencies, or rules. Instead, a context must be described which will allow for explanation of dynamics, of movement, of change, for that is the essence of development. One possibility is to describe local administrations as perceived decision systems.

In this sense, the context of administrative behavior is the type of decision process which exists in the particular local government. The dimension along which the types vary is the perception of the process by those who are being governed. The element

4. This formulation is consistent with that of Edward W. Weidner. For a more extended discussion of his ideas on the relation between system change and development see chap. i above.

of perception may be an additional factor which helps to bring about changes in administrative behavior.[5]

This approach is borrowed from an essay by Daniel Goldrich, who defines politicization as a continuum varying from "lack of perception of the relevance of government to one's life, through perception of it, to active involvement in politics." One mode of politicization posits the "administrative-oriented type versus the policy-oriented type."[6] For the present purposes these two types will be applied in a modified manner to help explain the context in which changing administrative behavior takes place.

Both the decision-making process itself and the perception of it are defined in the same way because they interact and the perception contributes to shaping the nature of the process.

Decision-making is administrative-oriented if it involves "relatively routine implementation of a prior, generally applicable decision; and if it implicates relatively minor values of a relatively few people at any one time, with 'technical' criteria available to guide the technically trained expert in his selection of one or another alternative outcomes as the decision." Decision-making is policy-oriented if it involves "relatively extraordinary review of an existing decision, or an entirely new decision, and (implicates) relatively major values or a relatively large number of people, with value judgments or preferences rather than 'technical' criteria as the major factors in determining the selection by 'policy-makers' of one or another alternative outcomes as the decision."[7]

The utility of these two types, it is suggested here, is to help account, in part, for one reason for administrative change. As

5. The emphasis on perception grew out of a previous attempt to use the concept in a different context which examined the differences between a Pakistani district and an American county in Harry J. Friedman, "The American County and Pakistani District: A Comparison of Administrative Impact," in Inayatullah, ed., *District Administration in West Pakistan* (Peshawar: Pakistan Academy for Rural Development, 1964), chap. xxvii.

6. "On the Concept of Politicization," in Robert S. Cahill and Stephen P. Hencley, *The Politics of Education* (Danville, Ill.: Interstate Printers and Publishers, 1964), chap. x.

7. *Ibid.*, p. 200. Goldrich cited these definitions from Robert E. Agger, "Political Science and the Study of Administration," in Lawrence W. Downey and Frederick Enns, eds., *The Social Sciences and Educational Administration* (Edmonton, Alb.: Division of Educational Administration, University of Alberta, 1963), p. 51.

perceptions of decision-making change, which may be caused by a great variety of factors summed up in Goldrich's concept of politicization, the conduct and consequences of administration change. This point will be dealt with at greater length below.

While it is primarily the *changes* in perception by the general public which help to bring about changes in administrative roles, there are also variations according to the *styles* of perception. The administrative-oriented citizen perceives government, the public ruling authority, primarily or even solely in terms of the functions of administrative agencies and officials. Government is pictured as the administrative official with whom the citizen has the most frequent contacts. This is usually in the areas of police, revenue collection, and, in recent years, some "development" programs of agriculture, health, education, etc.

Administrative-oriented persons tend to seek help for solution of public problems from one source only and in one way only, when they turn to government. They go directly to an administrative agency. They accept the terms of reference within which the agency operates. They judge the value of services rendered by the immediacy and efficacy of the response. Administrative-oriented persons do not attempt to find or create a variety of ways to make demands on governmental machinery. Neither do they look for mediating agencies to translate demands in varied forms.

The policy-oriented citizen perceives the relevance of government primarily in terms of the choices among policies aimed at broad social issues and the process of making such choices. This style of perception is concerned with goal-setting, the relation of leaders to alternative goals and the ways in which decisions are made as to one set of goals and leaders or another.

Private citizens with policy-oriented perception tend to behave in a greater variety of ways than administrative-oriented types. They may very well attempt to change the terms of reference for potential solution to their problems. For example, an urbanite seeking a zoning variance may not simply accept a negative decision from a regulatory body. If his outlook is policy-oriented, he may weigh and often pursue the gains to be derived from seeking assistance from political figures, such as a city council-man or party leader. He might also proceed through stages to an attempt to garner support for changes in the basic zoning policies.

In this sense, policy orientation is related to political participa-tion, meaning the attempts of private citizens to influence the formulation and outcome of public policy-making in one or more of a variety of ways, such as voting, joining pressure groups and political parties, or attending political meetings. The political behavior of policy-oriented citizens is more complex, more flexi-ble, subject to more changes and to more frequent changes, and more participant than that of administrative-oriented citizens.

Although the description above depicts two "ideal types," in reality perceptions and the forms of behavior motivated by the perceptions are often mixed. One form may dominate, even when aspects of the other are found occasionally. The policy-oriented individual, for example, will not always perceive, and act on, a variety of options, but he usually will.

To summarize, local government systems are decision-making processes which consist of both the choices (or decisions) made by public agencies and the perception of those decisions by the general public. Perception helps to provide the moving force which changes the nature of the process and the roles of adminis-trators within the system, but the reverse is also true. The types of structures help to determine the types of perception.

In their five-nation survey of the broader concept of political attitudes, *The Civic Culture*, Almond and Verba similarly de-scribed a set of relations in a section on local government:

one reason why individuals differ in the frequency with which they adhere to participatory norms is that the structure of government and community organization changes from one nation to another.

. . . even if the attitudes we describe are in part determined by the structure of government and social system in each nation, this does not remove the fact that these attitudes in turn affect these same structures.[8]

8. Gabriel A. Almond and Sidney Verba, *The Civic Culture* (Boston: Little, Brown, 1965), p. 125.

A local government system of a given society will not represent exclusively one type of decision process. Not only are there differences among nations, but there are also differences to be found within nations. To quote Almond and Verba again, "the structures of local government differ from nation to nation *and within the nations as well.* And these differences in structure partially explain differences in attitudes found among the nations."[9] They add that "the nations also differ in the extent to which the local decision-making apparatus is accessible to participation by local residents. In some communities—*and again this varies with nations,* but perhaps more sharply among nations—there will be greater opportunity for the individual to participate in decisions."[10]

Similarly, decision-making processes influenced by types of perception vary within a given society. In part, the variations reflect different stages of development, stages which are associated with greater or lesser amounts of participation and of complex organizations. For the purposes of description and analysis, however, we are considering local governments in given societies to be *predominantly* one type of decision process or the other.

It is within this context of two ideal types that administrative roles are played in local governments of developing societies. The administrative-oriented type is more descriptive of a process in the "folk" or "traditional" society, while the policy-oriented type describes a process more often found in a "transitional" or "developing" society. These types do overlap, however, and characteristics of both may be found at the same time.

Goldrich's use of these concepts indicated that an administrative-oriented form of politicization and decision process is more typical of the Westernized, industrialized society, but the modification used here is based on the contention that administrative orientation is characteristic of both folk and urban societies. There is a difference, however. Administrative orientation in an urban society is supported by a context of structural differentiation which changes the consequences of the process.

9. *Ibid.,* p. 121. Italics added.   10. *Ibid.,* p. 124. Italics added.

For the present, this description is being applied to the developing societies. Most start with an administrative-oriented decision process. Into this context is introduced the impact of central government development plans and other policies. These plans chart out not only economic goals but the institutions of a political and social infrastructure as well.

As central governments introduce such programs as community development and encourage the creation of local councils and agricultural co-operatives, they produce, among other things, two major consequences for administrative roles. One is the assignment of specific new tasks to local administrators. The other is the possibility of producing effects on environmental conditions and administrative roles not intended by the specific assignments.

The creation of a variety of representative institutions changes the environment of administration in such a fashion that the public official is specifically required to relate to the new public institutions in a particular way. For example, he may be directed to sit as a chairman of what appears to be a legislative body or he may be assigned the function of planner and co-ordinator of agendas for other organizations, not his own department.

Furthermore, these new assignments may not necessarily be substitutes for his previous work, but more often than not are tasks added to his traditional burden.[11] This factor, among other consequences, requires the administrator to make hard and explicit choices, raising the whole question of priorities. Rarely do government orders from above determine specific priorities for the civil servant; instead his choice of priorities will be determined by a combination of his own inclinations, the ideological atmosphere in which he operates, and the strength of immediate pressures.

Although the chief ostensible intention of new task assignments may be to associate government officials more closely with representatives of the public or to add development responsibilities to their legal duties, the central government may also find

11. Many government officers will point out these increasing burdens in private conversation. One example where the point is made in print is in Mohammed Anisuzzaman, *The Circle Officer* (Dacca: National Institute of Public Administration, 1963), pp. 6–7.

that the environmental changes it induces result in increasing demands on officials, rather than straightforward implementation of central programs. By providing a means for organized communication, the central government cannot predict all the forms such communication will take or all the forms of pressure which will follow.

What the central government aims for is an elimination of resistance to change by combining an educational process and a sense of participation in structural settings which place officialdom and public representatives in close proximity. In fact, a variety of responses is possible under such conditions. Some of these may be, and are likely to be, dysfunctional to the implementation of development goals, quite the opposite effect intended in the establishment of such structures. Increasing demands for particularistic "favors" are at least as possible a response to rudimentary forms of participation in policy-making as the hoped for universalistic criterion of demand-making.

The point is not that the end product of establishing new structures and assigning new tasks will necessarily achieve one result or the other. The point is that a fairly substantial portion of the results will be unpredictable, at least for a certain period of time covering the early to middle stages of such changes.

In summary, the impact of central government development policies on a local decision-making process produces explicit changes in the structural setting of administration, including the tasks of both administrative and non-bureaucratic agencies. Some consequences of these changes are fairly predictable and some are not, but all have a powerful effect on the public's perception of government, which in turn results in changing roles of public administrators.

Administrative Roles

In the administrative-oriented decision process in a folk or traditional society, the public official is regarded as the sole transmitter and interpreter of public policy. The private citizen who feels a need for government action of some sort turns to the administrator, not a politician or local council representative or private association leader. This is so partly because such structures exist only in rudimentary form and partly because the citizen's perception of the process is fairly simple, direct, and fatalistic. If he fails to secure a response, he is likely to withdraw from continued attempts.

The administrator, in turn, responds to the citizen's perception of the process by fairly routine behavior. He leans on precedent and on regulations promulgated by superior authorities to guide his decisions. Although an individual administrator may be imaginative and innovative on occasion, he performs that way only in isolated instances, not as part of a continuing process. He is constantly alert to the signal from the organizational hierarchy to condition his responses. Since the scope of government planning is narrow, the signals which are sent to the individual administrator rarely include substantial moves toward development. His own actions are therefore similarly non-developmental.

In the policy-oriented decision process, the civil servant is but one of a variety of public policy interpreters available to the citizen. If responses to a need for government action are not forthcoming from one source, the citizen will turn to another and still another. Alternatively, he may seek out different bodies for action on different types of demands.

The administrator, in this context, does not simply lean on standard rules or on precedent. He seeks accommodation among the more continuous pressures exerted on him from more and different directions. He becomes more of a competitor for both status and authority in his environment.

The different roles of the administrator under these two processes are not distinct and polar but represent some of the changes taking place under the impact of centrally induced transformations in local government systems. If placed on a continuum of changing roles, the movement would be from those characteristics found in an administrative-oriented process to those found in a policy-oriented process, but with considerable overlapping.

The major reason for the role changes, however, is the chang-

ing perceptions of government from one process to the other. As
both the citizens and the administrators see more values at stake,
involving more persons in decisions, the administrator must become more responsive to the complexity of his environment. To
continue to justify his position of authority, he cannot rely on his
office alone, but must rely on superior technical expertise in a
subject or expertise in knowledge of the administrative system's
operations.

Although these observations are intended to apply to all local
public administrators, there is a distinction between the generalist and the specialist. The generalist is more often the dominant
figure and relies more heavily on his hierarchical position for
authority than does the specialist, although the latter also is
dependent on hierarchy as well as professional expertise as a
foundation of authority.

Despite the continued dominance of the generalist, it is he who
is most affected by the variety of changes wrought in a policy-oriented process. The need for specialized knowledge and specialists grows, and therefore the number of specialists in the field
increases. The generalist has less specialized knowledge, by definition, to support his position, which must therefore be reinforced
either by constant reaffirmation from the central government or
by his sheer individual ability to manipulate subordinates, specialist departments, and public representatives. Differences in
individual abilities result in an uneven pattern of role adaptation
throughout the local government system.

These changes in administrative roles are not sudden or always
obvious. They cover a considerable period of time in response to
mounting pressures and an erratic course of demands. As the
administrator learns to rely more on technical expertise, partly by
his desire for retention of authority and partly by explicit training, he is laying the groundwork for movement toward a "modern" technical bureaucracy, one with a store of knowledge which
can be applied to increasingly complex problems. In this way,
changes in perception eventually contribute to changes in bureaucracy of the kind encompassed by the concept of development administration.

The changing process has additional consequences, however, some of which can block the immediate implementation of development programs. During the conversion of the decision process from administrative-oriented to policy-oriented, the public official at the local level learns to see the availability of more choices in his responses to public demands. Because increasingly he does not adhere merely to precedent or standard regulation alone, he seeks additional ways to accommodate the greater variety of pressures coming from new sources.

In doing so, however, he contributes to a growth of autonomy in local administration. The old basis of administrative continuity from central to local governments becomes disrupted, and a new basis must be found to insure the implementation of development, a foundation which is more likely to be built on the lines of value integration, as suggested by James Heaphey in his "Spatial Aspects of Development Administration."[12]

Although Heaphey points out, correctly, the difficulties of utilizing value-integrated administrative relationships in those "new states" which are postcolonial, the contention here is that the changes in administrative roles described above lay the groundwork for the new links.

Heaphey discusses value integration as a system potentially useful for successful decentralization, which, as he defines it, is the same as relations between a central government bureaucracy and a local government bureaucracy in this essay. "Decentralization," according to Heaphey, "should be conceived in terms of two roles; one being the role of responsibility for decision-making, the other being the role of decision-making. We define decentralization as the extent to which these two roles are assigned to concretely different persons and the extent to which the decision-maker is not bound by rules and regulations."[13] Heaphey adds that when decentralization exists as a result of value integration "the decision-makers make all of their decisions so that there is no difference between what they do and what the persons in

12. "Spatial Aspects of Development Administration: A Review and Proposal," *CAG Occasional Papers* (Bloomington, Ind.: Indiana University, 1965).
13. The discussion of value integration may be found in *ibid.*, pp. 14–18.

the role of responsibility for those actions want them to do."

Mutual confidence is the keynote to the use of value integration, and the implication obviously is that values must be demon-
strably shared for a considerable period of time to build this type
of integration. Furthermore, in order to produce the desired
results, not just any value is to be shared, but rather the particular value of favoring development.

Value-integrated administration cannot be counted on as the
basis for implementation of development plans in a policy-oriented decision process. As Heaphey points out, "the 'value-integrated decentralized' system will be susceptible to breakdown in
situations where local pressures on the 'man in the field' contradict the value integration that he needs to share with the central
authorities."

It is precisely such a situation which has been described as the
policy-oriented decision-making process. The consequences of
such a process, however, require that central authorities seek
value integration in the context of a stage beyond that of policy
orientation, a stage of administrative orientation in a differentiated society.

The Case of Pakistan

An administrative-oriented decision-making process of local
government existed in Pakistan prior to the introduction of several major programs by the central government, programs which
have been carried on under the supervision of both central and
provincial governments. To a considerable extent this process still
persists in many parts of the country and in several substantive
areas of public policy.

In the most traditional types of villages the level of politicization is still very low. Government may be perceived as relevant to
an individual's daily life, but government is viewed as monolithic
and limited in scope, an aid-giving agency. Government, too, is
caught up in a preordained set of inevitable relationships. As one
description has put it:

Fatalism is one of the most crucial factors in the villagers' belief system. This includes their complete dependence on God and unflinching faith in the efficacy of prayers and rituals. Fatalism has developed in them negative attitudes toward their own capabilities. They tend to depend on the government for all help and relief. The desire for improvement is there but the expectation is that the government should bring about the required improvements in their life.[14]

This is not to say that all local life or even all village life in Pakistan can be described in precisely this way today, but the description is applicable in many places and was, of course, almost universal at one time.

Furthermore, not only was the level of politicization low before the introduction of several major programs, but the mode of politicization was administrative-oriented in the modified sense used here. Perception was of a particular type: the administrative orientation of the undifferentiated society at the local level and, as previously stated, part of a decision-making process which can be described in the same way.

The following description of district administration in Pakistan is applicable also to the levels of government below the district level:

The authoritarian character of district administration was a product of the centralized alien rule and the passive, inarticulate, illiterate and unorganized peasant society. Besides the traditional, particularistic organizations of caste, class and tribe, there was no voluntary social and economic organization in the society which could articulate the interests and problems of the people. The few organizations which emerged were either bureaucratically controlled or represented the new professional skills in the urban centres. The informal and formal contacts between the district administration and the public were limited and were circumscribed by a psychological environment which did not permit two way communication. The people were informed regarding the amount of revenue they had to pay and what services were to be extended to them but an effective channel for communicating their feelings and problems back to the administration did not exist. Whatever communication did exist was through the upper rural class whose interest did not always harmonize with the remaining

14. S. M. Hafeez Zaidi, "The Village Culture in Transition: A Study of Two Villages in East Pakistan," unpublished manuscript, p. 175.

rural society. In the terminology of Almond and Verba the system lacked its "input" (political) aspect.[15]

This passage has been quoted at some length because it describes so well the nature of the process existent when distinct changes began to take place in the direction of policy orientation. Although such changes cannot be accounted for solely by the introduction of central programs, a great impact was in fact made by the broad-gauged approaches of community development (called in Pakistan Village Agricultural and Industrial Development or Village AID) and Basic Democracies, the system of councils in tiers which attempted to create a form of representation through limited local elections.

Pakistan's Village AID program from 1954 to 1961 was, like other community development programs, an attempt to draw villagers into a modernizing stream of activities and relationships in order better to achieve national economic development. It used a new bureaucracy to try to formulate and implement a large variety of economic and social projects, including the creation of such structures as village councils and co-operatives.[16]

Village AID became highly controversial with strong supporters and detractors. Its successes and failures could be measured by a number of different standards, but it is not the present purpose to develop a critique of community development goals and methods. The most relevant aspect of Village AID for the purposes contained herein is the extent to which it helped to lay a groundwork for movement toward policy orientation in both perceptions and local decision-making processes.

Central government leaders eventually tended to evaluate Village AID in terms of its physical accomplishments, but the secondary goal of stimulating the growth of thinking in terms of

15. Inayatullah, "Changing Character of District Administration in Pakistan," in Inayatullah, ed., *District Administration in West Pakistan,* chap. x. For a further description of district administration in Pakistan, see the discussion by Inayatullah in this volume, chap. ix. The two writers with the same name are not related.

16. Numerous articles, pamphlets, and books by Pakistani participants in Village AID and by American advisers document the course of Village AID. A recent work which places it in a comparative context and relates it well to development administration is Henry C. Hart, "The Village and Development Administration," mimeographed, pp. 26–30.

organizations may have been the long-run contribution of Village AID. Although the extent of such thinking has not been measured, the effect, at least in part, was to promote the *receptivity* of the general public to additional participation in representative institutions at the local level and to help condition perceptions of decision-making processes.

Village AID did not spring full-blown on the Pakistani scene and promptly change public perceptions of government. It grew out of a long history of attempts at village development on the Indian subcontinent, usually under the name of rural reconstruction and particularly during the 1930's in the Punjab. But Village AID reinforced the slim beginnings of the past and made a much more massive impact on shaping the receptivity of villagers to changing perceptions of government.

The process continued and began to become institutionalized through the structures created in the Basic Democracies Order of 1959. Although there was considerable discussion at the time of a sort of mystique of Basic Democracies—that is, an attempt to foster an atmosphere of excitement in charting new goals and a new way of life, backed by the prestige of President Mohammed Ayub Khan—the heart of the Basic Democracies system was the structural arrangements, by now widely described.[17]

Tiers of local councils, corresponding to a fourfold distribution of administrative levels, were established as settings within which government administrators and a limited number of elected representatives were able to meet to work out joint planning and implementing of development goals. The lowest rung of the ladder, the union councils, later was changed to consist solely of elected officials, and a percentage of their chairmen was appointed to the higher tiers of councils at the *Tehsil/Thana* (West and East Pakistan designations), district and division levels. An unimportant fifth tier existed for a time in the form of a

17. As in the case of Village AID, Basic Democracies has been thoroughly described in a variety of publications. For an early description, see Harry J. Friedman, "Pakistan's Experiment in Basic Democracies," *Pacific Affairs*, XXXIII (June, 1960), 107–125. To trace the course of events since then, a good source is the accumulation of publications from the two Pakistan Academies for Rural Development.

Provincial Development Advisory Council. Within these settings elected representatives were provided with the opportunity for making presentations to government officials, and most of the demands they made in this context were formulated in co-operation with their fellow villagers, not merely on their own whims.

A word of caution is necessary here before false assumptions become explicit. It should not be assumed that the process taking place under Basic Democracies is one of frequent and effective articulation of demands converted into public policies according to the desires of an elected majority. The contention here is that such a process is a long way off, if indeed it will occur at all, and that what is described instead is a rudimentary form of a new communication process which is likely to have effect on administrative roles.

For example, the public administration faculty member of the West Pakistan Academy for Rural Development at Peshawar discovered this gap between potential and practice over a period of time. Early in the Basic Democracies period, he hypothesized that

the significance of the Basic Democracies scheme lies in its ability to organize the rural middle class and open a two-way channel between tehsil and district administration, thereby unfolding a process of diffusion of power in the rural society of Pakistan. This, in turn, would tend to change the ecology of district administration converting an authoritarian system into one based upon democratic principles.[18]

In the same work, he added,

Also, Basic Democracies opens up more communications channels between peasantry and district officialdom, instead of just filtering peasant demands through landlords alone, such as selection of projects under Rural Works Program. BD also influences nature of officials' tours—places to go, people to be contacted. BD also influences selection and administration of projects through questions in council meetings.[19]

By following up these hypotheses in later empirical studies, he discovered considerable variations among responses of govern-

18. Inayatullah, *District Administration in West Pakistan,* pp. 116–117.
19. *Ibid.,* pp. 118–120.

ment bureaucrats to requests and demands channeled through elected representatives.

In one study of the communications from union councils to government departments in Nowshera *tehsil,* he found that 74 per cent were answered, of which 63 per cent were acted upon. On the other hand, there was wide disparity within the jurisdiction of the *tehsil,* as one union council received frequent responses to its communications and another appeared to be totally isolated. In the latter case, all members of the council resigned at one point in protest but withdrew their resignations when they were assured of more attention in the future.[20] In a separate study of union councils in Rawalpindi Division, only 25 per cent of their communications received replies, of which 66 per cent were acted upon.[21]

Although these studies were made only two years after the Basic Democracies system was put into operation and are therefore not necessarily descriptive of current relations among the public, their local representatives, and government officials, they do illustrate the mixed pattern of behavior. Basic Democracies, as an institutionalized communications link, does permit the public to perceive additional ways of influencing the government. A 1964 study in Lyallpur *tehsil* found that 53 per cent of 150 interviewees in three villages believed that Basic Democracies helped to establish closer contact between officials and the public.[22]

An additional factor should be considered in the Pakistani case of changing administrative roles. Various training programs, combined with an atmosphere of exhortation, have reinforced the impact of structural rearrangements and altered perceptions of the local bureaucracy.

Beginning with the first five-year plan, when the "administrative machinery" was informed that "its outlook has to undergo a change so that economic and social progress become its main

20. Inayatullah, *Study of Union Councils in Nowshera Tehsil* (Peshawar: West Pakistan Academy of Village Development, 1961), pp. 36–38.
21. Inayatullah, *Study of Selected Union Councils in Rawalpindi Division* (Peshawar: Pakistan Academy for Village Development, 1962), p. 35.
22. Zuhra Waheed, *Contacts between Villagers and Public Officials in Three Villages of Lyallpur Tehsil* (Lahore: Pakistan Administrative Staff College, 1964), p. 21.

purpose," public officials have been continuously urged to become "guides," "teachers," and "servants" of the people, instead
of "rulers" and "masters." They have been instructed and exhorted to be "development-oriented" instead of "law-and-order-
oriented." These terms, of course, not only lacked a universal
meaning for the bureaucracy, but they also had to be supported
by knowledge of how to change from one set of roles to another.
This factor called for a large-scale inauguration of in-service
training programs and institutions, ranging from visits to foreign
countries, through the establishment of a high-level staff college
and university departments and Institutes of Public Administration, to the creation of the somewhat unique Academies for Rural
Development.[23]

In all of these programs, the emphasis proved to be not only on
improved techniques of administration but also on changed attitudes and values deemed to be more relevant for the purposes of
implementing development. A bureaucracy well suited for revenue collection and law enforcement was undergoing a transformation to utilize new approaches, new techniques, and new organizational features. Once again, the consequence has been a
mixed one. During the early stages, administrators attempted to
unlearn familiar patterns and adopt unfamiliar patterns, a process
which was temporarily dysfunctional to the efficient and rational
implementation of programs. Pakistan's more recent successes in
economic development may be partly attributable to the fact that
bureaucratic role transformation is only now beginning to take
hold sufficiently to make the changes more functional to development. On the other hand, the fact that many problems still remain may indicate that the role-changing process is not yet sufficiently complete.

Who are these local administrators whose changing roles appear to be so vital to planned change?[24] In broad terms, they

23. A good brief summary of in-service training programs is Richard O. Niehoff,
"Technical Assistance in the In-Service Training of Pakistani Civil Servants since
1958," *Asian Studies Center Occasional Papers* (East Lansing, Mich.: Michigan
State University, 1966).

24. Among the many official and unofficial descriptions of administrative posi-
tions, one which relates the generalist to the specialist may be found in Henry
Frank Goodnow, *The Civil Service of Pakistan* (New Haven: Yale University
Press, 1964), chaps. v, vi.

include both the general civil administrators and the technical specialists. In Pakistani terms, the generalists are the dominant, prestigious, co-ordinating officials and the specialists are the technical experts guiding, advising, and supervising specialized activities.

The key individual is the historically famous deputy commissioner, the chief district official who, in British India, originated as a collector of revenue and a magistrate. Through the years, additional duties of general administration were superimposed on the office as, in fact, also occurred with other generalists below the district level. Today, the goals of development have been assigned to the deputy commissioner as one of his chief tasks, and attempts are continuing to do the same with his subordinates. Districts are subdivided into smaller units, and the officers who supervise them are known by different titles in various parts of Pakistan—assistant commissioners, subdivisional officers, circle officers, *tehsildars,* etc.

The specialists, who are controlled by their own departments for some purposes and by the general administrators within their jurisdictions for other purposes, are representatives of a number of old and new organizations which were historically known as the nation-building departments. These include agriculture, animal husbandry, education, co-operatives, fisheries, forestry, etc.

"Local government" is not synonymous with administrators alone. In fact, administrative roles are changing precisely because bureaucrats are part of a changing local government which, in turn, they are helping to change. Earlier, local government was defined for analytical purposes as a decision-making process. In structural terms, Nicolaas Luykx has defined rural local government in a way which makes clear the interaction of various elements in the system and which is useful to repeat here. Leaving aside the nature of government in cities, which may be different in structure but which is concerned with only a small percentage of the process we are attempting to describe and is therefore not as relevant at this time, the following six elements are included in Luykx' definition:[25]

25. Nicolaas Luykx, "Rural Government in the Strategy of Agricultural Development," in John D. Montgomery and William J. Siffin, eds., *Approaches to*

1. The smallest administrative authority recognized or established by the national government.

2. The representatives of the next administrative echelon higher than the village council or headman (if not an agency of the national government).

3. The representatives of central government agencies operating within rural localities either directly or indirectly, regularly or sporadically.

4. Special-purpose local organizations or activities promoted by or linked with the national government on an "unofficial" or "informal" basis.

5. Organizations or activities promoted, sponsored or regulated by the natural power structure (if different from formally recognized authorities).

6. Customary or traditional forms of public action which tend to determine the procedures which rural people will follow in their public activities.

These categories need only to be interpreted to include three levels of councils under Basic Democracies—union, *tehsil/thana,* and district—to cover well the nature of rural local government in Pakistan. The main point in this description is the emphasis on interaction of the general public and a variety of "governing" institutions. In Pakistan, as additional institutions have been introduced—local councils, co-operatives, special-purpose projects —the private citizens have had an opportunity to perceive that different types of governmental responses can be attained by utilization of structures additional to those of the traditional administration.

The well-documented activities of the East Pakistan Academy for Rural Development at Comilla exemplify a part of this process.[26] By using the limited model of a *thana,* an area containing between 200,000 and 250,000 persons, the staff of the academy, working with some government officials, stimulated the organization of village co-operatives, larger co-operative associations, and a more effective *thana* council to co-ordinate planning, supervis-

Development: Politics, Administration and Change (New York: McGraw-Hill, 1966), pp. 115–116.

26. Besides the academy's own publications and those of the government of Pakistan, again Hart's "The Village and Development Administration," pp. 31–46, is relevant here.

ing, and evaluating of governmental services. These were not merely paper activities. These were and are viable bodies perceived and used by villagers as relevant to their daily lives.

In turn, the combination of training at the academy of public officials and the increasingly frequent interactions of citizens and officials in a variety of ways influenced administrators to adopt new roles. One example of such a role change is forcefully described in the words of Akhter Hameed Khan, the director of the Comilla academy:

In such countries as Pakistan, there is a lot of talk about officers behaving like masters and lords, having a feudal mentality. The officers should adopt new attitudes, they should become "servants of the people." Servants of the people! When we talk of "servants," the word has very clear associations. A servant is a person who obeys your orders, who does whatever you want. One result of such constant talk about the officers becoming servants was that it demoralized them. So we said that the officers were to become teachers, not servants, but teachers; and they were to hold classes for the village representatives. This did much for the officers' morale.[27]

Furthermore, the accomplishments at Comilla are beginning now to spread beyond its immediate environs as the government of Pakistan has given its support to some programs tested at Comilla.

The academy has also re-emphasized the role of the generalist administrator, in contrast to criticisms which were popular during the Village AID era, but has recast that role in the form of a "team captain," particularly in the relations of the assistant commissioner and circle officer (the generalist at the *thana* level) with the *thana* council in the Basic Democracies framework. As Akhter Hameed Khan has said, "the first principle is coordination between the government departments; the second is coordination with the elected Councils."[28] He proceeded to implement these points by making the general administrator once again the chief co-ordinator.

27. "Rural Development in East Pakistan: Speeches of Akhter Hameed Khan," *Asian Studies Center* (East Lansing, Mich.: Michigan State University, 1964), p. 44.
28. *Ibid.*, p. 47.

Obviously, not all events in the changing patterns of local government move with ease toward the common goal of development implementation. As had been seen before, the picture is more often one of fits and starts, which is a pattern less conducive to rational implementation. One description of the circle officer's activities points to problems he encounters in dealing with elected officials in the union councils and raises unintentionally the issue of autonomy; that is, whether situations of conflict are more likely to lead to a breakdown of the value integration between various hierarchical levels as Heaphey indicated could occur.[29]

The circle officer's functions include not only those of a co-ordinator at the *thana* level but also those of an adviser to the lower-tier, fully elected union councils. The term "adviser" is a key one. He must rely on prestige and persuasive techniques in his relations with chairmen of the union councils to accomplish his program ends. Matters requiring administrative decision must be referred to his superior, a subdivisional officer.

When conflict occurs between the council chairman and members and the circle officer, the issue of value integration arises, because the extent of "trust," in Heaphey's terms, between the subdivisional and circle officers determines the extent of support provided for the lower-ranking official. In the case cited above, a circle officer was refused "access" by the council chairman to accounts and other official records, and the officer also failed to receive support from his superior. Although this may not currently be a frequent occurrence, repetition of such conflicts under the pressure of new demands from elected representatives could lead to a widening gap in the hierarchy, resulting from a breakdown in value integration.

In summary, Pakistan's administrative-oriented local decision-making process has been modified by the introduction of central government programs—such as Village AID and, especially, Basic Democracies—reinforced by deliberate attempts to redirect the roles of administrators through various training institutions,

29. Anisuzzaman, *op. cit.*, p. 46. For an extended discussion of the circle officer's relevant problems in the context of this chapter, see pp. 45–52, 57–60.

so that the predominant pattern at the local level is now policy-oriented, but with still some carry-over of perceptions from the administrative-oriented stage.

A Different Scale of Comparison

An attempt has been made in this chapter to focus attention on a limited range of alternatives in decision-making processes, which include public perception of those processes, at the local government level. For this purpose the concept of a continuum has been useful and the contention has been that local government processes move from administrative orientation to policy orientation as development programs are introduced by central governments into local traditional environments. As such changes take place, administrative roles undergo a variety of alterations, some of them functional to development and some of them dysfunctional.

A policy-oriented process is not an end in itself, however, and local government systems contain features of both processes. An ultimate goal of developing countries may be administrative orientation, but in a different context from the administrative orientation of the traditional society.

An administrative-oriented process may be seen as one which is more rational and more efficient for the purposes of implementing development plans. It means an ability to "program" as many decisions as possible, in the sense of Martin Landau's adaptation of the model fashioned by Thompson and Tuden.[30] Administrative orientation, in this context, resembles the "computation" process of decision-making, in which there is complete agreement on both (1) beliefs about causation and (2) preferences about possible outcomes, or agreement on facts and values of a given problem.

That type of administrative orientation, however, is different

30. James D. Thompson and Arthur Tuden, "Strategies, Structures, and Processes of Organizational Decision," in James D. Thompson *et al.*, eds., *Comparative Studies in Administration* (Pittsburgh: University of Pittsburgh Press, 1959, reprinted 1963), chap. xii. Landau's adaptation is presented in chap. iii above.

from the administrative orientation in a traditional society in that it must take place in a differentiated context. A society which distinguishes classes of decisions more sharply than a traditional or transitional one can also maintain differentiated institutions to process such decisions. Those decisions which must be made efficiently and rationally can be "programmed" (if there is agreement on facts and values) without excluding the private citizen from access to public policy-making. The reason is that in a differentiated society other classes of decisions can be processed by non-bureaucratic institutions.

When this second type of administrative orientation exists, public perception of the decision process again influences administrative roles. In this case, the direction of influence is likely to take the form of technical expertise; that is, private citizens will expect the public official to be technically expert in a specialized field, and he is likely to respond by playing that role or, in fact, to be required to play that role by the organization of which he is a part.

It should be pointed out, however, that administrative orientation in a differentiated context may not be simply an extension of the original continuum. The present examination of administrative-oriented and policy-oriented decision processes was confined to simply the transitional stage of development and is but one dimension of analysis. The introduction of differentiation as a variable would require a separate two-dimensional scale of analysis of the kind appearing in Fred W. Riggs's dialectical theory of development.[31]

31. Riggs's theory is presented in chap. ii above.

Chapter 9

Local Administration in a Developing Country: The Pakistan Case

Inayatullah

Introduction

Model-building and the search for theories of political development as evidenced in the recent writings of a number of eminent
political scientists[1] have resulted in major contributions toward
the understanding of the totality of the political phenomenon in
the developing countries. These studies provide valuable insights
into the process of political, and to some extent administrative,
growth in the "transitional" societies. There is, however, need for
simultaneous research and study which specifically aim at meeting "the more practical and precise requirements of development
administration."[2] Investigations into the processes of public administration in various parts of the world and particularly in the
developing countries can be highly rewarding. Exploration and
identification of major developments in public administration can
hopefully yield ideas and propositions which may help provide
the building blocks for the construction of a theory of comparative development administration.

Milton Esman in his elaborate article on the politics of development administration[3] has drawn attention to the "two funda-

1. Mention may particularly be made of Gabriel Almond, Ralph Braibanti, James
S. Coleman, Milton Esman, Samuel P. Huntington, and Fred W. Riggs.
2. Edward W. Weidner, "Development Administration," in Ferrel Heady and
Sybil L. Stokes, eds., *Papers in Comparative Public Administration* (Ann Arbor,
Mich.: Institute of Public Administration, University of Michigan, 1962), p. 111.
3. Milton J. Esman, "The Politics of Development Administration," *CAG Occasional Papers* (Bloomington, Ind.: Indiana University, 1963), pp. 1–2.

mental and interrelated goals" of the developing nations. These
are nation-building and socio-economic progress. Nation-building, according to Esman, "is the deliberate fashioning of an integrated political community within fixed geographic boundaries in
which the nation-state is the dominant political institution," while
socio-economic progress is "the sustained and widely diffused
improvement in material and social welfare." Public administration in these developing societies is, of necessity, closely concerned with the process of achieving these goals and emerges as a
major action instrument which in the course of time evolves its
dynamic and developmental dimensions. Development administration may thus be defined as the complex of organizational
arrangements for the achievement of action through public authority in pursuance of (1) socio-economic goals and (2) nation-
building. It presupposes policies, plans, and programs with a
distinct developmental bias as well as a bureaucracy which consciously and continuously seeks to modernize itself to meet the
demands of planned change.

This discussion attempts to analyze in very broad terms
the changing pattern of administration at the local level in one of
the developing countries, Pakistan. By administration at the local
level is meant district administration and the institutions of local
self-government. The major focus of the study is the emerging
role of the deputy commissioner. The deputy commissioner is the
leading representative of the national and provincial governments
in the district. The district is the principal unit of field administration.

Implicit in this study are certain assumptions which derive
validity from the conditions and experiences of such newly independent countries as Pakistan, India, Ceylon, Nigeria, and Ghana
—countries which were formerly a part of the British Empire and
share, in varying degrees, a similar colonial heritage. Experiences
and conditions of other developing countries such as the Congo
on one end of the scale and the Philippines on the other, being
different, these assumptions may not apply to them. These assumptions are:

1. The growth of development administration is vitally linked with the factor of political stability. In the absence of such stability, the scope of such growth is very limited. The history of Pakistan, before and after the 1958 Revolution, bears eloquent testimony to the validity of this assumption.

2. (*a*) Prefectoral or district administration is a necessary and important areal unit for insuring conditions of order and stability. (*b*) It experiences heavy stress and strain under the forces generated by democracy and development but has the potential and resilience of adjusting itself to the changing situation and growing into an instrument of development administration.

3. (*a*) The inherited colonial system of administration is not only generally capable of handling the requirements of the *take-over period*[4] but can also, without too many drastic changes, lend itself to be geared to the tasks of *experimentation* and *program control.*[5] (*b*) If soon after independence a condition of political instability prevails, bureaucracy under this system can make a major contribution toward keeping the state intact and to some extent filling the political vacuum by providing leadership and initiative at higher levels of national activity.

The price paid by bureaucracy in making such a contribution may be a general decline in the values and standards of integrity, solidarity, and cohesiveness. There is ample validation of this assumption in the first decade of Pakistan's political experience. Ralph Braibanti has observed, "the bureaucracy stood when other segments of society faltered and collapsed. It conducted the business of government. It helped forge a new state. It could not deal effectively with the burdens of internal stresses and strains; indeed no bureaucracy faced with a similar set of problems would have been able to meet the needs adequately."[6]

4. Edward W. Weidner, *Technical Assistance in Public Administration Overseas: The Case for Development Administration* (Chicago: Public Administration Service, 1964), pp. 235–237.
5. *Ibid.*, pp. 237–239.
6. "Public Bureaucracy and Judiciary in Pakistan," in Joseph LaPalombara, ed., *Bureaucracy and Political Development* (Princeton: Princeton University Press, 1963), p. 409.

Historical Background

For a clearer understanding of the current conditions, it is necessary to go back into history and look at the nature of the administrative system as it evolved during the colonial period in the Indo-Pakistan subcontinent and what happened to it after independence. The British rule was commercial in origin and military in character. Unlike the Moguls, the British did not make India their home. Their main purpose was to exploit, rule, and administer for the good and glory of the British Empire. Convinced of their superiority in various walks of life, they were also keen to spread their civilizing influence over the local population. Thus, despotism was tempered with paternalistic benevolence— the degree of benevolence varying with the individual administrator.

The British picked up the threads of the structure of administration as developed by the Moguls, modified it to serve their own requirements and thus over a period of time evolved a system which ideally suited their ends and goals. The system was a strong mechanism of control which vested all authority at all the strategic points in the hands of the British officers, leaving low-level routine to the local officials and clerks. The steel frame of the system was the Indian Civil Service (ICS), recruitment for which continued, till the early twenties of this century, to be made on the basis of a competitive examination in the United Kingdom. It was not until 1922 and as a result of strong and persistent political pressure from the subcontinent that the competitive examination was allowed to be held in India as well. Demand for Indianization of services which had started in the latter half of the nineteenth century was only partially met. In 1939, only one-third of the members of the ICS were Indians. New services were created at the lower levels which were manned entirely by the Indians. A highly stratified system with the ICS at the top and Class IV services at the bottom thus came to be established. There was very little social intercourse between the British officers and their Indian subordinates or even their Indian colleagues. Interest in people's welfare was paternalistic. Security and preservation of the status quo were the major concerns.

The district was the most important unit of administration. The strategic areal unit for the Moguls was the *suba* or the province. The British chose a smaller area with a population ranging from one to five million. The head of the district was a functionary called variously the collector, the district magistrate, and the deputy commissioner. He was usually a member of the ICS. Initially he was the be-all and end-all of everything administrative in the district. There was considerable differentiation of structure and function of his role in the course of time as new activities and increase in the volume of work brought new departments and agencies into existence. But right up to 1947 the deputy commissioner combined in his person the powers of the senior-most magistrate with supervision over other magistrates, powers of revenue collector, and all the residual authority of one who more than anyone else represented in his person the majesty of the British rule in the district. On his residence alone flew the Union Jack, and he was the *mai-bap* (mother and father) of the people. Above him was the commissioner of a division—consisting of four or five districts—and both were under the governor of the province and his secretariat. At the top was the governor-general and the viceroy. All of them were responsible to the secretary of state in London. The system was characterized by the supremacy of the generalist, who by virtue of his Oxford or Cambridge background and a rigorous competitive examination possessed considerable qualities of head and heart. He was generally intrusted with positions of high responsibility at a young age and provided with varied experience in the field and the secretariat.

The system as a whole was oriented toward law and order and provided ample means for the fulfilment of the ends and objectives of the colonial regime.

This very system continued after the independence. It proved its validity and strength in the building of Pakistan, beset as the new state was with tremendous problems of law and order and rehabilitation. The framework not only survived the jolts and jerks of a series of political crises which characterized Pakistan's first decade but also provided a firm basis for growth. Despite its shortcomings in serving the ends of planned development, it helped lay down the foundations of industrial growth[7] and proved resilient enough to secure such revolutionary changes as the merger of the provinces and states of West Pakistan into one unit. It suffered its share of damage, however, in this era of political instability and the re-emergence and assertion of the indigenous norms of ascription and parochialism.

In spite of the fact that two charismatic leaders[8] of national status were removed by death and assassination within four years of independence, that there was a serious shortage of senior officers and specialists, that there were differences in cultural background and comparative development between East and West Pakistan lying at a distance of a thousand miles from each other, that there were diverse problems of communication, integration, and development, that machinery of the central government had to be built up from scratch, that millions of refugees had to be rehabilitated under severely trying conditions—despite all these handicaps and difficulties, Pakistan managed to survive, notwithstanding the forebodings of many that the country would not last more than a few months. This is not the place to go into the causes for Pakistan's survival. A number of factors are involved, but it may safely be said that the bureaucracy made a major contribution toward keeping the state intact.

After the Revolution of 1958, the administrative apparatus was primarily geared to the task of economic development. The achievements of Pakistan in this sphere during the last few years bear eloquent testimony to the impressive contributions made by

7. Reference here is to the highly successful results achieved by the Pakistan Industrial Development Corporation, a semiautonomous body set up by the government of Pakistan to undertake essential industrial projects.
8. These leaders were Quaid-i-Azam Mohammad Ali Jinnah, commonly known as the founder of Pakistan, and his right-hand man, Liaqat Ali Khan. The former became the first governor-general of Pakistan and died in 1948, while the latter, who became the first prime minister of Pakistan, was assassinated in October, 1951.

the bureaucracy. Pakistan, in fact, is currently being cited as a model for rational absorption of foreign aid and for achieving a high rate of growth.[9]

An Interpretation of Politics and Administration in Pakistan in Riggsian Terms[10]

Public participation at higher and lower levels of government is desirable for various reasons. It is only natural that after independence the principle of popular sovereignty be acknowledged and established. Those who wield power are keen to have popular support. Economic development demands the co-operation of the people. These factors make it incumbent that there should be a sharing of power with people and their representatives. On the other hand considerations of national security and defense and the imperative of internal stability dictate the need for a strong centralized authority. Internal stability is also important for insuring rapid economic development and continuity of policies and programs. A strong authority at the center is a must if the parochial, regional, linguistic, and other fissiparous tendencies are to be held in check. The major conflict thus emerges in Riggsian terms between *capacity* and *participation*. More of participation without enhanced *integration* in the circumstances of a newly independent country may lead to a lowering of capacity. A lowering of capacity will lead to all-around deterioration, particularly if the various elements of participation are not adequately integrated. This is what happened in Pakistan between 1951 and 1958.

9. See Gustav F. Papanek, "Pakistan: Growth in the Mixed Economy," a paper read at the Conference of Planning and Growth under a Mixed Economy held in Istanbul, Turkey, in August–September, 1965 (Washington, D.C.: Embassy of Pakistan, 1965). To quote from page 3: "Yet recently, when pessimism about the growth of underdeveloped countries is general, Pakistan has been cited as an example of rare success. Its over-all growth, estimated at 5.5 per cent is approaching the rate at which it will be twice that of population growth."

10. See Fred W. Riggs, "The Theory of Political Development," in James C. Charlesworth, ed., *Identifiable Approaches to the Study of Politics and Government in America* (Philadelphia: American Academy of Political and Social Science, 1967). See also Riggs, chap. ii above.

The two charismatic leaders having gone, the major political party[11] having lost its hold on the people, there being a mushrooming of parties lacking popular support, the regional and local interests and forces emerged unchecked in a disorderly manner, and the political actors found themselves wrestling with each other with no holds barred. The referee himself became a partisan. The bureaucracy carried on the administration of the country but could not keep away from temptation to exploit the situation. It undertook, perhaps reluctantly at first, the responsibility of providing leadership and sought to infuse strength and order in the body politic. It did hold the fort but besieged as it was by the elemental forces of disorder and insecurity, it could not carry on for long. Weaknesses appeared within. The result was deterioration, a general feeling of frustration, and considerable uncertainty and confusion. Then came the Revolution. It brought fresh air, order, and certainty. It moved swiftly. It started off by cleansing the political and administrative systems. The inefficient and corrupt politicians and officers were screened out.

Too much of haphazard participation had had its toll. New forces of capacity emerged and restored stability. The new leadership was dynamic and in the short period of a few years achieved impressive results. The country's economy was put on an even keel. A series of reforms in the social and administrative spheres were devised and implemented. Ralph Braibanti, reviewing these developments, has referred to "the eminently rational spirit of self-criticism and reconstruction" which characterized the new regime. "This," he goes on to say, "has manifested itself in the creation of some twenty-five commissions of enquiry involving nearly three hundred experts to appraise all sectors of the nation's life and to determine basic policy. Of particular interest to bureaucratic reform are the three commissions dealing with administrative matters whose work, for the first time in Pakistan's history has been integrated into a cohesive pattern of reform

11. Reference here is to the Muslim League party, which, headed by Jinnah, fought for the creation of Pakistan.

which is as close to any rational plan" as any human organization can be.[12]

The new regime was also conscious of the need for taking concrete steps to promote political growth. The new Constitution of 1962 was a concession to the social and political realities of Pakistan. It was a blend of the American and British constitutional ideas and practices. It stood for a strong executive but also provided for an independent judiciary and representative legislature. A series of steps was taken at the provincial and local levels to decentralize authority, to experiment with new organizational devices for developmental activities, to strengthen the departments by evolving improved personnel practices and, most significantly of all, by introducing a viable and vital system of local self-government. This new system, commonly called "Basic Democracies," was, in its design and operation, in many ways a new beginning for a genuine participation of the people in the affairs of government and insured simultaneously a change in attitudes and influence of the local functionaries. It made the latter more and more exposed to local pressures and demands, thus initiating a process of partnership in the planning and implementing of development programs as well as in the management of local affairs.

Field Administration and Local Self-Government

What has been the picture at the local level? What has been happening in the districts—the most important areal unit of administration? Has there been any significant change in the structure and functions of the district administration? What new activities and complexities have emerged? How has the district as an important part of the field administration fared? How will it lend itself to be an instrument of development administration? The district is the level which bears the brunt of the pressures of

12. "The Philosophical Foundations of Bureaucratic Change," in Inayatullah, ed., *Bureaucracy and Development in Pakistan* (Peshawar: Pakistan Academy for Rural Development, 1963), pp. 88–89.

democracy and development, where administration comes closest to the people both in terms of expectations and continuous appraisal and criticism.

And what about the deputy commissioner—that living representation of the government in the district? Has there been any significant change in his authority, influence, and functions? What is his place in the changing patterns of activity? What sort of image has he now in the minds of his colleagues, his superiors, and the people in general? What sort of adjustment has occurred in his role in the context of increasing specialization in the developmental departments and of public participation? What will be the shape of things in the foreseeable future?

District Administration and Socio-economic Development

R. W. Gable has succinctly described the significance of the district, noting that it is "the fundamental unit of administration in Pakistan. . . . Policies are framed at the Central and provincial levels; they are implemented in the district. In the words of S. S. Khera, district administration is the cutting edge of the tool of public administration. The image which the people have of their government is the image projected by the district officer."[13]

The two provinces of East and West Pakistan have in all sixty-eight districts—fifty-one in the West and seventeen in the East. This number includes eleven political agencies in the tribal areas. These figures represent the present position. In 1947 West Pakistan had forty districts only. The addition of eleven occurred with the merger of the states as well as the provinces, in West Pakistan, into one unit.

There is a tremendous variation in the size, population, and topography of the districts and in their levels of industrialization and urbanization.[14] The average size of a district is about 6,015

13. "District Administration: Its Development and Its Challenges," in Inayatullah, ed., *District Administration in Pakistan* (Peshawar: Pakistan Academy for Rural Development, 1964), p. 1.
14. These facts and figures have been taken from different articles in *ibid.* and a paper by G. Yazdani Malik, "District Administration," *Public Administration Review*, XXIV (Lahore: NIPA, Oct.–Dec., 1964), 28–40.

square miles. In West Pakistan, which is six times the area of East Pakistan, the average size is about 16,079 square miles. There are, however, districts such as Mardan with an area of 110 square miles, while at the other end of the scale is the district of Kalat which covers more than 30,000 square miles.

Similarly there is a large variation in the population of a district. The statistical average is about 840,000, but the range varies from 41,000 in Chagai to more than 7,000,000 in Mymensingh. In West Pakistan itself the most populous district has sixty-five times the number of people of the smallest district.

There is also variation in the urban-rural complex from 1 per cent urban to 90 per cent. The urban component is around 22.5 per cent in West Pakistan and 5.2 per cent in East Pakistan. There are further differences in physical facilities such as communications and transportation, in the cultural heritage such as the language pattern, in the nature and extent of political expression, and in the attitudes of people toward government.

Three or four districts grouped together make a division. There are in all sixteen divisions in Pakistan—twelve in West Pakistan and four in the East. Each district is composed of subdivisions, *tehsils, thanas, qanungo* circles, and *patwar* circles.[15] These smaller units were primarily designed for revenue and police administration. Some of the smaller units of departments such as Irrigation, Communication, and Works have different areal subunits and cut across the revenue and police units. The figure below indicates the districts, their location, and the number of subunits in East and West Pakistan.

These territorial arrangements were subjected to a searching review by the Provincial Administration Commission (1960), on whose recommendations a number of changes and adjustments were made. New districts were created and new divisions organized. As a result of a policy decision steps are now being taken to create more subdivisions in West Pakistan by grouping two or

15. For an explanation of these terms, see glossary prepared by Ralph Braibanti in *Research on the Bureaucracy of Pakistan* (Durham, N.C.: Duke University Press, 1966), pp. 533–541.

Figure. *Administrative Structure of Pakistan*

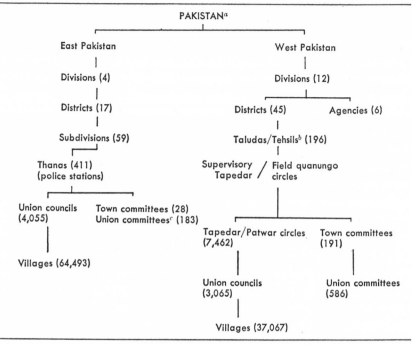

a. Excluding Jammu and Kashmir, Gilgit and Baltistan, Junagadh and Manavadar.
b. The *talukas* and some of the *tehsils* are also grouped into subdivisions.

three *tehsils* together. East Pakistan has no *tehsils* and instead has subdivisions.

The total number of villages in Pakistan is 101,560; 64,493 of these are in East Pakistan and the rest are in the western wing.

A district has normally thirty-two departments. They are: Criminal Administration, Civil Courts and the District Judge, Police, Jails, Revenue, Excise and Taxation, Anti-Corruption, Reclamation and Probation, Auqaf, Games, Food, Rehabilitation and Settlement, Civil Defense, Labor, Irrigation, Buildings and Roads, Electricity, Education, Fisheries, Agriculture, Animal Husbandry, Forests, Co-operatives, Basic Democracies, Urban Rehabilitation, Small Savings, Health, Transport, Information,

Social Welfare, Industries, and Family Planning. For purposes of classification the first fourteen (through Labor) may be described as regulatory and the last eighteen as developmental.[16] The districts were created primarily for the purposes of revenue administration. This accounts for the designation of "collector" used for the deputy commissioner in many parts of British India (and still current in India). Historically second only in importance to the revenue department was the magistracy headed by the deputy commissioner in his capacity as district magistrate. The remaining departments came into existence in the course of time as and when a specific need arose to provide a particular service or to control a certain activity. The departments which came into existence after independence are Rehabilitation, Auqaf (management of religious trusts and shrines), Urban Rehabilitation, Social Welfare, Family Planning, and Basic Democracies.

There are other activities such as land acquisition which are not departments as such, but for which there are a number of functionaries in the district. The supervision and, in differing degrees, the operation of these activities is the concern of the deputy commissioner. Mention may also be made of the works program,[17] to which about one billion rupees have already been committed. It aims at employing the idle labor in the villages as well as providing basic infrastructure in the rural and to some extent in the urban areas through the efforts of the Basic Democracies with the assistance of local government officers under the supervision and over-all direction of the district councils. All these new activities and the expansion of the technical departments have placed a heavy burden on the deputy commissioner both in the matter of operation and co-ordination.

A number of changes in the organization of the Provincial

16. Departments concerned with development work are commonly referred to as nation-building departments in India and Pakistan. Here the adjective used is "developmental" to distinguish its meaning from the word "nation-building" as used in defining the term "development administration."

17. The Rural Works program in Pakistan is discussed in Richard V. Gilbert, "The Works Program in East Pakistan," *International Labor Review*, LXXXIX (Mar., 1964), 213–226. Also see Inayatullah, ed., *Evaluation Report of Rural Works Program in West Pakistan* (Lahore: Government of West Pakistan Press, 1964).

Secretariat and the attached departments have occurred as a result of the recommendations of the Provincial Administration Commission and the Provincial Reorganization Committee.[18] These reforms, coupled with the changes which took place in 1955 in West Pakistan as a consequence of the integration of provinces and states and the functional adjustments made as a result of the promulgation of the new Constitution in 1962, not only have resulted in a rational rearrangement of territorial units—i.e., divisions, districts, subdivisions, as well as regions for such development activities as irrigation and communication—but have also brought about a considerable amount of decentralization and delegation of authority at various levels. Reference may also be made to a number of semiautonomous public corporations set up in the fields of industries, public transport, agriculture, and water and power development, all of which are represented at the district level and below and have a bearing on the growing volume of developmental activities at the local level.

Another way of measuring the over-all increase in these activities and the dynamic changes which have taken place to meet the demands of socio-economic growth would be the quantity of funds committed to developmental programs during the last decade and a half. The quantity allocated under each five-year plan is a good index of the rising volume and tempo of these efforts. These figures are:

	Period	Total developmental outlay in rupees (millions)[19]
First five-year plan	1955–60	10,800
Second five-year plan	1960–65	23,000
Third five-year plan	1965–70	52,000

18. For an account of the recommendations of these committees and commissions, see Braibanti, *Research on the Bureaucracy of Pakistan,* pp. 213–243.

19. These figures are derived from the government of Pakistan publications, especially the *Pakistan Economic Survey, 1964–65* (Karachi: Ministry of Finance, Manager of Government Publications, 1965), as well as Mahbubul Haq, *The Strategy of Economic Planning* (Karachi: Oxford University Press, Pakistan Branch, 1963). On pages 108–111 of his book, Mahbubul Haq discusses the inflationary trends in Pakistan during the period from 1951–52 to 1959–60. According to Table 23, with an index of 1951–52 = 100, the rise in the inflationary trend was 24 per cent in East Pakistan and 20 per cent in West Pakistan.

Amounts allocated to such programs as health, education, agriculture, and water and power were:

	Rupees (millions)
Education	
First plan (1955–60)	460
Second plan (1960–65)	1,055
Third plan (1965–70)	3,030
Health	
First plan	230
Second plan	420
Third plan	1,370
Agriculture	
First plan	970
Second plan	2,430
Third plan	8,670
Water and power	
First plan	2,160
Second plan	4,390
Third plan	9,070

In the province of West Pakistan, the annual development expenditure increased from 1,000 million rupees to 2,100 million between the years 1960–61 and 1964–65. During the same period the increase in East Pakistan was from about 550 million rupees to more than 2,000 million.[20]

Figures given below are a sample of the annual increase in expenditure and personnel in two departments in the Lahore District.[21]

	Budget			Personnel		
	1951–52	1963–64	Change	1951–52	1963–64	Change
Education	370,538	4,645,919	+1,154%	3,009	4,134	+37%
Health	188,060	947,050	+ 419	71	86	+21

Local Self-Government: The System of Basic Democracies

The system of local self-government during the British rule in India was by and large a failure. Tinker has described it thus:

20. See charts opposite pages 170 and 172 of *Pakistan Economic Survey, 1964–65.*
21. Anwar Tehmasp, "Structure and Functions of Nation-building Departments," in Inayatullah, ed., *District Administration in Pakistan,* p. 81.

"Indian Local Self Government was still in many ways a democratic facade to an autocratic structure. The actual conduct of business was carried on by district officials with the non-official members as spectators or at the most, critics."[22]

This statement pertains to conditions around the year 1908, twenty-six years after the promulgation of Rippon's Local Self-Government Act. Later on in the period between the two world wars, when the district boards and the municipal committees began having elected non-officials as chairmen, the performance of these local bodies continued to be poor and disappointing. Tinker ascribes this to difficulties arising out of "poverty, inadequate leadership, the failings common to that most delicate system of government—democracy and maladjustment between the custom of the East and the innovations of the West."[23] He goes on to indicate that "the aim of [British] policy was consolidation rather than experiment. . . . Policy making was further restricted by the narrow interpretation which was given to local governments. It was conceived in terms of sanitation, roads and 'improvements,' of chairmen, committees, minutes and resolutions. It was all as incongruous as the bizarre Victorian gothic town halls which adorn so many of the larger Indian cities."[24] The basic reason for failure was the fact that a foreign system of local management had been imposed by an alien power which could not function adequately in view of the mechanism of control at the local level—namely, the district administration, which was too strong and efficient to allow the growth of democratic local government institutions. The promise of the emergence of political responsibility at the local level thus remained unfulfilled, and local bodies, especially in the rural areas, were hardly more than a mere appendage of the district administration.

For reasons fairly obvious, little attention was paid to the reform of local self-government during the first decade of Pakistan. The organs of local government fell victim to the exploitationist designs of the politicians in the provinces and were used

22. Hugh Tinker, *The Foundations of Local Self-Government in India, Pakistan and Burma* (London: Athlone Press, 1954), p. 70.
23. *Ibid.*, p. 12.   24. *Ibid.*, p. 334.

for purposes of political bargaining. Most of these local bodies were inoperable by the time of the Revolution.

The system of Basic Democracies introduced by the new regime is in many ways very different from earlier experiments in local government. At the base of the new system in rural areas the union council consisted of ten or twelve members elected on the basis of adult franchise—each representing a population of about 1,000 people. The total number of union councils is 7,120—4,055 in East Pakistan and 3,065 in the West.[25] The union council has a number of functions both compulsory and optional. Councils perform routine civic duties such as street lighting and sanitation, building of roads, and school dispensaries, and also attend to general welfare measures and engage in the promotion of agricultural and other local developmental activities. The council elects a chairman who along with an appointed secretary runs routine business. The chairman and some members further act as a tribunal to settle petty local disputes and offenses. The chairman also administers the newly enacted Family Laws Ordinance which regulates divorce and second marriages. The union council enjoys the power of local taxation. It can seek and secure assistance from local government departments. The members of the union council are popularly called basic democrats.

In small urban areas there are town committees. These committees are restricted to small towns with a population of less than 14,000. There are 219 town committees in all. In the cities there are municipal committees. Both towns and cities are further subdivided into union committees which are the counterparts of union councils. There are 769 union committees in all.

The *tehsil* is a larger geographic unit than the senior council in West Pakistan. In the *tehsil* council are represented all the chairmen of the union councils and the town committees. The *tehsil*-appointed officials are also members of the council. In East Pakistan, instead of the *tehsil*, there is a *thana* council with a similar composition. These councils are mainly co-ordinating bodies, but they also supervise and guide the activities of union councils,

25. *Census of Pakistan, 1961* (Karachi: Manager of Publications, Government of Pakistan), I, 1–50.

particularly in the area of rural development. The *thana* councils in East Pakistan are emerging as active entities, more so than the *tehsil* councils in the Western wing, concerning themselves more dynamically with the process of development.

Above the *tehsil* or *thana* councils are the district councils which have a majority of elected members. The members of the union councils, union committees, and town committees constitute the electorate. The district councils are presided over by the deputy commissioner, but have elected vice-chairmen. A district council has wide powers of taxation and a large number of responsibilities and functions.

At the top of the local government hierarchy is the divisional council, with the majority of its members elected. The commissioner acts as the chairman. It is mostly a supervisory body and also has co-ordinating functions.

Thus, the union council is noteworthy since, unlike councils of higher tiers, it is a body completely elected. In all higher tiers, the councils are partly elected and partly official. While the number of appointive officials serving on the councils in each of these tiers has to be less than that of the elected non-officials, the mixed composition means that they are not the basic unit of the system; thus in many ways the union council is the most important body.

It is important to note that the Basic Democracies system is dynamic, not static. The relation of appointed officials to the elected bodies can change as conditions warrant. This has already happened. The system of nomination of some of the non-officials initially provided in the Basic Democracies order has been abolished. Currently, the union councils are asking for enhanced authority.

This, then, is the structure of Basic Democracies. The following salient features distinguish this system from the previous arrangement.

1. It does not rest on the idea of the village as a self-contained social and economic unit. It rather seeks to widen the area of active association to build up small communities in terms of common needs and problems.

2. It links one level with another. It does not leave them as isolated units as was the case before.

3. It brings the representatives of the urban and rural areas together as members in the district and divisional councils.

4. It is designed to encourage, perforce, a continuing dialogue between local officers and the people's representatives as members of the councils. It thus acts as an educating process both for the elected members and for the officials who sooner or later have to learn to shed their old attitudes and persuade themselves to be accountable to the people for what they do and how they do it.

5. The basic democrats are also the electors of the members of the provincial and national assemblies and the president. This makes them politically important and adds a tremendous weight to their voice. It makes it easy for them to have access to officers and ministers as well as the members of the legislatures.

6. The system has a unique developmental dimension which has been operative mostly through the highly successful Rural Works Program. This program has been practically run by Basic Democracies, primarily at the union council level. As mentioned earlier, large funds amounting to millions of rupees have been committed to the Rural Works Program since 1962–63. In its very first year in West Pakistan more than thirteen thousand schemes, mostly relating to link roads, water supplies, education, and agriculture, were planned and executed by these councils. The record of achievement in East Pakistan has been still better.[26]

It may also be mentioned that under a government directive the budgets of all the local departments concerned with development have to be referred to the district and divisional councils. The councils also have the right of discussing the performance of various departments and projects, raising questions, and demanding information about administrative and developmental matters. They are further privileged to address government in these matters and make recommendations for or against a policy issue even in regard to matters of provincial and national importance.

Thus, in addition to assisting in economic development, the

26. See Gilbert, *op. cit.*, and evaluation reports prepared by the Pakistan Academy for Rural Development, Comilla, East Pakistan.

Basic Democracies represent a process of partnership between government and people for political development. Through them official action at the local level is beginning to be responsible and responsive to public representatives. The system helps train the latter to handle and manage local affairs. It does more. It has been responsible for a new kind of leadership emerging at the village and district levels. The elected representatives come from different strata of society and are not restricted to the old landed gentry. Most of them are young and literate.[27] Basic Democracies have also provided new channels of two-way communication—there being only one channel before, the district and local officers, their subordinates, and their protégés.

Anxiety has been expressed[28] about the growth of the system of Basic Democracies in view of the element of official representation in the councils. Government functionaries, particularly the deputy commissioner, have been inclined to be hesitant to share authority and decision-making with local representatives. District administration has been essentially and traditionally authoritarian in character. Such apprehension is not without validity. Still, the features of the system and the importance which the national leaders attach to it augur well. The fact that the basic democrats wield considerable political influence by virtue of their right to elect the members of the legislature and the president provides a strong basis of hope for its growth both as a political institution and as an administrative arrangement.

In spite of these indications and the hopeful signs for the functioning and developing of Basic Democracies, ultimately much will depend on the manner in which the governing elites at the national and provincial levels and the officials at the district level conduct themselves and the willingness they show of speeding up the process of affording a larger measure of autonomy to these nascent organs of local expression. A lot will also depend on

27. See Braibanti's *Research on the Bureaucracy of Pakistan*, p. 205. "Nearly 70 per cent of those elected to the Councils are literate. Most of them are between the ages of thirty-five and forty and seem to come from the lower-middle and middle classes."

28. See articles by R. W. Gable, pp. 18–19, and Inayatullah, pp. 121–122, in Inayatullah, ed., *District Administration in Pakistan*.

the newly emerging local leadership and how these local leaders face the new demands through their imagination, initiative, and integrity. Expecting too much too soon will only stultify the steady growth of these local bodies. Therefore, their burdens and responsibilities should have some correspondence to their capacity in terms of knowledge, attitudes, skills, and experience. However, it is only with responsibility that individuals and institutions grow and attain their full stature.

The Deputy Commissioner: His Environment and Changing Role

The deputy commissioner was perhaps the most impressive of the institutions evolved by the British during their rule over India. He was practically the monarch of all he surveyed. He was the "kingpin" of the administrative system. "In all districts" Lord Macaulay is said to have remarked, "there is not a single village —there is not a hut in which the difference between a good and bad collector may not make the difference between happiness and misery. . . . Such power as that which the collectors of India have over the people of India is not found in any other part of the world possessed by any class of functionaries."[29]

The source of this authority lay in the formal powers he enjoyed and the commission he carried in his person as the embodiment of imperial strength and glory. His formal power rested on his being the head of the revenue administration, an activity which more than anything else touched the life of the people in the countryside where land had always been the primary source of sustenance and status. He was also the custodian of law and order; he was the district magistrate and held the powers of protection over the person and the property of the people. And last of all he was the chief representative of the government and as such possessed tremendous prestige and influence. He was the link between the government and the people and in this capacity performed the political roles of spokesman of the masses and interpreter of the policies of government. And besides being the patron of numerous voluntary and welfare organizations, he was

29. 128 *Parliamentary Debates, 3rd Series* (June 24, 1853), cols. 745–746.

also the district scout commissioner, the chairman of the Red Cross, and the president of the local club. He was the protector of people against natural calamities and disasters such as floods and locusts. It was within his power to distribute crown land by way of lease or outright grant, extend loans for agriculture improvement, and recommend names for the conferment of awards and honors. In the exercise of all these powers he was not accountable to the people. He was only remotely controlled by the higher authorities. His direct superior—the commissioner of a division —would normally not interfere in his work and decisions.

The nineteenth century marked the heyday of his glory. Already, however, forces of specialization had set in. New activities brought in new functionaries who were sharing power with him —the superintendent of police, the district surgeon, and later the engineer and the education and agriculture officers. His hegemony, however, continued. The demand for the Indianization of higher services and particularly the ICS and the introduction of reforms leading to an enhanced representation of the Indians in the processes of decision-making adversely affected his position as the blue-eyed member of an exclusive club. By 1921, the unquestioned authority began to be weakened by the emergence of Indian ministers at the provincial level and the increasing number of specialist services. Such was the impact of these developments that a large number of ICS officers resigned and left. The representative ministries elected under the Government of India Act of 1935 further lowered his status. By the time independence came, the deputy commissioner's position had been considerably shaken, although he still enjoyed his original powers and a great amount of prestige. The environment had changed, and with the departure of the British a transformation was under way.

The new administrative environment has been described very lucidly by Ralph Braibanti in an article on public bureaucracy and judiciary in Pakistan.[30] Briefly, the shortage of senior officers pushed young members of the civil service into positions of au-

30. "Public Bureaucracy and Judiciary in Pakistan," pp. 383–409.

thority including the office of the deputy commissioner. They were inexperienced, and the scope of guidance and training available to them was limited. The situation was so very different from the days before independence. There was urgency in the air. A new country, a new government was being born. Millions of refugees were to be settled. There was hardly time for elaborate training as in the old days.

Then, within four years of independence, soon after Prime Minister Liaqat Ali's assassination, Pakistan entered an era of mounting political instability. The politicians were out to exploit, and they did not spare the bureaucracy, particularly at the local level. The young officer felt himself torn between two worlds— the world of his ideals of high standards of service and integrity and the world of political pressure and demands for things to be done in ways unconventional and, to him, sometimes incorrect. If he resisted, he could be transferred, and there were frequent transfers. To stay in a district for more than a year was an exception rather than the rule. The old image of prestige and authority of the district officer was shaken. The effect went deeper. Officers from the provincial services[31] had to be posted to districts on account of the shortage of the CSP officers. These officers were different. They were more amenable to pressure and had greater experience of adjustment and compromise. They were older and comparatively less idealistic. They could be bent and used. Many of them were successful. The young officer, too, began learning ways of making his position secure and keeping the politicians and the senior officers happy. Tact was more important than integrity. Over-all efficiency was not as important as attending to certain tasks satisfactorily.

So far as the general public was concerned the deputy commissioner was still the government. If its expectations of great changes after independence did not come true then it was he who was to blame, particularly when in the public mind he was

31. For the relative number of PCS and CSP officers appointed as deputy commissioners in West Pakistan, see Minhajuddin, "Some Aspects of District Administration," in Inayatullah, ed., *District Administration in Pakistan*, pp. 30–39.

the symbol of an alien rule. In the meantime the Provincial Civil Services and the specialist cadres were demanding and claiming a share in the higher administrative posts, most of which had been reserved for members of the CSP. They did secure many. The general atmosphere for a young member of the "most distinguished civil service"[32] was thus one of discouragement and uncertainty.

The frequent transfers affected the deputy commissioner in other ways too. He could not make his full contribution to district affairs. He would hardly begin to know his area when he would be shifted. As one writer pointed out, he was gaining more experience in breadth than depth.[33]

The senior members of the civil service could not provide adequate leadership. They were too busy and were themselves affected by the changing environment. They had to unlearn a lot and learn how loyally to serve the politicians who had become so powerful since independence. There were thus no clear models to follow. Lack of security, lack of adequate guidance from seniors, inadequate training—all this led to the weakening of old traditions and lowering of values. This affected cohesiveness and the *esprit de corps.*

So far as the people were concerned the image of an impartial, upright, and paternal figure was distorted. The environment was one of "unstable equilibrium."[34] The civil services were not equipped to deal with the internal pressures generated by the instability of the society generally. Before independence the district officer could with advantage keep his distance from the people. After independence he had to learn to mix with the people and identify himself with them. A "posture of familiarity" in a society largely characterized by ascriptive and particularistic values could create a "reputation for partiality." "Since the natural barriers of background, colonial rule and cultural differences" were gone, the Pakistani official (and especially the district officer) was "almost helpless against this web" which threatened

32. Quotation from Sir Eric Franklin's *Statement on Careers in the Pakistan Central Superior Services* (Karachi: Government of Pakistan, 1).
33. Munir Ahmad, *The Civil Servant in Pakistan* (Karachi: Oxford University Press, 1964), pp. 226–234.
34. Braibanti, "Public Bureaucracy and Judiciary in Pakistan," p. 409.

to strangle him.[35] His aloofness was "his instinctive response to the need for self-preservation,"[36] but aloofness in the changed circumstances was often neither wise nor possible. The task of the district officer thus became more difficult and complex.

There was also a large increase in the work load of the deputy commissioner. This was a result of the increase in population, the emergence of new functions and activities, and the rising volume of funds devoted to development programs. The population had been increasing at the rate of about 2.8 per cent. A number of new departments and agencies came into existence after independence. Many of these were the direct concern of the deputy commissioner. He increasingly associated himself with welfare and developmental activities.

Simultaneously the size and number of technical departments was also expanding. The specialist was assuming more importance and was less inclined to accept the leadership of the deputy commissioner. He had the strong support of his senior officers who were fighting for a greater say in policy-making and a higher place in the hierarchy of power and status. With greater emphasis on developmental activities, which were becoming increasingly attractive to the politicians, the specialist officers were in a better position now to influence them and seek their assistance and patronage. All this made the tasks and problems of co-operation and co-ordination increasingly complex.

There were more and more visitors for the deputy commissioner, they were not satisfied to see his subordinates. He was after all a public servant and was to be accessible to them all the time. There was an increase in the protocol duties. Visits of VIP's, ministers, foreign dignitaries, and senior officers multiplied out of all proportion to what they had been before independence. The deputy commissioner also had to make a larger number of reports to the government. He was provided with some additional help, but his worries and involvement in these activities placed heavy pressures on his physical resources.

The picture of the deputy commissioner which emerged was one of attenuated influence, increasing burdens, complex tasks,

35. *Ibid.*   36. *Ibid.*, p. 394.

and loss of the old halo. The politician, the police department and technical departments were more than sharing his prestige and position. Young age, inexperience, increase in work, a more articulate public, lack of security, frequent transfers—all these weakened his position considerably. The rising importance and strength of the commissioner further prejudiced his leadership at the local level. It was in partial reaction to this deterioration that a former senior civil servant who had risen to the position of governor-general remarked, "You cannot have the old British system of administration [and] at the same time allow the politicians to meddle with the civil service. In the British system, the district magistrate was the kingpin of administration. His authority was unquestioned. We have to restore that."[37] It is ironic to find that he himself indulged in political maneuverings at the highest level.

The new regime which took over in 1958 was characterized by dynamism, and the district officer was expected to be equally dynamic and productive of results. Additional responsibilities ensued. Being the chairman of the district council and the project director of the Rural Works Programs, the deputy commissioner was continuously engaged in new tasks which demanded priority and full-time attention. The pressure of many activities mounted up. Election work increased considerably. Between 1959 and 1965 two country-wide elections were held. These related to election of basic democrats, members of the provincial and national legislatures, and the president of Pakistan. The deputy commissioner along with a number of his colleagues and subordinates acted as an agent of the chief election commissioner. If the burden of such responsibilities as the rehabilitation of refugees was lessening with the passage of time, there were many additional tasks and functions to keep him more than busy, new and novel tasks like helping the family planning, Auqaf, and land reform programs.

Efforts were made to rehabilitate the power and position of the deputy commissioner. The Provincial Administration Commission recommendations that he be specifically designated as the "head

37. Quoted by Keith Callard in *Pakistan: A Political Study* (London: Allen and Unwin, 1957), p. 285. The reference is to President Iskander Mirza.

of the district administration" and a captain of the team of the district officers were accepted and instructions issued accordingly. He was, at the same time, prohibited to "meddle in technical aspects of a program or the internal administration of other departments." These instructions have, however, not restored the previous dominant position of the deputy commissioner. The conflict is much deeper. It is the growing tussle between the generalist and the specialist. And if one looks at the concessions made to the specialists in the sharing of secretarial and other high positions, it is clear (and understandably so) that the generalist is losing ground. But such is the nature of activity at the district level that there is an obvious need for effective co-ordination, and the only government functionary who can perform the role of the co-ordinator is the deputy commissioner. The need for his playing this role has increased on account of the emphasis on development. There are many matters requiring the aid of his good offices, in the reconciliation of overlapping functions, in harmonizing efforts of different agencies, in reducing delay and expediting implementation of projects, and in securing co-operation for programs demanding involvement of several departments and the people at large. There are departmental jealousies, lack of co-operation, and therefore need for an authority which can remove bottlenecks in the matter of land acquisition required for development projects, problems of law and order, colonization of land, and mobilization of manpower. As Gable remarked in his article on district administration, "the specialist representatives of the various welfare and development departments in the field need the generalist district officer as coordinator, facilitator, influencer of public opinion. . . ."[38] The need of the generalist for making "overall sense"[39] out of a medley of activities and programs and therefore for co-ordination and guidance is obvious. It should be understood and translated into measures defining the new role of the deputy commissioner in a rapidly changing situation.

Earlier the deputy commissioner could secure co-ordination

38. Richard W. Gable, "District Administration," in Inayatullah, ed., *District Administration in Pakistan*, p. 11.
39. Paul Appleby, "Making Overall Sense," in A. Avasthi and S. N. Varma, eds., *Aspects of Administration* (New Delhi and New York: Allied Publishers, 1964).

mainly by his prestige. In the changed circumstances, how can co-ordination at the district level be achieved and the problems of relation of generalist to specialist eased? First, the deputy commissioner can be invested with certain specific powers. His relationships with other department heads in the district can be clearly laid down in the form of binding rules which leave no doubt about his functions and authority for insuring co-ordination. In India recently, a great deal of emphasis has been laid on this aspect of the role of the deputy commissioner.[40] Similar action can be taken in Pakistan also. Second, the deputy commissioner can be re-established as the head of the police administration in the district. Because of the power the police officials wield over the people and the capacity they enjoy of helping or harming the politician, the importance of the police has increased tremendously. Third, it would at the same time be appropriate if residential accommodation and adequate salaries are provided to technical officers at the district level. This would help allay their feelings of jealousy and inferiority vis-à-vis the generalist officers.

The role of the deputy commissioner in relation to the Basic Democracies is of special importance. He is the chairman of the district council and in this capacity as well as that of deputy commissioner has great power and capacity for good and bad. As indicated earlier, district administration has traditionally been authoritarian in character. Therefore, Basic Democracies, which are designed ultimately to take over a considerable part of the functions of government departments, may not find it easy to grow. This raises many questions. Should the chairman of the district council be non-official and elected? What should be the role of the deputy commissioner in such a situation? In India chairmen of most of the district councils are elected. In Maharashtra a novel approach has been adopted. The chairman is a non-official. The deputy commissioner has been removed from his position as co-ordinator of development departments. Instead, another senior officer of his status acts as the chief executive officer of the council, who also enjoys supervisory powers over all

40. This has been brought out in a number of articles in the special July–September, 1965, issue of the *Indian Journal of Public Administration* (published by the Indian Institute of Public Administration, New Delhi).

the technical and development departments. Thus, an element of bifurcation of functions and duality of control has been introduced. This change is significant and will be watched for results. There are already, however, voices of criticism against it, as it tends "to blur the focus of the district administration and makes it bi-polar."[41]

It appears likely, however, that in the current circumstances of Pakistan, the deputy commissioner will for some time to come continue to be chairman of the district council. The new concept of the officer as an agent of the administration as well as the people will be consciously developed. In the course of time, it is possible that most of the functions of the district administration will be taken over by the local councils. This hope has indeed been specifically expressed by the author of the idea of Basic Democracies. While inaugurating a seminar on Basic Democracies in 1963, President Ayub Khan spoke as follows:

Let us hope a time will come when these councils [Basic Democracies] would have attained such maturity as education spreads in the country that local administration almost withers away and they run their police, they run their own revenue system and they run everything. I like to see them go in that direction. In ten to fifteen years' time, a situation may arise when the officials are only there to guide and not as administrators and rulers.[42]

It is for the future to reveal whether or not this expectation will be fulfilled. The statement, however, does indicate the direction in which district administration will move.

Conclusion

Fesler[43] in his article on field administration has stressed the significance of prefectural administration both for maintaining the established order and creating a new one. Heaphy[44] in his paper on spatial aspects of development administration has also

41. Ram. K. Vepa, "The Collector in the Sixties: Andhra Pradesh," *ibid.*
42. *Pakistan Times* (Lahore), May 31, 1963.
43. James W. Fesler, "The Political Role of Field Administration," in Heady and Stokes, eds., *Papers in Comparative Public Administration*, p. 136.
44. James Heaphy, "Spatial Aspects of Development Administration," *CAG Occasional Papers* (Bloomington, Ind.: Indiana University, 1965).

stressed the importance of prefectural administration. In Pakistan, the district has proved to be an essential entity for keeping the forces of society in balance. As for its role in creating a new order, it is under severe strain. Doubts were expressed by the Food and Agriculture Commission of Pakistan regarding the instrumentality of district administration for development. As a result of its recommendations, the development programs in the field of agriculture have been transferred to semiautonomous agriculture development corporations. Still, the districts and the local councils do possess potential to become efficient instruments of development administration. The success of the Rural Works Program bears ample testimony to the validity of undertaking development activities through local councils under the guidance and with the assistance of the technical departments, with the deputy commissioner acting as the leader. With more training, with greater rationalization of the position of the deputy commissioner vis-à-vis other district departments, with the growing contribution the Basic Democracies are making in evolving a new administrative ethos in the district, and with provisions of help for relieving the deputy commissioner of routine and excessive duties, much can be achieved in meeting the existing deficiencies. In the context of the dynamic leadership of the present president of Pakistan and the achievements of his regime in various fields, the climate is conducive to rapid progress in this direction.

Field administration and local government today stand between the twin pressures of specialization and public participation. They must accommodate these pressures and take new demands in stride. The Basic Democracies scheme has provided a mechanism that permits such adjustment. Not only does it provide a means for social and economic progress; it also provides a method for nation-building and political development.

The range of the adjustment that is possible over the next few years without fundamentally changing the pattern of field administration and local government is illustrated by the range of suggestions currently made for improvement. Among the more promising are the following:

1. As more CSP officers are now available for district appointments, only senior officers with at least ten years of service should be posted as deputy commissioners.

2. In view of the varying nature of the districts, they should be divided into categories. Bigger and more complex districts should be intrusted to comparatively senior officers. Appointments to these districts should be considered as promotions.

3. Intensive training of district officers and, particularly, the lower-level officials should be undertaken. It is at this level that the public comes in direct and day-to-day contact with government functionaries. There should be special courses arranged for the deputy commissioners specifically concerned with the role they have to play vis-à-vis the Basic Democracies. Their attitude toward the Basic Democracies helps determine the behavior of their colleagues and subordinates.

4. A fresh assessment of the size and volume of work should be undertaken. Big and unmanageable districts should be split into two or three units.

5. All *tehsils* should be upgraded to the status of subdivisions. This would relieve the deputy commissioner of considerable work.

6. The emerging functions of the deputy commissioner should be redefined and incorporated in rules which are binding on all concerned, particularly in the case of the police and the development departments.

7. Elected non-officials should be appointed as chairmen of district councils in certain selected districts on an experimental basis to determine ways in which functions of district administration could be intrusted gradually to representatives, institutions, and individuals.

The requirements of order and stability and the forces and pressures of planned growth demand that field administration be strong and capable of absorbing tensions which arise out of programs of rapid economic development and enhanced public participation. In the newly developing countries, capacity and stability must be built and preserved if a new order is to emerge which will insure steady social and economic progress. Public participation must, at the same time, be encouraged and every possible step taken to insure its growth within a framework of order and capacity. Pakistan today provides an interesting instance of a developing country which is seeking solutions to these issues and problems on a realistic basis.[45]

45. This essay was written prior to the resignation of Ayub Khan as president in 1969. No changes in the text have been made to reflect this development.

Chapter 10

Indigenous Leadership in the Trust Territory of the Pacific Islands

Norman Meller

Milton J. Esman in his midterm appraisal of the Comparative Administration Group[1] prescribes for the further study of development administration and politics that "there must be greater emphasis on the statement of discrete problems and on empirical investigation, especially of the modest kind which do not immediately yield high level insights, generalized propositions, or sweeping prescriptions."[2] It is difficult to conceive of a more fitting response to this call for microcosmic study than to focus attention upon Micronesia, and more specifically, the Trust Territory of the Pacific Islands, whose 2,100 islands cumulatively constitute but 700 square miles of land scattered over 3,000,000 square miles of ocean in the mid-Pacific and are inhabited by only some 90,000 indigenes. Further, in view of the CAG's concern with development, where better to start for a basing point against which to measure political change than with a region still both relatively primitive and non-self-governing?

Introduction

This essay deals mainly with the legislature. Nevertheless, it is relevant to public administration, "broadly defined as being the

1. "CAG and the Study of Public Administration: A Mid-Term Appraisal," *CAG Occasional Papers* (Bloomington, Ind.: Indiana University, 1966).
2. *Ibid.*, p. 35.

activities performed by government executives."[3] It is relevant for
several reasons: (1) "legislature" as herein conceptualized delineates an institution with more encompassing functions than normally posited, which may include administrative decision-making
and performance; (2) even classical public administration recognizes as one of its areas of interest the articulation of the legislative and executive branches of government in the formulation
and implementation of policy; and (3) the study of development
administration of necessity has had to pace itself with a con-
comitant concern for development politics, and an essential element of the latter is the role of the legislature, regardless of its
definition.

The classifier "legislature" as normally employed confuses
function—that is legislating or lawmaking—with structure.[4] The
modern legislature had its inception before it had much concern
with legislating, and its product today is far outweighed in bulk
by the mass of governmental lawmaking occurring outside the
legislative halls. The anachronistic bar which graces the physical
chamber of the legislature bespeaks a judicial element not very
often displayed in the actions of the modern period. "Legislature"
here refers to the governmental institution which is consciously
designed to bring the element of representation into political
decision-making and is both collegial in nature and in the attendant processes it observes. The actual functions performed, be
they granting divorces, conducting wars, naming or recalling
chief executives, molding a nation's opinion, or directly administering a particular enterprise[5] will vary. Probably in any political
system, the "legislature" performs those functions appropriate to
that system as they have evolved by virtue of the legislative
body's representative nature and its characteristic group process.
To the discerning, it will be apparent that nominally executive

3. *Ibid.*, p. 6.
4. This is developed at greater length in Norman Meller, "The Identification and
Classification of Legislatures," *Philippine Journal of Public Administration*, X
(Oct., 1966), 308.
5. As illustration, Resolution 17, First Session, 1956, of the Palau District
Legislature of the Trust Territory names a legislative committee to administer the
district's rhinoceros beetle control program, including its awarding monetary prizes
for the collection of the largest number of beetles and larvae.

agencies, such as an elected school board, may fall within this structural classification of "legislature," and by implication it is thus suggested that their processes may be more fruitfully studied in the same manner as that of a whole subfield of political science.[6]

The classical view of public administration which sought to separate policy-making from administration, and assign to the administrator the execution of policy, has long since been routed by the reality that the administrator is ensconced in the center of policy formulation. How then to separate legislative from administrative policy-makers other than to view them from their respective institutional settings, as participants in a continuum of policy, and as players of roles appropriate to their particular institutions? This approach is particularly applicable to colonial areas, for the evolving legislatures may have no or only limited lawmaking powers, their members serving as champions of local aspirations vis-à-vis non-indigenous administrators sent from the ministering metropolitan nations, and the differences in interest ranging from the most far-reaching decision for future development to the minuscule of administrative detail and its implementation.

Finally, in a region's movement from colonial to politically self-governing status, the legislature plays a significant part in the political socialization of the area's leadership and in preparing it to assume the reins of government. In some cases, with self-government, the legislators have become executive heads while retaining their legislative status; in American-patterned systems this dual capacity is normally avoided because of the doctrine of separation of powers, although alternating service between one and the other branch is not uncommon. However, in the Pacific, American colonial practice temporarily permitted legislators to remain as important members of the administrative bureaucracy during the formative years of a legislative body, later requiring them to make a choice between the positions they occupied.

More broadly, it is the legislature which by virtue of its repre-

---

6. Norman Meller, "Legislative Behavior Research," *Western Political Quarterly,* XIII (Mar., 1960), 131, and "Legislative Behavior Research Revisited: A Review of Five Years' Publications," *Western Political Quarterly,* XVIII (Dec., 1965), 776.

sentative character frequently acts as the vehicle for political change. Its internal processes are uniquely adapted for bringing to the fore issues which a hierarchically structured bureaucracy may divert before they reach the centers of administrative decision-making. Its members more aptly communicate the needs of the people they represent[7] than a bureaucracy spacebound in centralized headquarters and so time-accelerated with future plans as to fail to comprehend the present hopes and fears of such as the subsistence farmer. In a region such as Micronesia, the legislature can and does concern itself with the details of executing policy, not alone through lawmaking and exercising administrative oversight, but at times by legislators voluntarily interposing themselves between levels of administrative officialdom as part of bureaucracy to help the new governmental activities function. And in those areas where law is enforced by social sanction apart from the existence of any specialized governmental institutions for administering it,[8] the legislator as law enunciator is an administrator to the extent that he communicates the law and thus articulates it within the existent social structure.

The Pacific Setting

The Pacific Basin today knows the ministrations of five metropolitan powers and encompasses the last two trusteeships of the original eleven established by the United Nations. Tonga, one of the oldest existing monarchies, is part of the Polynesian Triangle which cuts across this region, with its base running from New Zealand to Easter Island, and its apex in Hawaii. The other two major geographical groupings of Melanesia and Micronesia are both found to the west of the international date line, and, respectively, to the south and north of the equator; both contain minor Polynesian outliers. All provide examples of primitive societies undergoing acculturation in varying degrees. But it is probably in

---

7. This particularly applies to oral cultures such as in the Trust Territory of the Pacific Islands, with their dependence upon face-to-face-contact.

8. Bronislaw Malinowski, "Introduction," in Herbert Ian Hogbin, *Law and Order in Polynesia* (New York: Harcourt, Brace, 1934).

the area of political change that the rate is accelerating most rapidly: statehood for Hawaii in 1959, independence for Western Samoa in 1961, internal self-governance for the Cook Islands in 1965, and almost incredibly, nationhood for the little trusteeship of Nauru in 1968. The British government is pushing the Crown Colony of Fiji to greater self-governance as fast as the Fijians and Europeans there will accept it; in the same pattern, but at a slower pace befitting the aboriginal nature of many of the indigenous peoples, Australia is pursuing a similar course in Papua–New Guinea. More easterly, a new Legislative Council has just been established in the British Solomon Islands Protectorate to which the inhabitants may now send popularly chosen representatives. In both French Polynesia and New Caledonia majority political parties within the local legislatures have been agitating for the enlargement of political powers of these island areas.

Characteristic of the Pacific region is the diversity of colonial administrative policy and governmental structure. Colonial policy runs the gamut—from the French approach of political integration, to the English objective of independence bounded by the self-imposed frame of a Commonwealth, to the ambiguous American position between. The emphasis on speed of political change encountered in much of this region is as much externally generated as it is due to internal pressure; the dogma of colonial exploitation and indigenous dissatisfaction leading to uprisings against repressive government no longer fits. What coincides with reality is that while colonialism has been accompanied by a protracted period of transcultural contact and attendant induced change, Pacific colonialism today represents faster modification of both customary and introduced political institutions accommodating an ever expanding scope of self-government.

Throughout the Pacific there has been an eroding of traditional political forms and processes, and apparent substitution of Western-modeled replacements. These structural innovations are frequently mere layers of accretion introduced to provide functions not serviced in the traditional society; many indigenous processes continue to be observed with little fundamental modification.

Legislatures, looking for a consensus, may be found discussing a matter until overt unanimity is achieved, although parliamentary rules formally provide for definitive decisions with simple majority support. There may be an extension of traditional political structure alongside the new, as in the Crown Colony of Fiji where the Fijian administration constitutes a government within a government for the native Fijian living on *mataqali* (tribal) land. There may be a deliberate attempt to revive old forms such as the synthetic combination of *ariki* (chiefs) with the New Zealand high commissioner to represent the Queen under the new constitution of the Cook Islands. Or when the old political system dovetails neatly with introduced structure, the old political processes continue to furnish the motive power for introduced Western forms. In Western Samoa the *matai* system has been so interwoven with a parliamentary government that with independence one of the holders of the country's three highest titles has become prime minister and the other two joint heads of state hold ceremonial and limited veto powers, while Samoan suffrage and access to office is limited to the *matais* (family title-holders).

It is through the legislature, usually first as an advisory chamber and later as a limited law-enacting institution, that greater participation in policy formulation has been introduced throughout the Pacific. Sometimes this has taken the form of the British-model legislative council, with unofficial members gradually increasing and entering the executive council; the erection of a member-system; and finally the institution of a full cabinet government. Other times it is an advisory body that becomes a legislating chamber, separate from the executive, in which simultaneous membership in the two branches is precluded. In each case, the colonial administration has continued to staff the major posts of the executive and judiciary with non-indigenous persons until late in the shift to self-government, and it is through the institution of the legislature that local leadership has risen to the fore.

Before Western contact, the cultures of the Pacific did not correspond to generalized conceptions of the fused society—its limited specialization, place by ascription, and lack of formalism.

Mobility of individuals unassisted by hereditary status or super-natural assistance was not unknown. Democratic processes con-cealed by formalism—with chief in council unilaterally announc-ing the course to be followed only after the flow of discussion revealed agreement has been reached—have been well-authenti-cated. It is acculturation which may cause male-female task specialization to become less distinctive; and, the highly differen-tiated forms of kinship relationships unknown to the Western man give way to his nuclear family. Probably examples of every individual characteristic of a developed society may be encoun-tered in one or more of the Pacific areas. If a generalization can be attempted, it is that all societies contain within themselves the duality of attributes posited as distinguishing developed from undeveloped, and that it is the degree of internal consistency in their mix which classifies them toward one or the other pole, while it is the inconsistent society which best approximates Riggs's prismatic model.[9]

Not only are these Pacific areas undergoing change at different rates, but the change has not been unidirectional. The cargo cults of Melanesia[10] and the recent attempt of one to "buy" President Johnson from the United States[11] illustrate that social movement may also move in the direction of "retrogression" by seeking to incorporate a greater traditional component. However, common to all these Pacific societies is their increasing material complex-ity. This modification of material culture has been accompanied by the adoption of some new forms of specialization, and by the discouragement of others. Centralized and ever more complex governmental institutions have developed to cope with these material changes and attendant shifts in specialization. All these changes have been associated with authoritative reallocation of societal values over a period of time.

9. Fred W. Riggs, *Administration in Developing Countries* (Boston: Houghton Mifflin, 1964).
10. See Peter Lawrence, *Road Belong Cargo* (Victoria: Melbourne University Press, 1964), for consideration of the cargo movement as a rudimentary form of revolutionary "nationalism."
11. The Johnson Cult on New Hanover began before it decided to boycott the 1964 elections for the Papua–New Guinea House of Assembly and, instead, to bring President Johnson to the island.

The Trust Territory of the Pacific Islands

Micronesia is no exception to these generalizations about the Pacific Basin. Excluding Nauru—a miniscule nation existing on a single resource, phosphate mining; the Gilbert and Ellice Island Colony, part Polynesian and part Micronesian—administered by the English; and Guam—acquired by the United States after the war with Spain at the turn of the twentieth century; Micronesia falls within the Trust Territory of the Pacific Islands. Expansion of the legislative process has just occurred in Nauru. The Gilbert and Ellice Island Colony has recently established a House of Representatives as the first step to greater self-government. Currently the United States Congress is debating making Guam's Congress even more representative by deleting the requirement that its membership must be elected at large. By far the most spectacular of all the recent political changes in Micronesia has been the convening of a bicameral legislature for the Trust Territory of the Pacific Islands in the summer of 1965. This foreshadows a shift of political power from the American high commissioner to the territory's Micronesian inhabitants and raises a potential challenge to the entire course of the area's administration.

The trust territory lies in a geographically isolated portion of the globe, a factor materially contributing to the preservation of its many subcultures. It consists of mere dots of land that physically fall into three loose archipelagos—the Marshalls establish the eastern boundary, the Carolines stretch across the center and out to the southwest, while the Marianas mark the northwestern edge. Even within subunits of a chain, each island may be separated from the next by hundreds of miles of ocean, and the distance between the Marshalls and the Palaus in the Western Carolines compares to the sweep across the continental United States from Florida to California. Historical happenstance has artificially brought together islands which possess no traditional sense of commonality: first as a possession, then as a mandate under the League of Nations, and finally as a trusteeship under the United Nations.

Within this region will be found strong caste and class societies; leadership structures combining inherited status with mobility influenced by religious charisma and various forms of non-as-
criptive criteria demonstrating capacity; consensus processes denying authority to any man or single group of men; as well as
autocracy once possessing absolute, arbitrary powers of life and
death. Not only are the cultures diverse, but a great range of
acculturation is encountered today. These reflect the nature of
the indigenous systems existent at the time of Western contact,
the length and nature of cultural integration, and the degree to
which the dominant cultural configurations of each area have
proven flexible. The Hispanicized Chamorros of the Marianas
appear set on a course designed to "out-American" the Americans, while the conservative Yapese are fundamentally motivated
by the desire to permit adaptation only so far as is necessary to
shore up and retain Yapese culture.

Micronesia today is a coconut culture; its monetary income is
derived from the sale of copra and from United States expenditures in the conduct of government. The bulk of the population
still depends upon the products from its fields and forests and the
catch and gleanings from the reefs and adjacent ocean for the
bulk of its food. What the market economy provides is only
supplementary. But the enjoyment of introduced substitutes and
employment of labor-saving devices ever expand. Even the person who has not varied the tempo of his traditional daily rounds
has aspirations for better health, education, transportation, communication, and other government-provided services, which inevitably speed the course of acculturation and carry the certainty
of continued modification of the Micronesian way of life.

Until the advent of colonialism, Micronesia knew no central
authority. A chief's rule did not encompass within traditional
jurisdictions the whole or even a major portion of a single archi-
pelago. In some, loose confederations assured a degree of protection against rapacious neighbors. The vexing problems of transportation and communication assured that decentralization along
topographical lines would continue to characterize the governments introduced by metropolitan countries. The six administra-

tive districts today established by the American administration,[12] although, in varying degrees, arbitrarily clustering geographically adjacent but culturally diverse peoples, have their predecessors in the regional structures of former metropolitan administrations. They represent conglomerates of the little hereditary chieftainships, some best characterized as gerontocracies, that constituted precontact Micronesia.

The United States took possession of the region which now constitutes the trust territory as part of a military undertaking during World War II. Probably inevitably, a dispute arose between military and civilian authorities over the proper manner of resolving national security requirements with humanitarian objectives. The solution was found in development of the strategic trusteeship which permits the United States to withdraw parts of the area from international scrutiny and preclude visits to them by the tri-yearly United Nations missions. For the remaining territory the United States reports annually on its provision for the welfare of the indigenous inhabitants and their self-development. Its ministrations are thus subject to review before the United Nations, and the recent convening of the Congress of Micronesia in 1965 marks a response to United Nations pressure for establishment of a region-wide legislature to quicken the pace of political development and foster territory-wide cohesion.

From the outset, American policy was committed to equipaced social, economic, and political development, at a rate of change fundamentally reflective of local aspirations and mainly geared to local capabilities—a concept of development administration which proved to be unrealistic. Together with the physical destruction left by World War II and the debilitated traditional societies remaining after the ministrations of three previous metropolitan nations, this policy resulted in economic retrogression of those areas which had known relatively high living standards under the Japanese. With the gradual expansion of educational opportunities, and particularly with the quickening of political interest accompanying the institutionalizing of introduced governmental forms, the rate of economic development has been

12. The Marshall Islands, Ponape, Truk, Yap, Palau, and Mariana Districts.

far exceeded by demands upon it. A noticeable disparity exists between expressed desires and the current capacity of the territory to satisfy them. Massive injections of American funds will be required for an extended period before the territorial economy can, if ever, expand sufficiently to finance the services expected.

Initially, American policy was one of indirect rule, governing as much as possible through traditional chiefs. Mostly it sought to continue local political structures. Because of the wide diversity within the trust territory, this policy in some areas was meaningful, while in others it contributed unwittingly to the reinstatement of traditional institutions which had been eroded away under the Japanese, or to the reinstalling of customary leaders with authority sometimes greater than had been originally possessed. Although titles of village chief and village headmen had been given to those in leadership positions by the Japanese, they often were not allowed to retain their former power or social status, so that these new offices had not carried with them any traditional significance. The functional role of the chief, as revived under American administration, made him not only a symbolic figure but one who could now act without having to obtain approval of a local official of the administering government, as in the later Japanese period. In addition, the destruction of the traditional political infrastructure meant he was no longer effectively limited by the controls which had curtailed the exercise of power in the period before Western contact. Rather than constituting a threat the institution of centralized district government afforded a number of the hereditary chiefs an opportunity to enhance their powers by occupying top executive positions within that government. Some high chiefs established executive offices in district headquarters in order to facilitate their liaison in an advisory capacity with the American administrators. For administrative convenience in dealing with geographical units, in other areas of the trust territory, certain leaders were recognized as "island" chiefs although there was no aboriginal precedent for a paramount chief with island-wide jurisdiction. As a further complication, the highest chiefs in some of the more isolated parts of the territory had learned never to appear personally in regional gatherings unless it was the customary way of life, but only to appear through others with limited representative capacity. The latter frequently were mistaken by Americans as the representatives of traditional power. All of these incongruities demonstrate how the American scheme of following a course of indirect rule forcefully enhanced the weakened state of the traditional political structure. In a number of areas this structure was unable to fill the vacuum left by the withdrawal of German and later Japanese supervision. In a district of marked acculturation like Palau, the chiefs remained in political power only because of American support, but the American attitude toward democratic forms and processes foretold that this would not continue indefinitely.

The basic unit of government in the trust territory has been the municipality, consisting of one or more villages. To a large degree the boundaries of a municipality are coterminous with traditional geographic-political entities, and its community life proceeds according to culturally prescribed patterns modified to meet introduced needs. Gradually the political life of this unit has been systematized, the magistrate—in most cases initially a hereditary chief acknowledged by his people and recognized as magistrate by the administration—elected, a council installed when not already existent, and provision made for such subordinate municipal officers as secretary and constable. Despite secret elections, the people at first continued to return the incumbent chief to the post of magistrate. The cause was conservatism or skepticism. With the introduction of democratic processes which permitted competing leadership to emerge, in many municipalities those with highest ascribed status gradually lost control or retired without risking a test of strength. By 1957 the high commissioner could report to the Trusteeship Council of the United Nations that probably less than 20 per cent of the magistrates were also hereditary chiefs.[13] In outlying areas, far distant from district headquarters, the political life of the local unit proceeds in fairly

13. 802nd meeting of Trusteeship Council, May 29, 1957. TCOR, 20th Session, May 20–July 12, 1957; 51.

customary ways, adjusting itself to the new functions of government. Closer to the district centers the structural reforms have taken firmer hold, and tradition more subtly exerts its influence as the municipality tackles the problems of a more modern way of life. In highly acculturated areas such as Saipan, a wide array of municipal services requires the ministrations of personnel similar to those in any small American town.

Above the municipality is the district administration, headed by a generalist appointed by the high commissioner. The district administrator represents the latter by supervising the activities of district executive agencies, and also is the chief executive of the district with primary responsibility for enforcing all territorial and district laws. The district administrator oversees all programmatic services conducted at the district level, such as education, public health, and land management; he supervises the facilitating services of district finance, supply, personnel, public works, and other comparable agencies. District legislatures with advisory powers were introduced to break geographic and cultural insularity, and to encourage district integration as a prelude to regional integration. These popularly elected district legislatures[14] are beginning to exercise policy direction over district administration as well as to seek an advisory role in the preparation of the district administrator's budget. This is submitted to the high commissioner in support of requests for United States appropriations. The minor expenditures called for in the district legislature's appropriation of its own tax revenues are small in comparison. This legislative interest in greater participation is diametrically opposed to the tradition that district matters be referred to territorial headquarters for decision, and, therefore, for the staff of the high commissioner to exercise ever greater line supervision over the conduct of work in the field. Concomitantly, communication and transportation have improved, while augmented United States funds have expanded governmental serv-

14. Only Yap District does not have a district-wide legislature; here a Yap Congress serves the Yap Islands while the Outer Islanders enjoy no legislative representation.

ices. With some Micronesians beginning to call for the election of the district administrator, it is clear that his role must shortly be re-examined and rationalized.

At the Headquarters of the trust territory on Saipan in the Mariana District, the presidentially designated high commissioner is assisted by a deputy and a number of assistant commissioners who supervise administrative officers and technical directors of agencies with territory-wide concerns. In addition to providing staff aides to the high commissioner, many of these agencies provide technical guidance to their parallel units in the district administration. Supportive services of a general nature and specialized services beyond the capabilities of the district administration are also furnished from headquarters. A judicial system functions independently of the Office of the High Commissioner, while the establishment of the elected Congress of Micronesia has resulted in most of the lawmaking power, formerly exercised by the high commissioner, being transferred to the new Congress.

All of the top headquarter posts have been held by Americans. Gradually Micronesians are beginning to move up from clerical and semiskilled employment to middle management positions, and very recently a Micronesian was sworn in as deputy assistant commissioner—the first to be assigned permanent duties above a department head level at headquarters. In the district government this process of in-service advancement has occurred even more rapidly, and indigenes hold posts as high as district administrator in the Marshalls District and assistant district administrator in all but one of the remaining districts. All judges of the district and community courts (excepting the two Americans on the Kwajalein missile testing site) and all clerks of court are Micronesians, and they also assist in the functioning of the High Court. Micronesian medical practitioners supervise district medical systems, and indigenes occupy other professional and semiprofessional posts. The movement of Islanders into positions of administrative and professional responsibility has been noticeably accelerating.

The over-all direction of political change in the trust territory is toward the supplementation and gradual replacement of the locally dispersed, cellular, indigenous political structure with centralized, functionally specialized, and rationally integrated new forms and processes. This had started before the American period, and had proceeded faster in some areas than in others. The Chamorros of the Marianas and the Palauns of Palau differ markedly in their political acculturation from the rest of the territory. It is in these two regions that political parties have recently made their debut and where embryonic associational interests have voiced political demands. They contrast sharply with the outlying islands midway between Yap and Truk in the Central Carolines, where traditional political structures and processes continue with seemingly little modification. Concentric circles drawn so as to radiate out from district headquarters would probably measure fairly well the decreasing degrees of political acculturation found within any district, with marked chopoff occurring immediately outside the headquarters area and then graduating more evenly. Employment with the district administration and service in the district legislature have bridged the spatial dysfunctions of a primarily oral culture and provided the indigenous inhabitants with an opportunity to become concerned with areas outside their own islands. In the direction of ultimate political change, most of the people on Saipan wish to split the territory, to combine the Northern Marianas with Guam, to become American citizens, and to behave like them too. This sentiment is not shared by other areas, in which there is a nascent sense of territorial identification, if not nationalism. The first Congress of Micronesia adopted a territorial flag, designated the day commemorating the convening of the Congress as an annual territorial holiday, and proposed a number of measures designed to safeguard "Micronesia for the Micronesians."

Leadership

In Micronesia today "traditional" leadership in fact represents an adaptive variant of that which existed in precontact days. The authority of indigenous leadership was materially weakened by the ministering nations that forbade continuance of various customary practices and by their administrators who disregarded local ranks and kin relationships and considered all islanders equal under the law and subject to impartial treatment. In the Marianas the aboriginal political organization was early replaced by one structured by the Spaniards; all Chamorros, but a few on Rota, were removed to Guam, and for two centuries they amalgamated with the Spanish and their colonial troops. Paradoxically, the several administering countries strengthened as well as augmented chiefly authority by ascribing or extending political powers to the chiefs and, thus, consciously or unwittingly, undermined indigenous controls which had operated to keep them locally accountable. Repeated reference to conservative Yap and its traditional ways conceals the fact that it was the Germans and Japanese who divided Yap formally into today's ten *falak* (districts)—placing in each a *falak* chief in a position of power where he had to be obeyed. Judicial and administrative responsibilities were also assigned by the Germans to the Truk chiefs who since that time have been answerable only to the officials of the metropolitan authority. By the failure of the foreign administrators to shore up traditional counterforces which had served as sanctions against local excesses, indigenous political systems have tended to collapse. By the recognition of chiefs, traditional leaders in some areas came to be placed or confirmed in their office by the administering authorities and not by customary devices. Persons logically in line were bypassed or replaced by second- or third-ranking individuals without regard to hereditary status or local custom; appointments were made of those whose willingness to co-operate commended them to the administering officials. However, the Micronesians themselves were able to manipulate the traditional means for choosing chiefs in response to their need to articulate indigenous political systems with the imposed government.

During the Japanese period, in Palau, Saipan of the Marianas, and to a lesser degree in other districts, a Micronesian elite began to emerge whose place depended not upon traditional title or recognized role in the status society, but position in the Japanese-structured government. Top posts were reserved for Japanese, and village headships continued to be held by traditional chiefs so long as they remained in the good graces of the Japanese. In addition to these, indigenes served as policemen, as bureaucrats functioning within the Japanese officialdom (interpreters, medical assistants, schoolteachers, clerks, etc.), and as official advisers to the administration (court clerks and trusted free-lance politicians). Through access to the decision-making centers of the introduced government, they acquired power and prestige. Language skill often distinguished this group, and interpreters, in particular, became experts in offering advice that elicited favorable responses from the foreign administrators. At the district center level of government there was little place for the traditional chief, and the new elite—usually young, intelligent, better educated, and Japanese culture-oriented—endeavored to speed the transition from social obligations recognized within the authority of the chiefs to those appropriate to a Japanese society. For their part, the Japanese favored the development of a schism between generations by recognizing age-group differentiations and by encouraging young men's associations. This "pro-Japanese young Turk collaborator" group lost much of its *raison d'être* with the collapse of civilian government in World War II, while the chiefs were able to reassert the traditional powers appropriate to the care of their people during war period emergencies. Accordingly, when they first entered the area the Americans recognized the chiefs as entitled to exert political authority and utilized them in advisory capacities. The whole course of erosion of chiefly role in Micronesia was temporarily reversed; major chiefs began exerting an influence in some ways greater then they had ever possessed. The young Turk collaborator group, which was quite willing to transfer its orientation to American culture, found much of its work undone, and lacking a political or economic base, they became petty administrators who merely took orders.

The above pertains most particularly to the Palau District. Some chiefs in other districts mastered Japanese and functioned as part of the Japanese bureaucracy, while they retained their traditional authority where it was not proscribed by the Japanese.

Proving adaptable, they emerged in the postwar American period as advisers to the American administrators and, learning English, occasionally continued to act in the same capacity they had during the Japanese era. Kabua Kabua, an *Iroij Laplap* (paramount chief) from the Marshalls, served as a local judge under the Japanese and is now the district judge under the Americans. In both administrations he has helped to integrate the new with the traditional law and has helped to determine the viability of cusomary rights and obligations.

Gradually under the American administration a new elite has emerged, trained in American schools, able to understand or at least verbalize American principles and objectives. And, they are the individuals with whom Americans can identify. Possessing many of the characteristics and value orientations of the intellectuals described in the literature on developing areas, some became the first interpreters hired by American military government. Others graduated from teacher training and gravitated from the schools to work in the district office and later central territorial headquarters. Teaching dropped to a lower status than under the Japanese, when the prestige of the teacher extended far beyond that of the school. Because of their English language capability, from their numbers were selected those sent to Hawaii, Guam, the mainland United States, and the Philippines for college education and specialized training. Upon their return— no matter what their field of study—the Micronesians looked to them as resource persons able to suggest ways to solve difficulties and new problems that were beyond the ken of the traditional chiefs. Some received medical and dental training on Guam and Fiji; these professionals came to occupy the same political role.

During this period, a revival in the status of many of the young Turk collaborator group was seen. Some of them, promising young men in line for titles, had been placed in government service to prepare them for future roles in the indigenous political system, and could call upon their clan ties while they advanced within the American bureaucracy. Others relied upon private commercial activity, for, with Japanese competition removed and American precluded, their participation in Micronesian-conducted businesses, even though on a small scale, added wealth and access to their relative influence and potential political power.

Under American administration, legislatures developed out of district-wide meetings of magistrates. With their establishment in Palau, the Marshalls, and Ponape, the chiefs at first participated as full members along with elected representatives. Gradually, most voluntarily removed themselves or were eased out, according to the relative strength of the traditional chiefly system in a particular district. In some cases the chiefs saw no ultimate threat to their traditional powers; in others appreciating their inability to cope with the complexities of the introduced government, they were willing to leave this to more qualified persons. On Ponape the chiefs have lost all right of participation unless they are elected like other representatives; in Palau the chiefs may attend and debate but cannot vote on measures which may become law; on Truk a young group took over the district legislature, and the magistrates' council, consisting mainly of chiefs, faded in importance; only in the Marshalls did the *Iroij* (nobles) refuse to give up their legislative posts, and the Marshallese Congress was finally restructured, providing lifetime membership with full privileges for all hereditary *Iroij Laplap.*

Along with this structual modification of the advisory district legislatures, and the granting to them of limited legislating powers, democratic processes were introduced into the municipal government. The course of political change tended to push the high chiefs from positions of importance in the headquarters of the central district government back to the villages, where persons seemingly more knowledgeable in Western ways and possessing traditional legitimating characteristics came to the fore. If they ran for office, the chiefs did not always win local elections. However, the traditional institutions have remained, the chiefs exerting political influence by directing their people how to vote. Conflict was not inevitable, and many traditional leaders have been willing to forego all part in the introduced political institutions as they exert relatively little effect upon the tempo of life in the outlying reaches. Indeed, some chiefs have welcomed this introduced social and political change, for it offers some

areas more direct influence and participation: for example, the
Outer Islands in the Yap District are traditional fiefs of Yap, and
technically owned by the latter. On Ulithi, the most advanced
of the Outer Islands, the chiefs are encouraging the expansion
of education at a rate faster than on the Yap Islands, and have
taken the non-conventional position of favoring the erection of a
district-wide legislature in which the Outer Islanders would have
equal political status and, within the near future, equal voting
strength with the Yapese.

Finally, some of the chiefs have themselves been able to make
the transition from the old to the new leadership roles, emerging
as elected leaders in the district governments and, now, the
central Congress of Micronesia. They show by their conduct and
their actions that they understand the workings of the introduced
government and can deal with the Americans, but they also
retain full command of their traditional status and rights. Petrus
Mailo, respected throughout the trust territory as a man of
wisdom—what the Trukese call *itang,* a keeper of the traditional
lore and a master strategist—emerged as the magistrate of the
municipality in which the Truk District Headquarters are located, became first speaker of the Truk District Legislature, president of the Truk Trading Company (the largest commercial
operation by far in the district), and with the resignation of the
first speaker of the General Assembly of the Congress of Micronesia, temporarily speaker of that body as well. Too, Max Iriarte of
Ponape, the *Nanmarki* (king) of Net, similarly sensitive to the
dual role he plays, refuses to allow himself to be addressed in the
traditional noble language while performing as a government
official. Neither man can speak English, although each understands it a little. Nevertheless, standing for election to the Congress, they easily won their posts in the lower house.

Today, the position of the traditional leaders in the trust territory varies from culture to culture. In the Marshalls the old class
system remains fairly influential, with the *Iroij* entrenched, their
fulcrum for swaying political decisions based primarily upon
their residual control over land; in most of the atolls, the *alab*
(senior member of a senior lineage) plays the largest role, and

collectively they direct local affairs. In the Yap District the chiefs retain much of their power, on the Yap Islands frequently remaining in the background, as they oversee the course of the village political life and manipulate the course of the new elite's participation in the introduced, Westernized government. Not intractable, they preserve their traditional influence, bending as necessary. Symbolically, early in American period, many customs were terminated after protracted meetings between chiefs and a "Young Peoples' party." Low-caste people were permitted to attend school, and the prohibition on wearing American-style clothing was lifted. On Ponape, traditionally a highly stratified society combined with considerable internal mobility, the chiefs are withdrawing from their dominant position, but are also adapting by awarding titles to the new elite. In the Palaus, the traditional political system has been materially modified, and the chiefs are defensively seeking to stem their loss of influence in local affairs and in the direction of the observance of proper social conduct. The Truk chiefs were always relatively weak, and the newly introduced forms of government were easily established without travail; as a group they play no part in the district level of government except as magistrates. The chiefs of the traditional Chamorro political system in the Marianas had disappeared during the Spanish occupation, and their place was filled by prominent families with wealth, status occupation, education, and political leadership.

But what of the new elite, the group emerging into positions of political prominence as old influence ebbs and the Americans transfer ever greater power to the Micronesians? They tend to be relatively young, adapted to American customs and government, English speaking, better educated, traveled, and they possess personal access to decision-making centers either through employment in the government or through economic activity which brings them into association with American officials. Government employment provides an opportunity to demonstrate their capacity, establish contacts widely across the district, do favors which place others in their debt, and consolidate their positions. Training and practice as a medical practitioner, dentist, public defender, or other comparable position exempts no one—all Micronesian professionals today are in the service of the government. Many of this new elite also hold preferred traditional status; they may not be in direct line for chiefly title or even belong to a chiefly clan, but they frequently possess high ascriptive characteristics which legitimate leadership positions in their own native society.

Two ladders to social and political recognition still remain open in most of the trust territory. The traditional one depends upon hereditary position, covert political manipulation, overt demonstration of ability and compliance in customary skills and etiquette. The Western one utilizes advanced education, skill in American agency activities, and social intercourse with American personnel. Combining them is at times difficult and confusing— tensions arise out of the conflicting norms of the two roles; potentially, however, it offers the prospect of the broadest support and the biggest rewards to the aspiring politician. With American administration of the trust territory and the attendant political restructuring, traditional chiefs as well as low-status individuals of demonstrated capacity were brought forward, but within the foreseeable future each group will probably lose ground to an emerging leadership characterized by achievement criteria and buttressed by ascriptive legitimation.

Membership in the Congress of Micronesia

Most of the trust territory voters appreciate that the establishment of the Congress of Micronesia constitutes an important step in the political development of the area, although many do not understand exactly how the Congress will effect a change in self-government. They went to the polls intent on sending to Saipan those candidates standing[15] for office they considered most prepared to participate in the new governmental institution; with no counterpart in any traditional political system it was only partially paralleled by the district legislatures with their limited

15. The verb "standing" was deliberately employed as there was little overt campaigning or Western-style running for office in a number of the administrative districts.

jurisdiction. By their collective choice of two delegates[16] from each district and twenty-one assemblymen from as many constituencies, the voters were designating the nature of the new leadership they desired for a territory-wide government; they revealed too the extent to which they wished to observe traditional principles and values either in substitution for or in additon to those introduced by the Americans for political leadership. By the candidates elected, they showed a preference for the educated, the traveled, those with experience in the introduced government found at the district and territorial levels, and those

Table 1. *Spoken Language Ability of Congressional Candidates, 1965*

	Elected (33)	Defeated (62)
English	93.9%	93.5%
Japanese	72.7	66.1
Other Micronesian	21.2	29.0

who had also obtained prominence in district legislatures and territory-wide conferences. But they also demonstrated that they would choose traditional leaders not measuring up to all of these standards so long as they had recognized capacity to deal with American-sponsored political institutions.

The candidates put forward to run for congressional office were named in many ways—political party convention, nominating committee, chiefs' conference, self-nomination, or voluntary sponsorship by friends. No legal qualification of English-language proficiency was raised by the executive order creating the Congress; in fact, the reverse was expressly declared, and, although proceedings were to be conducted in English, the Congress was directed to provide interpreters for members lacking fluency in that language. Nevertheless, English-speaking ability was symbolically identified as essential for eligibility and practically all qualified with little to distinguish the elected from the defeated

16. On July 1, 1966, by secretarial amendment, the House of Delegates became "Senate" and the General Assembly was renamed "House of Representatives."

in any language skills. Significantly, both of the non-English-speaking members elected hold traditional chiefly status.

The voters seem to have preferred candidates with higher education. Sometimes, of course, all candidates running for office in a particular contest possessed similar educational backgrounds; in six House and eight Assembly contests the vote-obtaining value of education could not be measured. The Assembly seat in Ponape District B was uncontested, so must be disregarded. But in ten other contests, higher education candidates

Table 2. *Education of Congressional Candidates, 1965*

	Elected	Defeated
College graduation	12.1%	6.4%
Medical/dental school	12.1	9.7
Some college	66.7	50.0

prevailed, against eight without this advantage. The two candidates from royal (*Iroij*) families running from the Marshalls defeated more highly educated rivals, as did the two non-English-speaking chiefs from Ponape and Truk; the successful assemblyman from Yap who defeated a college graduate received strong chiefly support. The findings in Palau and the Marianas where the possession of higher educational attainment was not necessarily correlated with winning at the polls can be at least partially attributed to the political party development occurring in both areas, the party supporters being committed to vote their respective tickets. Chiefly status and party appeal thus appear to raise competing demands, and may have more influence on the voter in the trust territory than level of educational achievement.

The choice of candidates with extensive travel experience in the 1965 congressional elections probably reflects their level of educational achievement, for Micronesians must leave the trust territory for college and professional training. With travel to Guam, Hawaii, or the mainland United States, visits to Japan, other Pacific Basin islands, or elsewhere,[17] the successful candidates evidenced greater familiarity with non-trust territory regions than the defeated, and their success implies that this factor weighed at the polls.

The voters sought to return to the new Congress members whose service at territorial or district headquarters constituted preparation for tackling the problems attendant on running the territorial government. Teaching experience, which about half the candidates reported, was not related to election success, nor was association with the education function, such as educational

Table 3. *Governmental Employment of Congressional Candidates, 1965*

	Elected	Defeated
Present territory or district (excluding education)	54.5%	38.9%
Previous territory or district (excluding education)	72.7	46.8
Present and previous territory or district (excluding education)	75.7	54.8
Present teaching	9.1	21.0
Present education (including teaching)	21.2	30.6
Present and previous education (including teaching)	51.5	50.0

administration. Current or previous government employment, exclusive of education, differentiated the elected from the defeated.

And finally, the voters chose as their representatives those individuals who had achieved prominence in district legislative positions, and in territory-wide advisory conferences (as appointees of the district administrator, designees of the district legislature, and more recently in some districts through election). Comparable data for municipal office-holding fails to show any correlation to success at the 1965 congressional elections. Ability in local matters, if anything, apparently was considered unrelated to the assumption of territory-wide responsibilities.

Here emerges a new political elite, a rising to political power of

17. For accuracy's sake, the one exception is travel to the Philippines; in this case, for some as yet unexplainable reason, the defeated candidates slightly exceeded the elected.

Table 4. *Political Offices Held by Congressional Candidates, 1965*[18]

	Elected	Defeated
Seat in district legislature	75.0%	60.3%
Presiding officer, district legislature	34.4	13.5
Seat in territory-wide conference	51.5	17.7
Municipal office	46.9	63.0

individuals trained to "administrative" decision-making who become "political" decision-makers.[19] It is young, ranging from twenty-six to sixty-two years of age (median age—thirty-three, mean age—thirty-five), in a region where traditional leadership has generally been characterized by at least middle-age maturity, and where the customary political systems have afforded only minor roles to persons of such youth. This can be contrasted with the current median age of fifty-nine years for the thirty-five chiefs in the Outer Islands of the Yap District, with one-quarter over seventy! But this does not represent a group necessarily distinct from traditional title-holders, those in line for title or those possessing recognized high clan status; they, too, have been elected as long as they are distinguished by more than ascribed criteria. Of the seven Congressmen forty years of age and over, six hold chiefly title or are senior heads of their clans; excluding the Mariana delegation for which such analysis is inapplicable, at least thirteen Congressmen (46.4 per cent) possess well-recognized traditional status. Those with chiefly title were elected in spite of their lower formal educational achievement and their lack of governmental preparatory service—with prominence in district and territorial affairs they have demonstrated their competence to deal with the political institutions introduced by the Americans.

Felix Keesing noted in the 1940's that practically everywhere in the South Seas where provision was made for representation, it

18. In some cases *n* decreased due to lack of data; also, as Yap Outer Islanders are not under a district legislature, candidates from that constituency are excluded.

19. Fred W. Riggs, "Administrative Development: Notes on an Elusive Concept and the 'KEF-PRI' model," preliminary draft, Bloomington, Ind., Dec., 1963, pp. 3–9.

was the government employee who appeared in this new role.[20] The extension of representative institutions to Micronesia after World War II repeated this movement of the administrative bureaucracy into the legislative centers. However, the congressional elections in 1965 did more than mark the emergence of an American-trained, indigenous elite on the territorial level of government. Many of the congressmen had been educated across ethnic boundaries, living closely for protracted periods with Micronesians from cultures differing from their own. Many of them had later served in capacities which required broader vision than the parochial position of a particular district. As a result of their socialization they contributed to the Congress an element almost unique to the trust territory's ethnocentricism. They approached their new posts expecting to formulate their own policy decisions.[21] Since their numbers included persons peculiarly cognizant of the customary relationships and prescribed practices which still regulate much of the day-to-day life of the territory's various peoples, they also inclined toward an amalgam of the introduced and the traditional. But most important, this indigenous leadership brought with it to the Congress the foundation for a nascent, all-Micronesia identity, transcending the region's diverse cultures, which will materially contribute to shaping the ultimate political future of the trust territory.[22]

20. Felix M. Keesing, *The South Seas in the Modern World* (rev. ed.; New York: John Day, 1945), p. 165.

21. For fuller discussion of representational role orientations, see Norman Meller, "Representational Role Types: A Research Note," *American Political Science Review*, LXI (June, 1967), 474.

22. A fuller treatment of the development of the legislative process in the Trust Territory of the Pacific Islands and of many of the aspects only briefly touched upon in this essay will be found in my book *The Congress of Micronesia* (Honolulu: University of Hawaii Press, 1969).

Part III

Technical Assistance and
Development Administration

Chapter 11

Technical Co-operation in Development Administration in South and Southeast Asia

Shou-Sheng Hsueh

The increase in the variety, number and complexity of functions that have to be performed by the modern State has resulted in an administrative lag. A serious imbalance exists between aspirations and performance, between the needs to be met and the adequacy of the administrative machinery to carry them out. This imbalance constitutes a major obstacle to national development. To meet even a part of its growing responsibilities, the modern service State must develop the administrative capacity to implement its programmes of economic and social progress. Public administration is the machinery used by the service State to place itself in a position to make plans and programmes that can be carried out, and to carry out the plans and programmes it has made. To an ever-increasing degree, the effective utilization of national resources depends upon the adoption of sound economic and social programmes, whose success in turn depends upon an effective public service.

> Department of Economic and Social Affairs, United Nations, *A Handbook of Public Administration* (New York, 1961), p. 5.

Introduction

Development administration is not a new kind of administration separable from public administration in the general sense.[1] It

1. Compare the views expressed in "Development Administration," a report by a special committee under the chairmanship of Fred W. Riggs, *CAG Occasional Papers* (Bloomington, Ind.: Indiana University, 1964), pp. 6–8.

is goal-oriented and is intended to lay emphasis on a particular role of administration, namely, administration for development. As the word "development" is currently used to mean primarily economic, political, and social development, development administration within the reference of this essay deals basically with administration for development in the qualified sense.

The traditional role of public administration has been fundamentally related to the maintenance of law and order and collection of revenue. In other words, it is essentially a public administration to "maintain" the general activity of the government as a going concern. On the other hand, development administration, as the expression implies, lays emphasis on that role of public administration which is to "develop" the activity of the government, especially in the economic, political, and social fields. It should, however, immediately be added that "development" administration is by no means used to substitute or replace what one might call "general" administration or what B. S. Khanna refers to as "regulatory" administration. Even in its traditional concept, public administration does not necessarily preclude developmental activity. In practice public administration, whether called development administration or not, implies, in varying degrees in different countries, some developmental activity. It is not always easy to draw a clear line between developmental and general activity of administration.

The current use of the term development administration is designed to give more attention to the development aspect of administration than before, but this does not necessarily mean that less attention is being given to the general aspect of administration. Both the developmental and the general aspects of administration are important. Unless general administration is well insured, development administration cannot be effective. In other words, unless there is law and order, no country can succeed in economic and social development.

Most Asian countries are, economically speaking, developing nations and are engaged in developmental activity with the objective of raising the living standards of their people and improving their economic and social conditions as a whole. It is evident that their administrative machinery and systems, which until recently have been primarily geared to the fulfilment of the traditional functions of administration, need to be expanded and modified to be able to play the desired role in development. This involves not only elaboration, improvement, and possibly even basic reorganization of administrative machinery, system, procedures, and rules and regulations, but especially reorientation of the administrators in regard to their attitude toward development and also their retraining in technical knowledge and skills as required by development.

The significance of public administration to economic, political, and social development is being increasingly recognized in Asia. An agreed-upon concept of development administration is gaining ground in Asian developing countries, although its definition may be set forth in different words. The writer is grateful to his Asian colleagues of the seminar for their respective definitions of development administration:

José Abueva (Philippines) defines development administration as the administration of development programs in the economic, social and political spheres, including programs for improving the organization and management of the bureaucracy as a major instrument for national development.

Inayatullah (Pakistan) describes development administration as the complex of organizational arrangements for the achievement of action through public authority in pursuance of (1) social and economic goals and (2) nation-building. It presupposes policies, plans, and programs with a distinct developmental bias as well as a bureaucracy which consciously and continuously seeks to modernize itself to meet the demands of planned change.

B. S. Khanna (India) regards development administration as an administration geared to the tasks of economic, social, and political development, which has been induced by an increasing tempo, momentum, and diversity emanating from the elite and groups of people.

Hahn-Been Lee (Korea) defines development administration as the problems involved in so managing a government or an agency thereof that it acquires an increasing capability to adapt to and act upon new and continuing social changes with a view to achieving a sustained growth in the political, economic, and social fields.

Nguyen-Duy Xuan (Vietnam) considers development administration to mean the administration of development programs, that is, programs designed to achieve nation-building objectives and to promote socio-economic progress. It is a two-element concept: (1) the appropriate training of personnel and (2) the improvement of existing administrative organizations and establishment of new institutions for the implementation of development programs.

Although these views on development administration are personal, they broadly reflect much Asian thinking on the concept of development administration. The several definitions are in fundamental agreement; it seems clear that the objective is to encourage an effective administration capable of bringing about economic, political, and social development. These definitions underline the important role of public administration in achieving development in Asian countries.

Developing countries in South and Southeast Asia vary in traditions, cultures, political systems, social values, religious beliefs, languages, and degrees of economic development. However, most of them have a great deal in common in that they are relatively young countries, facing similar problems in public administration, sharing democratic aspirations, anxious to accelerate economic, political, and social development, and above all, recognizing, in varying degrees, the importance of development administration.[2]

Development administration as a field of study and research is gradually receiving recognition among Asian scholars, mainly as a result of their contacts with Western, especially American, scholars in the field. Similar recognition may also be discerned among professional and governmental circles. For instance, a National

2. *Technical Cooperation under the Colombo Plan,* report by the Colombo Plan Council for Technical Cooperation in South and Southeast Asia for the Year 1 July 1964–30 June 1965, p. 6.

Institute of Development Administration has been organized in Thailand, and a Development Administration Unit is being conceived of within the Prime Minister's Office of the Government of Malaysia. Development administration has indeed become important not only in theory but also in practice. To be effective, both the theory and the practice of development administration must combine to make a significant contribution to the development of Asia.

In sum, therefore, the term "development administration" has been increasingly used with a view to concentrating on the developmental aspect of administration. Development administration is receiving so much attention that it seems to represent a new dimension of public administration. This is especially true in Asia because of the importance of development in Asian countries.

The Basic Environment of Development Administration in South and Southeast Asia

There is great diversity of conditions in South and Southeast Asian countries in terms of political systems, levels of economic development, social structures, and cultural heritages. The following general observations are thus subject to exceptions.

Most developing countries in South and Southeast Asia are former colonies of Western powers. As such, they inherited colonial administrative systems at the time of independence. By definition, colonial administration is foreign in origin and is imposed on the colonial peoples by the metropolitan powers with or without due regard to the local conditions of the colonized territories. Although a good deal of effort has been put forth by developing countries in South and Southeast Asia to modernize their administration, few have yet succeeded in making their administration truly responsive to the needs of economic, political, and social development.

Several basic environmental factors—primarily political, economic, social, and cultural in nature—affect development administration in South and Southeast Asian countries. It is evident that these factors are not strictly separable, and their interplay is bound to produce a complex impact on development administration.

The importance to economic and social development of relationships between politics and administration is apparent and need not be emphasized here.[3] It would be idle to argue whether politics is more crucial to development than administration, or vice versa. In the light of recent developments, it seems clear that in South and Southeast Asian countries today politics not only influences but in many ways determines the success or failure of development.

Most South and Southeast Asian countries are developing or making efforts to develop, although in varying degrees of intensity and extent.[4] It may be true that political leaders in South and Southeast Asia are increasingly aware of the urgent task of development and of the important role of administration in development. As, however, such leaders are frequently transient, few of them are in a position to envisage long-term administrative development for economic, political, and social advancement, assuming that they are development conscious and that they are aware of the significance of administration to development.

Development and political systems are closely related in the sense that a stable innovating political system is conducive to development and that development contributes to further innovation and political stability. Political systems in South and Southeast Asian countries vary greatly. Development and political systems affect each other in different ways in different countries. It may be observed that in this region development occurs more rapidly in countries with political stability than in those without it. Too, the political party system is an important factor in achieving political stability. Development seems to be effective in a country without frequent changes of development policies. The continuity of development may be maintained in a country with a stable government—in countries with a major political

3. Fred W. Riggs, "Modernization and Development Administration," *CAG Occasional Papers* (Bloomington, Ind.: Indiana University, 1966), pp. 6–10.
4. Milton J. Esman, "The Politics of Development Administration," *CAG Occasional Papers* (Bloomington, Ind.: Indiana University, 1963), p. i.

party in power for a relatively long period of time, such as India, or in countries without political parties but under a strong political leader, such as Pakistan and Thailand in recent times. It may be true that frequent changes of government tend to disrupt development efforts as they often involve changes in development policies.

However, political stability is but one of the factors for development, and much also depends on such other factors as the will for innovation, capital, skills, natural resources, and technical assistance. South and Southeast Asian countries are developing to a greater or lesser extent. Key questions are how to accelerate the rate of development and in what ways administrators can help in such acceleration.

Administrators in South and Southeast Asian countries have a difficult and complex role to play. This is largely due to the need for their active participation in economic and social development. The primary responsibility for economic development rests with the private sector—industrialists, businessmen, financiers, technicians—in an industrialized country. The role of public administration is primarily related to the creation of a favorable climate within which the private sector can effectively engage in economic development. Such is the case in industrialized countries —for example, the United States or the United Kingdom. In a developing country, however, such a "private sector" is virtually non-existent or, where it exists, weak. Administration not only has to provide the favorable conditions for economic and social development but has virtually to take the leading role in providing or finding the capital as well as the know-how necessary for development.[5] Administrators in developing countries, therefore, also have an economic role to play.

Administrators in South and Southeast Asian developing countries play a very important social role. To begin with, these countries have a primarily agricultural economy based on a family or clan social system. Administrators in the rural areas are often at the same time leaders of certain families or those enjoy-

5. "Technical Assistance for Economic Development," *International Review Service*, V (1959), 1.

ing a high social respect or status among the rural peoples. Government dealings and transactions with rural people are seldom by official correspondence, but rather through personal contacts made by the administrators in the local districts. Official business may be transacted more expeditiously primarily because of the social relationships of the administrators to the people concerned. This social role is especially important as development frequently involves social change, and social change can be expedited through informal social relations between innovating administrators and the people to a greater extent than through formal, official channels. In a country where the people are largely uneducated, unused to administrative disciplines, and unconscious of development, it is all the more important that innovations for development be channeled through informal relations between the administrators and the people concerned. The social role of the innovating administrators in a country which is essentially an aggregation of village communities based upon family relations is consequently important in any effective development effort.

Culturally, many people in South and Southeast Asia are still illiterate and uneducated. Basically engaged in farming, they have neither time nor means for formal education. Being largely uneducated, the people are not politically informed and can hardly be expected to exercise their democratic rights intelligently. One basic condition for the practice of democracy is that the people should understand their roles in relation to the government. Administrators, being agents of the government, could play an educational role in the sense that they could, in frequent contacts with the people, help them to raise their political consciousness and ability, essential for the effective exercise of democracy.

Competent administrators are one important key to successful development. An imperfect administrative system may be made to work by able administrators, but a good administrative system will not function without competent administrators. This is one crucial area to which serious attention should be given if development is to have a chance of success.

Inasmuch as the behavior of the administrators in South and

Southeast Asian developing countries is conditioned by the traditional administrative system, they tend to be routine-minded, stagnant, and generally lacking in enthusiasm and ability for innovation. Development administration, on the other hand, requires an administrator who is dynamic, innovative, and development-conscious.

The basic question involved here is therefore how to convert the administrators in Asian developing countries, used to the traditional routine type of administration, into "development administrators," so that development administration can play its appropriate role in bringing about desired change, to pave the way for economic, political, and social development.

As has been indicated, the concept of and the strategy for development administration vary in developing countries in South and Southeast Asia, and even the degree of importance attached to development administration differs not only from country to country but also from time to time. It would not be easy to lay down the specific qualifications required of a "development administrator," as they obviously vary according to the administrative culture, social values, economic development, political conditions, and developmental needs of each country. According to Hahn-Been Lee, however, a development administrator should be innovative and should have a time orientation toward the future.

In conclusion, developing countries in South and Southeast Asia have an urgent need for a new kind of development administrator who is both technically competent and development conscious enough to perform his role in administration for development. This is indeed a most decisive area in development administration.

Technical Assistance in Public Administration in South and Southeast Asia

Technical assistance in public administration may take a variety of forms. Generally speaking, it involves the engagement of one or more foreign experts with or without additional assistance in the way of equipment and funds.

Technical assistance is extended from a donor country to a recipient country on the assumption that the former is able to help the latter fulfil a particular function which the latter is unable to perform on its own, primarily for technical reasons. This function may be performed by one or more foreign experts with or without a local counterpart. The foreign expert's role is, generally speaking, advisory, but in exceptional cases may even be operational for all practical purposes. By definition, technical assistance implies a more or less definite duration of time within which the function should be completed, and also that the country which originally requests the assistance should, by the end of such assistance, be able to carry on the expert's function on its own with no need for similar assistance in the future.[6]

Technical assistance may or may not involve public agencies on either side—the donor or the recipient of technical assistance— but it generally does, especially on the recipient side if it involves development projects. Technical assistance may be extended on a bilateral or multilateral basis.[7] The former was especially prevalent in the early years and of course continues today. The latter has been increasing as a result of multilateral diplomacy through international and regional organizations and conferences.

According to the United Nations definition, the objective of technical assistance "is to prepare more people to contribute towards the progress of their countries, either by advising them, showing them, teaching them or giving them the opportunity to exchange and develop the information which they already have."[8] The tone of the United Nations concept of technical assistance

6. H. J. Van Mook, "Note on Training Abroad in Public Administration for Students from Underdeveloped Countries," *International Review of Administrative Sciences*, XXVI (1960), 67.

7. See, for examples, David Owen, "The United Nations Expanded Program of Technical Assistance: A Multilateral Approach," *Annals of the American Academy of Political and Social Science*, CCCXXIII (May, 1959), 25–32, and Rollin S. Atwood, "The United States Point Four Program: A Bilateral Approach," *ibid.*, pp. 33–39.

8. United Nations Technical Assistance Board, *The Expanded Program of Technical Assistance for Economic Development of Underdeveloped Countries* (New York, 1964).

("advising them, showing them, teaching them or giving them") has been subjected to criticism among certain developing countries in Asia.[9] This feeling was reflected during the discussions which took place at a closed conference of the Asian Study Group on Technical Assistance held in January, 1965, in Bangkok, under the auspices of the Eastern Regional Organization for Public Administration (EROPA). The following statement is from the communiqué issued at the end of the conference:

Economic and social advancement of the developing countries, although the primary responsibility of the countries concerned, should also be the concern of the rest of the world. Therefore, the concept of Technical Assistance should be increasingly based on a spirit of partnership between those extending assistance and those receiving it. Only through this new concept of *Technical Co-operation* can maximum good results be achieved.[10]

It was stressed at the conference that more Asian countries were becoming donors and recipients of technical assistance at the same time although in different fields.

Most nations in South and Southeast Asia achieved independence after the Second World War. The immediate administrative responsibility of the governments of these new states was to carry on the administration inherited from the colonial powers and to cope with the new problems brought about by independence and the postwar conditions obtaining in their respective countries. Administration was essentially devoted to national reconstruction, and not specifically geared to development, although it was anticipated that development would follow. However, the immediate task of the government was obviously to get the new country on its feet. Thus technical assistance in public administration was initially related to the promotion of effective functioning of administration in the interests of economy and efficiency, as well as to the preparation of younger generations for future administrative careers.

Two parallel approaches have been adopted. In the first, for-

9. Compare the views of Fernand Vrancken, *Technical Assistance in Public Administration: Lessons of Experience and Possible Improvements* (Brussels: International Institute of Administrative Sciences, 1963), p. 35.
10. See EROPA Communiqué, TA/M/8/C, Jan. 23, 1965.

eign experts have been engaged to work directly with existing government agencies, generally in the central government. The nature of their services has varied. Several Asian developing countries have engaged foreign experts for the primary purpose of helping to examine the entire administrative system, with a view to planning a major administrative reorganization. During the present development decade, more and more South and Southeast Asian developing countries are aware of the importance of administration to development and are undertaking efforts for basic administrative improvement or reorganization geared to economic and social development. On the other hand, foreign experts have also been engaged to work in certain areas of public administration such as personnel administration or public finance. Foreign advisers are also frequently employed for short assignments, such as making a survey of a certain administrative situation, including recommendations for the consideration of the recipient country. There are also cases where foreign experts have been engaged as general advisers in a government ministry or department for a relatively longer period of time. As the major administrative difficulties in Asian developing countries are related to the implementation of developmental goals, the work of foreign advisers has been mostly concerned with techniques of implementation, although, to a small degree, also with planning. Some or all of such kinds of technical assistance may of course exist at the same time in a recipient country.

In the second approach, technical assistance has been extended for "institution-building" purposes. It is believed that institution-building is a "major instrument for the development of self-help" and that "it ensures continuity of operations for the effective transformation of the country towards achieving the goals of national development."[11]

One concrete form of institution-building has been the creation of a series of institutes of public administration in various countries of the region, their specific purpose to provide training for administrators as well as to prepare the younger generations for

11. *Ibid.*

future administrative responsibilities. These institutes provide training in administrative techniques but also opportunities for broadened outlook and experience. As of now, almost all South and Southeast Asian developing countries have at least one institute of public administration or its equivalent.

Technical assistance in the establishment of institutes of public administration in South and Southeast Asia has come largely from the United States, for several reasons. Primarily, the United States, more than any other country in the world, has developed the field of public administration, both as an academic discipline and as a practical profession. As a result, American academic institutions and professional bodies are in a position to provide experts, knowledge, skills, and experience useful to developing countries in South and Southeast Asia. Second, the United States government, universities, and foundations are willing and able to extend such assistance, although not without difficulties at its inception. Third, Asian governments and universities recognize the technical character of public administration. They acknowledge American competence in the field and are therefore ready to co-operate with the United States.

Among the countries receiving American technical assistance in public administration are not only those like the Philippines with historical links with the United States but also countries without similar links, including those with historical and political ties with Western countries other than the United States. The Philippine Institute of Public Administration, first of its kind in Asia, was created in 1952 within the State University of the Philippines with United States technical assistance. Similar assistance has also been received by such countries as Pakistan, Thailand, and Vietnam. The contributions of American government agencies, foundations, and academic institutions to South and Southeast Asian developing countries in the field of public administration should be duly recognized.

Technical assistance from other Western or foreign countries is of course not totally absent. The United Kingdom, for instance, is increasing its technical assistance in public administration to Asian developing countries, especially in the field of management. Likewise, France has been helping its former colonies in the development of public administration.

United States technical assistance in public administration has been extended to developing countries with French colonial background, such as Vietnam, and those within the Commonwealth, such as Pakistan. On the other hand, British technical assistance is slowly but surely increasing in South and Southeast Asian countries, including the Philippines. Asian developing countries can now be, and are, selective in technical assistance in public administration.

Although nearly all Asian developing countries have at least one institute of public administration, their actual locations vary. In certain countries, the institute is placed directly under or within the executive branch of the government as in Vietnam or Burma. As such, the primary objective of the institute is to provide in-service training, but this does not necessarily preclude academic research basically related to the needs of in-service training. In some Asian countries, the institute of public administration is essentially a professional institution as in India or Pakistan, but it may maintain effective working relationships with universities in the same field of interest. In still other countries, the institute of public administration is part of an institution of higher learning, notably a university, such as the Institute of Public Administration of Thammasat University in Thailand and the Graduate School of Public Administration (formerly Institute of Public Administration) of the University of the Philippines. Where the institute is part of a university, it generally is a graduate institute offering a master's degree curriculum in public administration.

Public administration courses are being offered in an increasing number of universities in South and Southeast Asia without an institute of public administration. Several universities have a separate department of public administration, for instance, Punjab University.

A few institutes of public administration in South and Southeast Asia were directed by foreign experts in the early stages.

Although such institutes are now managed by Asians themselves, several institutes still engage the services of foreign experts for varying lengths of time. And many Asians on the institute staff find it useful to maintain association with the former donor institution.

Technical assistance in public administration also involves the provision of opportunities for South and Southeast Asian scholars and administrators to learn modern administrative knowledge and techniques abroad by way of scholarships, fellowships, and observational or training tours. Although foreign visits help to broaden the outlook and experience of those concerned, such programs have their basic limitations. First, international travel is expensive, and few governments or universities in South and Southeast Asia can afford the expense with the general shortage of foreign exchange in these countries. Even if fellowships and assistance are provided by outside sources, such opportunities are generally few and the number of participants is limited. Second, administrative knowledge and skills learned abroad are not always applicable to local conditions in South and Southeast Asia. Unless the trainees are able to adapt Western techniques to Asian conditions, overseas training may not be effective. However, technical assistance of this type is valuable to senior administrators and scholars of public administration to help them broaden their contacts and outlook, which will be useful to their work at home. It is equally beneficial to specialized administrators and scholars to learn of Western experience and techniques. This may lead to appropriate adaptation in their own countries.

The basic objective of an institute of public administration as described above is to provide training or retraining for junior or mid-level administrators, with slight variations in different countries, and, in some cases, to prepare future administrators through a degree program. It has been increasingly felt that even senior administrators need some "training" in the broad sense of the word. Distinct in nature from the training provided by the usual institute of public administration, emphasis in "training" for senior administrators (or executive development) is laid on advanced administrative techniques as well as the reorientation of such administrators in the light of the need of their countries for economic and social development.

Against this background, a number of so-called staff colleges or executive academies have emerged in an increasing number of developing countries in South and Southeast Asia. Such institutions differ basically from the institutes of public administration not only in the level of participation but in purpose, professional composition, and methodologies used. The unique feature lies in the blend of government administrators and private industrial and commercial leaders, for the purpose of exchanging views and experience in management techniques and especially in problems of economic and social development. In other words, this type of college or academy definitely has a developmentalist approach, as distinct from the general approach of most institutes of public administration.

Foreign technical assistance in development administration to South and Southeast Asian countries is increasing. Development administration is itself a new field in the more developed countries; therefore, there is much room for close co-operation between Western and Asian scholars and administrators. One form of technical co-operation in this field has been the organization of conferences and seminars and the establishment of institutions of development administration. In the former case, the development administration seminar jointly sponsored by the Comparative Administration Group of the American Society for Public Administration and the East-West Center, involving both American and Asian participants, is a prominent example. In the case of the latter, with foreign technical assistance, a National Institute of Development Administration has been established in Thailand, and a Development Administration Unit is being planned in the government of Malaysia.

The establishment of institutes of public administration and staff colleges or executive academies is by no means a sufficient answer to the administrative problems of Asian developing countries. These institutes, colleges, and academies are, generally speaking, located in national capitals or metropolitan cities. The participants in their programs usually come from the departments and ministries of the central government. There is an obvious and urgent need for administrative development at the local and rural levels. In some countries, training is provided for local administrators, either by sending trainers to local districts or by receiving trainees from such districts. In either case, such training has its limitations and is not effective. The number of trainees is small, and training durations are necessarily short. Although the "training the trainers" methodology is being adopted more often in developing countries in South and Southeast Asia, the process is still slow and ineffective, especially in large countries like India or Indonesia. In this connection, the remarks made by Edward W. Weidner in 1962 are still valid today. "During the next ten to fifteen years, more emphasis should be placed upon institution-building and training the trainers in such a manner as to maximize local involvement and experimentation. As the world continues its course of bettering man's existence by ever more vigorous development programs, public administration must be related to them if it is to remain a vital and living field."[12]

The Role of EROPA in Technical Co-operation in Development Administration

Asian scholars and professionals in the field of public administration meet more often outside Asia than in it. This is largely due to the fact that most international conferences and overseas programs in which Asians participate have been held outside Asia. However, there has been an increasing number of contacts among Asians in Asia as a result of more regional conferences and programs. There is also a growing interest among Asian governments and institutions in the promotion of contacts among Asian professionals and scholars in public administration. The fact that many

12. "The American Education of Foreign Administrators: Lessons from American Training Programs in Foreign Countries," *Technical Assistance in Training Administrators*, Selected Papers on Public Administration, Institute of Training for Public Service (Bloomington, Ind.: Indiana University, 1962), p. 46.

Asian countries have institutes of public administration contributes to the establishment of some natural links among the
institutes. This has resulted in more frequent contacts among
Asians by way of exchange of visits, information, knowledge, and
views, thus paving the way for regional co-operation in public
administration.

Contacts between Asian administrators and scholars in the first
postwar decade primarily took the form of brief exchange visits.
A few years ago the Philippine Institute of Public Administration
with outside assistance launched a regional third-country participation program of short training courses lasting from three to six
months and open to participants from other Southeast Asian
countries. Such courses, basically organized and given by the staff
of the institute, were fairly general in nature. Occasionally, however, a specifically designed course was offered for a special
group of participants within the limit of available staff and resources. Because of the terminal nature of the grant supporting
this activity, the program was discontinued.

The emergence of regional organizations and regional offices of
international organizations has further helped contacts among
Asians in Asia. Such regional organizations include notably the
United Nations Economic Commission for Asia and the Far East
(ECAFE), the Asian Productivity Organization, the Asian Institute of Economic Development and Planning, the Colombo Plan,
the Southeast Asian Treaty Organization, and now the Asia Development Bank. The Association of Southeast Asia is being revived. An Asian Common Market is under discussion. Each of the
regional organizations has its own sphere of activity. None of
them has a specific interest in public administration, although a
few Asian regional organizations such as the Colombo Plan and
SEATO have in the past provided scholarships or fellowships in
public administration usable at universities in Asia or overseas.
Such opportunities are few, and the number of participants in
each case is small.

The United Nations has yet to show a substantial interest in
public administration in Asia. The activity of ECAFE in the field
is fairly recent, primarily consisting of occasional seminars, con-

ferences, and "working party" meetings. ECAFE has a public administration unit of one man, who is a regional consultant. Basically understaffed in the field of public administration, ECAFE is unlikely to be able to cope with the consultative responsibilities involving about twenty countries in its region. There has been some thought given to an increase in the manpower of the public administration unit of ECAFE, on the recommendation of a Working Party Meeting on Major Administrative Problems in Asia held in Bangkok in October, 1965.

Several Asian countries are members of or affiliated with international organizations of public administration such as the International Institute of Administrative Sciences or the International Union of Local Authorities. However, by virtue of the wide geographical coverage of these organizations with headquarters in Europe, Asia does not seem to receive much attention. One major conference has been held in Asia by the International Union of Local Authorities.

There was little organized regional effort to promote co-operation in public administration until the creation of the Eastern Regional Organization for Public Administration (EROPA) in 1960. According to the EROPA constitution, the primary objective of the organization is "to promote the adoption of more effective and adequate administrative systems and practices in order to advance and implement the economic and social development programs of the region."

The principal organs of the organization are the General Assembly, the Executive Council, and the Secretariat General, plus a number of specialized centers that may be created from time to time. The General Assembly is composed of all EROPA state, group, and individual members and meets every other year in the region. It formulates general policies, gives over-all financial direction to the organization, and elects the Executive Council and the Secretary General, who serve for terms of two years. The Executive Council directs the activities of the organization, determines the working procedures of the EROPA centers and services, prepares the budget, and administers finances under the authority of the General Assembly. The headquarters of EROPA are located in Manila. The secretary general is responsible for the execution of decisions and instructions of the Executive Council and for co-ordination of the work of the various centers and services. There are now five specialized centers: the Research, Documentation and Diffusion Center in Saigon; the Training Center in New Delhi; the Local Government Center in Tokyo; the Land Reform Center in Taipei; and the Organization and Methods Center in Seoul.

Two major fields of public administration constitute the main work of the organization. The first is concerned with development administration, and the second is related to the improvement of general administration. During the nine years of its existence, EROPA has been concentrating on development administration more than any other regional organization in Asia. On the agenda of the first regional conference in 1958 was "Administration of Economic and Social Planning and Programs." The major theme of the first General Assembly held in Manila in 1960 was "Strengthening Local Administration for Economic and Social Development." A seminar on "Urban Administration and Economic Development" was conducted the following year in Tokyo. The principal theme of the Third General Assembly, held in Seoul in 1964, was "Organizing for Development," which was subdivided into: (1) Planning and Policies for Development, (2) Administrative Machinery for Development, and (3) Financing Development. In 1965, two regional conferences on development were held: the Asian Consultative Conference on Foreign Service Development in Manila in September–October and the Seminar on Land Reform for Rural Development in Taipei in October. The land reform seminar was held in collaboration with the East-West Center and the Comparative Administration Group of the American Society for Public Administration. During 1966, a Seminar on Administration for Development was held in West Berlin and New Delhi in October, and the main theme of the EROPA Fourth General Assembly, held in December in Teheran, was "Administration for Social Development in Developing Countries." Another EROPA meeting on a theme related to development was the Conference of the Asian Study Group on

Technical Assistance, which, in January, 1965, in Bangkok, examined the problems of technical assistance and development from the point of view of recipient countries. As a general practice, the various conferences adopted recommendations for consideration by the governments in the region based on the findings and discussions.

Much emphasis has also been laid on the improvement of general administration. The agenda of the First Regional Conference on Public Administration, in 1958, included discussions on "Education, Recruitment and Training for the Public Service." The major theme for the Second General Assembly, held in Bangkok in 1962, was "Personnel Management and Administration," subdivided into (1) Organization of the Civil Service, (2) In-service Training of Government Officials for Economic Development, and (3) Academic Training of Government Officials. "Administrative Reform and Innovations in Asia" was the theme for the Fifth General Assembly held in Kuala Lampur in 1968.

One of the important projects being currently undertaken is on foreign service development. A team of senior consultants including former Asian presidents of the United Nations General Assemblies was constituted. The first regional foreign service course was conducted in 1967. The purpose is to inject a development-awareness in the foreign service. These courses are specifically intended for mid-level and senior officials of the ministries and departments of foreign affairs, with a view to stimulating the foreign service to play a more active role in promoting national development. The emphasis is on Asian problems of economic and social development, with a professional and interdisciplinary approach. A second course is being planned.

EROPA, like any other international organization, has its basic limitations. It cannot implement its recommendations in national territories without the co-operation of the governments concerned. Its main role is one of innovation, in the sense that after a careful study of the needs of Asian countries, a regional conference has been convened on a particular topic. The regional response has so far been encouraging in terms of participation and contributions. Apart from meetings which are strictly of a business nature, professional conferences are open to participants from all Asian countries, members or not, as well as participants from countries outside the region and international organizations, on an invitational basis.

EROPA meetings are held under joint auspices with the host country, generally a state member of the organization. Official government endorsement and support help greatly to attract international attention as well as effective participation. The various governments which have so far sponsored the EROPA meetings attach a great deal of importance to them. The President of the Philippines honored EROPA by his presence and address at the EROPA First General Assembly in Manila in 1960. The President of the Republic of Korea delivered a special address at the opening ceremony of the EROPA Third General Assembly in Seoul in 1964. His Imperial Majesty the Shah of Iran graced the EROPA Fourth General Assembly by his presence. This official blessing from the host governments, especially from such a supreme authority as the Head of State, has been an important contribution to the EROPA conferences.

Another basic limitation is finance. Membership subscriptions are relatively low. The income from membership dues can hardly support the existing small staff of the secretariat. The maintenance of the present secretariat has been made possible by a grant from the Ford Foundation.

EROPA has so far been successful in obtaining the necessary political support for its growth in terms of state membership as well as government participation and contribution to its work. EROPA, however, needs to sustain its work and to strengthen its professional character in the field of development administration if it is to have substantial impact. It has to consolidate its financial position and broaden official support. Above all, it should serve the countries in the region more effectively.

The participation of several Asian governments through state membership provides useful channels for effective co-operation with EROPA, and through EROPA, with the governments of the other states. The governments of all South and Southeast Asian countries have been invariably invited to EROPA's professional meetings, regardless of whether or not they are member states of the organization. This has made possible broader participation by governments, including those which, although not immediately interested in membership, may still lend co-operation in such areas of development administration as are of particular interest to them.

Since the primary objective of EROPA is to promote good administration for development, co-operation from the governments is of great importance. EROPA hopes that the governments will lend co-operation not only in becoming members of EROPA but especially in making the necessary contributions to facilitate the work of EROPA as an agency for technical co-operation in development administration in the region.

The various governments have frequently collaborated in EROPA professional conferences, particularly in making readily available their views and information for the purpose of conference deliberations and documentation. However, participation in EROPA activity should be a two-way process—a government should not only make its contribution but should also, through EROPA, derive benefit to its own administration. The participation of the governments is unlikely to continue for long unless they see the value of maintaining it. This value is to be measured by EROPA's contribution in professional terms.

EROPA is a professional organization. Being young, it has yet to build up its professional staff, especially in the various specialized centers. The Secretariat is essentially concerned with the general administration of the organization and also with co-ordination of the activities of the centers. Especially during the initial years, however, the Secretariat has felt a need to perform an active role in initiating projects in development administration in collaboration with the centers concerned, basically in the way of conferences, seminars, and research and training projects.

EROPA has the machinery for technical co-operation in development administration, but it needs to build up a deep professional root, primarily by strengthening the activities of its specialized centers. With effective co-operation among the centers and Asian countries, EROPA could indeed become a more effective agency for technical co-operation in development administration in Asia.

The organization is in a position to serve as an external agent for change for Asian countries in development administration. All Asian countries are making efforts toward change—change from developing countries into advanced countries and change from a routine-type of administration to development administration. EROPA, through its professional conferences and its other forms of activity, provides frequent opportunities for Asian countries to come together to share their experience, knowledge, and skills and to adapt them for their own benefit. The participation of advanced countries as well as interested international and regional organizations in the field further enriches the technical resources valuable to developing countries in Asia.

In view of the above, EROPA should be able to play a more effective role as an external agent for change by virtue of its contacts with the administrators and the academicians both in and outside Asia. This is perhaps a good time for EROPA to look back as well as forward at its activity and to work out a plan for action to strengthen its role both as an agency for technical co-operation in development administration in Asia and as an external agent for change for Asian developing countries in the interest of economic and social development. Being an Asian organization with the objective of promoting effective administration for economic and social development, EROPA is an agency par excellence for technical co-operation in development administration in Asia.

Conclusion

Both technical assistance and regional co-operation in development administration in South and Southeast Asia aim at helping the countries concerned improve their public administration, especially in making it more responsive to the needs of national development. The two approaches have been used to complement each other.

Nearly all developing countries in South and Southeast Asia have been receiving, in one form or another, technical assistance in public administration for a variety of purposes. It is hard to generalize whether or not technical assistance to Asian developing countries has been adequate and effective. Much depends upon the nature of the assistance, the qualities of foreign experts involved, and the extent of co-operation of the recipient countries. "There is no specific yardstick by which the total contribution of technical assistance can be quantitatively measured. There are, however, certain qualitative indicators: the increasing demand for technical assistance is a measure of its value to the recipient countries; its increasing scope and complexity is a measure of its vitality, while the increasing quantum of expenditure on technical assistance, as against other forms of aid, is a measure of the importance attached to it by the donor countries."[13]

The strength of technical assistance lies in personal contacts between foreign experts and local counterparts; expertise can thus be shared, selected, and adapted to meet the needs of a recipient country. The success of technical assistance, however, hinges on the presence of a number of factors: notably, that a developing country can identify its needs and specify the qualifications of experts required to help fulfil such needs, that a donor country is able to make available the services of the experts who can spend the desired lengths of time in a country requesting such services, and that a recipient country will provide all necessary facilities, especially in having qualified local counterparts who will work with foreign experts and carry on the latter's functions on completion of technical assistance.

Foreign technical assistance has been given generally to fulfil a more or less specific objective in a recipient country, usually in the form of a program or project. The objective is identifiable, and the task is considered to have been completed at the end of such assistance.

By the nature of technical assistance, contacts of foreign experts with the recipient country are generally limited to a small number of local counterparts who are to acquire or improve their

13. See *Technical Cooperation under the Colombo Plan,* p. 6.

technical knowledge and skills with the help of foreign experts. Institution-building, as another form of technical assistance, helps spread technical know-how thus acquired and maximize the impact of technical assistance within the country. For instance, the institutes of public administration in most South and Southeast Asian countries have been created with foreign technical assistance. Such institutes are playing a significant role in promoting knowledge and skills in public administration.

However, countries capable of extending technical assistance are relatively few, and the number of countries in need of such assistance, on the other hand, is great and increasing. There is a general shortage of experts everywhere in the world today. As funds available for technical assistance are limited and foreign experts are primarily needed in their own countries, technical assistance can only be given on a more or less *ad hoc* basis. Other approaches must also be tried to help strengthen public administration for development purposes.

Regional co-operation in public administration in South and Southeast Asia is a relatively recent development. The idea of sharing knowledge and experience among the countries of the same region has proved to be attractive. This has largely been based on the assumption that the countries in South and Southeast Asia, being newly independent and basically agricultural and having broadly common administrative problems in development, can benefit from one another's experience. The fact that government leaders subscribe to this assumption has contributed to the promotion of regional co-operation.

Regional co-operation in development administration, mainly through EROPA at the present, generally takes the form of conferences, seminars, training, and research. The strength of regional co-operation lies in intergovernmental contacts, usually at a high level. These contacts provide an important channel through which regional co-operation can produce significant impact on the governments involved in such co-operation. Ten states in the area are already members of EROPA, which also has institutional and individual members in other countries of the region.

There are, however, a number of weaknesses in regional co-operation in its present form. One basic difficulty is translating regional findings and recommendations into national actions. A regional organization can enforce its recommendations within national territories only with full co-operation of the governments concerned. Regional co-operation is also handicapped in its progress by the absence of sufficient funds with which to carry out its programs. So long as contributions from the countries of the region are small, foreign financial contributions can be an important source of assistance to the region as a whole. Inasmuch as countries in the same region share similar administrative problems in national development, foreign financial and technical assistance can, in some cases, be more effectively and economically used through regional co-operation. It can be especially useful in that regional co-operation can help maximize the use of foreign assistance to countries in South and Southeast Asia, both individually and as a region.

A proper combination of foreign assistance with regional co-operation in development administration can indeed produce lasting effects.

Chapter 12

Technical Assistance to a Public Administration Institute: The Vietnam Case

Nguyen-Duy Xuan

Introduction

The purpose of this essay is to review the major technical assistance programs relative to the public administration institute in Vietnam during the seven years of operations of the Michigan State University Advisory Group (MSUG) in Vietnam and to examine, in an indirect way, the impact of these programs as reflected in the role of the National Institute of Administration in Vietnam.

The factual information on which this study is based comes from the MSUG reports and various publications by former MSUG members during or after the termination of the MSUG technical assistance contract with Vietnam.[1] The study is divided into three sections. The first section, essentially based on the writings of Edward W. Weidner[2] and David S. Brown,[3] is de-

1. Robert Scigliano and Guy H. Fox, *Technical Assistance in Vietnam* (New York: Frederick A. Praeger, 1965); Jason Finkle and Joseph Zasloff, "The Case Method and Empirical Research in Vietnam," in Frank P. Sherwood and William B. Storm, eds., *Teaching and Research in Public Administration: Essays on Case Approach* (Los Angeles: University of Southern California, School of Public Administration, 1960), pp. 86–98; Howard L. Waltman, "Cross-Cultural Training in Public Administration," *Public Administration Review*, XXI (Summer, 1961), 141–147.

2. Edward W. Weidner, *Technical Assistance in Public Administration Overseas: The Case for Development Administration* (Chicago: Public Administration Service, 1964).

3. David S. Brown, "Strategies and Tactics of Public Administration Technical Assistance: 1945–1963," in John D. Montgomery and William J. Siffin, eds., *Approaches to Development: Politics, Administration and Change* (New York: McGraw-Hill, 1966), pp. 185–223.

voted to the emergence of technical assistance in public administration, the assumptions underlying it, and the techniques of providing technical assistance in public administration. The second section deals with what the MSUG accomplished in working with the National Institute of Administration in Vietnam. With a brief historical review of the founding of the National School of Administration at Dalat in 1953 and the subsequent transformation of that school into the National Institute of Administration now located in Saigon, the section examines the following program categories of technical assistance: (1) developing curriculum and teaching materials, (2) developing an in-service training program for civil servants, (3) promoting research, and (4) sending Vietnamese participants for training abroad. Reference is made to the difficulties with political elements which constrained the implementation of the MSUG technical assistance programs. The third section of the study focuses on the activities of the National Institute of Administration and the contributions of its graduates to the functioning of the administrative apparatus in Vietnam. In this concluding section a suggestion is made about the kind of technical assistance needed to enhance the role and improve the performance of the NIA.

The Problem of Technical Assistance in Public Administration

Emergence of Technical Assistance in Public Administration

To the layman the problem of technical assistance in public administration seems to have started or at least been conceived at the same time as that of technical assistance in agriculture, education, engineering, health, and the like. As a matter of fact it has not been so. The major emphasis of the numerous technical assistance programs launched in the early years after World War II was on social and economic development. The objectives of those programs were mostly related to the building of the economic infrastructure of the recipient country, its industry, its agricultural sector, and its public health and education systems. Only

gradually did public administration assume importance as a necessary field of technical assistance. "As programs of foreign aid
got under way, the inability of these countries to give effect to
new plans and projects caused some technical assistance experts
to turn to public administration for help."[4] The health and sanitation specialist who, according to Brown, stated that "the conduct of a DDT spraying program is 90% administrative and
10% knowing how to spray"[5] recognized the importance of the
relationship between a specific developmental program and the
administrative apparatus to carry it out. Thus, technical assistance in public administration emerged from a situation in which
problems of "organization, personnel, practices, and procedures
essential to effective performance of the civilian functions en-
trusted to the executive branch of the government"[6] were such
that they impeded the implementation of "genuine" technical
assistance programs in such functional fields as engineering, agriculture, health, and education. It later became a program by
itself with a clear purpose of improving the public administration
system per se of emerging nations. For more than a decade the
concern of technical assistance in public administration has been
the improvement of revenue and finance systems and specific
administrative procedures, the development of personnel systems
and the statistic services, the training of police, and the like. The
"philosophy of technical assistance in public administration"
is to convince leaders of the co-operating country that administrative weaknesses and inadequacies of government have a retarding influence upon economic and social development and
that the weaknesses can be corrected.[7] It is remarked moreover
that technical assistance in public administration in the last decade or so has focused primarily on the staff functions. As such the
adequacy of the approach of technical assistance in public administration has recently been questioned in terms of develop-

4. Weidner, *Technical Assistance*, p. 199.
5. "Strategies and Tactics of Public Administration," p. 188.
6. John A. Vieg, "The Growth of Public Administration," in Fritz Morstein
Marx, ed., *Elements of Public Administration* (Englewood Cliffs, N.J.: Prentice-
Hall, 1959), p. 6.
7. ICA Manual Order 2651.1, June 13, 1960, as quoted in Brown, *op. cit.*, p.
187.

ment administration, since the latter can be thought of "as the process of guiding an organization toward the achievement of development objectives."[8] There are also assertions that thus far very few technical assistance programs in public administration could be labeled programs in development administration.

In Vietnam, the problem of technical assistance in public administration was taken up seriously after the partition of the country by the Geneva Agreement in 1954. It was not a result of maladministration of functional technical assistance programs but a recognition of the importance and necessity of an efficient administrative system for the implementation of social and economic development programs.

Strategies of Technical Assistance in Public Administration

Brown in his study of the history of public administration technical assistance has identified six major strategies of technical assistance in public administration which he calls: (1) beachhead strategy, (2) power elite strategy, (3) multiplier effect strategy, (4) grass roots strategy, (5) program integration strategy, and (6) cultural accommodation strategy. All these strategies have not been used with equal frequency. In early technical assistance programs efforts were made to gain acceptability in a host country and therefore the beachhead strategy was undoubtedly used in most cases. Often a combination of strategies is used and sometimes there is no precise strategy in giving technical assistance in public administration. According to Weidner's experience with technical assistance in public administration, "goals must be determined before the best strategies can be determined." That could be done only if "public administration were goal-oriented" and thus far there are only a few technical assistance programs in public administration with a special purpose.[9]

Although the "strategies of technical assistance" hypothesized by Brown are not consciously used as such by operators of technical assistance programs, they are useful as a device for com-

8. Weidner, *Technical Assistance*, p. 200.
9. *Ibid.*, pp. 200, 226.

paring and guiding our observations with respect to the empirical phenomena of technical assistance. They will permit us to grasp more significant elements and to arrive at some generalizations and classification of problems germane to the field of technical assistance in public administration.

In the case of Vietnam under the First Republic of President Diem, in the first years of technical assistance in public administration the power elite strategy was heavily used owing to special circumstances conditioning the relationship between the early leaders of the technical assistance mission and the power elite of the recipient country.[10] It was combined with the beachhead and the multiplier effect strategies in most programs. In the early 1960's there was a switch from those strategies to the grass roots strategy, which may properly be called "rice roots" strategy, according to which AID representatives are stationed at the provincial and sometimes district level to help implement various technical assistance programs and accelerate achievement.

The Building of the National Institute of Administration (NIA)

Genesis of the NIA

Under French colonial control few Vietnamese were provided with training for high-level posts in the administrative services. For all Indochina (now North and South Vietnam, Cambodia, and Laos) there was only one School of Law and Administration, created in 1917 in Hanoi. In 1925 it was succeeded by the School of Advanced Indochinese Studies (Ecole des Hautes Etudes Indochinoises) and in 1932 by the Faculty of Law. Since the University of Hanoi and later the University of Saigon, set up in 1949, were organized according to the European educational system, only the traditional faculties of sciences, medicine, pharmacy, law, and letters were open. Economics was taught in the faculty of law, and other new social sciences were poorly covered.

10. Warren Hinckle, Sol Stern, and Robert Scheer, "The University on the Make," *Ramparts*, Apr., 1966, pp. 11–22.

There was little emphasis on public administration, and what little there was went in the direction of administrative law.

In 1950 it was realized by the government of the then Associated States of Vietnam that greatly improved public administration would be essential before Vietnam could hope to become a full-fledged independent nation. A plan to set up a school of public administration was drafted. The initial draft was studied by a commission, and in the spring of 1952 the National School of Administration at Dalat was authorized and its classes were opened in January, 1953.[11] The School of Administration at Dalat was directed by a high-ranking Vietnamese official. There was no consultation of any kind with the well-known Ecole Nationale d'Administration in Paris in the founding of the National School of Administration at Dalat for Vietnam. The Dalat school did not receive any kind of organized technical assistance except that a few high French officials working with the French Commissariat at that time were asked to give lectures to students.[12] In July, 1954, after the return to Vietnam of Ngo Dinh Diem as prime minister, a special four-man mission of the Foreign Operations Administration came to Vietnam. The mission was made up of Michigan State University professors. After two months' stay the FOA-MSU special mission submitted a report in October, 1954, in which it recommended a program to supplement the American assistance program. The proposed supplemental program was to be centered in the areas of public administration, economics, public information, and police administration. By late April, 1955, contracts between Michigan State University and the Foreign Operations Administration were signed, according to which the Michigan State University would operate an extensive program of technical assistance in public administration and economics. In the October, 1954, report of the FOA-MSU special mission it was recommended that an institute be established in Saigon with "complete training facilities, complete consultative

11. Walter R. Sharp, *A Public Administration Improvement Program for the Association States of Indochina,* report prepared for the Mutual Security Agency (Chicago: Public Administration Service, 1952).
12. This remark was made to the author by Professor Nghiem Dang, who was appointed vice-rector of the Dalat National School of Administration in 1954 and who has since remained in that capacity after its transformation into the National Institute of Administration.

services which it can extend to the government, and a reasonably complete set of research services in the government area."[13] Following the signing of the technical assistance contract between the Michigan State University and the government of Vietnam, the latter moved the National School of Administration at Dalat to Saigon (by Presidential Arrete, No. 483/PTT/TTK, August 8, 1955) and transformed it into the present National Institute of Administration. Thus, an organized program of technical assistance in public administration started only with the arrival of the Michigan State University Advisory Group in Vietnam in May, 1955.

As early as 1952, Walter R. Sharp had gone to Indochina to make a survey of public administration problems on behalf of the Mutual Security Agency. He had remarked that

a number of ministers and other senior officials in Vietnam would probably welcome concrete offers of help towards the solution of some of the staff and organizational difficulties. They expressed their eagerness to obtain American publications on technical, economic, and social problems and to learn about American and other non-French administrative concepts and practices. They seemed to sense that the oncoming generation of national leaders must become acquainted with other cultures if their peoples are to take their proper place among the free independent nations of the world.[14]

Sharp also proposed several forms of public administration assistance for Vietnam: training facilities for administrative personnel, special teaching materials and books on public administration, trainee grants for study and observation abroad, and development of an effective budget system for the country. Only with the arrival of the Michigan State University Advisory Group in mid-1955 did a systematic approach to technical assistance in public administration along these lines take shape. Although the programs of technical assistance in public administration of MSUG during their seven years of operations in Vietnam covered many areas, this essay will be concerned only with MSUG efforts to

13. Edward W. Weidner, "First Report of the MSU Vietnam Team in Public Administration" (Saigon: National Institute of Administration, Aug. 19, 1965).
14. See Sharp, *op. cit.*, for further details.

help the Vietnamese government build the National Institute of Administration.

Role of the Michigan State University Advisory Group (*MSUG*)

Technical assistance to a public administration institute is one form of the multiplier effect strategy of technical assistance now widely known as institution-building. In a paper prepared for the Special Studies Project of the Rockefeller Brothers Fund in 1956 titled "The Theory and Practice of Foreign Aid," Harlan Cleveland applied the term "institution-building" to the effort "to develop social institutions that provide a conduit for tangible benefits from a government to its people and for participation by people in their own government."[15] Since then it has become "something of a catch-word in aid circles." The term "institution" certainly has different meanings to different people. In technical social science literature it often "denotes the incorporation of values or norms into conventions and patterns of social behavior which are sanctioned and enforced by formal and informal authority." But in common usage it may be used "to denote a complex social system which incorporates values and discharges services to the community . . . and may perform economic, social, political or administrative functions either in the governmental or the private sector."[16] Thus technical assistance to a public administration institute is a form of institution-building.

In the case of Vietnam, one of the principal objectives of the Michigan State University Group was to make the National Institute of Administration an effective institution capable of developing the administrative skills and effectiveness of the Vietnamese Civil Service. The long-range purpose was to improve the administrative performance of the government of Vietnam and thus contribute to its social and economic development. An institution designated by the presidency to train high-ranking civil servants, NIA was to select its students by competitive examination and

15. *The Theory and Practice of Foreign Aid* (Syracuse, N.Y.: Syracuse University, Maxwell Graduate School of Citizenship and Public Affairs, 1956), pp. 43–51.
16. Milton J. Esman, "Institution Building in National Development," *International Development Review*, IV (Dec., 1962), 27–30.

they were to be obliged to work for the government upon completing their studies. The National Institute of Administration was also expected to be in charge of other programs for the improvement of governmental administration such as offering consulting and in-service training services, organizing a reference center for government agencies, and sponsoring a professional society and conferences on various aspects of administration.

The Michigan State University Advisory Group's activities during its seven years of technical assistance to the National Institute of Administration can be grouped into five basic program categories.[17] The first category was concerned with the development of curriculum and teaching methods. The second aimed at developing an in-service training program. The third consisted of promoting research and setting up a good social science reference library. The fourth concentrated on the training of the existing and future teaching staff, and was usually known as the participant's program. The fifth program consisted of providing material equipment to the National Institute of Administration. The order of enumeration of the programs does not mean that programs cited first were more important than the others nor that the programs were put into operation in that order. Almost all programs were implemented simultaneously in the early years of the MSUG's association with the NIA. Although it is not necessary to enter into the details of each program separately it is useful to review the salient aspects of each program.

Since the NIA originated from a two-year training school of civil servants set up when Vietnam was still an Associated State in the French Union, it was French-oriented in the sense that its course offerings were primarily juridical with very little instruction in public administration. Acting on MSUG advice, the NIA decided to expand its regular program from two to three years and to offer special evening courses for government employees. The curriculum approved by the presidency in May, 1957, comprised three years of study. A variety of subjects was taught,

17. The information used in this section is based on the semiannual reports of the Michigan State University Advisory Group in Vietnam. Altogether there are fourteen semiannual reports and a final report covering activities of the MSUG Vietnam for the period May 20, 1955–June 30, 1962.

among them introduction to public administration, economics, constitutional law, finance, statistics, practical drafting of administrative documents, and accounting. In the second year students were divided into two sections: general public administration and economics and finance. General public administration students concentrated on subjects germane to administrative sciences, such as administrative problems, civil service, labor relations, and law, while economics and finance students took courses in capital formation, economic planning, and the agricultural and economic problems of Vietnam. There were compulsory courses for students of both sections, such as human relations, office management, budget practice, and organizational methods. In their third year, all students were divided into small groups and sent into the field for special training for a semester. The field training had two phases: one in the provinces and one at the ministries of the central government. Field training at the central ministries was followed by seminars at the NIA. Periodic visits to central and field offices were made by the NIA teaching staff in charge of field training to observe the students' apprenticeship and working experience. In the second semester of the third year students returned to the NIA to take a few more courses in public administration, economics, and finance before their final examinations.

In 1960 the curriculum was revised again according to the recommendations of an NIA-MSUG committee. In the 1960 curriculum two courses in sociology were introduced in the first year, one of which was taught by an MSUG member. Later, new courses including research methods and a case-study seminar in public administration were given to students in their second year. In accordance with presidential instructions directing the NIA to provide a more "generalist" type of instruction, and in consideration of the fact that NIA graduates would be called upon increasingly to perform general managerial functions as provincial and district chiefs, the Academic Council of the NIA in 1962 decided to merge the general public administration and the economics and finance sections. When asked for an opinion regarding that pending decision, MSUG recommended that (1) the generalist dimension of administrative training might best be achieved by offering fewer courses in specialized and technical subjects and more courses in the liberal arts, (2) more reading of materials available in the NIA library be assigned, and (3) in order to train high administrators, who would be truly generalists in the sense of having attained a high level of well-rounded knowledge, it would be important to consider the addition of a fourth year of study. In MSUG's view, "the fourth year would be particularly beneficial both in terms of developing a curriculum stressing the Vietnamese cultural development and in enhancing the prestige of the credentials of the NIA graduates."[18] A merger of the general public administration section and the economics and finance section was made in 1966 upon instructions from the Prime Minister's Office—four years after the original decision was made.

Recognizing that the degree of success of a curriculum depends on teaching methods and teaching materials, MSUG also suggested to the NIA faculty less use of the magistral lecture system and greater employment of the discussion, seminar, term paper, and case methods. MSUG's help in preparing teaching materials consisted of writing complete sets of lectures or texts for various courses and collateral readings for others; all these materials were translated into Vietnamese, as were some selected textbooks and articles for classroom use. But owing to the woeful lack of Vietnamese textbooks most lectures continue to be written out. Still, most faculty members tend to make use of discussion methods as much as possible.

According to the 1955 contract between the government of Vietnam and the MSUG, Vietnamese civil servants already on the payroll were to become in-service trainees. In October, 1955, Frederic R. Wickert submitted a work plan for in-service training[19] which served as a guide for the introduction of in-service training in Vietnam. The work plan suggested that MSUG and NIA assume responsibility for selling the in-service training concept so that it might become an accepted personnel training

18. MSUG Vietnam, *Final Report* (Saigon, June, 1962), p. 28.
19. "Work Plan and Statement of Philosophy for In-Service Training" (Saigon: MSUG Vietnam, 1955).

policy in Vietnam. The recommendation made to the president in 1956 to set up a national in-service training program and establish advisory councils and in-service training staffs in each department and province to oversee program operations was not accepted. Therefore, it was necessary for the NIA to offer its services to governmental agencies interested in developing their programs.

With MSUG support, the NIA organized in-service training courses in accounting, budget administration, records management, and administrative and office practices. The NIA in-service training section was expanded and became a regular division of the NIA. In striving for government-wide in-service training even without the support of the Office of the President, an *In-Service Training Newsletter* was published and then was continued by a periodical called *Progress* with distribution of approximately six thousand copies throughout the government. Publication of *Progress* was discontinued after the departure of MSUG because of the lack of financial support.

In 1958 MSUG made new recommendations covering central and local government training. The most important recommendations were: (1) that departmental and semiautonomous agencies should create training centers and devise plans of action; (2) that the Civil Service Directorate should provide guidance, evaluation, and studies and issue appropriate regulations to increase the quality and scope of in-service training; (3) that an interdepartmental council on in-service training should integrate programs generally; (4) that the NIA should provide publicity, translation, and preparation of training materials and supervision. These recommendations did not receive formal acknowledgement or support, but many aspects of them were implemented. Seminars for employees at both central and provincial levels were undertaken in co-operation with the Ministry of Interior and the Civil Service Directorate, and interdepartmental seminars on in-service training were organized and attended by representatives from all provinces. With MSUG's support, twenty-one in-service training centers were built in the provinces and the NIA co-operated with the Ministry of Interior to develop training officers for most central ministries and for provincial administrations. More than 23,000 government employees participated in in-service training before the departure of MSUG—among them 4,500 who were section chiefs or members of higher groups.

According to the contract of April, 1955, between the government of Vietnam and Michigan State University, MSUG was to "assist the Government of Vietnam in establishing a comprehensive research and reference program in the problems of government in Vietnam, and in developing a reference library."[20] It was also felt that a survey of regional and provincial administration and their relations with the central government was needed. To cope with the new task, the NIA designated its chief of the Division of Research and Documentation to serve as counterpart to MSUG's technical assistance programs including public administration, police, and finance. Some early activities of MSUG were to assist faculty members of the NIA's research division and NIA's students to develop questionnaires, code the results, and familiarize themselves with the use of IBM machines for processing data.

An important feature of research promotion of the early stages was the development of the case study program. A Case Advisory Committee composed of three NIA and three MSUG staff members selected a series of cases for study, designed to illustrate administrative problems in Vietnam at the provincial level. Upon completion the cases were published in Vietnamese and in English.

In 1957 the NIA and MSUG embarked on a joint research program to gain much-needed information about sociological, economic, and administrative conditions in Vietnam. In a few years, roughly twenty studies were produced of various aspects of Vietnamese administrative and socio-economic conditions, based on field research in the Mekong Delta and in the coastal region of Central Vietnam. When in 1959 the NIA began to serve as the research and documentation center for the Eastern Regional Organization for Public Administration (EROPA),

20. Ralph H. Smuckler, "Work Plan for Research Coordinator" (Saigon: MSUG Vietnam, 1955).

MSUG's assistance was mobilized in the preparation of working documents and background papers for various EROPA meetings.

Essential to the NIA's teaching programs and research was the development of an adequate library. During the first four years of its operations, MSUG assigned a full-time adviser to library management. MSUG was also instrumental in sending two NIA librarians for training abroad. Thanks to MSUG financial support, the NIA has now an impressive collection of approximately 16,000 social science books, mostly in English but with some in French. In addition, the library has acquired about 1,000 United Nations documents and has more than 6,000 government documents and periodicals. It also has a microfilm reader and several dozen reels of microfilm. The library collections are catalogued and classified according to the Dewey Decimal System and have been constantly expanded through periodical subscriptions (150 different titles) and regular book orders.

Owing to rigid personnel regulations based almost entirely on educational background, it is not feasible to pay librarians and their assistants salaries commensurate with their proven competence and training. From its own funds, MSUG paid slightly higher salaries to the assistants than was otherwise possible. When MSUG funds were no longer available, some of the best assistants refused to become NIA personnel at lower salaries. The result was a shortage of qualified library attendants and restriction of the services of the NIA library.

The purpose of the participant programs was to put current or prospective staff members of the NIA abroad for observation or for advanced education. From the date of its creation until the middle of 1957, one of the NIA's most urgent needs was for staff to teach its new courses and to cope with its increased annual intake of students. Until the middle of 1957 MSUG staff taught an average of five or six semester courses to students in the regular program and in the evening classes. The MSUG teaching load was relieved when the NIA was able to add new faculty members working on a part-time basis. Efforts of MSUG to train the NIA staff consisted of sending NIA regular faculty members to the United States on four-to-nine-month observation and study tours and selected young prospective staff members for regular academic training in the United States. The training of Ph.D.'s for NIA teaching started relatively late, and only at the end of 1958 did MSUG help NIA embark on a systematic doctoral training program. Between 1958 and 1962 seventeen persons were chosen jointly by the NIA and MSUG, mostly from candidates in Vietnam and partly from Vietnamese graduate students already in American universities. By the end of 1965 eight participants had returned to work with the NIA, five with their degrees completed. Four other participants, of whom two earned the Ph.D., preferred to work with other government agencies. The remainder are still in the United States. Besides the training of the NIA teaching staff, the participant program included NIA administrators and librarians.

Acting on MSUG advice, the government of Vietnam in 1955 transferred the Dalat School of Administration to Saigon and transformed it into the present National Institute of Administration. With United States aid funds, MSUG helped the NIA establish its Saigon quarters in a former Catholic mission house with its library in a small chapel. It also provided the NIA campus with office and audio-visual equipment and funds to support NIA publication activities. The Catholic mission house soon became inadequate for the new programs being projected. It had only three classrooms, which were conspicuously insufficient for the instructional needs of a three-year degree program, several evening classes, miscellaneous in-service training courses, and other special programs. Only a single conference or seminar room was available, and there was no place large enough to accommodate the whole student body. In co-operation with the NIA, MSUG worked to replace the campus with a new one. By the end of 1961 a new plant was completed, consisting of four buildings on about nine acres of land. The first building was designed for offices and classrooms, and contained forty-eight offices of varying size and twelve classrooms, five of which could be used for seminars and discussion groups. The second building housed the library and auditorium. The two remaining buildings were a dormitory and a dining room. The cost of the new campus amounted to

$VN33,423,470$, including reimbursement for previously expended aid funds on the old NIA quarters and the cost of the land, which was supplied by the government of Vietnam.[21]

Achievements of the Michigan State University Advisory Group

MSUG technical assistance to the NIA in Vietnam was only part of the several programs that MSUG undertook in its twice-renewed contracts with the government of Vietnam. During the seven years of its operations in Vietnam, MSUG spent $5,355,000 for the salaries and transportation of its American staff and for miscellaneous campus-supporting activities, and $5,130,000 equivalent in Vietnamese currency for its Vietnamese staff and other expenses in the field. In addition, MSUG was allowed to spend about $15,000,000 of American aid funds for the purchase of equipment and materials. Altogether MSUG's cost for the seven years amounted to approximately $25,000,000.[22] Compared with the dollar costs of other universities' overseas programs, that of the MSUG is a sizable one.[23]

In 1957, after MSUG renewed its contract for the first time, its staff consisted, at its height, of 51 Americans and 151 Vietnamese.[24] The staff was almost entirely engaged in carrying out or giving administrative support to programs in two major fields: public administration and police administration. Advice and assistance to the NIA were, in the first contract, only a small part of the MSUG public administration activities, which included surveys and recommendations designed to improve government departments and the Office of the President, consultation with the government of Vietnam in the fields of budget and fiscal adminis-

21. *Fourteenth Report of the Michigan State University Advisory Group in Public Administration to the Government of Vietnam* (Saigon, Dec. 31, 1961), p. 4.
22. Scigliano and Fox, *op. cit.*, p. 4.
23. "ICA spent an average of roughly $115,000 per year on the University of California's public administration program in Bologna; $120,000 on Northwestern University's business administration program in France; $175,000 on the Georgetown University's language project in Ankara; $450,000 on the New York University public administration-law-commercial science project in Ankara; . . . some programs call for annual expenditures of more than $1,000,000" (Walter Adams and John A. Garraty, *Is the World Our Campus?* [East Lansing, Mich.: Michigan State University Press, 1960], p. 6).
24. MSUG Vietnam, *Final Report*, p. 1.

tration, taxation, personnel, and management. It would not be easy, therefore, to deduct from the total cost of MSUG's operations the cost of technical assistance provided to the NIA alone. Such questions as "How much does it cost?" and "Is the money well spent?" could not be answered accurately.

Even if the monetary cost could be ascertained,[25] major difficulties in the attempt to evaluate a technical assistance program still remain with us. If the tangible results could be pointed out, there would nevertheless remain the intangible effects which take some time to appear.

If goals must be determined before the best strategy and tactic of technical assistance can be determined, goals must also be recalled in order to enable us to make consistent judgment about the impact of technical assistance programs. In our case the goal of technical assistance was formally spelled out in the contract between the Vietnamese government and Michigan State University. MSUG's role was to assist the government of Vietnam in establishing and operating "a National Institute of Public Administration for purposes of improving the training and competence of government officials and employees, offering instruction at the university level related to a degree or certificate program in public administration . . . a comprehensive research and reference program in the problems of government in Vietnam and in developing a reference library."[26]

The questions to be answered now are: What in fact has been accomplished? To what extent do the results obtained correspond to what was expected? Aware of the methodological difficulties in the process of evaluating the effects of a technical assistance program in public administration, the author, nevertheless, will

25. It is possible to compute (1) the total of salaries of MSUG staff attached to the NIA and the cost of their supporting activities during the seven years, (2) the cost of the collection of books and documents paid by MSUG for the NIA library, (3) the financial support in carrying out the research projects jointly with NIA staff, (4) the cost of NIA's new buildings, (5) expense incurred by the sending of participants abroad, and (6) the cost of a few other miscellaneous items. The figure would represent only a small percentage of the total cost of $25,000,000. It would not be very meaningful, however, in view of the fact that MSUG's activities covered such a wide but interlocking scope that activities of one program overlapped with other programs.

26. See Guy H. Fox, John M. Hunter, and John T. Dorsey, "Work Plan, Degree or Certificate Program" (Saigon: MSUG Vietnam, Aug. 25, 1955).

try to point out through official reports, self-appraisals, and personal experience the solid and tangible results of the MSUG technical assistance programs at the NIA in Vietnam. Although the measuring of attitudes and attitude changes is particularly delicate and difficult, he has tried to obtain tangible evidence of the extent of the influence of MSUG upon the attitude, behavior, and general outlook of the Vietnamese at the NIA.

Using the institution-building concept to evaluate the achievements of MSUG's seven years' association with the NIA, it can be admitted that MSUG successfully attained its technical assistance goals for the NIA. The NIA seems to have satisfied, at least since departure of MSUG, almost all the requirements for a successful institution-building program noted by Edward W. Weidner: "Institution-building, however, requires more than establishment of a new organization. It must fit into local ways of doing things, be *staffed, supported,* and *wanted* by host country nationals, and *perform a useful function for the society.*"[27]

This point will be brought more into relief when we look at the current role of the NIA in Vietnam. However, in the current context, stress must be placed on the fact that MSUG in its association with the NIA played only an *advisory role.* It never participated in the administration of the institute as in the University of Michigan–Philippines case. Teaching of Vietnamese students by MSUG members was also limited to the years before 1957 when there was a shortage of NIA faculty staff.

Considering the political environment in which MSUG members worked—the cautious and legalistic leadership of the NIA resulting mostly from the attachment of the NIA to the presidency[28]—some of the results of the advisory role of MSUG are significant. For example, the adoption of a teaching curriculum emphasizing the social science approach, as advised by MSUG on the part of the NIA leadership which had previously been trained in traditional and legalistic academic disciplines, was indicative not only of a state of mind receptive to new ideas but also of the

27. *Technical Assistance,* p. 74. Emphasis added.
28. Robert Scigliano, *South Vietnam: Nation under Stress* (Boston: Houghton Mifflin, 1963), p. 65.

willingness to change. This may be considered as "a stage of innovation," to use Weidner's phrase, through which the French model was gradually replaced by the more Americanized model of training in public administration. The increased use of empirical research reports as reading assignments for students and illustrations in classroom lectures are certainly evidences of a change in the teaching method and of a new attitude toward learning (Lee and Weidner).

The permission granted to students to express their own views and raise questions in class constitutes a somewhat radical transformation of pedagogical techniques in a country where professors are accustomed to speaking from the podium without interruption from a docile audience. With the return of MSUG participants, who make up about one-third of the regular NIA faculty members, and with a leadership convinced of the necessity of research and its importance for the maintenance of a high academic standard at the NIA, a new attitude toward research has emerged among NIA faculty members. There is a healthy realization that in order to improve the standard and quality of one's teaching—let alone other beneficial aspects upon completion of the research project—one must undertake continuous research. This attitude is more significant in an institution where the slogan "publish or perish" is not as important as seniority. It would be too much to attribute this new attitude toward research entirely to the influence of the MSUG advisers, but their research activities at the NIA and the exposure of NIA faculty members to American university activities during observation tours organized under the participant programs have undoubtedly been among the forces for change (Hsueh).

A crucial aspect of a technical assistance program is human relations between the advisers and advisees. In the case of Vietnam, as in any other technical assistance recipient country, such problems as language barriers, cultural differences, and disparities in the standard of living[29] are the main obstacles in the early period of co-operation between the two parties. As impediments, these gradually recede into the background, although they re-

29. *Ibid.*, p. 195, for a comprehensive overview of the problem.

main present, for most advisers and advisees. The NIA being an agency attached to the Office of the President, the attitude of its leadership toward the MSUG's advisers primarily reflected the attitude of the president.[30] Although democratic institutions existed in form under the First Republic (1955–63), overwhelming power was in the hands of the president and members of his family. Most decisions were made at the presidential level. Moreover, the government's concern for internal security outweighed all other problems after 1959. Thus, the political system and circumstances were not conducive to academic research in public administration which would bring out many facets of government practices. It is worth noticing that the bulk of MSUG research projects in public administration at the central and local level was undertaken before 1960, when internal security was not a major threat to the government. After 1960, the government became more sensitive to any public criticism. It considered that security threats were too serious for it to permit impractical Western-style democratic liberties and that any criticism would be exploited by the enemy against the government. Although in the last few years of its operations MSUG concentrated its efforts on the NIA, little research in public administration was carried out, owing partly to physical security problems and partly to political constraints. It was thought that anything published which would lead to criticism of the government was a potential weapon for the Communists. The sensitivity[31] of the president toward criticism expressed publicly by MSUG members returning to the United States was the main cause for the failure of the renewal of the MSUG contract in June, 1962.

Because technical assistance given to the NIA was only part of the MSUG extensive program in Vietnam, what MSUG achieved at the NIA is somewhat blurred by MSUG's less successful enterprises in their advisory roles elsewhere in the Vietnamese government. As already remarked by Robert Scigliano and Guy H. Fox, a comparative study of the results of MSUG's association with

30. *Ibid.*, pp. 190–216.
31. Edward W. Weidner remarked that "handsome dividends" may be obtained in the counterpart system if "cultural sensitivity of the host countries" is absent (*Technical Assistance,* p. 114).

various agencies of the government of Vietnam would induce one
to hypothesize that:

i. Whenever and wherever the power elite strategy is applicable
there is great likelihood that technical assistance programs will be
implemented. In the case of Vietnam–Michigan State most of MSUG
recommendations were quickly adopted by the government of Vietnam in their early years of co-operation when the relationships between the president of the Republic of Vietnam and the chief adviser
of MSUG were more than friendly.

ii. Technical assistance programs which do not touch sensitive political nerves find greater receptivity than other programs. MSUG proposals for moving the Administration School from Dalat to Saigon and
expanding its scope and physical plants were more readily accepted
than other proposals concerned with civil service reforms or establishing provincial and village councils.

iii. Newly established agencies endowed with new leadership appear to be more receptive to technical assistance advice than older
ones. The reason is that resistance from old-line agencies and traditional civil service restraints render difficult the implementation of
technical assistance programs. The NIA may be considered as a relatively new institution with a new leadership, even though it belonged
to the traditional intelligentsia.

iv. The more violent and traumatic the overthrow of the colonial
power the more likely and readily will the new nation desire to become acquainted with cultures other than that of the former colonial
power.[32]

In the case of Vietnam, the overthrow of the French colonial
regime was violent and bloody; although the struggle against the
French during the period from 1945 to 1954 was under the
leadership of the Communists, the participation of nationalist
elements was vital to its success. With due consideration to the
above hypotheses and given the nature of the leadership and
political environment at that time, looking back to what MSUG
accomplished mostly as adviser and sometimes as operator at the
NIA, one can certainly say that it was a "good job."

However, there are a few areas to which MSUG advisers to the
NIA should have given more attention. For instance, the training
visits of NIA faculty members to the United States seemed to

32. Scigliano and Fox, *op. cit.*, pp. 25–26.

suffer the same defect as the training programs organized by MSUG for Vietnamese civil servants as a whole. As Nghiem Dang, vice-rector of the NIA, has pointed out, "the trips are sometimes conceived as a concession to the requirements of the social environment."[33] A study visit insufficiently prepared or granted to the wrong person would certainly reduce the potential value of the training. As recognized by a former member of MSUG, "there was no effective planning to achieve maximum results,"[34] and a few participants did consider the training trips as pleasure excursions.

Another problem in connection with training was the sending of doctoral participants to the United States. MSUG could have foreseen the possibility that these participants, because of the relatively long duration of training, would become familiar with a high standard of living in the United States and be reluctant to return to Vietnam. Another possible threat was that upon their return to Vietnam they would be attracted by other governmental positions and would not work with the NIA. An allowance should have been made in the number of recruits to make up for the loss of such participants. In the next few years the NIA will probably function with an understaffed faculty when the senior professors reach their retirement age.

An important problem that NIA has to face is procurement of teaching materials, particularly textbooks. In its seven years of association with NIA, MSUG should have helped solve the shortage of textbooks written in Vietnamese. It is true that the amount of teaching materials has tremendously increased with the assistance—particularly financial—of MSUG. But the existing materials are mostly translations of American textbooks and lectures given by MSUG professors to NIA students during the academic sessions of 1956 and 1957. The real need is for textbooks for the use of Vietnamese students. Undoubtedly incentives could have been found to induce economically overburdened and relatively low-paid NIA staff members to produce

33. Nghiem Dang, "Reflexions on Technical Assistance," *EROPA Review* (Saigon, National Institute of Administration), I (June, 1965), 20.
34. Waltman, *op. cit.,* p. 142.

such textbooks. Furthermore, MSUG's advice about the "content" of such textbooks would have been most valuable. If one of the functions of a technical assistance mission is to help the host agency to identify its needs and to try to satisfy them, then MSUG partially failed in its task of providing teaching materials to NIA.

Role of the NIA

When MSUG left Vietnam in June, 1962, NIA was well established and functioning. After the overthrow of the First Republic regime in November, 1963, the leadership of NIA was also replaced, but NIA continued to serve as a focal center for training and developing personnel for high-level positions.

NIA is still directly attached to the Office of the Prime Minister, although at times there have been strong suggestions that it be put under the jurisdiction of the Ministry of National Education.[35] It has four special-purpose divisions: the Academic Division, the On-the-Job Training Division, the In-Service Training Division, and the Research and Documentation Division. Since August, 1965, NIA has offered four training programs: advanced studies in government, economics and finance, and international relations (M.A. degree level); the field administration program (B.A. degree level); the chief clerk training program; and the proficiency in public administration program (evening courses). Students of the first division's three programs are recruited by competitive examination, given scholarships by the government during their study years at the NIA and upon completion of their study must work for the government in various governmental

35. The question of attaching an institute of public administration to a university or to a governmental agency is important in countries where the university enjoys an autonomous status. Attached to an autonomous university, the institute of public administration may have more prestige and more resources in supporting its academic research; furthermore, it may have more freedom to criticize governmental policies than institutes of public administration attached to a governmental agency. In Vietnam, universities are *not* autonomous and are under the jurisdiction of the Ministry of Education. It is probable that NIA's attachment to the Office of the Prime Minister enables it to have more influence upon decisions concerning the use and distribution of NIA graduates among various governmental agencies.

agencies in accord with their training. The proficiency in public administration program is designed to help increase the theoretical knowledge and technical skills of public servants and to prepare candidates for various public service entrance examinations.

The faculty of NIA has twenty-two regular members. Ten of them are holders of American or European doctorates. The teaching load is shared among the regular faculty members and seventeen part-time lecturers. In 1965–66 there were sixty students enrolled in the first year of the advanced studies program, and it is planned to recruit sixty students each year. There were almost three hundred students enrolled in the field administration program (one hundred in the first year, about one hundred in the second year, and ninety in the third year) and it is anticipated that one hundred students will be recruited every year. There were one hundred students in the chief clerk training program, and recruitment of one hundred students each year is planned. There were about two hundred students enrolled in evening training for the certificate of proficiency, and it is anticipated that almost that many students will be enrolled each year in evening courses. Thus, there are normally about seven hundred students every year studying at NIA. According to a census at the end of 1965, Vietnam has a total of 142,913 civil servants[36] of all categories.[37] Among them more than 2,500 are of Category A and approximately 41,000 are of Category B. Thus, the percentage of public servants to a population of 14.5 million inhabitants is just over 1 per cent.

Recently, according to a report of NIA to its Administrative Council,[38] there were 2,400 positions that needed to be filled by candidates having had training in public administration at a

36. Civil Service Supreme Council, "Tableau des effectifs annuels du personnel civil" (Saigon, 1966).

37. Recruitment of civil servants in Vietnam is usually based on the level of general and professional education. Personnel are classified into three categories: civil servants who have had a university education are classified in Category A, those who have had a secondary school education are classified in Category B, and those who have had a basic primary school education are classified in Category C. For a comprehensive discussion of the Civil Service in Vietnam see Dale Rose, *The Vietnamese Civil Service* (Saigon: MSUG, 1961), and Nghiem Dang, *Vietnam: Politics and Public Administration* (Honolulu: East-West Center Press, 1966), chap. v.

38. Report of the NIA to the Administrative Council Session, April 2, 1964.

university level, and there were only a little more than 600 candidates who satisfied the requirements, leaving nearly 1,800 to be recruited. NIA has been asked to recommend measures for solving that pressing need for administrators. The main reason for the opening of the advanced studies program in 1965 was to offer advanced studies in public administration and other related subjects to graduates of the faculties of law and arts and other qualified civil servants. Considering the need for high-level civil servants, if preservice training in public administration is required for government jobs, the annual output of NIA graduates is far from adequate.

In addition to its regular training programs, the NIA, at the request of various ministries since the overthrow of the First Republic, has organized many new in-service training courses in public administration, particularly for the military officers assuming responsibilities of province and district chiefs. As the country is now engaged in a survival struggle, there is a need for large numbers of political and administrative cadre mission- and program-oriented persons who will be in charge of implementation, direction, and supervision of pacification programs in recaptured villages and hamlets once held by the enemy. Therefore, besides the existing curricula, NIA is also preparing several new special in-service courses in countersubversion and pacification of former enemy territories for NIA graduates who are already in government positions and who will probably be reassigned to supervise political and administrative cadres whose training has been undertaken by the Ministry of Rural Reconstruction with the help of NIA staff members.

Since the overthrow of the Diem regime, NIA is no longer considered as a refuge of civil servant castoffs from other parts of the government. In October, 1965, when the prime minister created the Central Committee for the Improvement of Administrative Procedures, he appointed the rector of NIA as chairman of the committee. The members of this body consist of representatives of the Prime Minister's Office and of the Ministries of Interior, Finance, Economy, Psywar, Rural Reconstruction, Agriculture, Youth, Public Works, Public Health, and Social Welfare.

The rector of NIA has mobilized most staff members of NIA to help him in his new task. The committee meets once a week and discusses procedural administrative problems and bottlenecks brought to it by various ministries. A number of its recommendations have been ordered into effect by the Office of the Prime Minister or by the interested ministries.

In connection with the seminar movement organized within various governmental agencies "to build up ideas and to achieve a thorough understanding of the goals of national policy, to improve techniques, interchange experiences,"[39] the NIA rector was also appointed chairman of the Council on Documentation and Guidance. The members of this group include the chief of the Political Section of the National Defense Ministry and all directors of cabinet of the other ministries. The council is responsible for mapping out seminar programs and drafting all materials on general topics. It also holds weekly meetings at NIA.

These activities are indicative of the growing importance of NIA in the administrative system of Vietnam in terms of services rendered to various governmental agencies. However, its far-reaching impact upon the administrative apparatus lies mostly in the works of its graduates appointed to a wide variety of governmental posts (Lee, Abueva).

From 1953 to the end of the 1965–66 academic year, the NIA put out a total of 736 graduates from the regular three-year course of study in field administration. They have been trained to be administrators particularly responsible for the elaboration of proposals concerning general policy, for supervising the application of policy, and for maintaining liaison with other technical services in the government at various levels. Upon completion of their studies, NIA graduates are classified into Category A of the civil service, except for the graduates of the newly opened chief clerk training program who are classified in Category B. As of now, more than one-fourth of the civil servants of Category A are made up of NIA graduates. With a regular annual supply of about 150 new NIA graduates to Category A, the proportion of

39. Republic of Vietnam, Prime Minister's Office Communiqué No. 69/UBHP/ CT, Oct. 10, 1965.

civil servants graduated from NIA will increase considerably. Owing to their exposure to new subjects of study such as public finance, budgeting, accounting, organization and methods, and human relations, and particularly to their being familiarized with the practical aspect of public administration during their internship at central and local government agencies, NIA graduates are in high demand after graduation. It is confirmed opinion within government circles that in most cases an NIA graduate will learn his job more quickly than a new recruit from a faculty of law. This is undoubtedly because of the practical training that all NIA students must undertake.

According to an estimate made by the Social Services Bureau of NIA, up to 1964 about 53 per cent of the graduates served in the provinces as chiefs of provincial technical services, district chiefs (at present district chiefs are militarized and new NIA graduates serve as deputy district chiefs), and deputy province chiefs. At the central level, positions commonly held by NIA graduates are administrative bureau chief and service chief in the Ministry of Interior and in other (and technical) ministries.[40] As a result of personal connections, small numbers of NIA graduates are on detached service in various diplomatic missions abroad. Several have risen to the rank of director, secretary-general, and director of cabinet in the present government. An increasing number of NIA graduates are recruited by the Directorate General of Budget and Foreign Aid to work in its newly created corps of "budget examiners," whose function is to receive, examine, and modify the expenditure proposals submitted by various governmental agencies. Their role is undoubtedly important in following up on the execution of programs and in day-to-day control of the utilization of allotted credits.

In newly independent countries like Vietnam where there is a tendency for nationalist politicians to identify old-line bureau-

40. It is appropriate to recall that a ministry of the government in Vietnam is divided into directorates general, which are divided into directorates, which are further divided into services, and each service is composed of bureaus. For administrative purposes the country is divided into provinces which now number forty-three. Each province is divided into districts, each district is divided into villages and each village into hamlets.

crats with the ancient regime, the opportunities for NIA graduates to assume important responsibilities in the administrative complex are immense (Khanna, Inayatullah). With the military assuming political control of the government, the practice of appointing military officers to administrative roles now extends even beyond province and district chiefs, who were already largely military from the time of President Diem. The typical assignments now for NIA graduates in the current pacification and rural reconstruction programs of the government are thus typically restricted to deputy district chief for administration and deputy province chief for administration.

Conclusion

Some have agreed that an increase in bureaucracy tends to inhibit rather than encourage development.[41] In such a case, the main function of NIA—training more and more civil servants for the government—might be considered as having a negative effect on development. However, with a huge program of rural pacification and reconstruction and with the anticipated emergence of political institutions in the near future—i.e., with more differentiation in the political system—the number of well-trained government employees for the creation, maintenance, and improvement of regulative facilities and services needs to be greatly expanded. Looking at NIA from this angle, it can readily be seen that the organization is needed for development administration[42] and that it is performing a useful function for society (Khanna). It is necessary, however, to determine whether NIA is adequately staffed and supported in discharging its function and to suggest

41. Fred W. Riggs, "Modernization and Development Administration," *CAG Occasional Papers* (Bloomington, Ind.: Indiana University, 1966), p. A–25.
42. Here "development administration" refers to the administration of development programs: agricultural administration, educational administration, public health administration, community development administration, and the activation of economic development plans as well as the administration of rural pacification and reconstruction programs. See "Development Administration," report by a special committee under the chairmanship of Fred W. Riggs, *CAG Occasional Papers* (Bloomington: Indiana University, 1964), pp. 6–7.

the kind of technical assistance that is required to improve the level of its performance.[43]

The first problem to look at is that of staffing. With the introduction of two new training programs in August, 1965 (the advanced studies program and the chief clerk training program), the current faculty has to carry additional training loads and prepare material for new courses. Since the revolution in November, 1963, there have been several regular NIA faculty members detached from NIA to assume full-time positions in the government. The result is a reduction of the teaching staff. If the subject taught by the temporary on-leave member is highly specialized, a good replacement cannot be easily found at short notice, and the resulting consequence is a lowering of the course standard. The faculty must therefore be increased in size to cope with the increasing load. It must also be diversified in order to have enough instructors in each field. Currently, of twenty-two regular staff members, sixteen are in the field of law and political science; the remainder are in economics and finance. In the past there have been occasional shortages of instructors in these fields.

The present form of technical assistance for training future NIA faculty members does not seem to insure good results. Mainly because of the failure of a large number of Vietnamese participants sent to the United States for training to return to Vietnam upon completion of their studies, but in addition because of a desire to relate this training to Vietnamese conditions, it is now required that a Ph.D. participant must undergo two stages of training in American universities. In the first stage, the participant will stay two years or a little more to finish his Ph.D. comprehensive examination. Then he will return to Vietnam to teach at the NIA for one or two years, doing research or collecting data for his dissertation. Later, he will be sent back to his university for completion of the degree. The new scheme was

43. See Fernand Vrancken, *Technical Assistance in Public Administration: Lessons of Experience and Possible Improvements* (Brussels: International Institute of Administrative Sciences, 1965), pp. 143–144, for suggestions about possible improvements with regard to public administration institutes; François Gazier and Lucile Decoufle, "Les Ecoles et Instituts de Formation de Fonctionnaires dans les Pays en Voie de Development," *Tiers-Monde* (Paris: Presses Universitaires de France, 1963), pp. 59–83.

applied in 1965 by the Public Administration Division of the Agency for International Development mission in Saigon, and serious doubts have been expressed by NIA staff members as to its workability. Considering the relatively low salaries of NIA faculty members and the number of Ph.D. candidates unable to complete their degrees, the present Ph.D. training scheme for NIA is not realistic. Of course "high motivation" is a prerequisite for such training (Lee, Weidner), but more incentives and facilities should be given to a prospective NIA faculty member to attract him to the job. If the present training scheme continues, it is likely that the NIA will have, in the next three or four years, more unfinished Ph.D.'s; this will not strengthen a still weak and somewhat undertrained faculty. It would be feasible to set up a graduate school in public administration in a Southeast Asian country or in an EROPA member country with a faculty partially composed of visiting professors from the best schools in the United States or in Europe; the scheme would to some extent discourage participants from developing countries to remain abroad and would insure a level of training at an acceptable international standard.

The second problem which needs attention and assistance is research. Here there is a division of opinion. According to some NIA members, it would be idle to discuss field research problems when one cannot move safely and freely to the countryside to carry out field work. The prevailing opinion is that it is imperative for instructors of public administration at NIA to be informed of what is being done in the countryside and that it is useful to persuade governmental agencies to introduce a research component in a few important programs such as rural reconstruction at the provincial and village levels. Since teaching at NIA tends to emphasize the practical and factual aspects of public administration, research must be given special priority. As usual there is a need for financial support; budgeting procedures are such that it is not easy to get adequate funds at the right time. Research is not of equal importance to different people. There is particularly a difference of opinion between those engaged in academic work and those who hold the purse strings. NIA re-

search could be greatly facilitated if there were full-time advisers
stationed at the institute and directly involved in research in
co-operation with NIA members.

Directly associated with the research problem is that of the
library. The importance of a good library for an educational
institution and for the cultural life of a community in general
cannot be overemphasized. Since the departure of MSUG, there
has been a deterioration of the library and of the services it offers
owing to its being understaffed. In principle, the NIA library
should be an official depository of government documents which
are the chief source of current administrative data. Regulations
about the use of NIA's books and documents should be strictly
applied. Instances of books checked out and never returned to
the library are legion, and research work, especially in public
administration, is discouragingly hindered by missing official documents. If technical assistance is available, high priority should
be given to refurbishing the library and setting up a reference
service. The NIA library may be an example of external aid
designed to facilitate institution-building contributing to a society's development only if the society is capable of sustaining it.
Otherwise the impact of external aid becomes nil.[44]

The last but not the least important form of technical assistance NIA needs is a team of at least two consultants permanently
attached to it—one specializing in political science and related
fields and the other specializing in economics and finance, both
with sufficient experience in development work.[45] These two consultants would serve as a sounding board to those NIA staff
members directly assuming responsibilities in the government or
called upon by the government to advise on current administrative and economic problems. In addition, from an educational
point of view, the consultants would be an indispensable link
between NIA and the outside academic world—through numerous contacts with their place of origin and their professional field.
Especially to those NIA staff members who did not have their

44. Riggs, "Modernization and Development Administration," p. 23.
45. For the time being the NIA has an adviser in public administration, Dr.
Henry C. Bush, who shares his time between the NIA and the Public Administration Division of the AID mission in Vietnam.

training abroad the services of these consultants would be extremely useful. They would bring information about the theoretical development of certain subjects and data germane to such subjects. Ultimately they should be catalysts for change and for improvement (Weidner).

It is widely recognized that in transitional societies the developmental push must come largely from the government (Khanna) and that a two-element administrative base[46] is necessary for developmental action. The first element of such an administrative base is that "the administrative personnel must be sympathetic to and positively concerned with national development in addition to having administrative professional and technical capability." The second element is that "administrative organization, procedures and processes must be adapted to furthering development ends." These two elements are of course intimately interacting and somewhat complementary. In Vietnam the lack of security in some regions and the war conditions prevailing in many others are constantly obstructing the implementation of governmental programs in the rural areas. But in the kind of war now being fought in Vietnam—the objective of which is to win the support of the mass—socio-economic development programs must be prosecuted vigorously again and again. Therefore the need for an administrative base conducive to developmental action is obvious. NIA with its present staff, facilities, and experience could be more systematically used to provide the first element of such an administrative base.

In putting more accent on the teaching of countersubversion methods and techniques in its recently revised curricula, NIA is functioning very much as an instrument for development administration in the present Vietnamese situation. Of more importance in the long run is NIA's role as a center for professional standardization in public administration (Abueva). In effect, by stress on competitive entrance examination and preservice and in-service training, it is possible for NIA to limit the circle of eligibility and therefore to satisfy to a large extent the formal requirements of administrative professionalism (even apparent in a prismatic so-

46. Weidner, *Technical Assistance*, p. 207.

ciety).[47] As was pointed out earlier, NIA graduates are now much in demand by governmental agencies. This high level of demand for NIA graduates is beginning to confer upon them a kind of prestige which, if supported by merit and professional ability and widely recognized, would become a force in the professionalization of public administrators and ultimately a force for innovation (Lee and Weidner).

The type of technical assistance just suggested may be more appropriately called a form of technical co-operation in public administration (Hsueh). In addition to helping to improve the level of performance of NIA in its various teaching, training, and consulting functions, such technical co-operation will contribute to the building of an innovational force (Lee, Weidner, Khanna, Hsueh) and to the furthering of both development administration and development politics in Vietnam.

47. Fred W. Riggs, *Administration in Developing Countries* (Boston: Houghton Mifflin, 1964), p. 299.

Chapter 13

Development and Innovational Roles

Edward W. Weidner

Development means change. Whether endogenous or exogenous, whether carried out with or without technical assistance, development and change are inseparable. There are many environmental factors affecting or inducing change. Floods, famine, disease, and similar disasters bring both social and technological change. Population pressure may beget change. Changes in the biophysical environment are reflected in subsequent changes in the social environment. To a marked degree, change is a chain of interconnected conditions and events, one change bringing yet another.

The problem for development administration, however, is far more specific. Development means *directional* change. It carries with it the assumption that human beings can influence the course of events. They react to events and their environment, but they also initiate rather complicated and sustained changes in that environment. The process of planned or intended change in the direction of modernity or nation-building and socio-economic change is the process of innovation for development.[1] Development administration is concerned with maximizing innovation for development.

Planning developmental change and planning alterations in man's environment to produce such change are the normal means available to governments which wish to maximize attainment of

1. This definition of innovation departs from that of H. G. Barnett, *Innovation: The Basis of Cultural Change* (New York: McGraw-Hill, 1953). Barnett defines innovation as individual response in a divergent manner to universal change (p. 19).

development ends. Put another way, the essence of trying to accelerate national development lies in encouraging appropriate innovation and the conditions under which innovation can best take place. Governments or agencies with development responsibilities must be innovating governments or agencies if they are to be successful. After goals are agreed upon, and priorities determined, major innovation is likely to be required if major development is sought. Thus a primary task of development-oriented governments is to promote and carry out innovation.

A consideration of planned change and innovation for development requires emphasis on the group process of planning and the individual and group process of innovation. The two processes are linked through the innovational roles individuals play in organizations. We turn, then, to a discussion of possible innovational roles in a bureaucracy, with particular reference to innovation in the direction of developmental change.[2]

Innovational Roles

Innovation is not all of one piece. There are several roles that are more or less separable in any kind of innovation, even the simplest. The introduction of a new game to a group of teenagers requires an original idea for the new game, working it out, selling the group on the merit of the new game, organizing to play it, and its adoption by the group. In complicated social and physical technology such as is involved in development, these roles are more distinct, perhaps more numerous, less chronologically determined, highly interactive, infinitely more difficult of execution, and may be specialized according to the individual or agency performing each of them.

The role of *inventor* is performed when the innovation is something fundamentally new. By definition, invention is essentially an endogenous process. It is the invention of a new idea which, if

2. The concept of innovation used herein is consistent with that of Richard T. LaPiere, *Social Change* (New York: McGraw-Hill, 1965), p. 107. See also Everett E. Hagen, *On the Theory of Social Change* (Homewood, Ill.: Dorsey Press, 1962).

adopted, would break new ground for a particular organization and perhaps for the society concerned and for all societies. The inventor is the "man with an idea," a person who thinks along different lines, an individual who dares to explore strange paths. He may remain aloof from the society of which he is a part, or he may be an integral part of it, with heavy administrative and policy responsibilities. He may develop his ideas alone, or they may stem from a large and concentrated group research effort. The form and circumstances of the environment may be highly influential but are not crucial; the essential ingredient is creative thinking. To the extent that there is freedom for, and even encouragement of, such thinking, invention of social and physical technology as well as ideas for role or functional changes can no doubt be accelerated.

The truly original thought is indeed a rare prize. Rapid development in the world depends heavily upon borrowing ideas from others. However, there are elements of creativity in all such borrowing, since seldom if ever can any portion of social or physical technology be transferred without heavy adaptation. The *borrower* role is one that an individual or agency performs when some aspect of physical or social technology from one culture is proposed for application in another or some role or function is proposed for transfer. In Asia, the spread of new budget systems and institutes of public administration heavily exemplifies this process (Hsueh and Xuan).

In the last twenty years, the difference between invention and borrowing has become quite narrow in development administration in Asia. As a common body of knowledge has come to be shared by scholars and administrators in all the countries of the region, ideas for innovations in development administration have become more a matter of suggesting adaptations of practice elsewhere than the creation of strikingly new patterns of social integration and co-ordination. To view it another way, the inventors of one society increasingly perform a service for all. Subsequent adaptation to each country's needs is the role of the borrowers.

The essence of the roles of the inventor and the borrower is a spark of originality, an idea for a novel solution to a particular problem of development administration. Inventors and borrowers are not necessarily honored in their own societies. They may be looked upon as strange and different, apart from the main stream.

Closely associated with the inventors and borrowers and sometimes indistinguishable from them are the *culture transmitters.* Every teacher is a culture transmitter, and in the less developed countries as elsewhere the teacher transmits ideas regardless of the culture from which they originate. Education in all its forms is the transmission of all existing knowledge and the development of new knowledge. The idea-origination of schools and colleges is thus great.

Other culture transmitters are not conscious of their roles. The transmission of items may be almost incidental to their main concern. For example, the transmission of culture items may come about quite accidentally as the result of a business trip abroad or business activities and connections with foreign firms. All cross-cultural travel or other international intercourse is culture transferring to some degree.

An idea may die almost as soon as it is put forth. Most suggestions for change never receive substantial support. What makes some ideas different from others is that advocates for their adoption arise. The *advocate-leader* places his prestige and influence behind a proposal. Support may be necessary both within and outside the government before an idea becomes an integral part of development administration. The smaller and more technical the proposal, the more likely it is that the change can be made from within the bureaucracy itself. Any major change is likely to require approval from at least the top executives or task elite, and perhaps also from a legislative body or power elite. The latter might reflect substantial general public support or at least lack of public opposition. The role of the advocate-leader is to develop the support base for an innovation and to lend or obtain an adequate degree of legitimacy in regard to it.

An innovation must be put into such a form that it can be acted upon and implemented. Frequently, proposals for innovation are not completely thought through. The element of originality is not necessarily associated with detailing of a concrete proposal.

Original thinking does not carry with it any certain responsibility for spelling the ideas out or operationalizing them. Therefore, a specialized *detailer* may prepare statements, documents, and plans relating to a proposal. Such a function will be commonly performed separately from those of invention, borrowing, and culture transmission. The detailer may be called upon at several junctures: to spell out a proposal for formal consideration by advocate-leaders, to present material to a legislative body, to organize an agency to carry out a new program, and to prepare materials for consideration by potential adopters. While the function of the detailer is not nearly as original as that of the inventors and borrowers, it is nevertheless essential. Someone who can develop an idea and give it policy, procedural, and organizational expression is required as well as someone with creative insight. Of course, on occasion these two functions can be performed by the same individual or group.

Innovations requiring major changes in a substantial portion of the society require heavy inputs by government to induce change. If there is a problem of rural poverty in a country, one of the possible solutions may be to retrain a segment of the rural populace and give it incentives for migrating to certain urban centers where new jobs await it. To carry out such a program, a government might hire and train a number of *change agents.* The recruitment and training of thousands of village workers in India and Pakistan is a similar case. Thousands of new positions at the level of village worker were created and each government tried to make sure that those it recruited were both sympathetic to the task to be undertaken and otherwise suited to the role of village change agent.

A somewhat different situation arises where an established bureaucracy is present and is asked to perform the role of change agent. In such an instance, the employees concerned must be indoctrinated with the new approach or innovation. Where the principle of hierarchy is established and the employees concerned do not have much traditional freedom in carrying out their work, and where, furthermore, there is relatively little retraining and goal-shifting necessary, such a process may be easily carried out. But these conditions do not commonly obtain in a less developed country. There are strong forces resistant to change and favorable to continuance of traditional patterns. In such cases a two-step process is required. The change agents must first be adopters of a proposed innovation before they can extend still other innovations to the citizenry. If employees are specially hired to fill a change agent role, the step of adoption is avoided—or, more properly, is subsumed in the recruiting and employment process. The latter route may lead to much faster extension of innovation through change agents than the former. Existing occupants of established positions may find it painful and disadvantageous to perform different roles or existing roles in a new manner, especially if the goals or objectives are changed substantially.

An instructive example may be found in education at the elementary schoolteachers in a district or region. They may be asked to change their method of teaching and the content of what is being taught in order to make the education of the children more vocationally useful. The responsible government agency, the ministry of education, must first try to convince the teachers of the appropriateness of the proposed change and then develop special training facilities. Visits from supervisors are arranged, and explanatory leaflets distributed. Regional teacher-training institutes carrying out extension activities help to convince the teachers of the desirability of the new program. Hopefully the teachers become not only enthusiastic adopters of the new plan but competent in its execution. Not all will do so. The ministry formally implements the field aspects of the new curriculum and teaching methods, and the teachers perform their severely modified role of intermediaries to their pupils. They are both adopters and change agents, as well as intermediaries between the advocate-leaders (or detailers) of the ministry and the intended end targets, the pupils.

An adjacent district may not have any elementary schoolteachers. Because of the poverty of the area, schools were not previously established. A decision is taken to extend schools to the district, and an opportunity thus exists to create a curriculum from the very beginning and introduce such teaching methods as seem desirable. Potential candidates for teachers are screened and selected on the basis of aptitude and interest in the new system. The process of introducing the new curriculum and teaching methods is greatly simplified in such a situation. And the teachers perform only one of the roles of those in the neighboring district, that of change agents.

Upon reflection, the ministry of education or a community development ministry may not be satisfied with the total contribution of the teachers in the several districts to innovation. Wishing to see a more active role undertaken, they decide to work with an experimental group of teachers. The teachers are asked to develop skills in the organization of teenagers and adults to perform a variety of useful projects—chicken production experiments working with the teenagers, homemaking discussion groups among the women, and village organization and participation projects with the men. Again in these activities, the teachers are change agents.

Finally, no innovation can be complete without acceptance by the *target group*. The group is made up of the persons who are the objects of the change. If a new industry is to be established, the target group is composed of new managements and their workers. In community development, it is the villagers themselves. With institutes of public administration, it is the future public employees who are being educated or trained at the institute.

In a real sense, there is no such role as that of final or ultimate target. Particularly in the highly interdependent societies that are increasingly characteristic of Asia, every adopter is potentially an intermediary. Some of his associates, someone in a neighboring village, will observe his innovative behavior and be stimulated by the demonstration effect. The "target" becomes a "change agent" as well. Adopters can be grouped along a sliding scale from those who are clearly intermediaries by design to those who are intermediaries only by the normal working out of social intercourse. The latter can be considered as close to end targets as it is possible to come.

Intersector effects between target groups and others make the designation of the end target uncertain. An institute of public administration has as its immediate target the public employees. Ultimately, the target may be groups of citizens at the village level who will be affected by better development administration. In establishing a new industry, the government has as its immediate target the management and workers. Yet all of society that is affected by the business is also a target.

The seven major roles in innovation are overlapping. A particular person or agency may play only one role, or it may play several. Inventors and borrowers are sometimes advocate-leaders, and change agents may be detailer-organizers. Within any ministry or large agency all roles will be found.

Ideas behind innovations are not easily traced to their origins. The inventor and borrower make an original contribution, but not as a function unique to a few people, removed from society. Any major innovative idea is the product of many minds. The prime father of an idea may be unable to recognize his child by the time a new governmental program is launched. This may be so even though the proposal has in no way been watered down in the course of being considered, detailed, and structuralized. Aspects of creativity attach to numerous aspects of a social innovation, and the complete idea is seldom formulated in a single mind or a small government agency or private group.

The sequence in which roles are played also varies widely. Thus the role of the inventor may be followed by those of borrower, detailer-organizer, advocate-leader, borrower, detailer-organizer, culture transmitter, change agent, ultimate change agent, borrower, inventor, and finally the target group. An inventor may develop a brand new idea for community development. However, elements of the experience of other countries are subsequently woven into the idea (borrower). A staff is then assembled to work out the proposals in some detail for presentation to responsible political leaders (detailer-organizers). The task elite indorse the proposal and ultimately are able to convince the power elite of the wisdom of the idea (advocate-leaders). In the process of political discussion of the proposal, the experience of some of the influential members of the power elite leads to modification (borrowers). After political approval, the ministry of community development is given the responsibility of drawing up a detailed plan of operations and putting it into effect as soon as possible (detailer-organizers). Teachers, businessmen, and party workers are briefed on the new plan in order to solicit their support, ideas, and supplementary contributions (culture transmitters). Middle management of the agency is given extensive retraining so that it can help carry out the plan more effectively (change agents). It, in turn, begins to recruit village workers and give them appropriate training (ultimate change agents). In the course of their work in the villages, some village workers find that their previous experience and local conditions require a change in the plan (borrowers and inventors). As a whole, the workers have substantial success in introducing many changes in the practices of villagers (target group).

Innovation is a continuing process, not a discrete event. In the launching of a new community development program, there will undoubtedly be a series of innovations at different levels or steps, and a rather complete set of inventors, borrowers, culture transmitters, advocate-leaders, detailer-organizers, change agents, and target groups will be encountered each time. Initially, the roles of inventor, borrower, advocate-leader, detailer-organizer, and initial target group may all be found in the central offices of the minister and the permanent secretary. Later, there may be another similar grouping of roles as the technicians consider the proposal. A third grouping of roles may occur with the provincial and district representatives, and still another at the community level. If the concept of the innovational process is extended to include significant portions of the private sector, as indeed it should be, additional steps could be identified, during which the roles of inventor, borrower, advocate-leader, detailer-organizer, and target group would be found.

Nor does an innovation go through such a process only once. Constant reviewing, inspection, and checking are required, with appropriate reappraisal and modification. It is as stones dropping in a pond, the ripples intermixing. All roles of innovation may well be played simultaneously.

Sectoral Roles in Innovation

In the continuing process of innovation for development, government plays a major role in all Asian countries. By the very nature of the resources required for rational nation-building and socio-economic progress, government is required as a priority-setting and resource-marshaling mechanism as well as a mechanism for administering large portions of the resulting programs. It is thus important to consider the innovational potential of government and the extent to which innovational roles have been effective. However, it is not possible to ignore the innovational potential of the private sector. Most Asian countries have had important assistance from the private sector in their development efforts. Private innovational roles must likewise be assessed. And the roles of foreigners are occasionally key to Asian development efforts.

Within the public sector, certain innovational roles have been fulfilled less effectively than others. One of these has been at the leadership level of both the task and the power elites. The role of advocate-leader has not been a strong one. There is a dearth of strong advocate-leaders in Asia both at the government-wide level and at the ministry level. Task elites are not highly developmentalist and power elites are even less so (Lee). Almost all ministers and presidents or prime ministers are formally developmentalist, but many are not comfortable with innovation and are very reluctant to experiment within their respective spheres of authority. They are tied to power structures benefiting from the status quo or very mild departures therefrom. The strong national advocate-leader of innovation is the exception rather than the rule. This helps to account for the generally unbalanced nature of the development process in most Asian countries.

The charismatic leader is even more an exceptional case. Development goal achievement prospers when a charismatic leader sympathetic to modernity is identified, but an administrative system cannot be built upon that remote possibility.[3] Charisma may be usefully associated with pilot projects, providing that the usual bureaucratic controls are not present. In many Asian countries there are at least a few subnational charismatic leaders, often associated with a ministry or, more likely, with a particular region. However, regional leaders may pose a threat to the regime in power nationally. Hence, freedom to experiment extensively is normally lacking.

Another level in the public sector at which innovational roles have been weak is that of middle management, including provincial or district administration (Friedman, Inayatullah). In community development work, for example, it has been easier to secure national innovation-minded leaders and village-level workers devoted to bringing about change than it has been to provide a continuing chain of persons performing innovating roles between these two points.[4] This especially would indicate a breakdown in the roles of intermediary adopters and middle-level change agents.

The lack of a continuous chain of people performing innovating roles from the top national level to the village also suggests a serious lack of innovation-minded detailer-organizers. Traditional ways of performing these tasks are difficult to break. The role of detailer-organizers is less glamorous than most other innovational roles, and hence less likely to attract able people.

The military has been a very significant factor in innovation in Asian countries. Its innovational role has been enhanced in a dramatic and sweeping way when it takes over the government —as in Pakistan, Korea, and Indonesia. The modernizing military leadership then emphasizes invention, borrowing, and advocate-leadership on a national scale. In most other countries the military has stayed more in the background, but it has acted both as a stimulator and a diffuser of cultural change. It has been espe-

3. See the excellent study on Indian and Pakistani community development programs by Henry Hart, "The Village and Development Administration," *CAG Occasional Papers* (Bloomington, Ind.: Indiana University, 1967).
    4. *Ibid.*

cially active as an intermediary adopter and as a middle-level change agent. The nationwide and cross-section recruiting base of most Asian armies and the social and technological as well as narrowly military training in which they engage have strengthened these latter roles.

The private sector encompasses a number of elements of a society, of which the two most important for innovation are the business and intellectual communities. Despite the heavy involvement of government in nation-building and socio-economic progress, private business also has been quite active in innovational roles in most Asian countries. The Philippines and Japan are prime examples. Since the more imaginative portion of a business community tends to be among the principal gainers from economic development, businessmen have been prominent in suggesting new government policies and have been strong advocates of them. Through their trips abroad and their contacts outside the country, businessmen are important culture transmitters. Through their desire to use new methods they have been strong borrowers and occasional inventors, often having been able to move ahead even though the rest of the society has faltered. However, lack of capital, desire for too high a rate of return, and unwillingness to take a long-term view have hampered some of them in this respect. Traditional elements of business are to be found in most Asian countries, and innovational contributions have not come from them. They have been potential targets of government programs, since they have not played an aggressive role. In fact, the main beneficiaries of enlightened government policies have been the more modern elements of business, not the traditional ones.

Intellectuals may be classified as part of the private sector even though they may be employed by a public university. They have particularly performed the role of inventors (Lee); Korea is a prominent case in point. With their typically future time orientation, some of them have dreamed on a broad scale, thereby suggesting some broad new methods and goals for their country. Not all intellectuals are philosophers. The organization of universities is adapted to specialization of faculty members. Thus the innovative ideas from the intellectual community within institutions of higher education have been related to many aspects of nation-building and socio-economic progress: the economic system, the political system, education, works of engineering, medical and health services, and others. Of course, universities are normally culture transmitters. In addition, faculty members are likely to be borrowers, and possibly also detailer-organizers in support of certain government programs.

While university organization and faculty status vary widely from one Asian country to another, the innovative roles of faculty members have been quite different from those in the United States. In their roles as culture transmitters, faculty members have been less innovational, especially in certain traditional faculties such as law. Faculties in newer areas of study have been very innovational. In some countries, although not all, professors are not often used as consultants and hence are not frequently detailer-organizers of proposals. Universities are generally not considered to be change agents, and their extension activities are limited. So, too, have their research facilities been limited, restricting invention. Unlike the situation in Korea, faculty members have sometimes been kept away from government policy by the task or power elite which does not come from the same background.

Foreigners and foreign institutions have had significant innovational roles in many aspects of postcolonial Asia (Hsueh, Xuan). The formal programs of bilateral and multilateral assistance have been the largest sources of help in this regard. One measure of the extent of this process is the billions of dollars that have been put into foreign aid and the thousands of employees who have participated. Foreign aid is essentially an exogenous process, with ideas from one country being injected, with varying degrees of adaptation, into another. However, the roles of host country nationals and their institutions are always of major importance even in the most obvious cases of importation.

Foreign experts are usually invited only after a decision has been made to consider innovation in a given direction. An exploratory team may be sent to the country. In such a case, the initial role of borrower has already been played, and the experts who arrive later are more in the role of proposing supplementary borrowing and functioning as detailer-organizers or change agents. They commonly are invited to a country to reinforce a decision already taken or to give it more prestige and acceptance. Of course, they may sometimes find themselves a part of a largely formal modernistic veneer. An apparent decision to innovate may not be that at all, but may be a means of obtaining foreign aid.

The process of emulation goes far beyond the confines of formal programs of technical co-operation. The great majority of Asian students in the United States do not come under the auspices of a foreign aid program, and the great majority of foreigners in an Asian country do not have a connection with such an undertaking. Modern communications media strengthen person-to-person contact, and much diffusion of ideas is furthered by radio, television, movies, and the printed word. Inventors and borrowers from a foreign land may set forth some of their ideas through such media. Advocate-leaders of one country may have a direct effect on innovation in neighboring countries since communications media do not respect national boundaries. Thus innovation is not entirely under the control or determination of the persons residing within a country's boundaries. If other countries near or far are rapidly changing, and if ideas and information can be communicated across boundaries as they surely can, then a country cannot think of its innovational process and the several innovational roles as entirely local or subject to local control.

Strengthening Innovational Roles for Development

If a government or any part thereof wishes to adopt a conscious policy of maximizing development, it must necessarily be concerned with the strengthening of innovational roles for development. This is not a matter of indorsing all kinds of activity in regard to innovation, but rather of selecting those that will lead in a particular direction—namely, toward those aspects of nation-building and socio-economic progress that the government wishes to stress. In developing such a strategy, it must be kept in mind that the majority of tasks in a bureaucracy are not innovational in nature. Perhaps it is also true that the majority of tasks of any one member of the bureaucracy are non-innovational in character. Administrative process or routine, specialized or technical expertise, and political and administrative liaison require a great proportion of the energies of the bureaucracy. They are the bread and butter of administration. Innovational roles, while a small part of the whole, give the entire exercise meaning and validity.

Innovational roles may account at most for 10 or 20 per cent of the energy of the bureaucracy. Whatever the proportion, effective performance cannot be obtained simply by designating 10 per cent of the administrators as those who will perform innovational roles full-time. In a rapidly changing society, innovation permeates the entire administrative structure. The innovational abilities of a clerk granting a license are as essential, though in a way quite different, from those of a proposer of a new banking system. Viewed system-wide, innovation for development requires a kind of morale or orientation or *esprit de corps*. Each employee must play his appropriate part if innovation is to be maximized.

Similarly, citizens making up the target groups must be a part of the development process. Where broad goals of nation-building and socio-economic progress are embraced, few persons in a society are aloof from innovation. A citizenry must be receptive to change over a long period of time for most major changes to be consummated. How to bring about such a change lies outside the scope of this discussion, as does the broad problem of how to motivate the entire public bureaucracy to accept and play a role in major change. Instead, the focus is on a few courses of action available to public authorities that might serve to strengthen the role performance of inventors, borrowers, culture transmitters, advocate-leaders, detailer-organizers, and change agents in the public sector.

First, the roles of inventor, borrower, and culture transmitter can be strengthened by a number of means. There is quite a distance to go. Asian countries have relied heavily upon foreign assistance for sources of invention and borrowing. The performance of such roles within most of the host country bureaucracy has been more or less accidental.

Some Asian countries have used deliberate creation of idea-generating enclaves within—indeed throughout—an administrative structure. These idea-generating groups lie outside the operational arm of an agency. They may even lie outside the agency itself. Thus Korea has used parts of universities as idea-generating enclaves, and the Indian community development effort had an intellectual or elite enclave attached to it. Acceptance of many of the ideas put forth by an enclave must follow or otherwise it is useless. To succeed, substantial support must be given at a high level.

Pilot projects could be used far more extensively. The experience of Pakistan with the Comilla Academy for Rural Development is illustrative.[5] An innovative and development-minded leader was placed in charge of a pilot project which has served to better the conditions for the peasants in the area around Comilla, although that is not its central import. The significant aspect of the Comilla project is its demonstration effect. An innovational leader was selected, a rather independent pilot project was launched, and a system of evaluation was set up. Just as at Comilla, far more new approaches to rural development could be tried on a small scale, and they could be evaluated carefully for success. If the experiments pointed to the desirability of modifications of standard government policy and programs, the project might eventually have broad national significance.

There have been numerous other pilot projects in Pakistan and other Asian countries, but many, perhaps most, have not had the threefold characteristics of the Comilla Academy. Projects of this kind frequently lack effective innovative and development-minded leadership; this has been true of a number of institutes of public administration. Projects are often placed within the existing bureaucratic structure and not given enough effective independence to support substantial experimentation; this has often

5. *Ibid.*

been true of teacher-training projects. And evaluation has normally not been seriously and systematically tackled.

Aside from the failure to authorize an adequate set of conditions for pilot projects, the countries of Asia have hesitated to move strongly in this direction because of great pressures for nationwide programs as are found in India. Even where pilot projects exist, such pressures have forced governments prematurely to generalize nationally. Democratic forces must be reckoned with; the pressures for action from one region cannot be blithely put aside because the government sponsors pilot projects that happen to be in neighboring areas. However, any government can spread pilot projects over a wide area by sponsoring enough of them in different subject matter fields that they create a kind of balance in the various regions or districts. The pilot project idea can be applied equally well to community development, education, health, agriculture, and public administration. Two or more projects per subject matter field are not only possible but actually desirable, resources permitting, in order to test different approaches and different environmental influences. Even so, a pilot project approach raises the question of when and under what conditions the pilot experience may be extended to other areas—a difficult problem at best.

Innovational enclaves and pilot projects are not the only means of encouraging inventors and borrowers. A standard method in the United States has been to place an entire agency outside the regular control of administrative process, routine, and supervision. The emergency agencies of the New Deal era gave flexibility to the development of new public policies, and a similar path was followed in World War II. Classical administrative principles are contrary to such a practice, never being concerned with maximizing innovation for development purposes. Unfortunately, much technical assistance in public administration has tended to stress the classical principles, instead of seeking ways in which development can be encouraged, such as quasi-independent agencies.

An important variation of both the quasi-independent agency and the pilot project is the regional development authority. It is sometimes more possible to give a regional authority substantial independence and special powers to experiment than it is a government agency located at the center and administering a nationwide program. A regional authority is not unlike a greatly enlarged Comilla project. In the United States, the Tennessee Valley Authority broke new ground in a number of respects, particularly that of electric power production and distribution and its relation to regional development. It formed the locus for numerous inventors.

One of the simplest devices for encouraging experimentation for development is a conscious policy of extensive decentralization and regional and local autonomy. While the device is simple, its execution is not. Across-the-board decentralization may invite anarchy and strengthen political factions in some newly independent countries. In any event, a policy that affects all agencies at the center and regionally is difficult to launch. Nevertheless, Pakistan has carried out a measure of this through its Basic Democracies program (Inayatullah).

Landau has pointed out that one of the important attributes of an administrative system in a relatively more developed country is its greater reliance on a factual basis for decision-making. This suggests that another way of assisting development entrepreneurs is to provide generous resources for gathering the factual data needed for decisions in the appropriate areas of nation-building and socio-economic progress. Fact-collecting and analyzing enclaves can give the inventor and borrower the basis he needs for making more effective development decisions. Of course, the production of such information (e.g., additional budget analyses) will be perceived as a threat to those committed to old ways.

Finally, invention and borrowing roles can be strengthened from the outside through effective use of consultants and visitors. Whether these consultants are from within the country or foreigners, they may add new ideas to the proposals being discussed. They provide a valuable viewpoint from the outside of the innovative administrator. International intercourse can be an effective spur to invention, borrowing, and culture transmission. Traveling, seminars, conferences, publications, and correspondence could be profitably expanded.

Second, the strengthening of the role of advocate-leader in innovation requires far more than strengthening it in regard to national task and power elites. This role exists from the very highest posts in the nation to posts at the most local level. It is also present on both the administrative and political sides of government. The role of advocate-leader in innovation is one of leadership in regard to a proposed innovation among a large or a small group of people. A district or branch chief may be as occupied with such a task, at least in his own way, as a department secretary or minister. Developing a support base for the undertaking, legitimizing it, and popularizing it among those who must carry it out and adopt it are the most important functions of the role.

The transition from idea-generator to advocate is a major one. The inventor or borrower frequently becomes attached to a new proposal because of the values it contains in and of itself, although there is a wide range of variation in motivation. An even wider range of motivation exists at the level of advocate-leader, with emphasis on non-programmatic factors. Advocate-leaders may not believe in the particular aspect of nation-building or socio-economic progress that a proposal seeks to achieve. They may be more attracted to values that are supplementary or complementary to modernity. For example, they may embrace development because it makes them popular or because it adds to their own power and authority at a particular time or place.

Whatever their motivation, their responsibility as advocate-leaders is to enlist the co-operation of others for achieving development goals. In doing so, they must use a variety of appeals. There are two basic problems facing the advocate-leader. One is his own longevity in office or in his job if he pushes development values too vigorously. Protection from the power or task elite if he is a ranking officer of the government, or otherwise from his superiors (presumably also advocate-leaders at their respective levels) is required.

Assured of at least a reasonable chance to maintain his position, the advocate-leader must develop convincing methods to get others to co-operate in the adventure of innovation. To do so most effectively, he will have to appeal to a wide variety of values, including but not limited to those of development, such as non-development programmatic values and, most important of all, group and individual expediency values that are not inconsistent with development ends. In doing so he will be assisted by the fact that his own motives cover a wide range.

The most effective way of strengthening the role of advocate-leader in a less developed country is to create many more opportunities for individuals to perform such a function. In a highly centralized, hierarchical government there is a minimum of advocate-leader roles. In a government with some degree of decentralization both functionally and regionally, advocate-leader roles abound. It may be difficult for a society to obtain outstanding advocate-leaders at the very top, but every society has many persons who can fill such roles at lower levels, as long as the role is there to perform.

In addition to decentralization, the role of advocate-leader can be strengthened in many of the same ways that the roles of inventors and borrowers can be strengthened. More particularly, pilot projects, semiautonomous agencies, and regional authorities multiply advocate-leader roles. They give special opportunities to advocate-leaders both to put forth their programs clearly and to defend them with a minimum of other conflicting issues.

The advocate-leader determines whether an invention becomes an innovation. It is crucial that he have effective support from the outside if it may lead to an improvement in, or at least a sustaining of, his position. Competitive comparison often supports change. It is helpful to supply the advocate-leader with examples of innovations elsewhere that might be competitively stimulating to him and his support base. Similarly, forms of national and international recognition are important. Awards, travel grants, and visits by prestigious persons are among the devices that may prove helpful. They can readily be extended by any government seriously interested in development.

International seminars and conferences and executive development programs may multiply the number of advocate-leaders and strengthen their development orientation. There is an increasing number of international seminars in Asia in such fields as public administration, economics, agriculture, health, education, and land reform. The Eastern Regional Organization for Public Administration, the Agricultural Development Council, the East-West Center, and the Ford Foundation are among the several sponsoring organizations. Executive development programs have been established in several countries, those in the Philippines and in Pakistan being among the most prominent.

Third, the strengthening of intermediary adopter and change agent roles in the area of middle management and field supervision is another of the actions that would most likely lead to greater fulfilment of development goals. The inadequate transmission of innovative ideas from higher levels to field action levels has proved a serious problem. In addition, further innovation in the field, not mere transmission of ideas from above, is required if appropriate adaptation to local conditions of administration is to be obtained.

Why should middle management and field supervision pose such difficult problems for development administration? Perhaps the answer lies in the kind of people who hold these positions. Whether administrative specialists or generalists, public officials at this level more or less find themselves in one of two situations: either they are in positions they feel will be their life's work, or they have aspirations and expectations of moving up the administrative ladder in the years to come. Those in both categories, particularly the latter group, look upon their positions as inferior ones, and are likely to take their cues from their superiors. The former group do so for reasons of routine and not getting into trouble, the latter group because they do not want to do anything that might adversely affect their future transfer or promotion. It may be asked why they do not respond more appropriately when their superior is an advocate-leader. Two factors probably are paramount. First, they realize that innovators are greatly in the minority in the government. This they can confirm by simple observation. And this minority may not have a record of longevity for holding their posts. There may seem to be little reason to go out of the way to become unpopular as the advocate-leader may be doing when his days in that position probably seem numbered. Second, relatively few thorough retraining programs for middle management and field supervisors have been launched, especially from the standpoint of increasing receptivity to change. Even if outstanding training programs were put into effect, they would not achieve the desired result if there were no change in the reward pattern of the personnel system of the agency—reward for innovating and co-operating in carrying out innovation. Such changes in the personnel system are among the most difficult to secure. Thus a program to increase the effectiveness of intermediary adopters and change agents at the middle management and field supervisor level would have to include a broad new approach to retraining and a change in the reward pattern of the personnel system.

There are other alternatives, of course. New employees can be hired—as a part of an existing agency or as part of a new one. In either case, as new employees are added, attention should be given to recruiting those who would by temperament, education, and training make effective change agents. Two incentives or appeals would be helpful. If strong leadership prevails in the nation, reference to the official policies and public appeals of the task elite may sway a recalcitrant employee. And for those hopeful of progressing up the ladder, professional considerations may be persuasive, especially if strong professional organizations exist or can be organized. Their commitment to innovation can be a force that counters familialism and formalism.

Many supposed change agents do not have a proper self-image. They do not consider themselves to be change agents. They look upward and laterally but not downward; that is, they feel little responsibility to the people who constitute the target group. Rather, they are concerned with their standing vis-à-vis their contemporaries and their superiors. Their interaction with target groups can be cultivated far more thoroughly than it has been. Such a relation is greatly affected by cultural factors (Abueva).

Greater interaction can bring a tremendous stimulus to the change agents from the target group, which is far from being a mere passive recipient of government programs.

Fourth, the training of more effective detailer-organizers can make far more development possible. Here is clearly a case of upgrading the capacity of the bureaucracy to achieve development. The ability to get a new job done is not easily come by in Asian countries. For example, under the Sukarno regime in Indonesia, detailer-organizers simply did not exist. In the Philippines, the Program Implementation Agency had many inventors and borrowers and lots of ideas, but lacked follow-through.

In a way the position of detailer-organizer is less creative and exciting than other innovational roles. Still, it requires imagination and dedication and even some degree of inspiration to overcome the dead weight of past habits and practices. Intensive in-service training programs are the principal means of building up the capacity of detailer-organizers. Of course, no matter how able the detailer-organizers, they will be relatively ineffective unless capable advocate-leaders are present.

In sum, the problem of how to maximize the effectiveness of a bureaucracy so that it contributes to growth in the direction of modernity or nation-building and socio-economic progress is a problem of how to strengthen innovational forces in the bureaucracy. This, in turn, resolves itself into how a rather small minority can affect the behavior of the great majority. We have few partial solutions to these problems, and no complete ones. A broad area of experimentation by administrators and research by scholars lies ahead.

Index

Index